PHOTOSHOP®

MASKING & COMPOSITING

KATRIN EISMANN

New Riders

Berkeley, California

Photoshop® Masking & Compositing
Katrin Eismann

New Riders
1249 Eighth Street
Berkeley, CA 94710
510/524-2178
800/283-9444
510/524-2221 (fax)

Find us on the World Wide Web at: www.peachpit.com

To report errors, please send a note to errata@peachpit.com

New Riders is an imprint of Peachpit, a division of Pearson Education

ISBN 0-7357-1279-4

9 8 7 6 5 4 3 2 1

Printed in the United States of America

DEVELOPMENT EDITOR
Beth Millett

PROJECT EDITOR
Jill Marts Lodwig

TECHNICAL EDITOR
Wayne Palmer

PRODUCTION EDITOR
Hilal Sala

COMPOSITOR
Kim Scott

INDEXER
Karin Arrigoni

COVER DESIGN
Aren Howell

Contents at a Glance

Table of Contents

4

PEN TOOL POWER

PART II:
LAYERS AND MASKS EXPOSED

5

MASKS ARE YOUR FRIENDS

6

LAYERS ARE YOUR FRIENDS

7

THE POWER OF LAYER MASKING

PART III:
SELECTING AND PRESERVING FINE DETAIL

8

SELECTING HAIR AND FINE DETAIL

9

ADVANCED SELECTION TECHNIQUES

10

SELECTING TRANSLUCENCY AND GREEN SCREEN TECHNIQUES

PART IV:
SUBJECTIVE AND OBJECTIVE COMPOSITING

11

IMAGE EXECUTION AND PHOTOGRAPHY

12

PHOTOREALISTIC COMPOSITING

13

CREATIVE COMPOSITING

APPENDIX

DEDICATION

For my father, Alexander Peter Eismann, whose long life has inspired me to be caring, curious, and conscientious.

ABOUT THE AUTHOR

Katrin Eismann is an artist, author, and educator who loves to see the spark of inspiration in her students' eyes. Her other books include the first and second editions of *Photoshop Restoration and Retouching* (visit www.digitalretouch.org) and *Real World Digital Photography* (visit www.digitalphotobook.net). She has a Bachelor of Fine Arts in Photographic Illustration from the Rochester Institute of Technology and a Master of Fine Arts in Design from the School of VISUAL ARTS in New York.

Katrin is married to the most patient and insightful man on the planet, John McIntosh, with whom she shares a deep passion for art education, travel anywhere outside of New Jersey, and photography (his pictures are in focus; hers rarely are). Katrin and John are both card-carrying members of www.binge-golfers.com. To learn more about Katrin and her artwork, please visit www.photoshopdiva.com.

ABOUT THE CONTRIBUTORS

Mark Beckelman has been fascinated by the altered image since his first photography class in high school, where he sandwiched negatives and combined multiple images in his black-and-white darkroom. After graduating with a Bachelor of Fine Arts in Photographic Illustration from Rochester Institute of Technology, Mark embarked on a commercial photography career with numerous large photographic studios before starting his own business in the early 1990s. In recent years, he has rediscovered the joy and passion of his early illustrative work through Photoshop and the digital process. Using his surreal graphic style, he produces thought-provoking imagery for the editorial, corporate, and advertising community. In 2003, Mark's image *Thinking Outside the Box* was one of 12 winners of the Adobe International Digital Imaging Competition. To see more of Mark's work, visit www.beckelman.com.

Wayne Palmer has had a passion for photography all his life. He has a degree in education from Bloomsburg State College, but his interest in photography kept him in the darkroom as much as he was in the classroom. He worked for Guardian Photo, Inc. for 13 years after he graduated, marketing photofinishing services on a national level. Wayne started his own business, Palmer Multimedia Imaging (www.palmermultimedia.com), in 1994, offering customer photographic, videographic, and digital-photo restoration services. Wayne teaches Photoshop, Photoshop Elements, and Digital Photography in the Continuing Education department of the Pennsylvania College of Technology.

ACKNOWLEDGMENTS

This book has been on my "to-do" list for a very long time. I sincerely thank all the people who have supported me in crossing it off that list.

A heartfelt thank you to Mark Beckelman, whose images grace many of these pages. Your photography, insights, patience, and good humor made this project a pleasure to work on. Thank you to Wayne Palmer, technical editor: your queries, suggestions, and logic were essential to making the book such a valuable learning tool.

Thanks to all the artists and photographers who allowed me to feature the images and techniques that make this book shine. They are listed in the appendix, along with their contact info or Web sites. Thanks especially to Cathy Kudelko, Schecter Lee, and John Parsekian for facilitating some of the best images in the book.

Thank you to the many industry professionals who have answered questions and lent me equipment to work with: Thomas Knoll, Mark Hamburg, Marc Pawlinger, Russell Brown, John Nack, Myke Ninness, and Julieanne Kost at Adobe Systems; Richard LoPinto and Steve Heiner at Nikon; Debbie Rich at Digital Anarchy; Ted Lane at Dynamic Graphics; and Bill Lindsey, Scott Rawlings, and Mark Mehall at Wacom.

Thanks also to the many Photoshop users, students, and experts I have had the honor and pleasure to learn from: Kevin Ames, John Paul Caponigro, Jack Davis, Linnea Dayton, Jim DiVitale, Martin Evening, Bruce Fraser, Greg Gorman, Michael Kieran, Deke McClelland, Bert Monroy, Jack Reznicki, Andrew Rodney, Jeff Schewe, Eddie Tapp, Ben Wilmore, and Colin Woods.

Finally, a big thanks to everyone at New Riders and Peachpit for letting this book develop at an ice-age pace: Elise Walter (moving on but not forgotten), Steve Weiss, Jake McFarland, Kim Scott, Jill Marts Lodwig, Hilal Sala, and Jay Payne. And to Beth Millett: Your insights and suggestions made me make sense and helped me more than you know.

FOREWORD

Throughout the history of art, all major technological changes have brought major conceptual transformations as well. Moving from analog photography to digital photography is no exception. Of course, with digital photography you can still do all the same things you were able to do before, but it's much easier, faster and, very often, even cheaper.

Considering these benefits, we already have plenty of reason to be satisfied, but like other breakthrough moments, we also have the benefit of being able to explore entirely new creative ideas that have the potential to be new to the field of photography in general. It reminds me of the day often cited as the day when cinema was born: During the filming of *Birth of a Nation* in 1915, D.W. Griffith lifted the movie camera off the tripod and moved around freely with the camera in his hand. Up until that day, all films had more or less been theater in front of the camera. Griffith's single change of moving the camera off the tripod introduced a cinematic view that was a totally new means of expression.

Just as moving a camera changed the cinematographic world, working with silicon and software is radically changing photography. Rather than watching prints come up in trays of developer, we spend hours enraptured in the glow of computer monitors perfecting how images express our point of view.

Of course the idea of masking is not something new—we already had that in the analog world. Well, almost. If we compare what can be done with masking today to what could be done yesterday and then factor in the speed and ease of doing it, we are no longer even in the same ballpark.

It used to be that after having done one mask, that was it. So much time was spent doing just one that most photographers weren't inclined to try 22 other alternatives. With the newfound speed and ease of masking in the digital world, the "what if" scenario comes into play, allowing photographers to get even more creative.

Many of you know the experience of feeling your adrenaline pump as you dispatch one, and then another, and yet another alternative to just one image. You inevitably become better at whatever it is you're trying to achieve, and you feel a great sense of accomplishment.

On the other hand, how often have you had a wonderful idea but haven't been sure how to create it using Adobe Photoshop? Many times our ideas are more sophisticated than our skills. With this in mind, I am very happy to introduce you to Katrin Eismann, who I have known for many years as an artist, digital innovator, and most importantly, a patient teacher.

In this book, Katrin ushers you through all sorts of exercises aimed at pumping adrenalin through your creative neural system. We all love a bit of hand-holding, especially when entering unfamiliar territory, and Katrin provides all the hand-holding and gentle guidance anyone might need. As a smart, gentle, and nurturing woman, she anticipates your interests at every turn. By providing you step-by-step information and then encouraging you to look, explore, create, take risks, and listen to what inspires you, Katrin is not only your teacher, but your friend as well. In my eyes, this is what makes this book so special.

The tools Katrin explores fully in this book will bring you into a new relationship with your art. You will be encouraged to experiment and to test your ideas, only this time you need not transform your personality into some monastic creature with boundless patience, but into the fidgeting artist of today who wants his or her feedback now, in order to know which of the 22 alternatives is the best one.

When Katrin empowers you to follow your own bliss and let your imagination explore the limits of your own creative realm, you know that this book is more than just a how-to book. This book is about working with a friend who will not only assist you in achieving great results, but will also make the journey a really pleasant experience.

Pedro Meyer
Founder, www.zonezero.com

INTRODUCTION

IMAGES AND EXPERIENCE

The first time I went to college, I had the good fortune of being put on a one-semester academic leave of absence. The one semester turned into eight years, during which I delved into photography, worked in many aspects of the restaurant business, and traveled throughout Europe. When I returned to college to study photography, I was a thirty-year-old freshman with a deep passion for imagemaking that kept me in the darkroom and studio late into the night. In those first years at the Rochester Institute of Technology, I realized I couldn't adequately express my perceptions within the mechanical blink of a camera shutter, and I began to combine and composite images with scissors, tape, glue, and multiple exposures in the darkroom.

One night as I was leaving the darkroom, I passed by a small computer lab, where a few students worked in the weak glimmer of 13-inch Apple monitors on images similar to the ones I had struggled to create in the darkroom. The images were crude, yet exciting, and the energy in the room was contagious. At that very moment, I turned away from traditional photographic materials and processes and toward the future discoveries and potential that the digital realm offered.

I hadn't planned on "flunking out" of school the first time and I hadn't planned to walk down that hallway late at night, but in looking back I see that both moments were probably among the best things that happened to me. As imagemakers, we need to be open and ready to experience life, to learn from the world around us, and to be willing to take risks. Making art entails asking questions, challenging perceptions, and working with our craft to create compelling images.

IS THIS BOOK RIGHT FOR YOU?

This book is right for you if you have ideas to express and love images, or if you work with photographs as a dedicated amateur or full-time professional. This book is right for you if you're excited by the possibility of staying up late at night to finesse a perfect mask or to combine images in new and unusual ways. Masking and compositing requires flexibility and dedication—there is no "make great art" button on your keyboard, and it often takes a few attempts and approaches to get an image right.

This book is not for you if you don't have the time, curiosity, or patience to read through the examples, try them out and then—just as I push my students—take the techniques further by applying them to your own images.

You have three ways to learn the techniques in this book:

- By reading the examples and looking at the images.

- By downloading the images from the book's Web site, www.photoshopmasking.com, and with the book in hand, re-creating my steps.

- By taking the techniques shown here and applying them to your own images. As you work, you'll need to adjust some of the tool or filter settings to achieve optimal results. It is exactly at that moment, when you are working with your own images, that you're really learning how to mask and composite.

This is not an introductory book. To get the most out of it you should be comfortable with the fundamentals of Photoshop, know where the tools are and what they do, and know how to execute common tasks, such as how to activate a layer or color balance an image. I've been working with Photoshop for more than 14 years, but I still learned a lot just by writing this book. I tried to write a book that I would want to buy or that would interest the many intermediate and advanced Photoshop users that are looking for in-depth and challenging learning materials.

As you flip through the book, you'll see that all of my screen captures were taken on a Macintosh. If you're a Windows user, don't let that deter you from this book. Photoshop functionality, for the most part, is identical on the Macintosh and Windows platforms. All the features discussed in the book are available on both platforms, and the interface is nearly identical. When offering keyboard shortcuts, I give you both Macintosh and Windows commands. The command for Macintosh appears first, in parentheses, followed by the command for Windows, which appears in brackets, like this: (Cmd + Option + X) [Crtl + Alt + X].

THE STRUCTURE OF THE BOOK

Creating art is part craft and part imagination—one without the other gives you lifeless and banal results. With this book, I address both—sometimes with words, but many times more quietly and effectively by featuring images created by professional photographers, creative artists, and a number of my students. I am fortunate that they trust me with their work and that we all can benefit from the insights that the images reveal. Please refer to the Contributor List at the back of the book to learn whose work is featured in my book and what inspires them.

This book should really be called *Photoshop Selections, Masking, and Compositing*, but that title never appealed to me. Besides, it would be too long to fit on the spine of the book! However, the four sections of the book reflect how important and interrelated selections, masking, and compositing really are:

1. Selection Tools and Techniques

2. Working with Layers and Masks

3. Selecting and Preserving Fine Detail

4. Subjective and Objective Compositing

The first part of the book is aimed at helping you build a solid foundation in making accurate selections, followed by information on how to efficiently work with layers and masks. The second part delves into the professional techniques used to separate the finest details, including hair, translucency, and smoke, and continues with photography and advanced compositing techniques.

Each chapter starts with a brief overview of what will be covered in the chapter. I always start with a straightforward example that leads to more advanced examples. You may be tempted to jump to the more advanced sections right away, but I don't recommend it. The introductory examples serve as the foundation for the advanced examples, building on the same tools and techniques.

Although this book was an ambitious project from the very start, there are a lot of Photoshop aspects I do not cover. Throughout the book, I refer to additional references and books, including my other books *Photoshop Restoration and Retouching* and *Real World Digital Photography*. Rather than taking a general approach to Photoshop, I have opted to specialize, and now each one of my three passions has its own book. With this one, I concentrated on the most exciting aspects of imagemaking—combining, juxtaposing, and blending images to express new ideas and explore new worlds.

I did concentrate on the latest version of Photoshop CS when writing this book. If you are still working with version 6.0 or 7.0, you will still learn a lot, because the most important tools for masking and compositing—layers, alpha channels, and blending modes—are a part of those previous versions. And this book will also be useful long after the next release of Photoshop.

COMPANION WEB SITE

I designed and maintain a supplemental Web site where you can download many of the tutorial images featured in the book. Please visit and bookmark www.photoshopmasking.com to download images, view the reader gallery, follow links to additional resources, and contact me. Each chapter (except Chapters 1 and 11) has up to 12 JPEG images that you can download to work and learn along with as you read the book. In the book, images that are posted are signified with an icon and name, such as

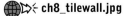 **ch8_tilewall.jpg**

Note

The images on the book's companion Web site are for your personal use and should not be distributed by any other means. If images are not posted on the Web site, it means that I do not have the copyright permission to post them and, therefore, I cannot legally make them available.

Many of the images in the book originated from my or my husband's own image and photography collection. The image stock collection Dynamic Graphics, Inc. and numerous professional photographers also have generously shared some of their images, many of which are also posted on the Web site. However, I was not able to procure permission to post on the Web site all of the images featured in my book—I would be breaking copyright agreements if I did. The copyright of all images used in the book and posted on the Web site remains with the originator, as noted throughout the book. On images for which it is not noted, the copyright belongs to me.

In the cases in which I didn't have permission to post specific images on the book's Web site, you can use similar images from your own photo collections to follow along. Although you won't be using the exact image I am using, the issues being addressed are so universal that I am sure you'll be able to learn the techniques using your own. After all, you'll probably be branching out to your own images sooner rather than later.

NOTE TO EDUCATORS

This book was built around the techniques that I have taught over the years to the numerous students in my digital and creative imaging classes. I hope that this book can help you teach Photoshop, and that the examples and images I have provided will help you learn and demonstrate the concepts and techniques of masking and compositing. As a teacher, I'm sure you know how much time and work is involved in creating exercises and preparing materials that fulfill all the needs of a classroom. I ask that you respect my work and the work of the many contributors and imaging professionals featured in this book by not copying pages of the book, distributing any images from the Web site, or otherwise reproducing the information, even if paraphrased, without proper attribution and permission. Of course, if students own their own copies of the book, they can freely download and use images from the Web site in the classroom.

I would love to hear from you. Please email your comments about the book and Web site to me at Katrin@photoshopmasking.com. Show me how you've taken the techniques in these pages and gone further with them. If you send me flattened JPEG files of the composite image (please keep them small—no more than 1 MB overall), I'll post them in the reader's gallery. Be sure to include information about how I can contact you; great examples of masking and compositing may be featured in the next edition of the book.

CLOSING THOUGHTS

It is the experience of life that the passionate visual artist reaches into to find the creative spark of self-expression. We create images to explore, discover, reveal, and express ourselves, and they often end up being more profound than our words. I hope this book inspires and encourages you to discover, create, and express your own images.

Best regards,

Katrin Eismann
Katrin@photoshopmasking.com
The Big Apple, New York City

Selection Tools and Techniques

1

THE CREATIVE PROCESS AND CONFIGURING PHOTOSHOP

Some of the best conversations I've ever had about images take place when I'm not near a computer—during a brisk walk or over dinner with friends and an intriguing red wine. I enjoy discussing how images come together to create new meanings as I work on and learn from them. Often the conversation includes long forays into Photoshop as we discuss the best way to approach an imaging challenge, such as isolating a delicate subject from the background. What is taking place during these dinners is something I would like you to do: enjoy imagemaking wherever you are and let Photoshop be a conduit to your imagination. One thing I've learned from the thousands of Photoshop aficionados that I've met is, "We eat, breathe, and sleep Photoshop." We have been known to ignore family, friends, pets, and plants as we work late into the night on a new creation.

Photoshop can never come up with an idea or create a compelling image on its own, and as I like to tell my students, "a keyboard shortcut for quality doesn't exist." Before we get into the nuts and bolts of Photoshop, we're going to take a brief foray into the history of combining images and discuss composite categories. In this chapter, you'll

- Learn about the types of composites
- Develop an imaging strategy
- Configure Photoshop preferences
- Learn how Photoshop handles color

A BRIEF HISTORY OF COMBINING IMAGES

The history of collage and montage is rich and varied. Its roots are in the history of painting, as painters often used symbolism and metaphor to convey a thought or perception. Photography is infused with artists who use combinations of printing, montage, and collage to overcome technical limitations or expand creative expression. Digital compositing continues this trend because the computer enables you to combine images from disparate sources, eras, and mediums to create new and compelling work.

In the 19th century, photographic materials were overly blue sensitive and couldn't differentiate between sky and clouds, causing the skies to be very white and uninteresting. Photographers used combination printing to add skies, as Camille Silvy (1834–1910) did with his highly regarded river scenes. Oscar Gustave Rejlander (1813–75) used combination printing and multiple exposures to choreograph and create complex images, which even today would be impossible to take with a single exposure. Rejlander often portrayed moral scenes that created quite a stir in the viewing public.

Note

Visit www.photoshopmasking.com for links to images and information on all artists discussed here.

Henry Peach Robinson (1830–1901) studied with Rejlander, and his images started with sketches and drawings in which he worked out complex scenes. His pictures told stories, including the famous "Fading Away" (1858), in which a young woman is seen lying on her deathbed surrounded by her mother and sister, as the distraught father gazes out the window. The image struck a deep nerve in Victorian Europe, as the death of children and young family members was something most families had personally experienced. Viewers were incensed that the photographer had been privy to and profited from such a personal event, even though the image was of willing models and at least five different glass plates were combined to create the final image. Interestingly enough, painters at the same time also portrayed this subject without creating an uproar. Because the image was photographic—that is, realistic—viewers imbued the image with truth and related to the situation much more keenly than when a similar subject was portrayed with oil on canvas.

But it wasn't until after World War I that artists began to use montage as a truly new art form, one that tore, questioned, and challenged existing perceptions. The Dadaists in Berlin, including Raoul Hausman, Hannah Hoch, Kurt Schwitters, and John Heartfield, used photomontage in new and exciting ways. Of this group, John Heartfield is the most well known and revered. Not one to shy away from expressing his political views, Heartfield exposed and criticized Adolf Hitler's reliance on German industrial wealth and the horrors of war. Heartfield's work was banned during the Third Reich, and then rediscovered in the late 1950s. Since then, his powerful use of image and type has greatly influenced many artists and graphic designers.

In the late 1950s, two American photographers were beginning to emerge as montage artists. Jerry Uelsmann (**figures 1.1 and 1.2**) and Duane Michaels composed evocative, dreamlike images with traditional black and white materials. Both of these men, but especially Uelsmann, created the very foundation of contemporary photomontage; Uelsmann, in his multiple enlarger, traditional black-and-white darkroom, created decades ago what we are trying to do with Photoshop today.

© Jerry Uelsmann

© Jerry Uelsmann

figures 1.1 & 1.2

Created in the classic darkroom with multiple enlargers, Uelsmann's images have inspired countless artists to explore combining images.

From scissors and pots of glue, to sandwiching negatives, to working with high-end digital equipment, the images we create by combining, juxtaposing, and colliding pieces and influences are insightful and intriguing. Many contemporary artists are using Photoshop to create artwork with great depth and character; some of my favorite artists include Diane Fenster (**figure 1.3**), Maggie Taylor (**figure 1.4**), and Lyn Bishop (all of whom are featured in Chapter 13, "Creative Compositing"). In commercial

figure 1.3

One poster of a series for the Seattle Opera Company. This one is for the opera "Carmen."

work, the images of Glenn Wexler, Daniel Clark, David Bishop, and Nick Vedros (**figure 1.5** and featured in Chapter 12, "Photorealistic Compositing"), are shattering the boundaries of the imagination. I admire and enjoy their work with great respect as they portray the world with intelligence, humor, and compassion. For additional information on the history of collage and montage, please visit this book's Web site where I have provided numerous links to the artists mentioned.

© Maggie Taylor

© Nick Vedros

figure 1.4

Maggie Taylor uses a flatbed scanner to input image elements and then creates the collages in Photoshop.

figure 1.5

The idea of frogs enjoying surfing is quirky and fun.

TYPES OF IMAGE COMPOSITES

For me there are two primary types of composites—*subjective*, or creative surreal, and *objective*, or photorealistic. I'm not saying that photoreal images aren't creative or that people don't plan the process of making surreal images. As an image-maker, I approach these two types of composites differently with distinct strategies.

Subjective Composites

The subjective-creative approach involves taking risks, a lot of experimentation, and listening to and learning from the images as they progress. For example, suppose I have photographed some appealing textures and I'm curious to see how they'll look combined with another picture. I'll open the images in Photoshop and use the Move tool to drag them into one file. By experimenting with opacity, layer blending modes, and the advanced blending options, I am often surprised by the images that appear. I find them liberating and relaxing, and the image juxtapositions create meanings I never would have conceived of without this experimentation, as shown in **figure 1.6**. We'll delve into creative-surreal composites in Chapter 13.

figure 1.6

My parents and I live on different sides of the Atlantic Ocean, and this image represents my reaching out to them.

Objective Composites

Objective, or photorealistic, composites are meant to convey an illusion of reality. For instance, I know that the little girl is not holding the moon on a string in **figure 1.7** by Mark Beckelman, but the size relationships, lighting, and gesture let the viewer experience a suspension of disbelief, which makes the image more effective. Photorealistic compositing is the bread and butter of the advertising and movie industry. In many Hollywood movie posters, the pictures of the stars are not really pictures of the stars. Rather, a photographer such as Lee Varis photographs a body double and then "zippers" the star's head onto the stand-in's body.

Photorealistic composites are also very creative and are produced with the same tools and Photoshop techniques as creative-surreal images. Like all Photoshop composites, they require a lot of planning and pre-production to be successful, which is addressed in Chapters 11 and 12.

Additional Definitions

John Paul Caponigro developed the following image composite categories for the online exhibit, "Deus Machina," that he judged in 2002:

- **Lumine (made by light):** Recording the imprint of light on a sensitized surface makes a strong connection between the image and what we know or think we know about reality.

- **Colligo (collage):** This category could involve combining images from separate sources that use very different visual vocabularies (text, diagram, drawn images, generated images, photographic images) in ways that make no attempt to integrate them into a single reality. Rather, it holds the separate realities together by the substrate(s) or frame(s).

- **Mixtura (montage):** This category combines images from separate sources to create a new, seamless visual reality—a montage.

As you delve into the art and technique of combining images, John Paul's distinctions may prove to be valuable and insightful.

© Mark Beckelman

figure 1.7

A multilayered image composite that plays with size relationships and the impossibility of what is being portrayed.

THE IMAGEMAKING JOURNEY

Before you start digging into image pixels, it's a good idea to have a plan. The foundation of my Photoshop strategy is to work flexibly, nondestructively, and safely. I never work on the background layer because it is my original image data. Photoshop layers, layer masks, and alpha masks offer you tremendous flexibility, and you are working nondestructively, as long as you don't flatten the file. I am also a compulsive "save as" and data backup person. While I've never regretted having too many layers or file backups, I've always regretted not having an image backed up when I needed it or when the client wanted a change made.

Removing Creative Roadblocks

If you are too busy making excuses to work creatively, or if cleaning the bathroom just sounds better than working on images, do not lose hope. We often put off creative work out of fear of failure, perceived lack of ideas, or personal inhibitions. The first thing I do to get over empty computer-screen phobia is to "just work through it," something I learned from an experienced photography teacher. When I felt empty or uninspired, he encouraged me "to get out there and take pictures." The actual act of working often frees me up to keep going, and once I have momentum, there's no stopping me.

I learned another helpful concept from Julieanne Kost at Adobe Systems. In a nutshell she advises, "Identify the primary distraction that keeps you from your creative work and deal with it. If you have an issue, be it weight, lack of exercise or family worries, do your best to resolve that issue or reduce its power of distraction on your time and energy."

It's important to remember that creating images is a worthwhile endeavor in and of itself. Being creative, expressing yourself, and learning about the world we live in through imagemaking is a positive way to spend your time. So turn off that nagging voice of distraction and doubt and get to work.

Inspiration

I often come up with my best ideas while on a morning run. Others get their inspiration from rummaging through a flea market to find objects and images to create with, while still others turn to their family history or dreams. Pay attention to what triggers an idea or flips your creative switch—is it a quiet afternoon spent gardening, or would you rather page through magazines, go for a walk, or visit museums?

I teach a freshman imaging class in the Computer Art department at the School of VISUAL ARTS in New York City, and last semester I gave an assignment called "Free Inspiration." The students had to find three objects they did not pay for and create images that portrayed those subjects in a respectful manner. Many students found interesting objects on the streets of Manhattan, which they used to create very beautiful images (**figure 1.8**). So if trash and leaves inspire college freshmen, just think what you can use for inspiration. Nurture the subjects or pastimes that inspire you—they are your personal wellspring of ideas and insights.

Swipe and Snap

As you page through magazines, tear out the images, words, advertisements, and articles that catch your eye. Collect these swipes in a large artist's notebook (as shown in **figure 1.9**) or sort them into file folders. I'm always looking and collecting. Often I don't even know why I like an image—it may be the color, the focus, the light—it doesn't matter. Allowing your eye and mind to let go will produce a wealth of ideas and inspiration.

I try not to leave home without a camera because I never know what texture, play of light, or window display will trigger my fancy. The camera doesn't have to be big or expensive—my husband John McIntosh carries a small digital camera, the Fuji F700, with him all the time, making quick visual

© Seung Hyung Lee

figure 1.8

Starting with a found leaf, one student created a fascinating environment to show to the viewer.

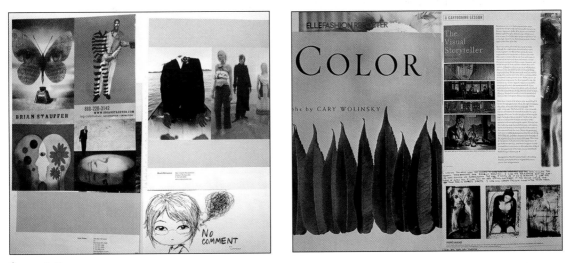

figure 1.9

A student's swipe book with pictures, sketches, and notes.

notes on his way to work. I use a variety of digital cameras to collect stock images, textures, or interesting image elements while waiting for a flight, as shown in **figures 1.10** and **1.11**, while walking to the dentist, or in-between business appointments. As New York photographer Jay Maisel says, "I always carry a camera with me, as it makes it much easier to take photographs."

figure 1.10

The untouched snapshot of an antique toy exhibit at the San Francisco Airport.

figure 1.11

To make the image more playful, I interpreted it with sharp, blurred, and colorizing layers.

Observe

Similar to swiping and snapping, take the time to relish looking, gazing, and really seeing the world. Notice how the light plays with a wine glass (**figure 1.12**), how pearls of water cluster and collect on a metal surface (**figure 1.13**), how the sky changes over the course of a few minutes (**figure 1.14**), and how shadows differ depending on the time of day and time of year. Observing nature and studying art will make you a better imaging artist.

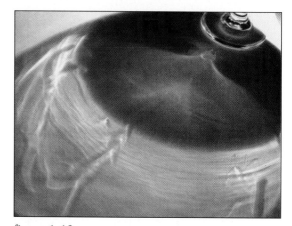

figure 1.12

Notice how the light bends and plays within the traces of the red wine.

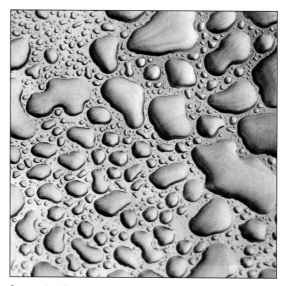

figure 1.13

The cliché of water on a metal surface is evenly dispersed round droplets, but as you can see the shapes are irregular and random.

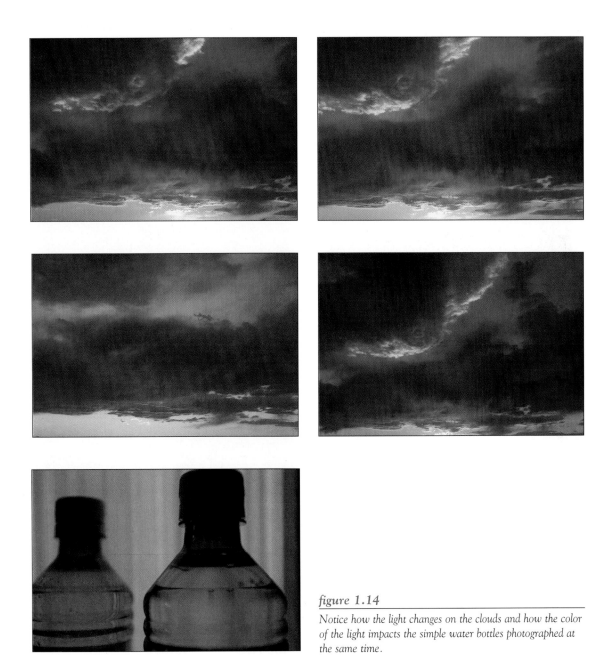

figure 1.14

Notice how the light changes on the clouds and how the color of the light impacts the simple water bottles photographed at the same time.

Brainstorm and Concept Development

This is the time to turn off the TV and quiet the voice in your mind that keeps saying, "That idea is stupid," or "Who are you kidding?" or "I don't like that idea at all." Just let yourself imagine the unimaginable. Who says pigs can't fly? The only rule in brainstorming is that negative words such as *no*, *impossible*, and *stupid* are banned.

In developing a concept, some people like to write about it, while I like to discuss ideas and inspiration with John. We talk and brainstorm, and one thing leads to another. Just let yourself go, and you'll be surprised at the ideas, images, and solutions that come up. Stop making excuses or finding flaws in an idea.

Doodle and Sketch

Grab a pencil and paper, yes—the actual materials you can hold—and start doodling. What elements do you want to include? Think about scale, position, shape, lighting, textures, and color, which we'll discuss in Chapters 12 and 13. If you feel dry or uninspired, grab your swipe book or folder of images and page through the images. Often, I'm surprised by an image I swiped a few years ago and how it triggers a new idea. *Please note:* I am not saying to copy someone's images in any way, because that does break international copyright laws, but take a look at the image in **figure 1.15**, which I swiped from a magazine a few years ago for its beautiful blue color. **Figure 1.16** shows the image that it inspired. Is there a direct connection? Well, both images are blue, but after that the similarities stop. The blue image encouraged me to experiment with color.

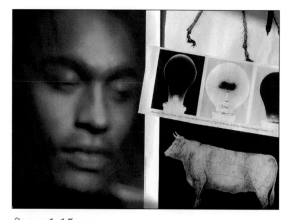

figure 1.15

A *few pages from my swiped image collection. The blue portrait on the left inspired me to experiment with color.*

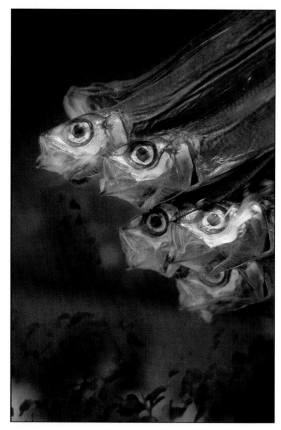

figure 1.16

The playful fish image relies on composition and color.

Proof of Concept

I've had many ideas for images that looked great in my mind's eye but were (much) less than stellar when I actually created them. I've learned that doing a low-resolution, proof-of-concept run-through of an image often helps me develop an idea, plan the image, or even sometimes not pursue the project at all.

By doing a rough (a proof of concept) you are practicing with the image to determine whether the idea has legs. During the proof-of-concept stage, you'll also see what elements are missing, how they need to be photographed, which models need to be cast, and whether you need to go back to step one. Believe me, skipping the proof-of-concept step is like going to a foreign country without a map, guide, or local currency. Take the time to make low-resolution proofs of concept files, and you will be able to approach the final image with much greater confidence because you'll know where you need to go—that is, how to photograph a subject and whether you need to put a lot of effort into a complex mask.

Plan and Collect

The concept is developed, the idea holds water, and you have the green light to create the image(s). Now you need to plan and do the photography or collect and scan the image elements. I address planning for photography and taking pictures to use in composites in Chapter 11. Once again, it makes a lot of sense to carry a camera with you whenever possible. For example, why would I need to buy stock images of clouds when I have gathered a collection of my own images that I can use without worrying about image release or paying the copyright holder? So take pictures of interesting textures, shadows, reflections, buildings, and landscapes. If you do photograph a person, you will need a model release to use the image commercially. Even if you don't plan on using the image commercially, if there's any chance it may be published, it is always a good idea to have a standard model release signed by the model or the model's guardian. See www.asmp.org for additional information on forms for photographers.

Caution

You can't scan images from magazines, books, or stock image catalogs because they are protected (rightfully so) by international copyright laws. To play it safe, if you didn't create the original image or image element and it's less than 75 years old, assume that you can't use it for commercial purposes. Only use copyright-free stock images or your own photographs, drawings, and images. See www.photoshopmasking.com for additional information on copyright rules.

Digitize and Back Up

If you've shot film, it's time to scan for the composite. Scanning and calculating the optimal image resolution is addressed in Chapter 13. If your images are from a digital camera, you'll need to download, acquire the RAW file, and save the files. (Please see *Real World Digital Photography, 2nd Edition*, from Peachpit Press, for a comprehensive book on working with digital cameras). Every project I work on has a dedicated folder, and within that folder there are subfolders named originals, WIP (work in progress), and finals. I put the scans, stock images, and digital camera files into the originals file, and as soon as I open a file and modify it in any way it goes into the WIP folder. I save all layered files that are pertinent to that project in the WIP folder. The final folder has only the final flattened version of the image. By creating this simple folder hierarchy, I can quickly find the images and files I need. After making the scans or gathering the images I need for a composite project, I always burn a CD or a DVD to ensure I don't need to start over if I encounter a computer or hard-drive error. During the project, I regularly back up to an external hard drive, and at the end of the project, I burn two sets of DVDs: one remains in my studio and the other is stored offsite in a safe location.

Cleanup and Color Correct

Before doing any creative work, remove dust, damage, or artifacts with the Clone and Healing Brush tools and apply global tone and color correction with image adjustment layers. One of the dead giveaways of poor compositing are images that have different and distracting colorcasts, so taking some time in the initial phase of image creation will pay off later many times over. Additionally, the time I spend cleaning up files gives me the chance to "get to know the file," and plan how to approach making the selection or mask. My book, *Photoshop Restoration and Retouching, 2nd Edition* (New Riders Press) addresses image cleanup and color correction, which is why I am not including the information in this book.

Select and Mask

Finally, you get to dive into making selections and masks. I very often take the time to isolate the individual elements before combining them. The process of selecting fine detail or drawing a precise path once again gives me the chance to familiarize myself with the image. If you've spent more than a few minutes making a selection or if you know you'll need to reassess it, then I suggest you save the selection as an alpha channel, which is addressed in great detail in Chapter 3, "The Essential Select Menu," and Chapter 5, "Masks Are Your Friends." When you have an active selection, use Select > Save Selection to store the selection with the file to ensure you don't have to make the same selection repeatedly.

Composite and Refine

Let the fun begin! As discussed in Chapters 12 and 13, there are many approaches to making image composites. While I work on a project, I never flatten the file or merge layers, as shown in **figure 1.17**. I never know when a specific layer will have a tidbit of useful information or a layer mask that I can reference. If a layer seems unnecessary, I make it invisible rather than throwing it away.

To refine the image, I do the following: Take a break, get a second opinion, and make a print. Taking a break for a few hours or coming back to an image the next day lets me see the image with fresh eyes. Asking for a second opinion is a must. I always ask the person to tell me what they like about the image and, more importantly, what they don't like. It's important to find someone who has a good eye and is willing to discuss the image without thinking they need to protect your feelings. After all, it's an image, not a marriage proposal. Finally, I make a workprint to really see the image because I just don't see the details or glaring errors on screen. Making the print gives me an object to look at, live with, and learn from. If you can, make workprints and tack them onto a wall. As you study the images they will "tell" you what they need changed. Go ahead and mark these prints so that when you return to the computer you can fix and refine the details efficiently.

Of course, you'll adapt this creative process to fit your own working style, and as you work, steps will blend together. Just make sure you give yourself the time, space, and opportunity to work and be astounded by image creation.

PHOTOSHOP PREFERENCES

Before you start working on your images in Photoshop, you need to configure the behind-the-scenes settings that control how different aspects of the program behave. I like to think of this routine as being similar to picking up a rental car at the airport. There are always a few things—positioning the mirrors, adjusting the seat, finding the headlight switch, checking the gas level, and choosing a decent radio station—that I like to do before I drive out of the parking lot and hit the open road.

Photoshop provides numerous ways for individual users to customize the program. From actions that record commonly performed tasks, to user-defined keyboard shortcuts and saved workspaces, there are different avenues to getting the program set up just

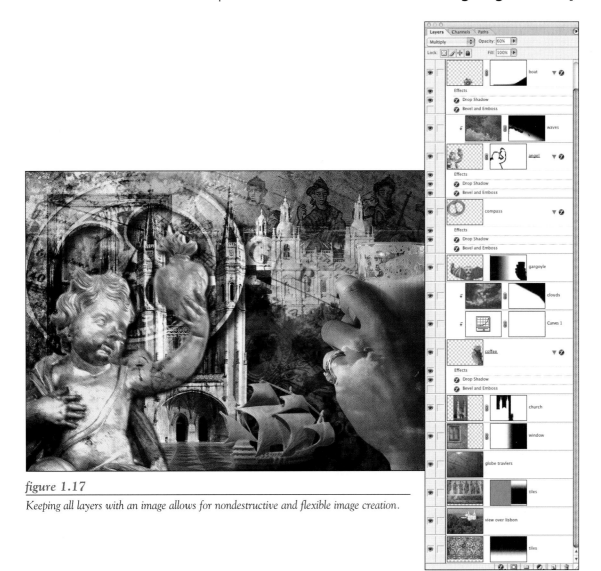

figure 1.17

Keeping all layers with an image allows for nondestructive and flexible image creation.

the way you like it. The place you should start, however, is with the Preferences settings. On Mac OS X, Preferences are located in the Photoshop menu; on Windows systems, they can be found under the Edit menu. There are a lot of preferences, and many of them are specific to tasks and work-flows that are more for graphic design and Web-related fields. So I won't discuss each one in minute detail. Instead, I'll address the most important pref-erences that pertain to the overall operation of the program in general, and more specifically, to those items that have the most impact on the type of work that digital artists and photographers are likely to do. The following text on preferences and color set-tings is excerpted with permission from my book, *Real World Digital Photography*.

General Preferences

The following list briefly introduces the general preferences that will help you work efficiently.

- **Image Interpolation.** Interpolation refers to the method by which new pixels are created or existing pixels are thrown away when an image is sized. Choosing an interpolation method here will affect how interpolation is done in other areas of the program, such as when you scale an image or transform an image element. The change is immediate and does not require a restart of the program. If you are using Photoshop 7 or earlier, you should choose the Bicubic method because that is the most accurate algorithm for photographic images.

    Photoshop CS has introduced two new interpolation methods: Bicubic Smoother and Bicubic Sharper. For upsampling images (which means making them larger), Bicubic Smoother is almost always the better choice. Bicubic Sharper will often provide the best results for downsampling (or for making an image smaller), although the results can vary from image to image, so the choice is not as clear as Bicubic Smoother is for upsampling. All of the interpolation options are available in the Image Size dialog box (see **figure 1.18**) and can be chosen for specific images as the need arises. If you choose to scale an image larger or smaller using the Free Transform tool, there is no way to specify an interpolation method. The preference setting is the default, which is why I leave it at Bicubic and adjust the Image Size setting as needed.

- **History States.** At the most basic level, the History feature in Photoshop is a super undo command that lets you move backward through the editing steps and undo changes. Photoshop refers to every separate change as a history state, which can be anything from a

tonal correction, to a paintbrush stroke, to resizing the image. As you might imagine, this provides great flexibility and insulation from "no way out" mistakes that occur during the editing process. The default number is 20, and the maximum number of history states is a whopping 1,000. Whether you'll actually be able to get by with the maximum amount will depend on a number of factors, including the size of your image, how much RAM you have, and how much free disk space is available for Photoshop to use as a Scratch Disk. Until you get a better idea of how many history states is a good number for you, I suggest beginning with 50.

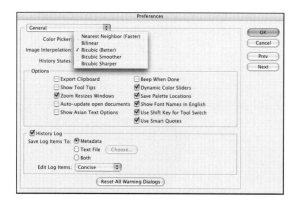

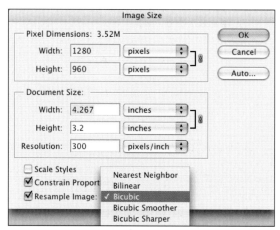

figure 1.18

The image interpolation algorithms are available in the main Photoshop CS Preferences and the Image Size dialog box.

- **Export Clipboard.** This setting lets you copy pixels from Photoshop and paste them into another application. Keep in mind, however, that this process can put a large chunk of pixels on the clipboard (the computer's copy buffer) and create a brief lag when you switch to another program. Unless you specifically need to do this, I recommend you leave this preference unchecked. In many cases, what you have copied is too large for the clipboard, and you will see a "clipboard export failed because it is too large to export" warning, which only serves to slow you down as you move between programs. Unchecking this feature still lets you copy and paste within Photoshop itself.

- **History Log.** New to Photoshop CS, this preference lets you save a record of what you've done to an image. You can choose to save this information to a file's metadata, to a separate text file, or both. The details can be restricted to the following: Sessions Only, which simply records when you open and close a file; Concise, which tracks session info and keeps a record of every step you perform, similar to the record you see in the History palette; and Detailed, which tracks session info similar to the way the Actions palette does it, keeping a surprisingly detailed record of everything you do to an image, including filter and color correction settings. If you want to remember what you have done to an image, the Detailed option can be very useful.

File Handling

The second preference screen controls how Photoshop manages file saving and compatibility issues.

- **Image Previews.** If you want Photoshop to save small versions of the image to be used as icons or preview thumbnails by your computer's operating system, the Image Preview setting is the place to go. Note that this preference has nothing to do with the thumbnail previews generated by the File Browser. If you're generating images for the Web, you usually won't want to save either previews or icons because no one visiting a Web page will see them, so they needlessly increase the file size. If you want to choose on a per-image basis whether these items are generated, select the Ask When Saving option.

- **Ignore EXIF sRGB tag.** Color tags are used to give meaning to the color numbers in a digital image so that the appearance of an image will be consistent on different color-managed computers. Some digital cameras will automatically tag their images with an sRGB color profile, even if you have specifically chosen Adobe RGB in the camera's setup menu. While the sRGB profile may represent a correct interpretation for the images a camera produces, it is just as likely to be no more than a "default" tag provided by the camera that does not necessarily reflect the best way to interpret the colors in an image. If you determine that another color profile, such as Adobe RGB or ColorMatch RGB, works well with the images from your camera, you can use this preference to have Photoshop ignore the sRGB tag contained in a camera's EXIF data. If you are using Photoshop 7, you can add this functionality to the program by downloading a special Ignore sRGB Profile plug-in from the Adobe Web site (www.adobe.com/products/photoshop).

- **Ask Before Saving Layered TIFF Files.** In the old days, only Photoshop's native PSD format could save layers. Now the club is not so exclusive, and the TIFF specification has the ability to support layers, too. This is really only an issue if you're using TIFF files in page layout programs. In the past, some layout applications would get downright cranky if they encountered a layered TIFF. Photographers and production artists would also use the TIFF format for the flattened images that were placed in the layout program and reserve the PSD format for the work-in-progress layered image. The different file formats were another way to keep it clear that the correct, nonlayered file was placed in the page layout. Although programs like InDesign can handle layered TIFFs and PSDs, many designers and prepress businesses still use flattened TIFF files to minimize workflow confusion. If you want a reminder that you're saving a layered file in TIFF format, turn this option on. I leave it off.

- **Enable Large Document Format (.psb).** New to Photoshop CS, this preference lets you save very large files (300,000 × 300,000 pixels), which was not possible in earlier versions. The previous 30,000 pixel limit is still the largest size that can be saved using the standard PSD format, but larger files can now be saved as TIFF (up to 4GB) or the new PSB format. This new format and the new image size limits are not backward compatible with earlier versions of Photoshop. The number of people who have a need for such gargantuan files is very small, and I recommend that you leave this preference unselected, simply to protect against accidentally creating a file this big. If you feel compelled to stitch together 97 6-megapixel photos into a single, monumental image, however, this is the preference you need to set to make that possible.

- **Maximize PSD File Compatibility.** This option has been around in several versions of Photoshop under a variety of names, and it controls whether Photoshop will include a hidden, composite layer along with the regular layers when you save a file. The composite layer is essentially just a single layer that represents what the image would look like with all the visible layers flattened. This preference is primarily for people who need to use their layered PSD files in other applications, which claim to read PSD files but need that composite layer in order to do so. The main problem with this option is that the extra composite

layer will make your file size much larger—up to 33 percent larger—than it needs to be. Although this is not much of an issue with small files, it can quickly become a big issue with larger documents. If you're working on your images only in Photoshop, I recommend you leave this preference turned off and save some disk space.

Display and Cursors

The third preference panel controls how Photoshop displays image channels and tool cursors.

- **Color Channels in Color.** I feel strongly that this preference should be left unchecked. When turned on, it displays the individual color channels with bright-colored overlays to match their names. The channels have names that identify them, and the colored overlays actually make it much harder to evaluate the tonal detail in the channels. You're better off leaving this unchecked and viewing the default grayscale versions of the color channels (**figure 1.19**). In addition, we'll often use the image channels as a foundation to create an alpha channel, as discussed in Part Three of the book, "Selecting and Preserving Fine Detail." Being able to inspect the image channels is always the first step in building a good alpha channel.

- **Painting Cursors.** This is probably the most important setting on this panel. When you set the painting cursors to Brush Size, you can see a circular cursor that represents the actual size of the brush you're using. If the cursor is the default brush symbol icon, you won't know how large your brush is until after you've painted on the image. The Other Cursors preference lets you choose between standard, which is the tool icon, and a precise crosshair.

Tip

You can always access a precise crosshair cursor by pressing the Caps Lock key. To return to your regular cursor, simply press Caps Lock again.

figure 1.19

Leave the display of the color channels set to the default grayscale view. The RGB colored overlay makes it hard to evaluate the tonal detail.

Transparency and Gamut

The fourth preference screen controls how Photoshop displays areas on layers without information and gamut warning color.

- **Transparency Settings:** Grid Size & Colors. When you have an image element on a separate layer, it can either fill the entire size of the image or occupy only a portion of the image area. If the pixels on the layer do not fill up the full image area, Photoshop uses a checkerboard pattern to represent the transparent pixels that surround it. You'll only see the pattern if you turn off the eye icons in the Layers palette of any underlying layers. If you're new to Photoshop or Photoshop Elements, the checkerboard pattern may be confusing at first. Essentially, the program needs to have something there so that you

can see there is nothing there. I have found that the default colors and grid size work fine for most images. Clicking in the colored swatches will take you to the Photoshop Color Picker where you can choose new colors for the grid.

- **Gamut Warning.** When the Gamut Warning is activated (from the View menu, choose Gamut Warning), Photoshop will place an overlay tone over any colors in the image that are out of gamut for the current CMYK setup specified in the Color Settings dialog box. You can also use it to display the out-of-gamut colors if you have selected an inkjet profile as the current proofing space. The default battleship gray at 100% works pretty well for most images...unless you have a photo of a battleship on a foggy day, in which case lime green or shocking magenta might be a better choice.

Units and Rulers

As its names implies, the fifth preference screen controls how Photoshop measures image and document information.

- **Units.** I prefer to change the ruler units in the main Photoshop interface, either by (Control-clicking) [right-clicking] inside the rulers, or by accessing the units in the XY section of the Info palette (see **figure 1.20**). If you'll be printing most of your images, use the measurement system you are most familiar with. If you were raised in the United States, that's likely to be inches; if you're from almost anyplace else in the world, you might be more comfortable with centimeters. If you need to prepare images for the Web, pixels are the best choice.

figure 1.20

Changing units of measurement via the Info palette is faster than changing the preference setting.

- **Column Size.** If you are doing any work on a publication that uses columns for arranging text on a page, such as a newspaper, specifying the exact size of your columns here lets you resize images or create new files, based on the column width used in your publication. If you want to resize a photo so that it is two columns wide, for instance, the column size preference tells Photoshop how wide to make your image.

Plug-Ins and Scratch Disks

Photoshop is a memory-intensive application, so this preference pane lets you assign separate hard drives to increase Photoshop's memory allocation.

- **Scratch Disks.** When Photoshop runs out of RAM, which is the fastest memory in your computer, it uses empty hard drive space as temporary RAM. The preference options let you assign first, second, third, and fourth choices for which hard disks, called *scratch disks*, Photoshop should use as scratch space. You should always assign your fastest drive with the largest amount of free space as the primary scratch disk drive.

T i p

Adobe recommends you have at least five times the size of your image in available RAM, meaning the RAM remaining after your operating system, Photoshop, and any other application have taken what they need to operate. Of course, more RAM is always better.

Memory and Image Cache

The eighth preference pane is very important to set up correctly.

- **Cache Settings.** The image cache enables Photoshop to increase the apparent speed with which it deals with large images. Using the number specified here, Photoshop saves several smaller versions of the image at different zoom percentages (that is, 25%, 33.3%, 50%, and 66.7%). When viewing the image in a zoomed-out view, the program can apply the changes to a smaller, cached version first and update your screen preview faster. The default setting is 4 cache levels, which works just fine for most images. If you find that you're working on really large images and you have a good allocation of RAM, you might try increasing it to 6.

- **Use Cache for Histogram in Levels.** This preference should be turned off! Its sole purpose is to speed the rendering of histograms in the Levels dialog box when you are working on your image at views other than 100%. Although the speedier histogram may seem like a good thing, you're not getting the real histogram from the full image. Rather, you're getting a histogram rendered from whatever cached version happens to be presently in use. If you're going to make the effort to understand what the histogram is telling you, you might as well be getting the accurate data.

- **Memory Usage.** This section shows you how much available RAM you have and how much of it should be assigned to Photoshop. Both Windows and Mac OS X use dynamic memory allocation, so the number is not necessarily as specific as it may seem in this preference. I generally use 90 percent of available RAM for Photoshop. If you are running a lot of programs or you find your system getting cranky, you may need to lower this amount, install more RAM (always a good idea), or try closing some applications. Of these options, getting more RAM is the best one. You can never have too much RAM with Photoshop, especially now that you can work on 16-bit layered images.

File Browser

New to Photoshop CS, this group of preferences influences various aspects of File Browser behavior.

- **Do Not Process Files Larger Than...** If you have certain folders that contain really large image files and you don't want the browser to get bogged down in generating high-res previews and thumbnails, you can specify a file size cap here. The default is 200MB.

- **Allow Background Processing.** This preference tells Photoshop to grab on to any extra available processing power and use it to generate previews and thumbnails for the selected

folder of images, even if you're not currently working in the File Browser or Photoshop. This is very useful for setting up the File Browser to work on a large folder of new images before you actually start browsing the files. I like to target the folder in question and then work on other tasks (or just go have dinner), so that when I return, all the thumbnails and high-quality previews are ready to use.

- **High-Quality Previews.** As the name implies, this preference directs the File Browser to build a higher-resolution preview. This is an essential feature for evaluating images before you open them—I recommend you turn on this feature.

- **Render Vector Files.** If you have Illustrator, FreeHand, or CorelDRAW files and want to see previews of them in the File Browser, turn this one on.

- **Keep Sidecar Files with Master Files.** The sidecar files contain additional information about images generated by the File Browser. By default, this preference is turned on. It lets you move, copy, delete, rename, or batch rename the data, along with the associated image files. I suggest leaving this option on.

COLOR SETTINGS

The Color Settings dialog box is mission control for how Photoshop handles the display and conversion of color in your images. Understanding what goes on here and choosing the appropriate settings is key to controlling color in Photoshop and maintaining the color fidelity of your photographs. Although the settings are executed in the background, this dialog box is one of the most important areas in the program: The settings you choose here affect how images are opened, what happens to pixels when you paste from one image into another, how colors are displayed on your monitor, and how much notice you get if a particular process may change the colors in an image. It's well worth your time to get to know the different options in this dialog box and understand how they impact your image-editing workflow.

How Photoshop Handles Color

Before I get into the details of the Color Settings dialog box, let's pause for a moment to get a good overview of the terrain I'll be exploring. It doesn't do any good to simply tell you what settings to choose, which checkboxes to check and what radio buttons to enable if you don't have an understanding of the conceptual foundations of the Color Settings dialog box and Photoshop color management in general.

When distilled to its most basic components, a digital image is nothing more than an electronic paint-by-numbers kit. The image is made up of a grid of pixels, with each pixel's color, or tone if it's a grayscale image, represented by a number. In the case of an RGB image, each pixel has three values, one each for red, green, and blue. True, when you're working on an image in Photoshop, it probably feels a lot more high-tech than a paint-by-numbers kit, but all you're really doing when you edit a digital image is changing the color of the pixels. The numbers that are assigned to the pixels tell Photoshop how to display each pixel on your monitor, or they tell an output device what color each pixel should be when the image is printed.

The problem with this arrangement is that it comes with a certain amount of ambiguity. A paint-by-numbers picture, divided into separate areas that call for specific colors, will look very different depending on whether you use watercolors, oils, acrylics, colored pencils, or chalk pastels. With digital color, the actual color you get, whether displayed on a monitor or printed by an inkjet or photographic printer, will vary from device to device, simply because different devices interpret the numbers and render color in different ways.

In an effort to standardize how digital color is displayed and printed, color management in Photoshop revolves around four key principles:

1. Controlling your working environment with consistent lighting and neutral-colored walls.

2. Having a properly calibrated monitor with an accurate profile that tells Photoshop how your specific monitor displays color.

3. Using an RGB Working Space that is device-independent; that is, its interpretation of how a given set of color numbers should be displayed is not constrained by the limitations of a particular device, such as a monitor, printer, scanner, or camera.

4. Adding ICC profiles, or color tags, to your image files that tell Photoshop and other ICC-aware applications how the color numbers in your file should be displayed. These color tags give meaning to the color numbers in your image.

The Importance of Monitor Calibration and Profiling

The importance of controlling your viewing environment and having an accurately calibrated and profiled monitor cannot be emphasized enough. Simply put, if your monitor has not been properly adjusted (calibrated) and the profile that describes it is not accurate, no amount of color management diligence and use of image color tags farther down the pipeline will give you predictable color. If you have never created a profile for your monitor (at the very least you should use the calibration utility that comes with your computer's operating system), I recommend postponing any serious printing of your images until that vital piece of the puzzle has been resolved.

Note

The Adobe Gamma monitor calibration utility is included with the Windows versions of Photoshop and Photoshop Elements, but not the Mac version. This is because Adobe Gamma does not run on Mac OS X. If you are not using a third-party calibration package to calibrate and profile your monitor, Adobe recommends using the ColorSync calibration utility that is included with OS X.

The Importance of Working Spaces

A working space defines how Photoshop will interpret the color numbers in a file and gives some visual meaning and consistency to the numbers that make up a digital image. The working space will affect any new images you create in Photoshop and images that do not already have a profile associated with them (as is often the case with files from a digital camera). Because the working spaces that are available in Photoshop do not represent color as defined by a particular device, such as a monitor or printer, as long as an accurate monitor profile is being used and an image is saved with a color profile (more on that shortly), then the display of the image will be consistent when viewed on other calibrated and color-managed systems.

The Importance of Color Profiles

If you gather five people in a room and ask all of them to close their eyes and think of the color purple, it's very doubtful that everyone would imagine the exact same color. Apart from obvious brightness differences such as light purple and dark purple, there are also subtleties of hue and saturation to consider. Is it a deep bluish purple, or a purple with traces of intense magenta? With no way to precisely define the color, the range of imagined purples would be all over the map. To accurately convey a more specific idea of what type of purple you are talking about, you would need to provide some additional information. In a digital image, an ICC profile is the additional information that ensures the colors in the image are being interpreted properly.

A color profile is essentially just a label that describes how the colors in an image should be displayed or printed. Along with a monitor profile and a device-independent working space, it represents the third crucial component in how Photoshop handles the colors in the images you work on. Any file you work on in Photoshop should be saved with an embedded color profile (this option can be found in the Save As dialog box). The presence of a profile tells Photoshop and other ICC-aware applications how the colors should look. I cannot stress enough the importance of having a profile associated with your image. In the words of color management experts Bruce Fraser and Andrew Rodney, without an embedded profile, your file is just so much RGB "mystery meat." Photoshop has no idea how to display the colors, so it just displays them according to the working space, which may represent a correct interpretation, but then again may not.

CONFIGURING THE COLOR SETTINGS

With that history lesson and important background information out of the way, let's turn our attention to the actual Color Settings dialog box and discuss some of the choices there. On Mac OS X, this dialog box can be found under the Photoshop menu; on Windows, it's found in the Edit menu. Or you can simply press (Cmd + Shift + K) [Ctrl + Shift + K].

The Settings Menu

The settings pop-up menu is at the very top of the Color Settings dialog box and contains a collection of preset configurations tailored for different purposes. If you have never changed these settings, it's likely they are still set at the defaults, which, while not catastrophic, are certainly not the best settings for serious photographic work with Photoshop. In Photoshop 6 and 7, the default settings are configured to Web Graphics Default unless you customize them when you first open the program after installation or later on. In Photoshop CS, the default settings have been changed to North America General Purpose Defaults, which for all practical purposes are no different than the previous set of defaults. Again, while use of these default settings doesn't herald the end of the world in terms of color quality, they're not ideal.

To quickly get to most of the settings that I recommend for photography, you can choose U.S. Prepress Defaults from the Settings menu (**figure 1.21**).

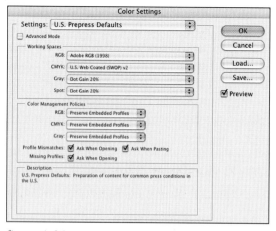

figure 1.21

View of the opened Settings menu from the Color Settings dialog box, with U.S. Prepress Defaults active.

RGB Working Spaces

Photoshop provides you with four choices for RGB Working Spaces and of these, only two are serious contenders for those who care about good color reproduction. Unfortunately, neither of them is included in the default settings. Let's take a look at them in greater detail. I'll list them in order of preference, rather than how they appear in the Working Space pop-up menu.

- **Adobe RGB (1998).** This is my preferred working space and, with few exceptions, it's the one I recommend for digital photographers. If you chose U.S Prepress Defaults from the settings menu, Adobe RGB (1998) is already selected for you. This RGB working space has the largest color gamut of any of the four spaces provided by Photoshop. If you're producing images for reproduction on a printing press, the gamut of Adobe RGB includes nearly all of the colors that can be found in the most commonly used CMYK gamuts. The only potential drawback of using Adobe RGB for prepress work is that it extends pretty far out into the brightly saturated greens—colors which in most cases would be impossible to reproduce on press.

For any printed output of your photographs on RGB devices, whether that be on inkjet printers or photographic printers such as a Lightjet 5000, Adobe RGB (1998) encompasses most of the color gamuts of those devices and is the best choice of the available RGB working spaces in Photoshop. But if you're preparing files for specific output devices, it's always a good idea to check with your output provider to see whether they have different recommendations. Many consumer digital photo printers, such as the Fuji Frontier, use sRGB as their target output profile.

- **ColorMatch RGB.** This working space is based on the gamut of an actual device, the Radius Pressview monitor that was once ubiquitous in prepress shops. After Adobe RGB (1998), this is the other logical choice to use, particularly if you are preparing images for press reproduction. Although the gamut of ColorMatch is much smaller than Adobe RGB (1998), it does include most of the common CMYK gamuts. Because it does not include as many intense, saturated colors as Adobe RGB (1998), some people prefer this space for work that will end up on press because the saturation of some of the colors they see on their monitor will more closely resemble what the image will look like when it is finally converted into CMYK.

- **sRGB.** This is Photoshop's default RGB working space, so if you have never changed it, or if you just accepted the defaults when you installed the program, it's probably still set to this. If I had to describe this working space in a few words, those words would be "the lowest common denominator." In an effort to place some reference on what they felt most of the world was seeing on their monitors, Microsoft and Hewlett-Packard developed the sRGB space to represent the gamut of the "typical" monitor. Because most of the world is probably using cheap monitors that are not designed for imaging work, sRGB is nothing to write home about. If your work is destined for a printing press, sRGB is not advisable because it produces considerable clipping of colors (that is, it cannot reproduce them), especially in the cyan range.

With prints made from desktop inkjet printers, which is arguably what many digital photographers are most concerned with, sRGB is similarly gamut-challenged. Because most cameras use a variation of sRGB as their internal space for creating photos from the data produced by the CCD, you might think it makes sense to simply use sRGB in Photoshop as well. While not catastrophic for casual use (that is, emailing photos, dropping them into a Microsoft Powerpoint presentation, Web graphics, or hobby-printing), it's not ideal for printed output. Suffice it to say, if you really care about color quality, you can do much better. I recommend Adobe RGB (1998) over sRGB any day.

- **Apple RGB.** I'm not sure why Apple RGB is still offered in Photoshop. In computer terms, it's something from the fossil record (the polite way of referring to it would be to call it a "legacy" working space). In Photoshop 4 and earlier, the default color space (it didn't let you choose your own back then) was based on an Apple 13-inch monitor, hence the inclusion of Apple RGB in the list of choices here. Unless you're just nostalgic for the past (otherwise known as the "dark ages before color management"), there is no good reason for you to choose this as a working space.

- Many people assume that the best working space to use is one that describes their monitor, camera, scanner, or printer they will use to print the final image. This is a false assumption. You should never, ever use a device profile as a working space in Photoshop. For one thing, a working space based on a specific device, especially a monitor, may not contain all the colors your output device can render. Another reason is that

device profiles are rarely neutral (also known as *gray-balanced*), which means that equal amounts of red, green, and blue yield a neutral color. Photoshop makes this critical assumption in color correction and blend mode calculations. To play it safe, stick with one of the four working spaces that ship with Photoshop. My recommendation is Adobe RGB (1998).

CMYK Working Spaces

Before I get into the different factors that determine what CMYK working space you should choose, let's get one thing straight: You only need to be concerned with this setting if the images you're working on will be reproduced on a commercial printing press. Even though desktop inkjet printers use cyan, magenta, yellow, and black inks, they are considered to be RGB devices because they do such a great job of taking the RGB data you give them, converting the RGB information into the color of ink they use, and most importantly making nice prints. If you don't need to convert images to CMYK for prepress purposes, you don't need to trouble yourself with this setting, and you can safely skip ahead to the next section.

Although RGB working spaces are device-independent, CMYK is very output specific, and the settings are influenced by such things as the type of inks, the paper being used, and, in some cases, the characteristics of the individual printing press. So it's not as easy to give a one-size-fits-all recommendation for the best space to use. This is also not a CMYK book, so our coverage of this area is not indepth. I can, however, talk about the default settings and some of the presets that are included with Photoshop that represent a good start. Knowing a bit more about these will help point you in the right direction should you find yourself having to prepare images for reproduction on a press. I also believe in acknowledging the expertise of those whose experiences and advice I value—*Real World Adobe Photoshop* CS by David Blatner and Bruce Fraser is an excellent resource for anyone who needs to use Photoshop with CMYK.

If you're in the United States, using the default U.S. Web Coated (SWOP) version 2 is probably as safe a choice as any for a default setting. The term *web* here does not refer to the World Wide Web, but to a web press, which uses huge rolls of paper fed through the press at incredible speeds (think of those montage shots in old movies where you see the newspapers flying by on the printing press in the background and the momentous front page spins into view in the center of the screen). The term *coated* refers to the fact that paper has a very thin coating that is designed to produce sharper text and images with more saturated ink coverage. This book is printed on coated paper, for example, as are most magazines and high-quality publications. If the press uses individual sheets of paper, as opposed to the large rolls on web presses, you might choose U.S. Sheetfed Coated v2. If you were printing on uncoated paper, which is generally duller and less glossy, you would use one of the settings for uncoated paper stocks.

Because CMYK settings are so tied to how the job will be reproduced, any setting you choose should be thought of as no more than a general place-holder that will suffice for the most common printing situations. Depending on the work you do and the type of publications in which it appears, one of the supplied presets may be just fine, but you should always maintain good channels of communication with your publisher or printer and verify you are using the right setting. While I was working on this book, for instance, I used two specific CMYK setups supplied to me by the publisher: one for images and the other for screenshots.

Gray Working Spaces

Gray working spaces can be selected to reflect specific dot-gain characteristics or display gammas. *Dot-gain percentages* refer to the fact that when printed on a press, a dot of ink will increase in size, and therefore become darker, as it is imprinted and absorbed into the paper. The gamma settings are designed for images that will be viewed on a monitor but also work well for images that will be printed on an inkjet printer (more on that shortly).

If your primary output is to a printing press, choose a dot gain that matches the same figure in your CMYK setup. For instance, a common percentage for coated stock is 20, which is the default in Photoshop CS. As with CMYK, however, mileage and dot gain may vary depending on the particular inks and paper being used, so consult your printer to get as much information as possible.

If you're printing black and white images to a desktop inkjet printer, I recommend setting the Gray Working Space to Gray Gamma 2.2. This is true even if you're on a Mac, which still uses a default display gamma of 1.8. A gamma of 2.2 (here and in your monitor calibration) will produce smoother gradients than a gamma of 1.8. If you're on a Mac and will be opening earlier grayscale files created using a gray gamma of 1.8, you will be notified that the embedded profile does not match the current gray working space of 2.2. In that case, just choose Convert to Profile, and the tones in the photo will be converted with an eye toward preserving the appearance of the image.

Spot Working Spaces

This setting is very specific and refers only to specialized prepress situations where custom inks (that is, other than the standard process colors of CMYK) will be used. It does not apply to working on your digital photographs. Because you'll probably never use it, the default setting is fine. If you need to use it at all, check with your printer about the specific dot-gain characteristics of the ink, paper, and press that will be used to print the job.

COLOR MANAGEMENT POLICIES

This section of Photoshop's Color Settings tells the program how to behave when it encounters an image that either does not have a profile (untagged) or has an embedded profile that does not match the currently selected working space (mismatched). This is the place that controls those annoying warnings that appear when you open an image in Photoshop. Well, some people feel they're annoying, but once you understand what they're telling you, they're not so bad.

There are three separate pop-up menus for setting the policies for RGB, CMYK, and Gray working spaces (**figure 1.22**). All contain the same three choices: Preserve Embedded Profiles, Convert to Working RGB (or CMYK, or Gray), and Off. These choices are the same ones that appear in the warning dialog boxes when you open images, although the exact wording is a bit different What you select here just determines which radio button is selected by default when the warning dialog box pops up. Let's take a look at exactly what these choices mean. I'll discuss them in order of our preference, rather than how they appear in the menu.

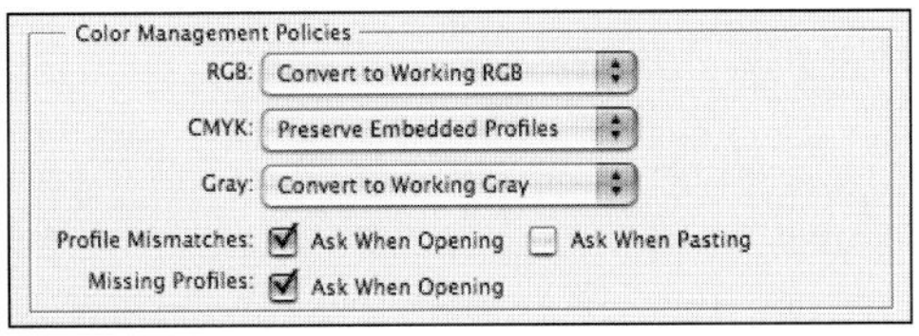

figure 1.22

The Color Management Policies control whether you see a color profile warning dialog box when you open a file.

- **Convert to Working RGB.** When a file is opened that has a different color tag than your working space, this choice will convert the image from the embedded space into your currently selected RGB working space. This is your best choice if you're working in a closed loop system (that is, you're generating all of your images from your scanner or digital camera), you know where all of the files are coming from and that they have accurate profiles, and you're using a working space such as Adobe RGB (1998).
- **Preserve Embedded Profiles.** When opening a file with a color tag that is different from your working space, any embedded profile (like sRGB, or ColorMatch) is not touched. The image opens into Photoshop, and you can work on it in its own color space without having to convert to your working space.

Assuming that you have a properly calibrated and profiled monitor, the display of the image should be correct. This setting is useful if you get files from different sources and only want to make a conversion to your working space after you have had a chance to see the file.

- **Off.** If you open a file that contains an embedded profile, Photoshop will throw away the profile and regard the image as untagged. The color numbers in the file will be interpreted according to the currently selected working space, even though that may not be a correct assumption. Because I believe profiles (if they are accurate) can help you take control of the color in your digital images, it's probably no surprise that I think this is a really bad idea. By stripping the profile from the image, you are flying blind as to the true meaning of the color numbers, and Photoshop can only display the file as if it matched your working space. There is no good reason to choose this setting.

Profile Mismatches and Missing Profiles

These three checkboxes control whether you see those pesky missing or mismatched profile notices when you open a file. If you can't stand them and never want to be bothered by them again (and I hear this sentiment a lot!), you can turn them off here. I recommend you leave at least two of them on, however, because it's always good to be informed about what's happening with the color in a file. The most important ones are the Ask When Opening options that trigger a notice if you open a file that either has no profile or has a profile that does not match your working space. The last one, which you can safely turn off (it drives me crazy!), is the Ask When Pasting option. This triggers a notice when you paste from one image to another and the profiles of the two don't match. In nearly all cases, the answer to the question it poses is the default one, which is to convert the color numbers so that the image appearance is preserved.

How to Deal with Profile Warnings

One of the most common questions I get from students and new Photoshop users is what to do about the missing profile and profile mismatch warnings that seem to pop up every time you open a file, as shown in **figure 1.23**. If you don't know what they're telling you or what the right answer should be, encountering these can be very frustrating. To make matters more perplexing, they use language that is slightly different from that used in the Color Management Policies section. In an effort to clear up some of the confusion surrounding these warnings, here are some recommendations on which choices are appropriate when you run into them.

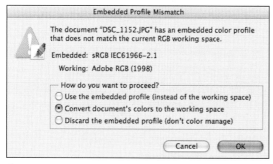

figure 1.23

The Embedded Profile Mismatch dialog box.

Profile Mismatch situations are the easiest to deal with because Photoshop detects a profile associated with the image, which gives it the necessary information to convert the color numbers from the existing profile into your current RGB working space. Of the three choices presented to you, only the first two are really an option.

The Use the Embedded Profile option will honor the existing color tag and you will be able to edit the image in its native space, as though your working space had been temporarily changed to match the profile of the image. This choice is the same as the Preserve Embedded Profiles menu option in Color Management Policies.

The Convert Document's Colors to the Working Space option is probably the more logical choice for most digital camera owners (assuming that the profile is correct). The most likely scenario you will encounter is opening a digital capture where the camera has tagged it with an sRGB profile. Because it's far better to edit an image in the Adobe RGB (1998) space than in sRGB, converting to the working space makes a lot of sense. The conversion will preserve the image's appearance, so while actual color values in the image may change, it should look exactly as though you had opened it by choosing to preserve the embedded profile. This choice is the same as the Convert to Working RGB option in Color Management Policies.

The final choice, Discard the Embedded Profile (Don't Color Manage), should not be used. This is the same as the Off choice in the Color Management Policies. The profile is removed from the image and the colors in the file are interpreted according to the working space, which is essentially just Photoshop shrugging and saying, "I dunno, let's try this." The only reason I can think of to ever use this option is when you're certain the embedded profile is wrong and you want to remove it so that you can assign a new one.

If you open an image that has no embedded profile, Photoshop has no reference to rely on. In the Missing Profile dialog box, it asks you how you want it to interpret the color numbers in the file. If you are only opening files from your digital camera, you can usually figure out the right choice with a little testing. For one thing, most consumer level digital cameras create files that look pretty good when opened as sRGB files. If your camera lets you shoot into the Adobe RGB (1998) space, you can always select that, or simply convert into the working space if you're using Adobe RGB (1998). The next few paragraphs detail what the three choices in the Missing Profile dialog box (see **figure 1.24**) mean.

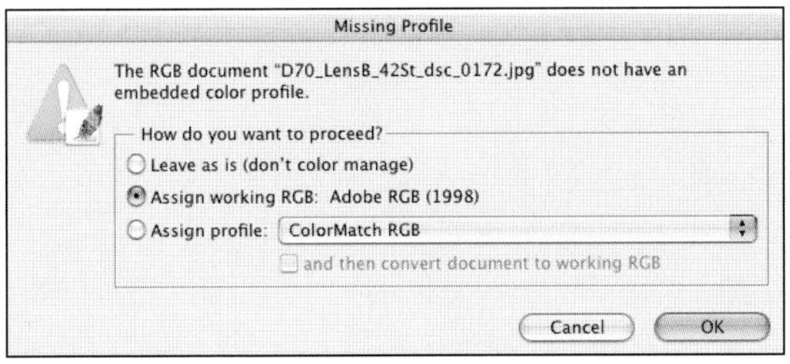

figure 1.24

The Missing Profile dialog box.

The Leave As Is (Don't Color Manage) option is similar to Off in the Profile Mismatch Warning dialog box, with the exception that because there is no profile to start with, nothing gets stripped from the image. Photoshop opens it, interpreting the colors according to how the working space thinks they should be displayed, whether that is correct or not.

The Assign Working RGB option essentially does the same as the previous choice, with the only difference being that it slaps the profile of the working space onto the image. Because no color numbers have changed and the image is being displayed based on the specification of the working space, the appearance of the image will be identical to how it would look if you had chosen Leave As Is. This choice is appropriate only if you know that the file matches your working space.

The Assign Profile option lets you choose a specific profile and then convert to the working space after the profile has been assigned. This is a good choice if you know, for example, that sRGB works well for your camera's images but they still open up as untagged. You can choose sRGB from the pop-up menu and then click the Convert to Working RGB checkbox. The momentary presence of the sRGB profile gives Photoshop enough information to make a correct conversion to the working space. The only thing missing from this choice is a preview so that you can see how a different profile is affecting the image. But, because the image isn't even open yet, there's no way to see a preview.

When opening the tutorial images from this book's Web site, please choose the Use the Embedded Profile option to maintain the color integrity of the images.

Color Companion by Tim Grey and *Real World Adobe Photoshop* CS by David Blatner and Bruce Fraser are both great references if you want to delve deeper into Photoshop's handling of color.

CLOSING THOUGHTS

Learning about the history of photomontage and setting up Photoshop preferences and color settings is only the beginning. So grab your mouse and let's dive into mastering the tools and techniques you'll use to create the images in your imagination.

2

SELECTION STRATEGIES AND ESSENTIALS

For me, one of the very best aspects of Photoshop is that there are usually three to five ways of accomplishing anything. This flexibility means I can approach each image with a variety of tools and techniques to create an intricate selection or seamlessly combine images. But on the other hand, that flexibility can be very frustrating when you're working under a deadline or trying out something new. You can avoid the frustration by developing a selection strategy.

In this chapter, you'll learn how

- Photoshop sees and handles selections
- To analyze an image to make the best selection
- To work with the Marquee, Elliptical, and Lasso tools
- To use the Magic Wand and Quick Mask tools to make refined selections
- The value of combining tools and techniques

The great majority of image composites are based on masking, and masking is based on selections. So before you can dive into masking and compositing, it is essential to appreciate and practice the art of making better selections.

WHAT IS A SELECTION?

You can work with an image in two ways—either globally or locally. The global approach affects the entire image or active layer, and it's something I'm sure you've done while experimenting with Photoshop filters. Working locally begins by selecting part of the image and then applying a filter. See **figure 2.1** for examples of both. Without a selection, Photoshop will always work globally and change all the pixels of the active layer. To control where Photoshop applies a change, use a selection or a mask to "tell" Photoshop exactly where the change should take place. The changes you make can be as subtle as lightening up part of a landscape or changing a section of a color image into black and white, or it can be as radical as the limits of your own imagination, such as superimposing a decrepit skull onto a person's face to imply mortality.

So exactly what is a selection and how does Photoshop "see" it? The selection edges, which in the past have also been referred to as *dancing ants* or *marching ants*, signify an active selection, but they are not how Photoshop actually recognizes a selection. Internally all Photoshop selections are grayscale files that Photoshop references to designate active and inactive image areas. If you want to change a specific image area, you start by selecting it; but what Photoshop is seeing internally is that the active area is white and the inactive area is black, as shown in **figure 2.2**.

To create a soft transition around a subject, you could feather a selection to soften the edges. Photoshop doesn't know what feather really means, but it does know that lighter shades of gray are more active and darker shades of gray are less active, which is exactly what feathering does. Feathering adds a tonal transition from the black inactive to white active area by blurring the internal grayscale file to create softer edges and transitions, as shown in **figure 2.3**.

TYPES OF SELECTIONS

Making a good selection—whether it's selecting a geometric street sign or a finely detailed dandelion seedpod—doesn't begin with the mouse. Rather, a good selection involves first assessing the image and the subject and then, based on that assessment, deciding on the best selection tool(s) or technique(s) to use. Once you've selected the subject, the fun begins. You can change its color, replace it completely, or add it to another image to create fantastic images that are uniquely yours.

© John Macintosh

figure 2.1

From left to right: Original, Filter applied globally, and Filter applied locally.

In the following section, I introduce the five primary types of selections and explain which tools and techniques to use, as listed in **table 2.1**. The five primary types of selections are based on shape and form, tone and color, edges and detail, translucency and light, and opposites and differences. To make life interesting, images often combine more than one of these selection types, and you will need to use more than one tool or technique to make the best selection.

figure 2.2

Left: The active selection. Right: The internal grayscale file Photoshop creates to record the active (white) and inactive (black) areas.

figure 2.3

The internal grayscale file Photoshop creates when a feather of 25 is applied to the active selection. Notice the soft transition from filtered to non-filtered areas in the image.

table 2.1

Types of Selections

Type	Example	Tool or Technique	Chapters
Shape and Form	Street signs	Rectangular and Elliptical Marquee	2
	Fruit, sculptures	Lasso and Pen tools	2 and 4
Tone and Color	Highlights and shadows Brightly colored clothing	Magic Wand, Magnetic Lasso, and Color Range	2 and 3
Edges and Fine Details	Hair and fur	Extract, Luminance Masking, and Image calculations	8, 9, 10
Translucency and Light	Glassware and smoke	Channel masks, Green screen, and Image calculations	9 and 10
Opposites and Differences	Subject on contrasting background	All of the above	2, 4, 8, 9

Shape and Form

Shape-based and form-based subjects are the easiest to recognize because the subject is usually a clearly defined object. Shape selections are usually geometric and man-made, while form selections often have curved and more organic lines. Both shape-based and form-based selections have smooth edges and contours. In addition to shape, you need to study the edge characteristics of the subject—for instance, even though both apples and kiwis are round fruit, the smooth apple is a good example of a form-based selection while the fuzzy kiwi isn't. **Figure 2.4** shows shape-based and form-based subjects. Other examples of shape-based selections include buildings, automobiles, and sculptures; other examples of form-based selections include nudes; planets; and sea life such as fish, porpoises, and whales. We'll be working with a variety of shape-based and form-based selections later in this chapter and in Chapter 4, "Pen Tool Power."

Tone and Color

Images are primarily split into three tones: shadows, midtones, and highlights. Digital photographers often need to select an image tone to improve specific values in an image. For example, I wanted to lighten up the darker values of the castle image shown in the before and after example in **figure 2.5**.

Color selections are based on (you guessed it!) color. Although they may seem straightforward, working with color selections requires a keen eye and an understanding of how light bounces and reflects onto both the image subject and the image environment. Making tone and color selections is addressed in this chapter; Chapter 3, "The Essential Select Menu;" and Chapter 10, "Selecting Translucency and Green-Screen Techniques."

figure 2.4

The antique sign is a shape-based subject, while the curved pear is based on organic form.

BEFORE

AFTER

figure 2.5

Lightening up the darker areas of the castle guides the viewer's eye to the center of the image.

Edges and Fine Detail

Everyone wants to select edges and fine detail, but once they try to select a model's hair they start tearing out their own. Some of the more challenging things to select are people (figure 2.6) or animals with fine hair; winter tree branches and soft edged subjects such as motion-blurred automobiles; and images with a shallow depth of field, as shown in figure 2.7. Chapter 8, "Selecting Hair and Fine Detail"; Chapter 9, "Advanced Selection Techniques"; and Chapter 10, "Selecting Translucency and Green-Screen Techniques" are dedicated to mastering these demanding selections, where you must select the finest details while preserving the look and feel of the original edges in the image.

© John Macintosh

figure 2.6

Extracting a person with fine hair can be challenging.

figure 2.7

Maintaining fine detail and soft edges when making selections requires a careful eye and delicate mouse.

Translucency and Light

Translucency and light are very challenging selections to make. The flowing veil of a bride's wedding dress, a wisp of smoke, or the transparent nature of a beautiful crystal glass all need to be selected while maintaining the delicate characteristics of the subject. **Figure 2.8** is a beautiful composite by Mark Beckelman that illustrates the refreshing quality of natural spring water. Can you see how the water is flowing in and around the bottle? We'll be working with making similar selections and images in Chapters 10 and 12.

© Mark Beckelman

figure 2.8

Working with clear objects and translucent materials can try anyone's patience.

Opposites and Differences

Opposites and differences are selections in which you select the parts of the image you don't want, and then inverse the selection to make the selection of the things you do want. For example, take a look at **figure 2.9**—would it be easier to select the red flower or the blue sky? If I need to select the red poppy, I can achieve a better selection more quickly by selecting the smooth blue sky and then inversing the selection. Working with opposites and differences is just one example of learning to think like Photoshop, which I'll address later in this chapter.

figure 2.9

Selecting the opposite is often quicker than selecting the actual object.

You may be wondering why I'm spending so much time and so many pages on selections when the book is called *Photoshop Masking and Compositing*. It really should be titled *Photoshop Selections, Masking, and Compositing*, but that is simply too many words to fit onto the spine of the book. Making appropriate and accurate selections is an essential Photoshop skill that may not seem as exciting as creating a surreal illustration, but the great majority of composites start with the artist isolating and selecting the individual image elements before bringing them together.

GEOMETRIC SHAPE SELECTIONS

The Marquee, Polygon Lasso, and Pen tools are the best tools for selecting geometric shapes. The following section discusses the Rectangular and Elliptical Marquee and Polygon Lasso tools. The Pen tool is such a precise and important selection tool that I've dedicated an entire chapter to it (see Chapter 4).

The Rectangular and Elliptical Marquee selection tools have been in the Photoshop toolbar since version 1.0 and are ideal tools to use when selecting geometrically shaped objects such as planets, balls, and individual signs, as shown in **figure 2.10**. When I use either the Rectangular or Elliptical Marquee tool, I start by clicking the upper-left corner and pressing the mouse button while dragging diagonally down and over to the bottom-right corner, as illustrated in **figure 2.11**. Starting in the same corner every time gives me a sense of orientation, allowing me to concentrate on the selection task at hand.

⊕⊳‹ **ch2_signs.jpg**

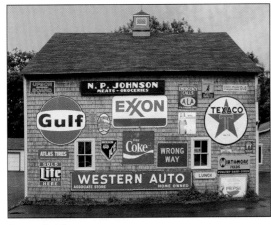

figure 2.10

The signs are ideal subjects to select with the geometric Marquee and Elliptical Marquee tools.

figure 2.11

Clicking and dragging from the upper-left corner to the lower-right corner to select the sign.

🔍 **T i p**

To create a perfect square or circle:

1. Hold the Shift key while dragging with the Rectangular or Elliptical marquee.

2. Press (Option) [Alt] to start the selection from the center.

3. Press (Option + Shift) [Alt + Shift] to draw a perfect square or circle from the center of an object.

4. Press the spacebar while dragging out a selection to move the selection while drawing it.

Fine-Tuning a Marquee Selection

If you miss the exact area you want to select, you have a number of options:

- Click next to the inexact selection to deselect it and try again. (Cmd + D) [Ctrl + D] also deselects the active selection.

- Click a selection tool in the toolbar and use the arrow keys on the extended keyboard to nudge the active selection into position.

- Transform the selection to fit the position, shape, and angle by using Select > Transform Selection, which will add a transform boundary with eight handles and a center point.

  1. Grab a handle to pull or push the selection outline into place.

  2. To rotate the selection, move the mouse 1/2 inch (1 cm) away from one of the corner handles. When you see the curved arrows, hold down the mouse button and pull in the direction in which you would like the selection to rotate.

  3. (Control-click) [right-click] near any of the handles to bring up the context-sensitive controls, as shown in **figure 2.12**, to scale, rotate, skew, distort, apply perspective, rotate in exact increments, or flip.

  4. Once you are satisfied with the transformed selection, press the Enter or Return key to apply the Select Transform.

figure 2.12

The context-sensitive menu gives you access to all the controls of the Transform Selection command.

In the example of the Enjoy Coke sign, I used the skew and distort controls to make the selection fit the angle and shape of the sign. To further refine selections, please see "Adding, Subtracting, and Intersecting Selections," later in this chapter.

Caution

If your Marquee selections have unwanted rounded corners or are not shaped correctly, check the Options bar. Often a previously dialed-in feather or style can interfere with making rectangular selections.

The Secret Identity of the Elliptical Marquee Tool

The Elliptical Marquee is really the Rectangular Marquee tool in disguise. Treating it like the Rectangular Marquee with extremely rounded corners makes it easier to use. Try the following two exercises to feel and understand how the Elliptical Marquee tool is working.

ch2_arrowsign.jpg

1. The Elliptical Marquee tool is nested under the Rectangular Marquee tool. Select the Elliptical Marquee tool, position the mouse at the center of the sign and (Shift + Option) [Shift + Alt] click and drag straight up toward the top of the image. Notice how small and tight the circle is and that you're pushing without a lot of results.

2. Release the mouse and click outside the selection to deselect it.

3. With the Elliptical Marquee tool, position the mouse at the center of the sign and (Shift + Option) [Shift + Alt] click and drag up and over to the upper right or left corner, as illustrated in **figure 2.13**. Notice how quickly and easily you can draw the circle.

Tip

When using with the Elliptical Marquee tool, work diagonally from corner to corner for the best results.

figure 2.13

Dragging diagonally toward the fictitious corners of the Elliptical Marquee lets you make a round selection very easily.

Selecting Circles and Ovals Without the Guesswork

ch2_markfoo.jpg

The poignant memorial to world-class surfer Mark Foo shown in **figure 2.14** is in Hawaii. To select just the gray marble of the tablet, follow these steps:

figure 2.14

Framing the object with guides to make the best and fastest selection.

1. Select View > Show Rulers and drag out four guides that just touch the four outermost curves of the dark marble, as shown in figure 2.14.

2. With the Elliptical Marquee tool, click the upper-left intersection of guides and drag down to the lower-right intersection, as shown in **figure 2.15**.

figure 2.15

Start at the upper-left intersection and drag down toward the lower-right guides.

3. If necessary, fine-tune the selection with Select > Select Transform to scale and shape the selection outline. (Control-click) [right-click] any of the handles to access all possible controls. In this case, I selected Distort and finessed the upper-left and lower-right sides of the selection in toward the marble to make a better selection.

Tip

When using the Elliptical Marquee tool, select View > Snap to > Guides to help keep the selection within the boundary defined by the guides.

Rectangular and Elliptical Marquee Tool Options

The Options bar shown in **figure 2.16** contains all the settings for controlling the active tool. The three state-change buttons are addressed in "Adding, Subtracting, and Intersecting Selections", later in this chapter. Here I'll address the options that are relevant to the Rectangular and Elliptical Marquee tool—Feather, Anti-aliased, and Style.

figure 2.16

Before you use a tool, use the Options bar to control the tool's behavior.

Feather

Feathering softens a selection edge to both the inside and outside of the initial selection. As discussed earlier in this chapter, Photoshop sees all selections as grayscale channels—black represents unselected areas, shades of gray are partially selected areas, and white areas are fully selected. Feathering creates a transition between the white and the black areas. The lower the feather value, the shorter the transition; the higher the feather value, the wider the transition. The file resolution also affects the visual effect a feather has. For example, if you apply a feather of 10 to a selection on a low resolution, Web-graphic-sized file, it will have a very visible effect. If you use a 10-pixel feather on a high-resolution 100MB or larger file, that feathering will have much less visual impact.

In figure 2.17, you see a tight crop of a stained glass window that I created with four different feather settings of 0, 5, 20, and 50. The higher the feather value, the softer the transition is into the white background and the more diffuse the subject becomes.

To Feather or Not to Feather?

When using the Marquee tools, I recommend you don't use the Feather control in the Options bar. When you dial in a feather setting in the Options bar, you cannot see the actual effect of the feathering. To state it bluntly, you are working blindly. Rather, use the Gaussian Blur filter on a Quick Mask of your selection to visually control the amount of feather, as described Chapter 3.

figure 2.17

By changing the feather, you influence the edge quality of objects. From left to right, I used a feather of 0, 5, 20, and 20.

Anti-Aliased

When using the Elliptical Marquee and Lasso tools, the Anti-aliased check box is selected by default. Anti-aliasing adds a subtle transition between pixels when working with these tools. It's important to understand that anti-aliasing is not the same as applying a feather. **Figure 2.18** illustrates this—the left circle was made with the standard elliptical selection with Anti-aliased selected and a feather of 0. The right circle was made with the Elliptical Marquee tool when Anti-aliased was not selected. The bottom circle was made with the Elliptical Marquee tool with Anti-aliased deselected but with a feather of 1 applied after the selection was made. As you can see in the close-up in figure 2.18, the initial anti-aliased selection is smooth, the second selection is jaggy, and the feathered selection is quite soft. The only time I deselect Anti-aliased is when working on tiny image icons or thumbnails or when designing Web or multimedia graphics that require precise color placement.

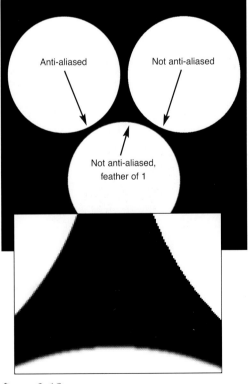

figure 2.18

With careful examination, you can see the differences in edges when anti-aliasing or feathering is applied.

Style

When the Rectangular or Elliptical Marquee tool is active, you have a choice of three styles—Normal, Constrained Aspect Ratio, and Fixed Size—to control the shape and size of the next selection. Normal lets you draw a freehand selection of any shape or size. When you change the style to Constrain Aspect Ratio, the default is set to a width of 1 and a height of 1, which is a perfect square. By changing the aspect ratio to 3 for width and 2 for height, you will create a selection with that aspect ratio when you click and drag the Rectangular Marquee. This may seem obscure, but any photographer quickly translates this to 35-mm film aspect ratio. To select the area for an 8 × 10-inch print, set the width to 10 and the height to 8 (or use the lowest common dominator of 5 and 4).

Fixed Size is very useful. If you need a rectangular image that is exactly 4 × 5 inches, enter 4 *in* and 5 *in*. With the Marquee tool active, click the mouse in the image and the next selection you make will be exactly 4 × 5 inches in size. I use Fixed Size quite often, especially when I need to make identically sized selections from multiple files to mock up a page layout or to prepare files for an on-screen presentation by using a setting of 1024 px × 768 px. The Fixed Size width and height measurements will default to the settings that the ruler Photoshop preferences are using, unless you type the abbreviations after the number value, as shown in **table 2.2**.

table 2.2
Fixed Size Terms and Abbreviations

Pixels	*px*
Inches	*in*
Centimeters	*cm*
Millimeters	*mm*
Picas	*pica*
Points	*pt*
Percentages	*%*

Selecting Non-Geometric Shape-Based Objects

Not all shape-based subjects are circles or squares, and I use both the Polygon Lasso and the Pen tools to make nongeometric shape-based selections. The Polygon Lasso tool is nested under the standard Lasso in the toolbar. It makes perfectly straight selections between clicks of the mouse. If the object you are selecting also has a curved edge, press (Option) [Alt] to change the Polygon Lasso into the standard Lasso tool. The biggest difference between the Polygon Lasso tool and the standard Lasso tool is that if you let go of the mouse, the Polygon Lasso doesn't race back to your starting point. To close the selection, you can either click once next to the origin point or double-click any-where in the image; Photoshop will close the selec-tion by drawing a straight line between the first and last points.

Figure 2.19 shows an ideal use for the Polygon Lasso tool, because I would like to select the small church to isolate it from the background.

⊕↳✕ **ch2_church_model.jpg**

🔍 T i p
_____

To work efficiently with the Polygon Lasso or the Pen tool:

- (Cmd + Opt + 0) [Ctrl + Alt + 0] (zero) to view the image at 100%.

- To see more detail, (Cmd + +) [Ctrl + +] to zoom to 200%.

- If you run out of monitor space, press the spacebar to turn the Polygon Lasso into the Hand tool and drag the image towards the center of the monitor to see more of the image. Releasing the spacebar returns the Hand tool to the previously used tool.

figure 2.19
_____

The original photograph and the isolated church.

1. Select the Polygon Lasso tool and click in the lower-right corner of the church. Release the mouse button, move the mouse up, and click the corner where the church building and roof meet, as shown in **figure 2.20**.

figure 2.20

Starting the selection.

2. If you run out of monitor space, press the spacebar to turn the Polygon Lasso into the Hand tool and drag the image toward the center of the monitor so that you can see the upper portion of the church, as shown in **figure 2.21**.

3. Continue clicking point to point until you have the entire church selected.

figure 2.21

Zoom and position the image to see the image edges.

4. Continue clicking around the church until you reach the starting point. To close the selection, either click as close as possible to the starting point or double-click (**figure 2.22**).

figure 2.22

The completed selection.

5. Zoom in and carefully inspect the selection to see if areas are missing, such as shown in **figure 2.23**, where the top of the steeple is not accurately selected. If the area you wish to add is not a straight line, select the standard Lasso tool. While holding down the Shift key, start in the existing selection and draw along the desired area to include the missing areas. When you release the mouse, Photoshop will add the missing area to the active selection (**figure 2.24**).

6. If parts of the selection include unwanted areas, use the Lasso tool to correct. While holding (Option) [Alt], start drawing from the existing selection along the areas to remove and return to the existing selection. When you release the mouse, the unwanted area will be subtracted from the selection. Adding, subtracting, and intersecting selections will be explained in greater detail later in this chapter.

figure 2.23

Inspecting the initial selection reveals that the tip of the steeple is missing.

figure 2.24

The refined selection.

7. Once the selection is complete, you can copy the church and paste it into another image.

8. To save your selection with the image, click the Save Selection as Channel icon in the Channels palette (**figure 2.25**). Now when you close the file and save it as a PSD or TIF file, the alpha channel will remain with the image, and you can reactivate it by choosing Select > Load Selection, as shown in **figure 2.26**.

9. Selections that are complex, that were time consuming to make, or that that you will need again are best saved as alpha channels for future use. I will be covering alpha channels in great detail in Chapters 5, 8, and 9.

figure 2.25

Click the Save Selection as Channel icon to create an alpha channel.

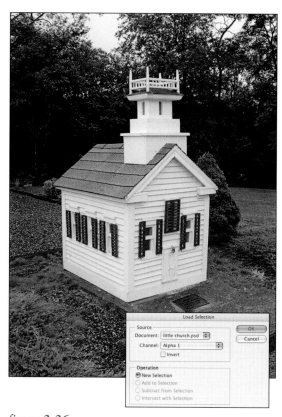

figure 2.26

Loading the alpha channel restores the original selection.

FORM-BASED SELECTIONS

Form-based selections usually work well for smooth, organic objects that are not geometrically shaped. The primary tool I use for these tasks is the Pen tool, as explained in Chapter 4. However, many people find the Lasso tool very useful to make and refine form-based selections as described here.

The Standard Lasso Tool

The standard Lasso tool lets you select objects that are organically shaped (*not* geometric shapes, which are best selected with the Rectangular and Elliptical Marquee tools). On its most basic level, the standard Lasso is a very straightforward tool to use. Click and hold the mouse button and drag around the object you want to select. When you reach the starting point, let go of the mouse button and Photoshop will close the loop to complete the selection.

Combining Straight and Curved-Edged Selections

The best aspect of the standard Lasso tool is that you can turn it into the Polygon Lasso tool by (Option-clicking) [Alt-clicking] your way around an object. Use the Lasso tool to select objects that have both straight edges and curved contours like the tombstones in **figure 2.27**.

⊕▷⊱ **ch2_tombstones.jpg**

figure 2.27

The tombstones have both straight and curved contours.

1. Using the standard Lasso tool, press (Option) [Alt] and click on the lower right-hand corner of the tombstone. While keeping the (Option) [Alt] key depressed, release the mouse button, move the mouse to the corner of the base of the tombstone, and click once.

2. Repeat this once more until you reach the curved, chipped contour (**figure 2.28**). Release (Option) [Alt], but keep the mouse button depressed.

3. Click and hold down the mouse button and trace along the curve (**figure 2.29**). At the end of the curve, release the mouse button and continue using the Lasso tool like the Polygon Lasso tool. Whenever you reach an irregular or curved area, press the mouse button and trace the desired contour.

figure 2.28

Pressing (Option) [Alt] changes the Lasso tool to the Polygon Lasso tool.

figure 2.29

Pressing the mouse button lets you trace the curved details.

4. At the top of the curved chipped area, press (Option) [Alt] again and release the mouse button. Move the cursor up to define the straight side of the tombstone, click the mouse button once, and move to the next corner. Pretend you're connecting the dots by clicking from dot to dot.

5. When you reach a curved area, release (Option) [Alt] and hold down the mouse button. The Lasso tool will behave like the standard Lasso tool, enabling you to trace along any irregular or rounded edge.

6. When you reach another straight area, simply press the (Option) [Alt] key while releasing the mouse button and clicking to connect the dots between the straight areas. When you're finished, you should have a completed selection like the one shown in **figure 2.30**.

figure 2.30

The final selection.

When using the Polygon Lasso tool, whether directly or by toggling to it from the Lasso tool, you can't use the spacebar to access the Hand tool for moving the image around the monitor. Instead, as you reach the edge of the monitor, nudge the cursor to the edge of the image, and the image will scroll in that direction.

Adding, Subtracting, and Intersecting Selections

Wouldn't it be wonderful if making a good selection took just one click of the Magic Wand or a quick drag with the Marquee tool? Well, most images you work with just aren't that simple. To make the best selection, you'll often need to add or subtract from the existing selection. You can do this by either pressing the corresponding button on the Options bar as shown in **figure 2.31** or using the modifier keys, which I prefer to do as follows.

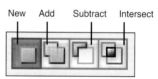

T i p

Sometimes I get confused about what's selected and what isn't. To see whether an area is selected, move any selection tool into the area in question. If the tool cursor changes to a small white arrow with a dashed rectangle next to it, you are inside the active selection. If the tool icon doesn't change and looks exactly like it does in the toolbar, you are outside the active selection.

figure 2.31

The Options bar buttons used to modify a selection.

T i p

To avoid inadvertently deselecting the active selection (also referred to as *dropping the selection*) when modifying a selection, always press the modifier key first, then use the tool, release the mouse, and then release the key.

Adding to a Selection

If an area you want to be included in the selection is not selected, add it by drawing along the missing contour with the Lasso or Marquee tool and generously drawing *into* the active selection, as illustrated in **figure 2.32**. When using the Magic Wand, hold the Shift key while clicking the areas that are not selected to add them to the selection.

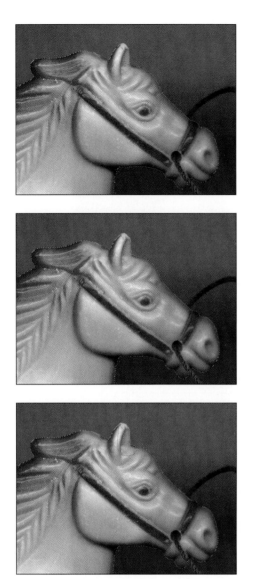

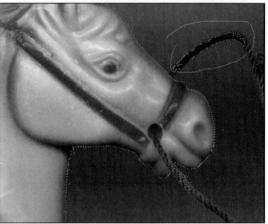

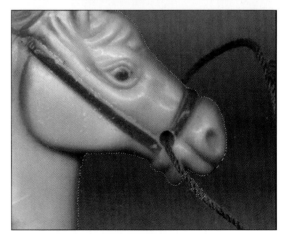

figure 2.32

To add to a selection, hold down the Shift key, start in the selection, and trace along the desired contour and back into the active selection.

Subtracting from a Selection

To subtract from an active area, hold down the (Option) [Alt] key while using any selection tool. With the Lasso tool, hold down the (Option) [Alt] key and draw along the correct contour and generously encircle the area that is incorrectly selected as shown in **figure 2.33**. With the Magic Wand, press (Option) [Alt] while clicking the area to be subtracted.

figure 2.33

To subtract from a selection, hold down (Option) [Alt] and circle the unwanted active areas.

Figure 2.34 shows a figure that I needed to separate from the wall. I started by roughly outlining the angel with the Polygon Lasso tool, as shown in figure 2.35. Then to subtract the wall but leave the angel selected, I switched to the Magic Wand and pressed the (Option) [Alt] key while clicking inside the selection on the white wall areas (figure 2.36). With a few clicks the work was done. This is a great method to quickly lift and separate objects from uniform backgrounds.

ch2_angel.jpg

figure 2.35
Roughly outline the figure with the Lasso tool.

figure 2.34
Original image.

figure 2.36
Subtracting the unwanted wall with the Magic Wand is fast and easy.

Intersecting with a Selection

You probably won't use intersect as often as add or subtract, but it comes in handy to select part of a selection. For example, I needed to select just the upper part of the Statue of Liberty. I started by selecting the sky with the Magic Wand and inversing the selection (**figure 2.37**). Then I pressed (Shift + Option) [Shift + Alt] and used the Marquee tool to frame just the area of the statue that I needed, as shown in **figure 2.38**.

ch2_liberty.jpg

Additional methods exist to modify and refine a selection, and using add, subtract, and intersect is only the beginning. As discussed later in this chapter, you can combine any selection tool with Quick Mask to paint in selection modifications. As shown in Chapter 4, the Pen tool is a fantastic tool to add, subtract, or intersect an active selection without running the risk of deselecting it.

T i p

When using the Marquee or Lasso tools to add, subtract, or intersect a selection, make certain the feather amount in the Options bar is the same as the feather setting on the original selection tool. For example, if you use the Marquee tool to make the initial selection and then add to the selection with the Lasso tool, the selection edge quality will not be the same if the Lasso tool has a different feather setting than the Marquee tool.

figure 2.38

Use the Shift + (Option) [Alt] key to intersect a selection and isolate it.

figure 2.37

The original photo.

COLOR AND TONE SELECTIONS

Making good color and tone-based selections ranges from very straightforward to intricate and complex. The simpler color-based selections are made with the Magic Wand. The Magnetic Lasso tool is a good choice for images in which the color or tone of the subject is too similar to the image background for the Magic Wand to be useful. For more intricate color-based and tone-based selections, use the Color Range command found under the Select menu, as discussed in Chapter 3.

The Magic Wand

The Magic Wand seems to be everyone's favorite selection tool…well, except for me. I understand how it works but it never seems to work as well as I want it to. Rather than relying on it, I prefer to use the "magic wand with brains"—more commonly called Color Range, as described in Chapter 3. Perhaps you will have better luck with the Magic Wand, so I've included both technical and practical information for you to get to know the tool and make your own decisions about it.

The four settings that influence the Magic Wand's behavior are Tolerance, Contiguous, Use All Layers, and, oddly enough, Sample Size on the Eyedropper tool.

The Tolerance Setting

The Tolerance setting is the primary setting to control how many shades of brightness the Magic Wand includes in a selection. The settings range from 0 to 255, with 0 selecting only one tonal value, the default of 32 selecting 32 shades, and 255 selecting all the shades of the image (basically, the entire image). The Magic Wand stops the selection where the tonal difference is higher than the Tolerance setting. Please note: I refer to shades of brightness instead of color because the Magic Wand doesn't really look at color. Rather, it looks at the image channels, which in an RGB image are three grayscale images stacked on top of one another.

When working with grayscale images, the Tolerance setting is pretty straightforward. As shown in **figure 2.39**, I used the Magic Wand with a Tolerance setting of 16 and clicked once in the center of the grayscale ramp, which selected 16 shades of gray above and 16 shades of gray below where I clicked. After choosing Select > Deselect, I increased the tolerance to 32 and clicked on the identical spot shown in the figure, which selected 32 shades above and 32 shades below the point where I clicked.

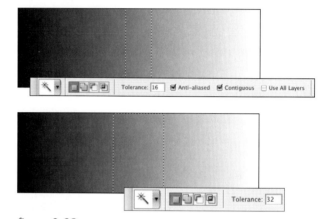
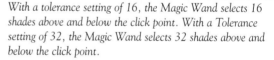

figure 2.39

With a tolerance setting of 16, the Magic Wand selects 16 shades above and below the click point. With a Tolerance setting of 32, the Magic Wand selects 32 shades above and below the click point.

When working with color images, predicting what the Magic Wand tool will select becomes a very complicated mathematical calculation, making its behavior much more difficult to foretell. The Magic Wand looks at all three channels in a RGB image or four channels in a CMYK image and selects the average of the Tolerance setting. That's why the Magic Wand sometimes works as expected and sometimes seems to have a mind of its own.

Helping the Magic Wand

Because the Magic Wand is easier to control and predict when working with grayscale images, I first inspect the three channels by pressing (Cmd + 1, 2, 3) [Ctrl + 1, 2, 3] and then use the single channel with the greatest tonal difference to make my selection. **Figure 2.40** shows a comparison of the three RGB channels. As you can see, the red channel offers the greatest tonal difference. I activated the red channel by clicking the word *red* in the Channels palette and used the Magic Wand with a Tolerance setting of 40. With one click, I created the selection (**figure 2.41**). After returning to the composite view by pressing (Cmd + ~) [Ctrl + ~] or clicking the word *RGB* in the channel palette, the selection is still active.

Red channel

Green channel

Blue channel

figure 2.40

Inspect the grayscale channels and use the Magic Wand tool on the channel with the greatest brightness difference.

figure 2.41

The final selection in the red channel and in the composite image.

Additional Magic Wand Controls

Understanding the parameters that control the Magic Wand make it a more useful tool.

- Anti-aliased smoothes the edge transitions between what is selected and what isn't. Unless you are selecting flat graphic colors, such as for a Web graphic, I suggest you leave this on at all times.

- Contiguous is on by default, and it tells the Magic Wand to select only tonal areas that are directly connected to the point you click. If you want all similar tones in an image to be selected, uncheck Contiguous.

- Use All Layers determines whether the Magic Wand looks only at the active layer or searches all visible layers in a document, which can be very useful if you are trying to change a specific color or tone that exists on multiple layers.

- Oddly enough, the Sample Size setting on the Eyedropper tool (yes, the Eyedropper tool!) influences how large the initial area will be that the Magic Wand uses for its calculations. Point Sample will use the exact pixel you click; 3 × 3 Average will use a nine-pixel square; and 5 × 5 Average uses 25 pixels to start the Magic Wand calculations. I usually have my Eyedropper Sample size set to 3 × 3, because that is the most useful setting for color and tonal corrections. This is a setting I am aware of but do not to change because it would impact my other Photoshop work.

The Magnetic Lasso Tool

The Magnetic Lasso tool is a good choice for selecting tone and color-based images. Although it's not as straightforward to use as the standard Lasso or Polygon Lasso tools, it is well worth it to understand how its settings, shown in the Options bar in **figure 2.42**, work. In fact, the Magnetic Lasso tool is a great tool for selecting image elements that are very similar to their environments and for images in which the Magic Wand would have difficulty.

The Magnetic Lasso tool has six primary parameters that influence how it works. You can adjust them, depending on how close the subject and its environment are in tone, color, and contrast.

- Feather and Anti-aliased work exactly the same way in the Magnetic Lasso tool as they do with the other selection tools.

- Width tells the Magnetic Lasso how far from its center point (between 1 and 40 pixels) to detect an image edge. Use lower settings when the area you need to select is close to areas you don't want to select.

- Edge Contrast tells the Magnetic Lasso tool how much difference there needs to be between the object and the background. Use higher settings (30% or more) to select images or objects that are well defined from the background, and a lower edge-contrast setting for images or areas that are less defined or similar in tone to the background.

- Frequency controls how many anchor points the Magnetic Lasso lays down. The higher the frequency, the faster the anchor points will be laid down.

- Stylus Pressure is important if you work with a pressure-sensitive tablet. When the option is selected, pressing harder with the stylus will decrease the edge contrast setting.

⊕↘ꜰ **ch2_stonelion.jpg**

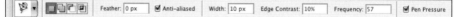

figure 2.42

Understanding the settings of the Magnetic Lasso is essential for getting great results from this tool.

The stone lion encompasses quite a selection challenge, one that I would not want to try to outline with the standard Lasso tool. However, the Magnetic Lasso tames the challenge in no time at all.

1. Because the tone of the stone lion is so similar to the background, start with lower Width and Edge Contrast settings of 30% and 5%. To see the size of the Width setting, press Caps Lock so that the Magnetic Lasso cursor is shown as a circle with a crosshair.

2. Click where the lion's back meets the stone wall, and then release the mouse and drag to the left. Notice how the Magnetic Lasso is laying down a wire-like line that follows the tonal contours (**figure 2.43**). Click the locations where you want to make sure the Magnetic Lasso lays down a point. You don't need to be compulsively perfect—just drag around the object and let the Magnetic Lasso find the edge for you.

3. When you've traced around the figure and are close to the starting point, either single-click over your starting point or double-click to close the selection (**figure 2.44**).

4. Inspect the initial selection and use the standard Lasso or Magnetic Lasso tool to refine the selection as described previously in the "Adding, Subtracting, and Intersecting" section of this chapter.

figure 2.44

After refining the selection with the standard Lasso tool, the stone lion can be copied and pasted into another document.

To really understand how the Magnetic Lasso tool works, change the tool settings one at a time to see how the change impacts tool behavior. For example, leave the Width at 40 and set the Edge Contrast to 40%. Taking a few minutes to experiment with these settings is well worth it. I like the Magnetic Lasso because it is easier on my wrist. By just clicking once and then casually dragging around an object, my hands are relieved of the tension required to click, hold, and drag with the standard Lasso tool to make a good selection.

I often use it to make a quick selection of a subject when I'm in the planning or proof-of-concept stage of an image: Rather than spending a lot of time on a complex selection, I'll do a quick rough of an image composite to see whether the idea is working. If it is, then I'll return to the image elements and take the time to make a perfect selection. If the composite isn't working, I haven't wasted a lot of time finessing a selection that in the end I didn't use.

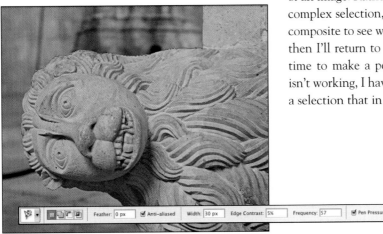

figure 2.43

Pull the Magnetic Lasso around the object without pressing the mouse button down.

Magnetic Lasso Tips

- On images with well-defined edges, use higher Width and Edge Contrast settings and trace the border quickly and roughly. On an image with less defined edges, use lower Width and Edge Contrast settings and trace the border more precisely.

- Press Caps Lock to change the Magnetic Lasso cursor from the lasso cursor to a circle with a crosshair in the center. The size of the circle reflects the Width settings, which is very helpful for seeing where the tool is looking to find an edge.

- While creating a selection, press the right bracket key (]) to increase the Magnetic Lasso edge width by 1 pixel; press the left bracket ([) key to decrease it by 1 pixel. Press Shift + right bracket to increase the Edge Width setting to the maximum of 40, and Shift + left bracket to drop it to the minimum of 1.

- While using the Magnetic Lasso tool, (Option-click) [Alt-click] to access the standard Lasso tool to hand-select areas that the Magnetic Lasso is having problems with.

- If you don't like the position of the anchor point that the Magnetic Lasso is laying down, press the (Delete) [Backspace] key to delete anchors points as you work.

- In case you're completely frustrated with the Magnetic Lasso (don't worry, we've all been there), press Escape to cancel the current selection. Modify the tool settings and try again.

COMBINING TOOLS

Making a good selection often requires that you mix and match tools and techniques. Start the selection process by making the initial selection with the tool that will grab the largest area of the object or image. Then choose the second tool that will best refine the selection. In **figure 2.45**, the challenge is to select the blue door and include the archway above the door.

ch8_bluedoor.jpg

figure 2.45

The original photo.

1. Verify the Marquee tool is set to default settings—something you can quickly do by clicking the small triangle next to the Marquee icon in the Options bar and dragging over to and highlighting the Reset Tool, as shown in **figure 2.46**.

2. Select the doorway with the Rectangular Marquee tool (**figure 2.47**).

3. If necessary, use Select > Transform Selection to make the perfectly geometric selection fit the idiosyncratic shape of the door. You can access all the controls of Transform Selection by (Control-clicking) [right-clicking] anywhere in the image to bring up the context-sensitive menu (**figure 2.48**).

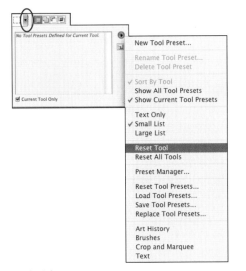

figure 2.46

Resetting the Marquee tool is useful to avoid style or feathering surprises.

figure 2.48

The Transform Selection command adds handles for tweaking your selection.

figure 2.47

Start by making a generous selection.

4. Press (Return) [Enter] to accept the transformation.

5. Select the Polygon Lasso tool. Start inside the existing selection, and Shift-click along the top of the archway (**figure 2.49**) to complete the selection of the arch.

figure 2.49

Clicking along a slightly curved area in half-inch increments makes a perfectly acceptable selection outline.

Many times you'll start a selection with one tool and then use a different selection to refine it. As mentioned earlier in the "Adding, Subtracting, and Intersecting Selections" section, when combining tools you need to verify that the settings between the tools match up. For example, if you start a selection with the Magic Wand (which doesn't have a feather setting) and then continue the selection with a Lasso tool that might have a feather, the two edges won't match up and may cause problems in your final composite. **Figure 2.50** shows what happens if you mix and match selection tools without checking the settings. I started the selection of the pastel with the Magic Wand tool and then used the Polygon Lasso with a 10-pixel feather to add to the selection. As you can see, the quality of the edges varies widely—the top part of the pastel is jaggy and the center part is much too soft. **Figure 2.51** shows the results of selecting the same pastel, but using no feather with the Polygon Lasso tool.

WORKING WITH QUICK MASK

Quick Mask is one of the very best selection tools in all of Photoshop. I use it all the time to create and refine selections and to verify the quality and accuracy of selections I made using the standard selection tools discussed previously in this chapter. In a nutshell, Quick Mask lets you see which image areas are active (selected) and which ones are inactive (not selected) via a transparent overlay. Quick Mask is tremendously flexible and powerful; you can use it with or without an existing selection, you can use many painting tools and filters on it, and you can also save a Quick Mask as an alpha channel to save it for future use. Sadly, many people belittle Quick Mask as a tool for beginners or amateurs, but I say let them make fun of the ugly duckling—we know that Quick Mask is really a swan in disguise.

figure 2.50

When combining selection tools, you need to pay attention to the settings to avoid mismatched edges.

figure 2.51

Consistent selection tool settings will create selections with similar edges.

T i p

To practice working with Quick Mask in the exercises that follow, first make sure you're using the default settings for Quick Mask. You can do this by double-clicking the left Quick Mask button under the color picker in the toolbar and making sure the settings you see match the settings shown in **figure 2.52**.

figure 2.52

Quick Mask's default settings.

Starting with a Selection

After making an initial selection using any selection tool, click the Quick Mask icon under the color picker in the toolbar or press *q*. Photoshop displays the image using a red transparent overlay, similar to a shield of clear film, to cover the inactive areas, leaving the selected areas unaffected. Notice that the dancing ants have disappeared. Quick Mask lets you modify and refine the selection without inadvertently deselecting it. Best of all, you can easily see which areas are selected and which ones aren't and work back and forth by painting with black and white to create accurate selections.

Separating Image Elements

In the following example, we need to separate the small leaf from the background.

ch2_leaves.jpg

1. Outline the leaf on the left using the Magnetic Lasso tool or select it using the Magic Wand to create the initial selection (**figure 2.53**).

2. Press *q* to enter Quick Mask mode (**figure 2.54**). Everywhere you see the red overlay, the selection is inactive—that is, not selected. Everything that is not red is selected—that is, active.

figure 2.53

Start with an initial selection.

figure 2.54

Enter Quick Mask mode.

3. To further separate the leaf from the sidewalk, paint over the sidewalk that's still showing with a black brush. In this instance, use a hard-edged brush to mimic the crisp contours of the leaf. By painting over the image areas that should not be selected, you are subtracting from the selection.

4. If there are areas that you want to add to the initial selection, paint over them using white. For example, zoom in on the bottom of the stem of the leaf. Painting with a 100% white hard brush adds the lower end of the stem to the selection as shown in **figure 2.55**.

figure 2.55

Refine the Quick Mask by painting with black and white brushes.

5. When you are satisfied with the selection, press *q* again. Photoshop will convert the Quick Mask into an active selection (**figure 2.56**) that you can use to copy and paste the leaf to another image.

Tip

As soon as you enter Quick Mask mode, Photoshop resets the color picker to the default colors of white foreground and black background. While you're painting, press *x* to switch the foreground and background colors to black or white as needed. Use the left bracket key to make the brush smaller and the right bracket to enlarge the brush as needed.

figure 2.56

Pressing q exits Quick Mask mode and activates the selection.

Checking Selections in Quick Mask

No matter which tool I use to make a selection, I always check it in Quick Mask mode to verify that the selection is accurate and the edges are smooth, and to determine if any telltale artifacts will interfere with my planned composites or effects. The following example illustrates how useful this habit is, especially when using the Magic Wand, because it can be difficult to know what is selected and what isn't.

1. After clicking with the Magic Wand to create the general selection, press *q* to enter Quick Mask mode.

2. Often the color and transparency of the mask makes it difficult to accurately access the selection. To see the selection in black and white, open the channels palette and click the eyeball icon in the View column next to the word *RGB*. This shows you the mask in pure black and white, making it easier to see any defects (**figure 2.57**).

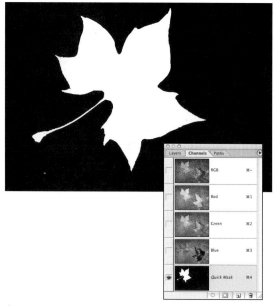

figure 2.57

Viewing the mask in the Channels palette in black and white can reveal small problems and specs of dirt.

3. Viewing the selection in black and white clearly shows the specs of dust and grit that need to be cleaned up before continuing with the selection. You could use a small paintbrush to dab over the specs or use the Dust & Scratches filter to remove the small specs very quickly, as I've done in **figure 2.58**.

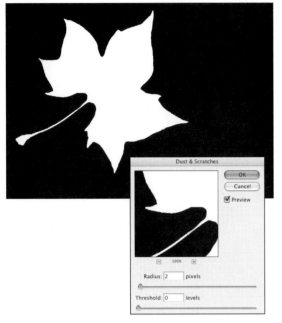

figure 2.58

Use a low radius setting to clean up dust and dirt very quickly.

4. Choose Filter > Noise > Dust & Scratches and move the radius slider up until the dust specs disappear. In most cases, a radius of 2 will do the trick. Use as low a radius as possible so that the edge quality of the selection is not softened too much.

5. After cleaning up the artifacts, click on the RGB view column again to see the image with the Quick Mask overlay (**figure 2.59**) and press *q* to exit Quick Mask mode to create an active selection (**figure 2.60**).

   Figure 2.61 shows the leaf on a new background.

figure 2.59

Click on the RGB View column to see the Quick Mask overlay.

figure 2.60

The fine-tuned final selection.

figure 2.61

A playful leaf.

Checking selections in Quick Mask mode is very easy and fast and I've often caught dirt or mistakes that would have caused problems if I hadn't fixed the mask before continuing with the composite. Please see Chapter 3 for additional information on using Quick Mask with a variety of filters if you want to be able to refine selection edges like a pro.

Starting Without a Selection

Some people are very comfortable with the Photoshop painting tools and prefer to use them to make selections. I often do this when working with a Wacom pressure-sensitive tablet, where painting comes as naturally to me as it did during my kindergarten days.

 T i p

When using Quick Mask in painting mode—that is, starting without an active selection—it is useful to change the defaults in the Quick Mask Options dialog box so that Selected Areas in the Color Indicates section is selected, as shown in figure 2.62.

figure 2.62

If you're using Quick Mask without a selection active, change the Quick Mask defaults.

 T i p

If the object you are trying to select is red, choose a contrasting color like blue for the mask by clicking the color picker and choosing a blue tone. Use the color that is the opposite of the image or subject to make it easier to see through the Quick Mask. If you're not sure what the opposite color is, choose a color that could not be mistaken for part of the image, such as pure cyan, hot pink, etc.

To select the water lily blossom in **figure 2.63**, it is easier to paint it than to use the Lasso or Magic Wand tools.

figure 2.63

The original image.

 ch2_waterlily.jpg

1. Make sure there is not an active selection by choosing Select > Deselect. If the menu command is grayed out, no selection is present. Also make sure the Selected Areas default in the Color Indicates section of the Quick Mask Options dialog box is selected. Click the red square and select a contrasting color to the lily—I chose a bright blue, as shown in **figure 2.64**.

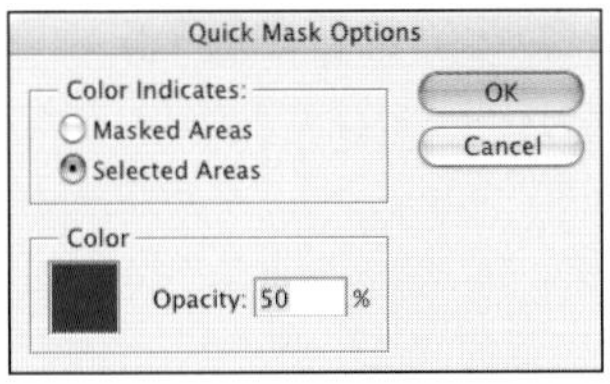

figure 2.64

Select a contrasting color to help you see the image through the mask more clearly.

2. Press *q* to enter Quick Mask mode; the image will be unchanged.

3. Zoom in on the lily blossom and use a black, hard-edged brush to trace along the inside of the blossom, as shown in **figure 2.65**.

figure 2.66

Fill the lily with black to complete the selection.

figure 2.65

Paint around the inside edge of the lily with a hard-edged black brush.

4. After completely encircling the blossom, choose a larger hard-edged brush and quickly paint the entire inside of the flower with black (**figure 2.66**).

5. After covering the lily with black—which in this case will look blue—press *q* to exit Quick Mask mode. Only the lily blossom should be active (**figure 2.67**).

figure 2.67

The selected lily.

6. To interpret the image, you could apply a filter to the selected part of the image or convert the background to black and white, which is what I did. Choose Select > Inverse and Layer > New Adjustment Layer > Channel Mixer. Click monochrome and adjust the sliders to mute the green leaves. After clicking OK, I adjusted the channel mixer layer opacity to 75% to let a hint of green shimmer through, as shown in **figure 2.68**.

CLOSING THOUGHTS

Making good selections takes practice and patience—and delivers a dose of frustration—but learning how is well worth the time saved in retouching ragged edges or telltale transition halos that poor selections cause when combining images. In the next chapter, we'll continue exploring how to manage and refine selections via the Select menu.

figure 2.68

By converting the background leaves to black and white, the lily flower pops off the page.

3

THE ESSENTIAL SELECT MENU

I go into New York City almost every day, and on most days I go to the same two areas of town: midtown and Chelsea. At some point I became aware that I had fallen into a rut—every day I was taking the same subway and walking the same route. On the few occasions when I went uptown or down to Greenwich Village, I was always amazed at the different faces the Big Apple has. Each neighborhood has its own smells, textures, and feelings.

Working with Photoshop can be a lot like a daily commute—in no time it can seem like you're in a rut. When making selections, most people simply grab one of the familiar selection tools from the toolbar and hope a quick drag or click will get the job done. However, the selection tools usually just aren't sophisticated enough to make finely tuned selections.

Selections in Photoshop have an entire menu devoted to them, called the *Select menu*. Oddly enough, it seems that not a lot of users ever wander into this neighborhood to take advantage of the power the Select menu offers.

In this chapter we'll work with a variety of images to learn about

- Using the Color Range to select both tone and color
- How to control the Feather command
- When to use the Modify commands
- Saving, loading, moving, and storing selections

SELECT MENU INTRODUCTION

The first four options in the Select menu are so fundamental—I use them every time I launch Photoshop, even though I never use the Select menu to access them. Learning to use the command keys in **table 3.1** will speed up your selection work.

table 3.1

Select Menu	Command Keys
Select All	(Cmd + A) [Ctrl + A]
Deselect	(Cmd + D) [Ctrl + D]
Reselect	(Cmd + Shift + D) [Ctrl + Shift + D]
Inverse	(Cmd + Shift + I) [Ctrl + Shift + I]

Select All

In a nutshell, Select > All selects the entire active layer, active image channel, or the entire document if it has only one layer. This may not seem that exciting, but it is very useful.

In the creative process of combining and moving image elements around, I often have large portions of images that hang over the edge of the image area, like the cupid in **figure 3.1**. Photoshop maintains image data outside of the edge of the visible canvas by supporting what Adobe calls *big data*. This is a great feature because it lets you move image components around without the fear of having them chopped off at the visible image edges. However, a disadvantage of big data support is that the extra, unseen image information adds to the file size.

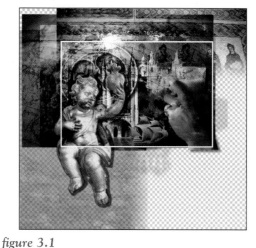

figure 3.1

Extra image information is maintained outside of the visible image canvas.

Once you have the image composition in place, like my example in **figure 3.2**, it is a good idea to trim away the big data, which will remove the extraneous image information and reduce your working file size.

Select All plays into this process by selecting only the content of the image area and disregarding anything you don't want in the final composition. To locate and trim extra image information that may be bloating your composited files and slowing down your work, follow these steps:

1. Select Image > Reveal All to see image information that is hanging over the visible edges. Reveal All increases the canvas size, which also increases the file size.
2. (Cmd + Z) [Ctrl + Z] to undo the Reveal All.
3. Select all (Cmd + A) [Ctrl + A].
4. Select Image > Crop to crop away the extraneous information.

In this example, the layered image file went from a hefty 283 MB down to a more manageable 188 MB file—a savings of almost 100 MB.

Deselect and Reselect

Many times when I have an active selection, I find I need to work on the entire image or simply want to start a new selection. To deselect the active selection, use (Cmd + D) [Ctrl + D]. You can also click outside an active selection with any of the selection tools to deselect it, but in most cases, this click technique just gets me into more trouble: I either end up moving a selection or starting a new selection. So I recommend using (Cmd + D) [Ctrl + D] to deselect a selection and be a more efficient Photoshopper.

Reselect is another indispensable command. How many times have you been working on a selection and by accident deselected it or, thinking you didn't need it anymore, deselected it and kept on working only to realize that you need the exact same selection again? Don't panic—use Select > Reselect (Cmd + Shift + D) [Ctrl + Shift + D] to resurrect the last selection you made.

figure 3.2

By cropping the final composition down to just what is visible, the file size is reduced.

 N o t e

The Reselect command only works on the very last selection you made, but here's a trick to retrieve "older" selections: Open the History palette and click on the desired selection, as shown in figure 3.3 (provided you haven't exceeded the number of states you have assigned to the History palette).

Inverse

Often the best way to make a selection is to first select the opposite of what you want, as you already know from reading Chapter 2, "Selection Strategies and Essentials." In combination with the Magic Wand, Select > Inverse lets you quickly select objects on simple backgrounds.

figure 3.3

Taking advantage of the History palette to reload selections.

For example, I showed you a red poppy in Chapter 2 that I really wanted to select but didn't want to have to do a lot of work to get there. So I selected the blue sky using the Magic Wand, set to its default setting of 32 Tolerance. Then with a quick Select > Inverse (Cmd + Shift + I) [Ctrl + Shift + I], I had the red poppy selected in no time (**figure 3.4**). So on those occasions when you need to speed the selection process, think *opposite*.

⊕▷⊱ ch3_poppy.jpg

figure 3.4

Inversing the selection of the sky selects the poppy.

COLOR RANGE

The Color Range command is "the smart Magic Wand" because it lets you select and preview selections of colors and tones with greater precision and control than the Magic Wand. The Magic Wand either selects a pixel or it doesn't, while Color Range selects pixels both entirely as well as partially, letting you create selections that maintain subtle color transitions.

When you choose Select > Color Range, Photoshop examines your foreground color and references it to create an initial selection. You can select other colors or add or subtract colors using the dialog box.

For example, look at the difference of the initial Color Range selections in **figure 3.5** and **figure 3.6**. In figure 3.5, the foreground color is the default black, and Color Range selected the darkest

specs of sand, which isn't very useful. In figure 3.6, I sampled the purple from the center of the image before selecting Color Range, and the selection is now based on purple.

To harness the power of Color Range, it helps to understand the primary controls in the Color Range dialog box.

⊕▷⊱ ch3_bucket.jpg

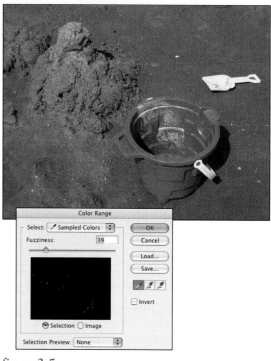

figure 3.5

With black as the foreground, Color Range selects the blacks in the image.

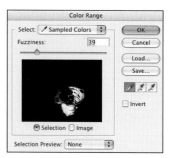

figure 3.6

By sampling the color of interest before choosing the Color Range command, you start with a better initial selection.

Selecting Sampled Colors

The three eyedroppers in the Color Range dialog box are for selecting, adding, and subtracting colors from a selection. You can use them directly on the image or within the Color Range dialog box, I prefer to use the eyedroppers on the image and to watch the dialog box, which shows a black and white rendition of the selection as a mask.

Figure 3.7 shows what happened when I clicked on the center area of the purple bucket to make my initial selection using the default eyedropper. Because I wanted to select all the purples, I needed to add to the selection. The middle eyedropper with the plus sign might seem like the logical choice for adding color, but it's actually faster to just press the Shift key while selecting more colors using the default, as I have done in figure 3.7.

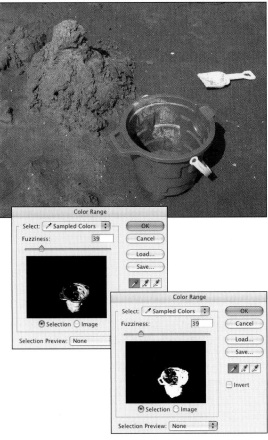

figure 3.7

The initial Color Range selection and the expanded Color Range selection.

To take away from a Color Range selection, (Option-click) [Alt-click] in the image and Photoshop will subtract those colors and tones from your selection. These keyboard shortcuts also work when you are dragging across a part of the image.

Tip

If you mistakenly click on a color or tone in the Color Range dialog box that you don't want selected, use (Cmd + Z) [Ctrl + Z} to undo the last sample point.

Controlling Color Range

You can define the area that Color Range examines by making a marquee selection of the subject *before* choosing Select > Color Range. Because sand is inside of the bucket, every time I click on the sand in the bucket, Photoshop also selects sand of the same color outside the bucket, adding unwanted colors to the desired selection, as shown in **figure 3.8**.

1. Before using the Color Range command, select the bucket with the Rectangular Marquee tool.

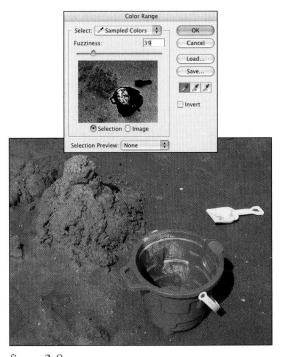

figure 3.8

Using the Color Range command on this whole file would select a lot of pixels that I do not want to alter.

2. Use the default eyedropper in the Color Range dialog box to select the purple bucket (**figure 3.9**).

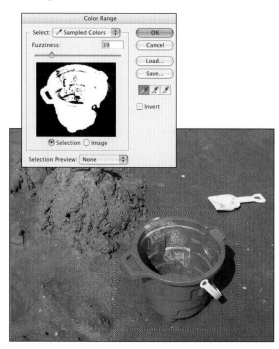

figure 3.9

Selecting the bucket before entering the Color Range command focuses Color Range on the bucket.

figure 3.10

Before and after—using the Lasso tool to add the missing areas to the selection.

3. Click OK to accept the initial Color Range selection. Then, while pressing the Shift key, use the Lasso tool to circle the missing areas to the selection (**figure 3.10**).

Fuzziness

Many people and books equate the Fuzziness setting of Color Range with the Tolerance setting of the Magic Wand. If that were true, why wouldn't it be called Tolerance? Like Tolerance, Fuzziness controls whether a pixel will be selected. However, Fuzziness also controls how much of that pixel is selected by controlling the degree to which related colors are included in the selection. Keep in mind that Color Range can select pixels fully and, more importantly, partially to create selections with realistic color and tonal transitions.

Figure 3.11 illustrates how increasing the Fuzziness setting increments of ten changes the tonal transition of the resulting selection, as shown in the grayscale mask. Making a good Color Range selection requires finding a balance between the Fuzziness setting and how many color samples you take. To select large, general areas of similar color, start with a lower Fuzziness setting and sample often. To select a color in a finely detailed image, use a higher Fuzziness setting, because finely detailed areas most likely will contain color contamination from adjacent areas of the image.

I prefer to sample more often rather than cranking the Fuzziness setting too high to make a Color Range selection.

0 Fuzziness

50 Fuzziness

100 Fuzziness

150 Fuzziness

figure 3.11

Increasing the Fuzziness value increases the percentage amount of the selected colors.

Selection Preview

The Color Range dialog box includes a number of options for displaying the selection in progress. There are two radio buttons—Selection and Image (**figure 3.12**)—under the primary image. Clicking Selection displays the selection in progress in black and white, and clicking Image displays the actual image (albeit in miniature format).

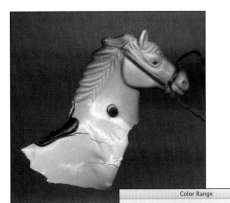

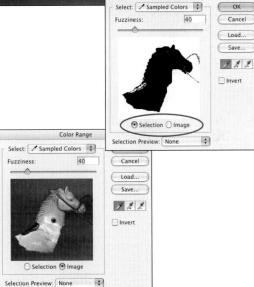

figure 3.12

What you see in the preview window of the dialog box is controlled by the Selection and Image choice.

Tip

To toggle between the Selection and Image displays without having to click the radio buttons, press (Cmd) [Ctrl].

To preview the selection in the image, you have five options. The default is none. The four additional previews give you a range of choices:

- Grayscale shows what the selection mask will look like if you save it as a channel mask (**figure 3.13**).

- Black Matte shows what the selected image area will look like when pasted onto a black background (**figure 3.14**).

- White Matte shows what the selected image area will look like when pasted onto a white background (**figure 3.15**). This can be useful for previewing the edge pixels when compositing onto light backgrounds.

- Quick Mask previews the selection in Quick Mask mode, as shown in **figure 3.16**. The Quick Mask default display color is 50-percent red. To change the display color while in the Color Range dialog box, press (Option) [Alt] while selecting Quick Mask, and the setting will pop up.

When working with any of these four preview settings, select the Image radio button to see the original image. When working with the Selection Preview, set to None, I suggest you use the default Selection radio button to see the selection in black and white and how changing the Fuzziness setting is influencing the selection outcome.

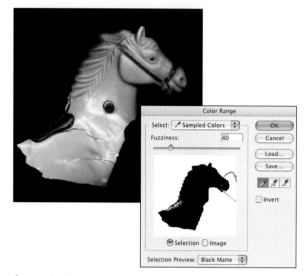

figure 3.14

Previewing the image on a black background.

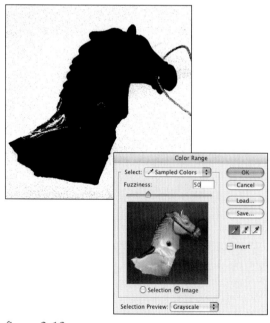

figure 3.13

Previewing in grayscale shows you what the grayscale mask will look like.

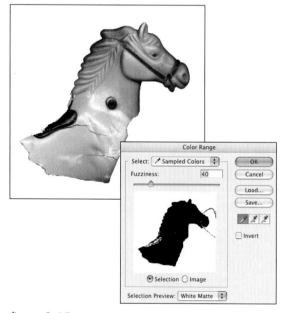

figure 3.15

Previewing the image on a white background.

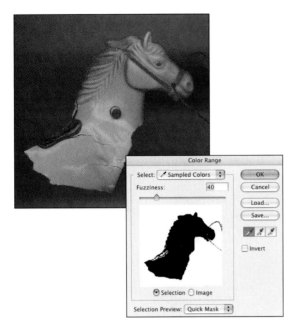

figure 3.16

Previewing the selection as a quick mask.

Tip

While the Color Range dialog box is active, you can use (Cmd + Space) [Ctrl + Space] to zoom the image up and (Cmd + Option + Space) [Ctrl + Alt + Space] to zoom the image down.

Default Colors and Tones

Many Photoshop users pooh-pooh the canned Sample Colors, but they have helped me select subtle colorcasts or diffuse tones so often that I've learned to appreciate them a great deal.

When you select one of the default colors, Photoshop looks through the entire image and only selects a pixel if it has a majority of that color in it. The greater the difference between the selected color and the other primaries, the more that pixel will be selected. But enough of the mumbo-jumbo! Let me show you how you can use the default colors to create a selection to improve a person's skin tones.

The portrait of the woman shown in **figure 3.17** is fine, but her skin tones are too warm. Reducing the red makes her look much more comfortable and less flushed (**figure 3.18**).

 ch3_maturewoman.jpg

1. Choose Select > Color Range, and from the Select options, choose Reds. Then click OK (**figure 3.19**).

figure 3.17

figure 3.18

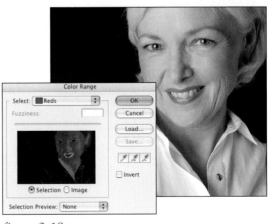

figure 3.19

Selecting Reds.

2. Select Layer > New Adjustment Layer > Hue/Saturation and click OK. As soon as you add an Adjustment Layer with an active selection, Photoshop transfers the selection to the layer mask. Where there are active selections, the mask is light; the inactive areas are dark.

3. Adjust the Hue and the Saturation to reduce the overall saturation by 30 percent and the red saturation by 25 percent (**figure 3.20**).

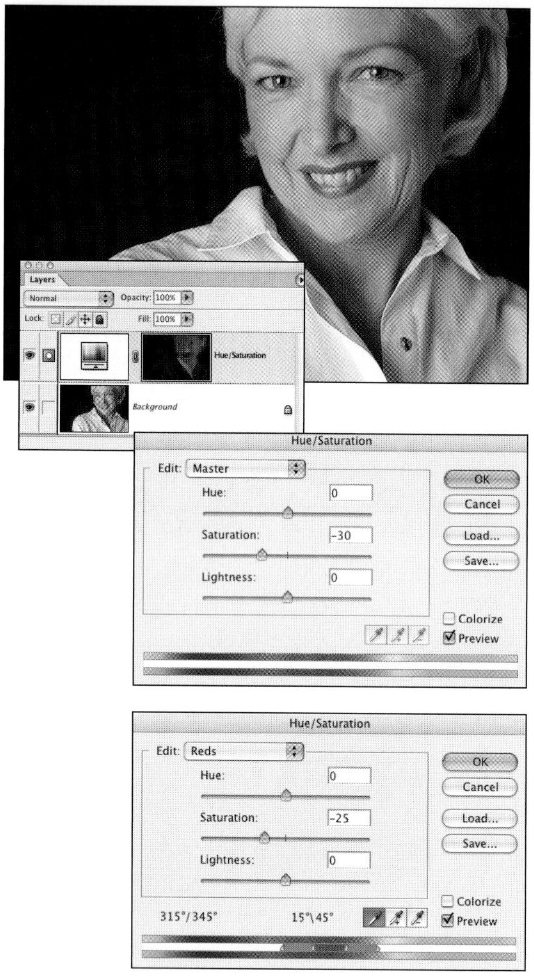

figure 3.20

Using a Hue/Saturation Adjustment Layer to reduce the red saturation.

The Highlights, Midtones, and Shadows presets are also very useful for selecting tonal areas and then using the ensuing selection to control the contrast of the selected area in conjunction with Levels and Curves Adjustment Layers.

Tip

If you ever catch yourself using Color Range and then inversing the selection, you can achieve the very same effect more efficiently by selecting Invert in the Color Range dialog box before clicking OK.

Grow and Similar

A bit further down the Select menu are the Grow and Similar commands, which are precursors to Color Range. I used to use them all the time to make tone-based and color-based selections, but because they do not have a preview or offer the controls of Color Range, I rarely use them now.

Grow and Similar share two attributes: they both require you start with an active selection, and they both reference the Magic Wand Tolerance setting to determine how far to extend the selection. The Grow option only looks at image areas that are directly connected to the original selection; whereas Similar looks throughout the entire image for color and tone that fall within the parameters of the Magic Wand Tolerance setting.

FEATHER

Softening selection edges with low amounts of feathering is a useful technique for creating subtle transitions between image elements or, when pushed to the extreme, for easily and quickly creating dream-like image composites. As discussed and illustrated in Chapter 2, feathering a selection creates a transition between active and inactive image areas. As the feather amount increases, the transition between active and inactive pixels increases—something you can take advantage of to enhance creative effects.

Although I like a soft edge, I can't stand the "no preview," feather interface shown in **figure 3.21**. When you change the numeric value, you get absolutely no visual feedback as to what is going to take place until you click OK. So from here on out, we will never, ever feather a selection again! But we will soften selection edges with visual acumen and control by combining Quick Mask and Gaussian Blur.

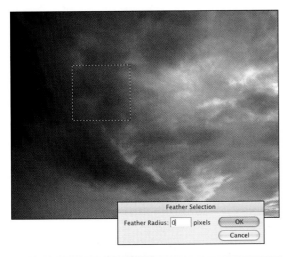

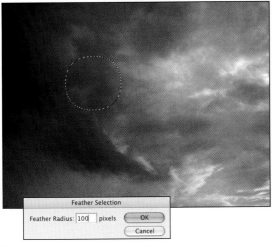

figure 3.21

Whether the feather is 0 or 100, the Feather dialog box provides no preview of its effects.

Smart Feather

To see what effect feathering is having, use the following technique. You can experiment using your own images or use the example I'm using by downloading it from www.photoshopmasking.com.

ch3_playhorse.jpg

1. Select the play horse shown in **figure 3.22** with either the Lasso, Magnetic Lasso, or Pen tools converted to a selection. If you are using the Lasso tools, make sure no feather is dialed into the Options bar.

2. Since we'll be reusing this selection, choose Select > Save Selection to save and name the selection into a new channel, as shown in **figure 3.23** (this command is discussed more thoroughly in the "Save and Load Selection" section, later in this chapter). Saving the selection lets you reload it whenever you need to.

figure 3.22

Start by selecting the play horse.

figure 3.23

Save the selection for future use.

3. Double-click the Quick Mask icon to verify Quick Mask is set to Masked Areas, and then click OK (**figure 3.24**). Don't worry about the color—it is just a preview option and doesn't affect how Quick Mask works.

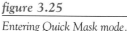

figure 3.24

Double-checking the Quick Mask settings.

4. Click the Quick Mask icon on the toolbar (**figure 3.25**) or press *q*. Quick Mask is an impermanent mask you can use to modify selections with filters, image adjustment controls, and painting tools.

5. To apply the visual feather, select Filter > Blur > Gaussian Blur. The softer the desired edge, the higher Gaussian Blur setting you should use, as shown in **figure 3.26**. The big, big difference is that you can zoom in on the image edge and see the effect of the setting.

6. To see how the feather will affect your composite, click the Standard Mode icon to activate the selection. Using the Move tool, drag the active image area over to another image or to a new blank document.

7. To really understand how well Quick Mask and Gaussian Blur work together, return to the original image and choose Select > Load Selection to activate the original, non-feathered selection. Click the Quick Mask icon again and experiment with more extreme Gaussian Blur settings.

figure 3.25

Entering Quick Mask mode.

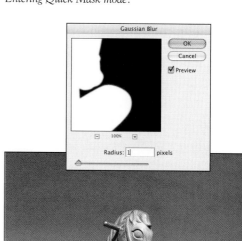

figure 3.26

Applying a Gaussian Blur of 1 pixel is the same thing as applying a feather of 1.

As you can see in **figure 3.27**, the differences in feather are very apparent when the horse is placed on a plain white background. When the same horses are placed on stormy cloud backgrounds, the images interact beautifully.

So from now on, avoid the Feather command. Instead, take advantage of the ability to actually see the softening of the selection via this Quick Mask and Gaussian Blur technique. In the following section, we'll be using Quick Mask and other filters to control additional edge qualities of active selections.

Radius of 1   Radius of 20   Radius of 75

figure 3.27

Experiment with the Gaussian Blur settings for a variety of edge transitions.

THE MODIFY MENU

Making the very best possible selection before compositing images is always better than trying to fix sloppy image edges after the elements are composited together. As with Feather, many of the Select > Modify commands can be re-created and improved upon with Quick Mask, filters, and tonal controls as discussed here. Remember, all of the Select > Modify commands require that you start with an active selection.

Border

When you select Modify > Border and type in a numeric value, you are telling Photoshop to redraw the selection as a double-edged selection that is the width of the value you typed (**figure 3.28**). Using a small border selection can be very useful when you need to carefully blur, darken, or refine image edges.

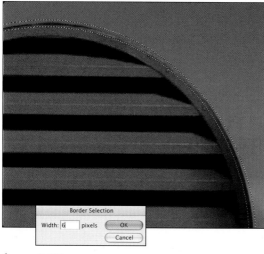

figure 3.28

The Border option redraws the selection outline into two separate outlines.

Figure 3.29 shows a composited image with a harsh edge. Figure 3.30 shows how I used a border selection to soften the edges of the crossing guard figure, making the visual character of the edges match the softness of the background image. To apply edge softening, the individual image elements need to be on separate layers. Make sure you take care of image-edge quality before you flatten the Photoshop layers.

figure 3.29

figure 3.30

1. (Cmd-click) [Ctrl-click] the Layer icon of the crossing guard to make a selection based on the transparent areas of the image, as shown in **figure 3.31**. This is called *loading the transparency* of a layer.

2. Select > Modify > Border and set the Width to 4 pixels. Then select Layer > New > Layer (Cmd + J) [Ctrl + J] to place the bordered selection onto its own layer (**figure 3.32**).

figure 3.31

Loading the layer's transparency.

figure 3.32

Using the Border option to outline the initial selection.

3. I used a very low Gaussian Blur to soften the bordered edge ever so slightly, as shown in **figure 3.33**.

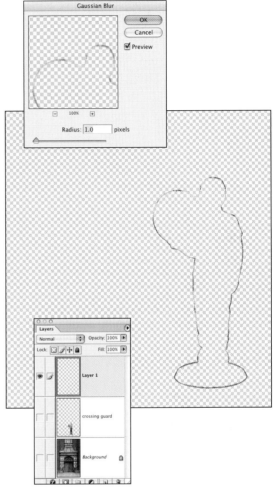

figure 3.33

Apply a low Gaussian Blur to the bordered layer.

The beauty of applying the Gaussian Blur to a separate layer is the ability to control the strength of the effect by adjusting the layer opacity and layer blending mode to improve edge quality. In this case, I used the Multiply blending mode to darken the image edges down ever so slightly, as shown in **figure 3.34**.

The technique of bordering an image edge in combination with blurring and blending modes is an effective method for finessing image edges to match and blend with image backgrounds.

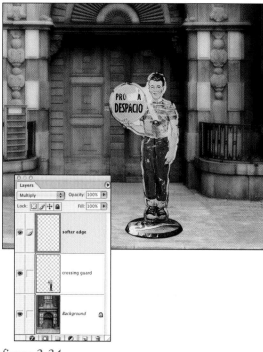

figure 3.34

Adjusting layer opacity and using the Multiply blending mode darkens and softens the edge of the crossing guard.

Smooth

Have you ever been frustrated with a Lasso or Magic Wand selection because it is too jumpy, lumpy, or bumpy? If so, then you will love the Modify > Smooth command, which does exactly what is says—it smoothes out rough selections.

Figure 3.35 shows a quick selection I made of the kewpie doll using a combination of the Magic Wand and Lasso tool. As you can see, the selection edge of her arms is very ragged.

To even out the rough edges, use the Select > Modify > Smooth command. In this example, I used a value of 10 to achieve the results shown in figure 3.36.

The Smooth command will affect sharp corners and rough edges much more than straight line selections.

figure 3.35

figure 3.36

The problem with the Smooth command is that you cannot see how the values you choose are affecting the selection. Behind the scenes, when you use Smooth, Photoshop looks at the pixels along the selection border and, depending on the Sample Radius setting you used, it selects or deselects pixels to even out the selection. Internally, Photoshop is really running the Median filter on an internal grayscale channel, which also means you could smooth a selection by combining Quick Mask and the Median filter (Filter > Noise > Median).

⊕⊏⟩⊰ ch3_doll.jpg

1. To work along with me, recall the initial selection by clicking on the History state that contains the first selection of the doll shown in **figure 3.37**.

   Note: Your History palette may have different steps than mine, depending on how you made the initial selection.

2. Press *q* to enter Quick Mask mode and choose Filter > Noise > Median. By adjusting the radius setting, you are adjusting the amount of smoothing that Photoshop applies. You can see the effect of increasing or decreasing the setting in **figure 3.38**.

Using Quick Mask in combination with a filter is a more predictable and controllable method for modifying a selection than using a command without a preview. Using the Median filter in a quick mask is also a great way of removing small specks of dust or dirt from a selection, as shown in **figure 3.39**.

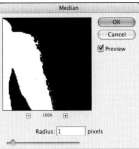

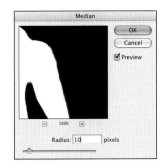

figure 3.37

Use the History state to recall the initial selection.

figure 3.38

Use the Median filter combined with Quick Mask to re-create the Modify > Smooth command.

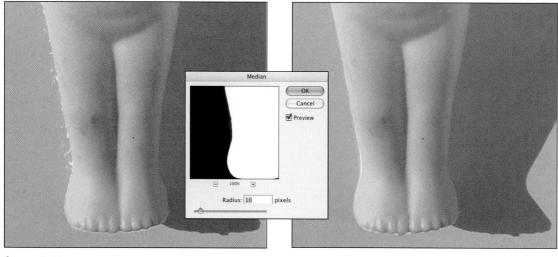

figure 3.39

The Median filter also smoothes and cleans up dust-specked selections.

Expand and Contract

Expand and Contract are very useful selection modify commands. For the most part they do what their names imply—you can use these commands, or the Quick Mask and filter equivalent, to enlarge or tighten selections.

Using the Expand command is the same as using Filter > Other > Maximum on a quick mask, and using the Contract command is the same as using the Filter > Other > Minimum filter. Once again, the difference is that when you use Quick Mask mode in combination with these filters you can see exactly what you are doing.

Do you have the feeling I really like being able to see and control an effect rather than having to guess at it?

Figure 3.40 shows two stock images I wanted to composite together. The wedding couple was photographed on a white backdrop, and I figured it would be a piece of cake to combine it with the lightning image. I used the Magic Wand to select the white background, inversed the selection, and then moved the "happy couple" over to the lightning picture. Figure 3.41 shows the poor results. Look at the terrible edges that just scream, "Look here: bad composite!"

© PhotoSpin

figure 3.40

Two stock images.

figure 3.41

The white edges make the wedding couple stand out too much against the blue lightning.

To avoid unpleasant surprises, including white halos, review the selection in Quick Mask and adjust the mask to refine the selection as described in the steps that follow.

1. Returning to the original wedding couple, where the selection is still active, I enter Quick Mask mode by pressing *q* and choose Filter > Other > Minimum with a setting of 1 pixel (**figure 3.42**).

2. I pressed *q* again and dragged the second couple over to the blue lightning image. As you can see in **figure 3.43**, the second couple on the right has no telltale halo and the edges are clean.

figure 3.42

The minimum filter contracts the mask.

figure 3.43

On the left, the original wedding couple with the terrible white edges; on the right, the same wedding couple with the contracted and much better edges.

Using Curves to Expand and Contract Selections

Often the Expand or Contract command or their Quick Mask equivalents, Maximum and Minimum, are adequate to clean up basic edge problems, but they are also limited to working in exact increments of 1 pixel, which may remove too much image information or edge detail. To expand and contract edges with greater finesse, I use Gaussian Blur and Curves in Quick Mask to finesse selections and edges that fit snuggly along the edge of an object.

Figure 3.44 shows a garlic still life, from which I needed to separate the garlic clove for use as a design element in a cookbook project. I started the selection with the Magnetic Lasso and refined it with the Freeform Lasso, as illustrated in **figure 3.45**. To see how it would look dropped out to white, I copied and pasted it onto a new document. The results are ragged and distracting (**figure 3.46**).

⊕⟩⋇ **ch3_garlic.jpg**

To refine the edges, do the following:

1. Make the initial selection using the Magnetic Lasso, refine it with the Freeform Lasso tool, and press *q* to enter Quick Mask mode.

figure 3.44

The original still life.

figure 3.45

The selected garlic clove.

figure 3.46

Unacceptable black and white edge fringe artifacts.

2. To create slightly soft and fluid selections, start with a low Gaussian Blur setting between .5 and 1 pixel, as shown in **figure 3.47**.

3. To snuggle the selection to the inside of the garlic, use Image > Adjustments > Curves and the Midtone handle to increase or decrease the quick mask, as shown in **figure 3.48**.

Note: Depending on how your Curves defaults are set, you may need to pull the Midtone handle to the left. The results, however, will be identical.

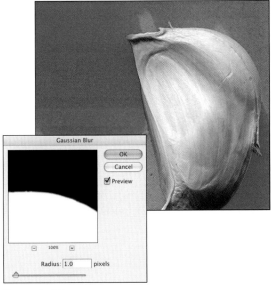

figure 3.47

Using a low Gaussian Blur on the quick mask adds gray value transitions for the next step.

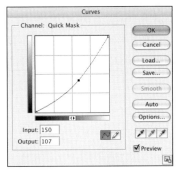

figure 3.48

Using Curves to expand the dark areas of the mask tightens up the selection.

4. Press *q* again to exit Quick Mask. In my case, I copied the garlic clove onto a white document and compared the edges to the initial selection (**figure 3.49**).

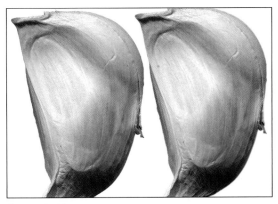

figure 3.49

On the left, the initial selection created rough and ragged edges. On the right, the refined selection maintains the edge quality of the garlic without looking artificial.

Table 3.2 lists the Select menu commands and the filter equivalents you can use in combination with Quick Mask to make better selections.

table 3.2
Select Menu Filter Equivalents

Select Menu Command	Quick Mask and Filter
Inverse	Image > Adjustments > Invert
Feather	Filter > Blur > Gaussian Blur
Modify > Border	Filter > Stylize > Glowing Edges
Modify > Smooth	Filter > Noise > Median
Modify > Expand	Filter > Other > Maximum
Modify > Contract	Filter > Other > Minimum
Refine Selection Edges	Gaussian Blur and Curves

Using your Photoshop discretion to refine selection edges requires some practice and a critical eye. But believe me, making a good edge is so much better than trying to fix a bad edge with tedious cloning or erasing pixels. The time you spend making the better selection now is time saved in refining composites later on.

TRANSFORM SELECTION

One of the most useful yet underrated commands is Transform Selection. As you saw in Chapter 2, not every Elliptical or Marquee selection I make is perfect, and often the object I need to select is crooked or cock-eyed. On these occasions, I use Select > Transform Selection to finesse the shape of a selection into place.

To access the power of the Transform Selection command, use the context-sensitive menu key (Ctrl-click) [right mouse button-click] anywhere inside the selection, and then drag down to the required option (**figure 3.50**).

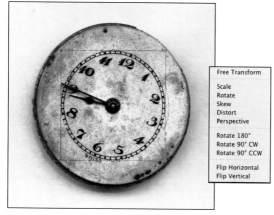

figure 3.50

Assessing the Transform Selection controls.

The first five options are the most important:

- **Scale:** Pull on any handle to size the selection. Hold the Shift key to maintain the original aspect ratio and (Ctrl) [Alt] to apply the same change to the exact opposite handle.

- **Rotate:** Move your mouse about half an inch away from the corner handles, and the cursor will become a little curved arrow. Click and drag up or down to rotate the selection. The small crosshair in the middle of the selection controls the axis point of the rotation.

- **Skew:** Moves the center handles to the left or right or up and down.

- **Distort:** My favorite—lets you position each handle independently.

- **Perspective:** Useful for finessing images with keystoning, but used less often now that the Crop tool has a perspective feature.

SAVE AND LOAD SELECTION

Imagine you've spent the better part of 15 minutes making a perfect selection, and for some reason you inadvertently quit Photoshop or shut down the computer. You don't want to have to make that selection all over again. To preserve your selection work and sanity, you should use the Save Selection command to save and name your selections as alpha channels, which are visible on the Channels palette.

Use Save Selection whenever you've made a complicated, sweat-inducing selection; think, feel, or know that you'll be use a selection again; or when you need to stop working and want to continue where you left off in the selection process.

When you choose Select > Save Selection, you're not saving the dancing ant outline. Rather, Photoshop is taking the internal grayscale channel and saving that as an alpha channel. An alpha channel is a grayscale addition to the file that does not make up the image as the red, green, and blue or cyan, magenta, yellow, and black channels do. The alpha channels control where an applied image effect takes place—but we'll get to all that great stuff in Chapter 5, "Masks Are Your Friends."

For right now, it is important to know that you can save yourself a lot of frustration, heartache, self-deprecation, and sometimes tears using the Save Selection feature as follows:

1. Open an image and make a selection. To make this exercise meaningful, you need to make a selection that takes some time to make, such as a good Color Range selection.

2. Choose Select > Save Selection to open the Save Selection dialog box (**figure 3.51**).

3. Name the new channel and click OK.

4. As you can see in **figure** 3.52 and your Channels palette, Photoshop has added an alpha channel with the name you typed. Notice that Photoshop doesn't deselect the selection when you save it.

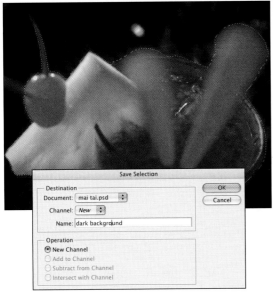

figure 3.51

The Save Selection dialog box.

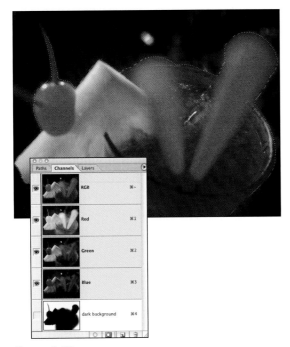

figure 3.52

The named alpha channel.

I have a confession to make: I rarely use the Save Selection command. Whenever I have an active selection I need to save, I open the Channels palette and click the Save Selection as Channel button (**figure** 3.53). This saves the selection as an alpha channel without a name. You can always rename an alpha channel later by clicking on the name and typing. To name the channel without using the menu command, (Option-click) [Alt-click] on the Channel button in the Channels palette and Photoshop will produce the New Channel dialog box (**figure** 3.54).

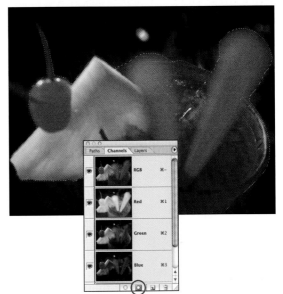

figure 3.53

Clicking on the Save Selection as Channel button on the Channels palette.

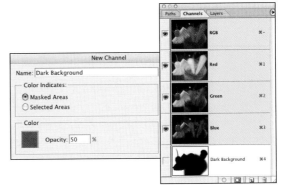

figure 3.54

Naming the channels while you save them will reduce frustration later on.

Load Selection

When you save a selection, you can reactivate the alpha channel at any time by choosing Select > Load Selection and selecting the name of the desired channel, as shown in **figure 3.55**. Using the Load Selection command—or in Photoshop parlance, *loading the channel*—is another way of saying, "Photoshop, please turn the alpha channel into an active selection so that I can get on with my work."

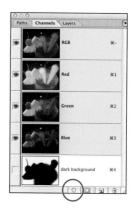

figure 3.56

Loading the alpha channel by dragging the channel down to the Save Selection as Channel button to activate it.

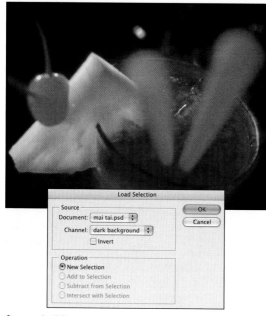

figure 3.55

Loading the alpha channel to create an active selection.

Once again, I rarely use the Load Selection command—there are a number of options to make your work more efficient. From less efficient to more efficient and professional, here is the order I prefer:

- Click and drag the desired channel to the Load Channel as Selection button (**figure 3.56**). To work efficiently, avoid clicking and releasing the mouse button and then dragging the channel down to the button. Instead, you want to click, hold, and drag with confidence, or, as I like to say, with *schwung*.

- (Cmd-click) [Ctrl-click] on the alpha channel you want to turn into a selection.

- (Cmd + Control + #) [Ctrl + Alt + #] is my favorite method for activating an alpha channel. For example, if I need to activate channel 7 in an image, I would (Cmd + Control + 7) [Ctrl + Alt + 7] to load the alpha mask as a selection. I prefer this method because you don't need to have the Channels palette open to use it—anytime I can avoid a menu or a click and drag, I'm all for it. Sadly, this only works for up to nine alpha channels.

Just the Alpha Facts

A Photoshop CS document can support up to 53 channels, an RGB file can have 50 additional alpha channels, and a CMYK image can have 49. Each alpha channel will add 25 percent to the file size, but only when the image is open.

When you save and close the image to your hard drive, Photoshop uses a very efficient run-length encoding to reduce the amount of information needed to describe the file. Don't worry, all the data and all your work is still there—Photoshop is just being smart about how the information is being saved. But be a channel hamster and save those selections. Believe me, while you'll never regret saving a selection, you will regret not saving one.

When saving files with alpha channels, use the native Photoshop file format. Although TIF supports alpha channels and PICT saves one, these formats don't take advantage of Photoshop's alpha smarts when efficiently encoding the file.

MOVING CHANNELS AND SELECTIONS

If you're tormented watching the progress bar crawl across your monitor, you can offload alpha channels to reduce file size and speed up your work. For example, a few years ago I was working on a high-resolution imaging project and just did not have enough RAM to work efficiently. So I separated the alpha channels from the image document and then loaded the selections only when I needed them. This reduced my working file size and I was able to get the job done.

To save alpha channels into separate documents, use the following steps:

1. Select the channel you need to duplicate.

2. In the Channels palette fly-out menu, select Duplicate Channel.

3. Make sure to select New from the pull-down menu, name the file, and click OK (**figure 3.57**).

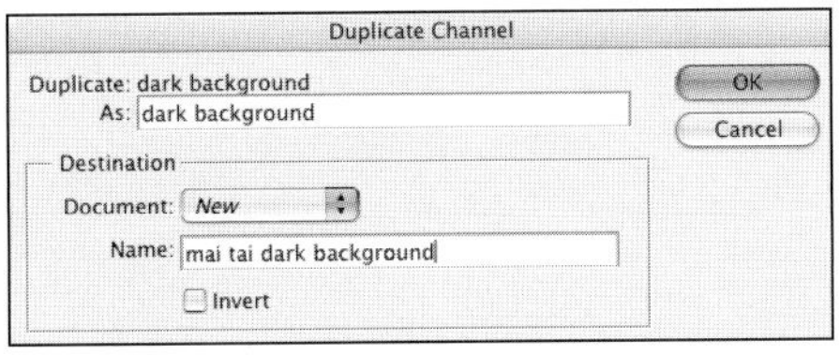

figure 3.57

Selecting New to create a new document from the duplicated channel.

To save file space in the original file, drag the channel you duplicated to the small trashcan on the Channels palette. To load this file into the original file or into any other open file that has the exact same pixel dimensions, just duplicate the original channel into the desired destination file.

 T i p

You can copy and paste alpha channels from one document into another, but this will bog down the Photoshop clipboard and use up available RAM, which is why I avoid the copy and paste method whenever possible.

Presently, RAM prices have dropped so much and hard drives are so large that you may never need to worry about file size or offloading a channel to reduce file size. On the other hand, if you have a selection in one image that can be used to mask out an image in a different file, I suggest moving the channel into the image and starting the masking process with the initial work already done for you. Chapter 5, "Masks Are Your Friends," delves into all the beauty, power, and intricacy of alpha channels. For right now, remember to save those selections as alpha channels and you'll appreciate how often you'll use them.

CLOSING THOUGHTS

Taking advantage of the Select menu is a fantastic way to explore new neighborhoods in Photoshop and not get into an imaging rut. Of course, there are always new neighborhoods to explore, so take your time, look around, and don't forget to come back once in a while to rediscover the tools and commands in the Select menu. In the following chapter, we're movin' on up to the East Side to the exclusive real estate location of the powerful and precise Pen tool.

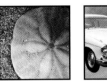

4

PEN TOOL POWER

We all have certain "to do" chores that we keep putting off. For me, its sorting through our storage unit. For my husband, John, just the idea of sorting through dusty golf clubs and the possibility of parting with a never-used putter brings on cold sweats.

I also used to have a list of "to learn" chores in Photoshop. I worked with Photoshop for three years before I touched Curves and it took me even longer to get up the nerve to learn how to use the Pen tool. Every time I tried to use it, the Pen tool and I ended up having a fight, and, in most cases, the Pen tool won. If tangled Pen tool loop de loops covering your image sounds familiar, then you know what I mean.

Learning the fundamental power of the Pen tool takes about 90 minutes. Just 90 minutes, and you will be able to use one of the best selection tools in Photoshop.

In this chapter, you will learn how to

- Recognize the types of images that make ideal Pen tool candidates
- Use the Pen tool to silhouette simple and complex objects
- Work with paths, the Paths palette, and the Path Selection tools
- Combine paths and selections

WHEN TO USE THE PEN TOOL

At first glance, the Pen tool doesn't look like a selection tool: It's not positioned with the other selection tools on the toolbar, it doesn't create a dancing marquee outline when you use it, and it doesn't respond to the Select menu commands. So is it even a selection tool? Absolutely.

The Pen tool works well for selecting shape-based and form-based image elements. For example, you will use the Pen tool in the following situations:

- To select smooth, mechanical edges, such as buildings, cars, bottles, windows, etc.
- To select smooth, organic forms, including rocks, nudes, fishes, flowers, planets, etc.
- To select elements in images where the color and tones are so similar that the standard selection tools don't have enough difference to create an accurate selection.
- To silhouette an object by dropping out the image background.
- Most importantly, when you need extreme precision. It is exactly here where the Pen tool shines high above the other selection tools.

Do not use the Pen tool to select image elements with the following characteristics:

- Images with delicate or complex detail, such as puffy dandelions or winter tree branches
- Portraits of people with fine hair or furry animals
- Images with tonal subtle gradations, such as a sunset, water reflections, or a foggy landscape
- Areas in an image with soft edges such as a natural shadow or photographic motion blur

Once you have created a path, you can turn it into a selection to use for a mask or composite or to create a path for any painting tool to follow. In other words, the Pen tool is an end to a means—use it to make exact outlines of form-based and shape-based objects and control where image effects take place.

Pen Tool Essentials

The Pen tool is not a drawing tool that lays down ink; rather, it is a mechanical drawing tool used to precisely outline an object or define a smooth curve with anchor points and mathematical vector curves. The vector aspects of the Pen tool enable it to work independently from the pixel information of the underlying image, which is exactly why the outlines created with the Pen tool are much smoother than outlines created with a pixel-based selection tool, as illustrated in **figure 4.1**.

On the top is the dolphin that I selected as carefully as possible with the standard Lasso without any feather. As you can see, the animal looks cut out and the edges aren't smooth.

On the bottom is the same dolphin, but this time I used the Pen tool to outline it. The edges are smooth and flowing without any telltale lumps or bumps that working with a pixel-based selection tool may create.

Pen Tool Settings

Before you use the Pen tool to outline an image subject, it is important to click the Path icon on the Options bar (**figure 4.2**). The Pen tool also has a dedicated palette called the *Paths palette*. I suggest you open it and keep it on your desktop for the remainder of the chapter.

Clicking and holding the Pen tool in the toolbar reveals the standard and freeform Pen tool and the Add, Delete, and Convert Point tools.

figure 4.1

The top dolphin was selected with the standard Lasso tool, while the much smoother
selection on the lower dolphin was made with the Pen tool.

figure 4.2

*Before beginning, double-check that the Pen tool options are
set to paths.*

Straight Paths

Working with the Pen tool is akin to the childhood
game of connecting the dots to reveal the picture—
the only issue is that the dots aren't on the paper.
The "dots" are the anchor points that you add with
a single click of the Pen tool. By clicking around an
object from point to point without holding down
the mouse button, you create a path defined by a
series of corner points and straight lines. To practice
along, please download the templates from
www.photoshopmasking.com. I've also posted additional templates for you to use when you practice
your Pen tool skills.

Ch4_pentool_1.jpg

Start in the upper-left corner and, working from
corner to corner, click once on each corner to add
an anchor point. When you return to the initial
anchor point, a small circle will appear next to the
Pen tool. This is the symbol to close the path. Click
once more on the first anchor point to close the
path. Open the Paths palette to verify Photoshop
has added a Work Path, as shown in **figure 4.3**.
Double-click Work Path to rename the path.

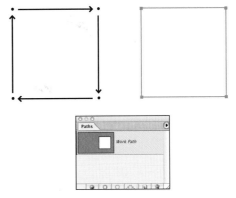

figure 4.3

*Clicking each corner dot creates anchor points and straight
lines. I moved the square path to the right so that it would be
visible in the illustration.*

Photoshop can support up to 32,000 paths (a mind-boggling concept). Naming paths takes only a moment, but it is extremely helpful in navigating the Paths palette with ease. Naming the Work Path also ensures it will not be overwritten when you start a new path.

Simply click from point to point to outline straight-edged objects, such as the individual signs in **figure 4.4**.

 Ch4_foursigns.jpg

figure 4.4

The hard-edged signs are ideal candidates for a Pen tool path.

1. Start by outlining the shipping sign by clicking each corner point of the sign.

2. After closing the path, open the Paths palette and name the Work Path *shipping sign*.

3. To create a separate path outline for the office sign, it is very important that the shipping sign path is not active; that is, not highlighted in the Paths palette. Deactivate the shipping sign path by clicking in the neutral gray area under the named shipping path in the Paths palette.

4. Outline the next sign and name the path.

5. Repeat the process for the remaining two signs.

Creating a path for each separate sign or image element gives you greater flexibility when selecting the individual image elements. Your final result should be the signs image with four separate paths, as shown in **figure 4.5**.

figure 4.5

Each sign has a dedicated path, which will make selecting each sign much easier.

 T i p

To create extremely precise paths, zoom in to a 200% to 300% view and stay one pixel inside of the object you're selecting, as shown in **figure 4.6**.

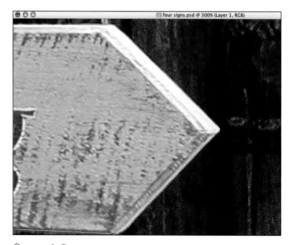

figure 4.6

Zoom in to select the object with precision and remain one pixel inside of the object edge.

Curved Paths

Using the Pen tool to outline straight-edged objects is a good place to start learning, but when it comes to outlining curved objects, the Pen tool really shines. To create a curved path, click and hold down the mouse button while dragging in the direction of the next anchor point along the edge that you are outlining. The initial anchor point changes from an anchor point to a smooth anchor point, with direction lines and direction points that control the curve. While drawing the initial path, ignore the direction points and concentrate on where the next anchor point is to be placed. After you have closed and named the path, return to the path and you can move the direction points and anchor points to refine the path.

🌐▷✂ **Ch4_pentool2.jpg**

We'll practice with curved paths.

On the circle practice template:

1. Start on the top dot (at the 12-o'clock position) and click, hold, and drag to the right.

2. At the tip of the arrow, release the mouse.

3. Move the mouse to the second dot at the 3-o'clock position and click once.

4. Release the mouse and click and hold on the third dot (at the 6-o'clock position).

5. Drag the mouse to the left, and you'll see how beautifully the curve is describing the circle.

6. Release the mouse and click the third dot (at the 9-o'clock position) and then release the mouse.

7. Return to the initial anchor point and click once on the first anchor point to close the path.

8. Open the Paths palette to see that Photoshop has added a work path, as shown in **figure 4.7**. Rename the path.

As you can see, it only takes four anchor points to describe a complete circle. Take this tidbit of information with you as you work with the Pen tool and use as few anchor points as possible to outline an object. The goal is not to rivet around the object but to gracefully and efficiently outline an object, which can be done with just a few anchor points.

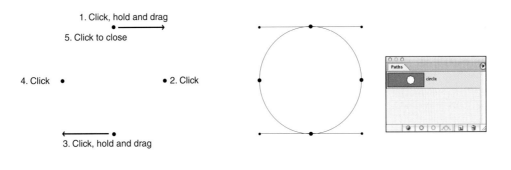

figure 4.7

The practice template and the ensuing circle in the Paths palette.

Combining Curves and Corners

Most of the objects you'll need to outline won't be perfect squares or circles. The following exercise shows you how to make a path with both curved lines and sharp corners.

 Ch4_pentool3.jpg

On the practice template:

1. Start at the top-left corner and click, release the mouse button, and click the junction of the curve to the right (**figure 4.8**).

2. Release the mouse and click the apex of the curve, hold down the mouse button, and drag to the right to define the curve on the left side of the arch.

3. Release the mouse button and click the junction where the arch meets the angle.

4. Click once on the corner point and continue working your way around this shape, as shown in figure 4.8.

5. Return to the initial anchor point and click once on it to close the path.

Tip

To practice your Pen tool skills:

1. Create a new 8-inch × 10-inch 150 ppi Photoshop document.

2. Click the Type tool and type in one single letter. If you're a beginner, type in a capital L in a simple sans serif font. If you feel more confident in your Pen tool skills, try using an S.

3. Make the letter huge—in **figure 4.9** on an 8 × 10 page, the S is 500 points.

4. Trace the letterform. Start with straightforward letters, such as *l* and *z*. Move on to curved letters, such as *j* and *s*, and then practice on letters that have inside and outside areas, such as *a*, *b*, and *o*.

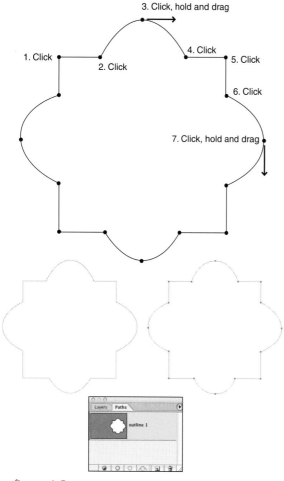

figure 4.8

Practice outlining the curves and the corners of this template.

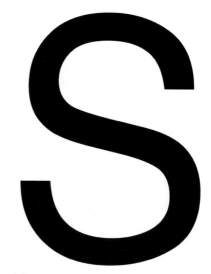

figure 4.9

Practice tracing large letterforms to hone your Pen tool skills.

The doll's head in **figure 4.10** is a perfect image for the Pen tool—it is a man-made, hard-edged object, and it doesn't have strong tonal or color differences you can use to separate the head from the background.

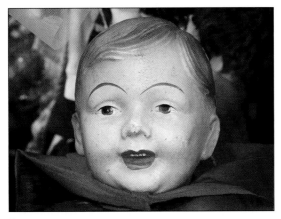

figure 4.10

The doll's head is an ideal subject to outline with the Pen tool.

⊕▷✂ **Ch4_dollhead.jpg**

⊕▷✂ **Ch4_dollhead_dots.jpg**

Take a moment to plan ahead and visualize where you will be placing the anchor points. In **figure 4.11**, I added dots to show where I would place anchor points—on points where there is a dramatic change in direction, like the earlobes, and where the curve is distinctly defined. For best results, work between 200% and 300% zoom view. As you can see in **figure 4.12**, you'll only see part of the doll's head. Once you've clicked, held, and dragged your way toward the edge of the image frame, hold down the spacebar to access the Hand tool and scroll down to the lower part of the image.

Start with the Ch4_dollhead_dots.jpg file and then practice creating the path on the Ch4_dollhead.jpg without the dots.

1. Starting at the top of the dolls' head, click, hold, and drag to the right. While dragging the handle to the right and along the doll's head, look ahead and plan where your next anchor point will be.

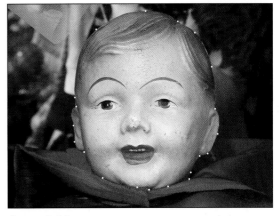

figure 4.11

Look at the object and imagine where you would place the dots—that is, the anchor points to plan out the path.

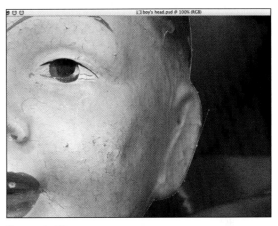

figure 4.12

Use the spacebar to access the Hand tool and scroll the image into view.

2. Release the mouse button and move the mouse to where the second anchor point should be. Click, hold, and drag down toward the doll's ear.

3. Continue down and around the doll's head, being careful to stay just inside of the edge by one pixel between the doll and the background.

4. When you reach the corner by the top of the doll's ear, press (Option) [Alt] while clicking and dragging along the edge of the ear (**figure 4.13**).

   This technique adds a corner anchor point with direction handles that you can fine-tune after you've closed the path.

5. Work your way up and back to the origin point of the path. Click the initial anchor point to close the path.

6. Open the Paths palette and name the path *Doll Head*, as shown in **figure 4.14**.

figure 4.13

Pressing (Cmd + Option) [Ctrl + Alt] while clicking and dragging adds a corner anchor point with a direction handle.

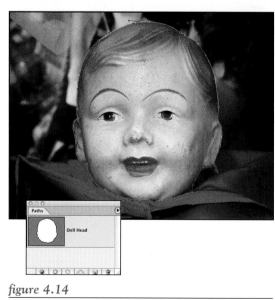

figure 4.14

After closing and naming the path.

 T i p

Use my Pen tool mantra to keep track of where you are while creating your first paths: "Click, hold, drag. Click, hold, drag. Click, hold, drag." This will help you to become a smooth and confident Pen tool user.

In a nutshell, sharp 90-degree corners require one click; curves require a click, hold, and drag to form a smooth contour; and changing direction requires that you either double–click or (Option-click) [Alt-click] an anchor point to draw out a direction handle as you make the path.

When working with the Pen tool and paths, use the command keys in **table 4.1** to make your Pen-tool time more efficient and your paths more precise. The Add Anchor Point, Delete Anchor Point, and Convert Anchor Point tools are nested under the Pen tool.

table 4.1
Pen Tool Command Keys

Task	Action
Activate Pen tool	P
Switch between Pen tool and Freeform Pen tool	Shift + P
Switch between Pen tool and Direct Selection tool	(Cmd-click) [Ctrl-click]
Switch between Pen tool and Hand tool	Press and hold the spacebar
Move individual handles	(Cmd-click + drag) [Ctrl-click + drag]
Convert anchor points	(Option-click) [Alt-click] anchor point
Select multiple anchor points	(Cmd + Shift-click) [Ctrl + Shift-click] on desired anchor points
Select entire path	(Cmd + Option-click) [Ctrl + Alt-click]
Duplicate a path	(Cmd + Option + drag) [Ctrl + Alt + drag]
Delete anchor point	(Control-click) [right-click] to open context-sensitive menu
Add anchor point	(Control-click) [right-click] to open context-sensitive menu
Close an open path	Click first open end and then the second
To continue a path	Click open end and continue the outline

Fine-Tuning a Path

After you close a path, inspect it to see whether the outline needs to be finessed.

Zoom in and take a close second look at your doll head path, as shown in **figure 4.15**. Look for sections of the path that are outside or too far inside of the doll head areas.

figure 4.15

The initial path is all right, but it needs refinement before it looks professional.

To fine-tune the path, use the Direct Selection tool, fondly called the *white arrow tool*, to move anchor points and adjust direction handles. You'll find it nested under the Path Selection tool (the *black arrow tool*), directly above the Pen tool. When initially creating and refining a path, the active anchor point is solid and an inactive point is hollow.

Here are some tips for refining your paths:

Refining a path with the Direct Selection tool:

- Move anchor points by dragging them so that the path outline conforms to the object more precisely.

- Move direction handles up and down in a seesaw manner to make the angle of the curve steeper or to bend them into form-fitting position. You won't need to move the handles very much to achieve dramatic results.

- If a curve is too steep, shorten the direction lines by pushing the direction handles in toward their anchor point.

- To increase the arch of a curve, lengthen the direction lines by pulling them away from the anchor point.

- Move direction handles independently to affect only the curve on one side of the anchor point by (Cmd + Option-clicking) [Ctrl + Alt-clicking] one handle and pulling.

- If the handles are longer than half the length of the curve that they describe, add a new anchor point by (Ctrl-clicking) [right-clicking] the curve where you need a new anchor point. Then select Add Anchor Point from the pop-up menu.

- If there are too many anchor points, simplify the path by deleting unnecessary anchor points. Use the Direct Selection tool and (Ctrl-click) [right-click] over an existing anchor point and select Delete Anchor Point, as shown in **figure 4.16**.

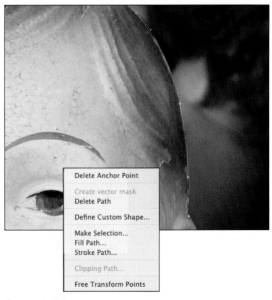

figure 4.16

Use the context-sensitive menu when refining a path.

- Change the attributes of anchor points as needed. To convert an anchor point to a smooth anchor point, use the Direct Selection tool and (Cmd + Option + drag) [Ctrl + Alt + drag] to pull out the handles. To convert a smooth anchor point to an anchor point, use the Direct Selection tool and (Cmd + Option-click) [Ctrl + Alt-click] the anchor point to convert it.

Refining a path with Transform:

- To transform the size or shape of the entire path, use the Path Selection tool (black arrow) to select the path by clicking anywhere on the path. Select Edit > Free Transform Path to scale the path.

- To transform a group of points on a path, use the Direct Selection (white arrow) tool to click and drag over a number of adjacent points. Select Edit > Free Transform Path to scale just part of the path, as shown in **figure 4.17**.

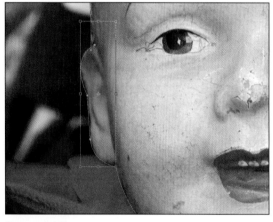

figure 4.17

Transforming a selected group of adjacent pixels.

Hints for Pen Tool Success

Over the years I've developed and used these hints to help make me a better Pen tool user:

- Use as few anchor points as possible.
- Place anchor points as far apart as possible.
- Place anchor points at significant changes in curvature inflection.
- While drawing the initial path, pull the handle in the direction you want to continue the path.
- The handles that define the curve should not be longer than half the length of the curve they are describing.
- Close the path before going back to fine-tune anchor points or handles.
- Name all paths.
- Before creating an additional path, double-check the Paths palette to make sure no other path is active.
- Work at 200% to 300% view and stay one pixel within the object to be selected.
- Learn the essential Pen tool command keys.
- While making a path, use the Pen Tool mantra, "click, hold, drag," to meditate yourself into a calm Pen tool mindset.
- With one eye, look ahead along the path to see where the next anchor point should go. This is akin to driving on the highway—you don't concentrate on the asphalt 10 feet in front of your car but rather look ahead to observe the traffic flow.
- Do not fight the Pen tool—it will win. If the Pen tool is winning and your curves and handles look like a plate of spaghetti, press the Delete key twice to delete the offending path, take a deep breath, smile, and start over again.
- Remain calm—the Pen tool is very forgiving. It doesn't race back to the starting point like the Lasso tool and it doesn't create unpredictable selections like the Magic Wand. Carefully click your way around the object, knowing that you can always return to a specific point to fine-tune the anchor point after closing the initial path.

The Freeform and Magnetic Pen Tool

The freeform Pen tool is nested under the standard Pen tool, and using it is akin to drawing with a pencil on paper. You have no control as to where the anchor points are laid down, but you can fine-tune the paths and points with the Direct Selection tool. I personally do not use the freeform Pen tool very often because the time needed to refine the paths it creates would be better used to make a precise path with the standard Pen tool. On the other hand, the Magnetic Pen tool is a handy tool to use when outlining images with distinct tonal differentiation and smooth edges.

When the freeform Pen tool is active, select Magnetic in the Options bar to draw a path that snaps to the edges of defined areas in your image, similar to the way the Magnetic Lasso tool works. To control the Magnetic Pen tool, click the geometry options triangle, as shown in **figure 4.18** and explained here.

figure 4.18

The Magnetic Pen tool controls.

Use the fly-out menu to adjust the parameters of the Magnetic Pen tool:

- For Width, enter a pixel value between 1 and 256. The Magnetic Pen detects edges only within the specified distance from the pointer. Use Caps Lock to turn the Magnetic Pen Tool icon into a circle whose size reflects the width.

- For Contrast, enter a percentage value between 1 and 100 to specify the contrast required between the pixels to be considered an edge. Use a higher value for low contrast images.

- For Frequency, enter a value between 0 and 100 to specify the rate at which the Pen sets anchor points. Higher values anchor the path in place more quickly.

- When working with a stylus tablet, selecting Pen Pressure determines that as you increase the pen pressure you decrease the active width of the Magnetic Pen tool.

🌐▷⟨ **Ch4_shrimptruck.jpg**

With its smooth edges and well-defined contrast, the shrimp truck is a perfect image to outline with the Magnetic Pen tool:

1. Click the upper-left corner of the shrimp sign to set the first anchor point.

2. Without pressing the mouse button, drag to the right along the top edge of the shrimp sign. As you move the mouse, the Magnetic Pen tool snaps to the strongest edge in the image.

3. When you get to the right corner, click once to add an anchor point and continue down the side of the truck.

4. If the border doesn't snap to the desired edge, click once to add an anchor point manually and to keep the border from moving. Continue to trace the edge and add anchor points as needed. If needed, press Delete to remove the last anchor point.

5. The area under the driver side door isn't as well defined as the rest of the truck (figure 4.19). To temporarily change the Magnetic Pen tool to the freeform Pen tool, press (Option) [Alt] to draw along the dark lower edge.

6. Complete the path by clicking the starting anchor point and naming the path, as shown in figure 4.20.

T i p

When the Magnetic Pen tool is not working as desired or when you just need to start over again, press the escape key to delete the path in progress.

figure 4.19

Press (Option) [Alt] to draw along less well-defined areas.

figure 4.20

Close and name the path.

COMPLEX PATHS AND COMBINING PATHS

Up to this point, you've learned to outline a single solid-shaped object with one path. But there are many objects that have both an inside and an outside. For example, the shape of a coffee cup consists of the actual coffee cup and the hollow handle area. Or think of Superman standing broadly with his hands on his hips, ready to save the world. The Superman form is made up of his body and the three triangles of negative space formed by the two arms on his hips and widely spread legs. Believe it or not, many composites have given themselves away when the artist outlined the figure but forgot to outline the hollow negative spaces, resulting in a composite where the figure is in an environment but the studio backdrop between the triangle formed by their arms or legs is still visible.

For practice, we'll separate the lion head doorknocker (figure 4.21) from the background to place it into a different picture, as shown in figure 4.22. We'll start by outlining the outside contour and then the inside contour that makes up the shape.

Ch4_doorknocker.jpg

Ch4_clouds.jpg

1. Outline the outside of the doorknocker. Outlining the area of the knocker handle is straightforward, while the intricate areas created by the lion's mane require the use of modifier keys. When you reach a corner where you need to move in a different direction, click to set the anchor point and (Option + drag) [Alt + drag] in the direction of the angled path to create a directional anchor point as shown in figure 4.23.

2. Close and name the outside path (figure 4.24).

3. In the Options bar, click the Subtract from Path button (figure 4.25).

figure 4.21

figure 4.22

figure 4.23

On distinct changes of direction, (Option) [Alt] drag to change direction and add an angle anchor point.

figure 4.24

Start by making and naming the outside path.

figure 4.25

After clicking the Subtract From Path Area button (circled), outline the interior space of the doorknocker.

4. Outline the inside of the doorknocker. Notice that the icon of the existing path changes as you outline the hollow area (**figure 4.26**). Make sure to close the inside shape path.

5. Activate the Direct Selection tool and zoom in on the path. Fine-tune the path by adjusting anchor points and direction handles. In **figure 4.27**, you see two extraneous anchor points that I need to delete. (Ctrl-click) [right-click] the anchor point to bring up the context-sensitive menu and choose Delete Anchor Point.

figure 4.26

Subtracting the hollow negative area from the outside path is clearly visible in the Path icon.

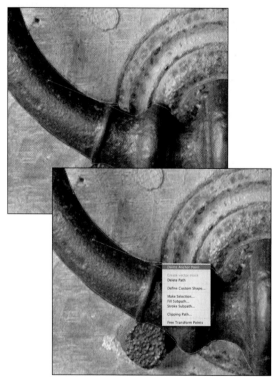

figure 4.27

Fine-tuning the path now will help make your composites more successful.

Making the path in and of itself doesn't change the image. So after making a path, naming it and saving the file as a PSD or TIFF file, you have a number of creative options for altering the image, as discussed throughout the book. To create the simple composite of the doorknocker in the sky, follow these steps:

1. Click the outside path in the Paths palette to activate it. Use the fly-out menu and choose Make Selection (**figure 4.28**). Use a feather of 1 to very subtly soften the edge of the selection and click OK.

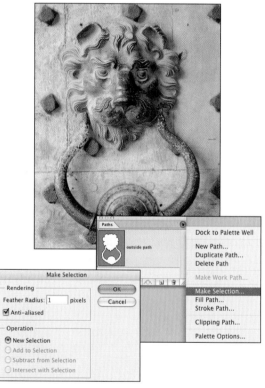

figure 4.28

Turning the path into a selection with a subtle feather of 1.

2. Open the clouds file and return to the lion head image. Use the Move tool to drag the selected lion head pixels to the new background (**figure 4.29**). Dragging with the Move tool makes a duplicate of the selected pixels and moves them, leaving the original file intact.

3. I added a slight drop shadow using the layer styles to create a subtle separation between the doorknocker and the clouds.

figure 4.29

Adding layer effects is a flexible way to enhance an image.

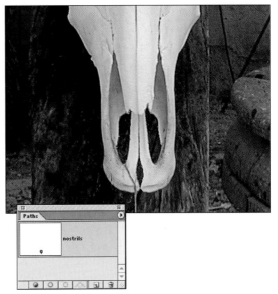

figure 4.31

Outline the three nostril areas as one path.

Intersecting the Details

When an image has numerous hollow areas, as is the case with the nostrils in the steer skull shown in **figure 4.30**, I find it easier to use the Pen tool on these areas first (**figure 4.31**). Then I click the Intersect Path Area button, as shown in **figure 4.32**, and draw the outside path around the steer's skull to create the path in which the interior hollow areas are removed from the exterior path.

Ch4_steerskull.jpg

figure 4.32

Click on the Intersect Path Area button in the Options bar to create paths that describe complex inside and outside relationships.

figure 4.30

The original digital camera snapshot of the steer head.

To Specify How Overlapping Areas Interact

Create a path or select an existing path in the Paths palette, activate the Pen tool, and choose one of the following options in the Options bar:

- Add to Path Area to add the new area to the existing path.
- Subtract from Path Area to remove the overlapping area from the existing path.
- Intersect Path Area to restrict the area to the intersection of the new path and the existing path.
- Exclude Path Area to exclude the overlapping area in the consolidated new and existing paths.

Figure 4.33 shows an industrial oven that Mark Beckelman had to photograph and then separate from its industrial environment. Because of the reflective surfaces, he photographed the oven twice—once using the fluorescent room light and once using his strobe equipment. He then combined the two exposures with an image of a kitchen, as explained in Chapter 6, "Layers Are Your Friends." Figure 4.34 shows the oven in a clean environment and the path that Mark used to silhouette the oven.

figure 4.33

The oven in the manufacturing environment.

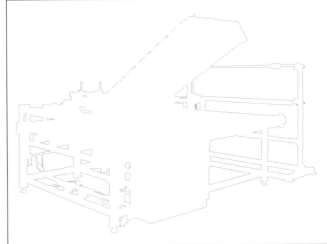

figure 4.34

The isolated industrial oven.

When Are Separate Paths Needed?

In the previous examples, we added to, subtracted from, or intersected paths to isolate an object with both the positive and negative space outline on one path in the Paths palette. When you are selecting an object with elements that interact, such as objects with translucent attributes like the windows of a car or someone's eyeglasses, it is better to have each element outlined with its own path.

The advantage of having separate paths is that you can convert each path into a selection, enabling you to handle each image element differently. In the following example, we will be treating the windows of a classic Studebaker differently than its solid body parts.

To separate the car from its environment, shown in **figure 4.35**, I first outlined the car and then made sure the car path was not active when I created a separate path for each window. To control each image element separately, it is *very* important that after creating and naming the initial exterior path, you select the Add to Path Area button in the Options bar and deactivate the initial path before outlining the interior areas to create separate paths for each window. Separate paths, which will be converted into active selections, enable you to control the density of the car windows in the final composite (**figure 4.36**).

figure 4.35

BEFORE

figure 4.36

AFTER

1. Outline the entire car body with the Pen tool.

2. Make sure the car path is not active and that the Add to Path Area button on the Options bar is selected (**figure 4.37**). Outline the front windshield and name the path.

3. Continue making and naming a separate path for each window of the car. **Figure 4.38** shows the resulting Paths palette.

figure 4.37

Make sure that the initial path is not active (not highlighted) before continuing.

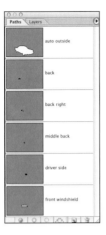

figure 4.38

Each aspect of the car requires an individual path.

4. To complete the image as shown, save the file and continue on to the next chapter. When the image background is replaced, you can control the density of the windows with the density of the layer mask, as shown in **figure 4.39**. By using shades of gray in the layer mask, the feeling of the glass windshield is maintained. If I move the car to another part of the picture, the scene behind it changes appropriately (**figure 4.40**).

If I just cut out the car and left the windows solid, the composite would look wrong—the original background would show through the car windows, as shown in **figure 4.41**.

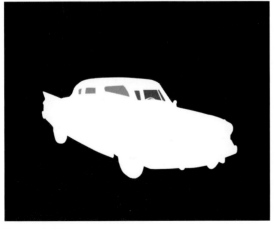

figure 4.39

Varying the shades of gray in the car's layer mask controls the density of the windows.

figure 4.40

Upon moving the car, you can see how the background changes show through the windows.

figure 4.41

If the car windows are not masked out, the original environment causes a visual disconnect.

Creating every outline on a separate path gives you greater flexibility, and because they are so easy to combine, move, and activate, many photographers are in the habit of making one outline per path.

Combining and Moving Paths

As you create more and more paths, you'll find that you have a path in one file that would be useful in a different file. Rather than redrawing the path, you can drag and drop the path from the first file to the second.

Moving paths is a practice frequently used in studio still-life photography (**figure 4.42**), such as when a photographer makes a path of an object and then decides to work with a different frame of the same object.

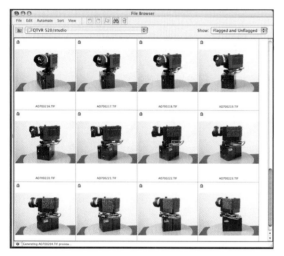

figure 4.42

The camera was photographed on a turntable to create a QuickTime VR and it now needs to be isolated.

To move the path from the first file to the second, use the Path Selection tool (black arrow) to activate the path you need to transfer, drag the path from the image or the Paths palette into the target file. Photoshop will add the path to the active path or, if no path existed before, create a Path that you then name.

You can also stack the individual shots in a layer stack and create a path for each layer. If the path doesn't fit perfectly, use the Direct Selection tool to select the points that need refinement. Select Edit > Free Transform Points, press (Cmd + T)

[Ctrl + T], and transform the path into place (**figure 4.43**) to create the final path (**figure 4.44**). When the second path is completed, duplicate it by dragging it down to the New Path button on the Paths palette and then refine it for the next layer.

For each layer, start with the path from the previous layer and refine by transforming, adding, or deleting points, and bending the direction lines into position until each layer has a corresponding path (**figure 4.45**).

figure 4.43

Transforming the path into position.

figure 4.44

The refined path.

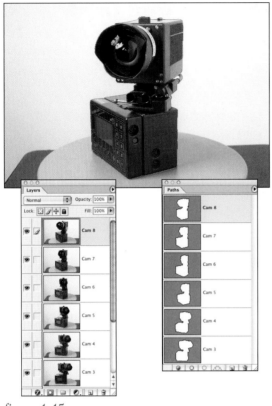

figure 4.45

Each camera layer has a corresponding path, which is carefully named to minimize confusion.

If the Path Fits

When you are copying and pasting or dragging paths between files, both images must have the same pixel resolution for the path to fit the target image—something I forgot to check before dragging the bottle path from the wine1.psd file into the composite file shown in **figure 4.46**.

To fix this oversight:

1. Delete the mismatched path and use Image > Image Size with Resample Image unselected to make the pixel resolution of the origin and target files identical.

   In this case, I changed the pixel resolution of both files to 266 per inch, a common size used in magazine printing (**figure 4.47**). Resizing the image with Resample Image unselected will not degrade the quality of the image or the path.

figure 4.46

For the dragging of paths to be predictable, image resolution must be identical. Notice the teeny path in the center of the image.

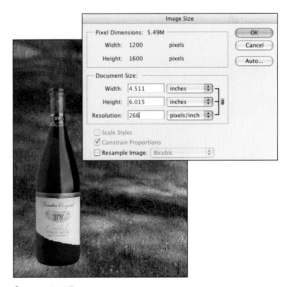

figure 4.47

Use the Image Size dialog box to make sure that both files have the same pixel resolution.

2. Return to the original file—in my case, the wine bottle image—and drag and drop the path from the Paths palette to the target image. Voilá, the path comes in at the correct size, as **figure 4.48** shows.

3. Use the Path Selection tool (black arrow) to move the path into position as I did in **figure 4.49**, and continue with your work.

figure 4.48

After adjusting the image resolution, dragging paths between files yields useful and predictable results.

figure 4.49

After using the Path Selection tool to position the path.

WORKING WITH PATHS

After making and fine-tuning the path, it is time to do something with it. For compositing artists, the most useful choices are these:

- Convert a path to a selection
- Stroke or fill a path
- Create Image Clipping paths

Converting a Path to a Selection

Converting a path into a selection is the option I use all the time. The ability to combine Pen tool precision with selection flexibility is an almost intoxicating combination.

To convert a path to a selection, use one of the following techniques:

- With the desired path active in the Paths palette, click the Load Path as Selection button on the bottom of the Paths palette.
- Drag the Path icon down to the Load Path as Selection button in the Paths palette.
- (Cmd + Return) [Ctrl + Enter] to convert the active path into an active selection.
- (Cmd-click) [Ctrl-click] the Path icon in the Paths palette.
- Choose Make Selection from the fly-out menu on the Paths palette.

Once the path is a selection, use all of the finesse and controls discussed in Chapter 2, "Selection Strategies and Essentials," Chapter 3, "The Essential Select Menu," and in the following chapter "Masks Are Your Friends."

Filling a Path

Once you've made a path, the Photoshop world is your oyster. You can fill or stroke a path to create special or photorealistic effects. **Figure 4.50** shows the original photograph of a branding exercise I worked on. As part of the project, I showed that the New York Waterway ferryboats would look much nicer with a bit of clean up and pizzazz. After cleaning up the boat, I outlined the side of the boat, and defined a number of patterns, such as the ducky and fern image that come with the Photoshop sample images. To define and name a pattern to use on an image, follow these steps:

1. Use the Rectangle Marquee tool on any open image to select an area to use as a pattern. Feather must be set to 0 pixels.

2. Choose Edit > Define Pattern.

3. Enter a name for the pattern in the Pattern Name dialog box and click OK.

N o t e

To work along, download the two files Ch4_ferryboat.jpg and Ch4_patterns.pat. Load the pattern file into your patterns library.

 **Ch4_ferryboat.jpg**

Ch4_patterns.pat

 figure 4.50

After cleaning up the boat and making a path, it was child's play to create theme variations by filling the path with a pattern.

To fill a path with a pattern:

1. Make a path around the side of the ferry and name the path. Select Layer > New Fill Layer > Pattern, click OK, and choose and scale the desired pattern as shown in **figure 4.51**. Click OK.

2. To allow the ducks to interact with the ferry, I changed the Fill layer's blending mode to Multiply, as shown in **figure 4.52**.

Please keep in mind that while Multiply is an appropriate blending mode for this image combination, you'll need to experiment with the blending modes to achieve the best results for your images.

3. The ducks are now sitting in a straight row and don't look as though they've actually been painted on the boat. To rotate them into position, rasterize the Fill Layer (Layer > Rasterize > Fill Content) and rotate and transform the duck layer to create the final image (**figure 4.53**).

figure 4.51

Selecting and scaling the pattern.

figure 4.52

The Multiply blending mode lets the layers interact realistically.

figure 4.53

The final image.

Color and Gradient Fills

You can also fill a path with solid colors (Layer > New Fill Layer > Solid Color) and gradients (Layer > New Fill Layer > Gradients), which in combination with blending modes gives you a fantastic and flexible method to experiment with images.

Figure 4.54 is a beachside snapshot of a sand dollar. **Figure 4.55** shows the accentuated version, in which I made a path for the sand dollar and used a Gradient Fill layer to frame the image with color.

Ch4_sanddollar.jpg

figure 4.54

figure 4.55

1. Create and name a path for the sand dollar.

2. Convert the path into a selection and invert the selection (Cmd + Shift + I) [Ctrl + Shift + I].

3. Rather than using the Layer menu, click the Adjustment Layer icon in the Layers palette and select Gradient.

   As soon as you add a Fill or Adjustment layer with an active selection, Photoshop automatically creates a layer mask based on the selection. The black area is inactive—that is, protected—and the white area is active and is where the effect will take place.

4. Photoshop will bring up the standard Gradient Fill dialog box, which is a good starting point from which to develop gradient variations. In this case, I started with the standard Copper gradient set to Radial, shown in **figure 4.56**.

5. Clicking the color bar of the gradient brings up the Gradient Editor, where you can change the color of the gradient by clicking on the small color squares and choosing a new color from the Color picker (**figure 4.57**).

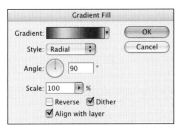

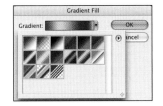

figure 4.56

Selecting the Copper gradient, set to Radial.

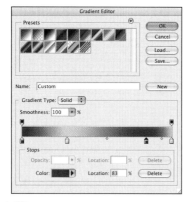

figure 4.57

Experimenting with colors and spreads helps produce unique image effects.

6. Experiment with the colors and scale to your liking. In my case, I used the complementary colors of blue and magenta so that they would visually offset each other, and I scaled the gradient by 200%.

7. Click OK. **Figure 4.58** shows the results of my tinkering—the gradient is 100-percent opaque and rather ugly. By changing the gradient layer's blending mode to color and dropping the opacity to 40%, I achieved a more subtle effect, similar to using a gradated filter when photographing with traditional gels or filters. With further adjustments to the gradient, I achieved the effect as shown in **figure 4.59**.

The potential of using the Pen tool to precisely outline an object in combination with the flexibility of fill layers may cause many a sleepless night of Photoshop experimentation and adventures.

Stroking a Path

You can stroke a path with any of the painting, toning, and focus tools shown in **figure 4.60**. In compositing, you can use this lesser-known feature with the Blur, Burn, Healing Brush, Clone Stamp, and Airbrush tools to refine image edges and darken areas of contact to create a contact shadow.

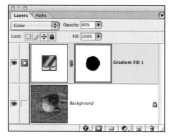

figure 4.58

The opaque blend is very ugly.

figure 4.59

After some experimentation, a pleasing colorization effect is achieved.

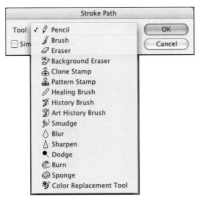

figure 4.60

The choices for stroking a path.

figure 4.62

Without the contact shadow, the wine bottle hovers.

Take a look at the coffee cup in **figure 4.61** and notice that where the cup meets table there is a very small contact shadow—it is exactly this shadow that gives the cup its visual weight. Now take a look at **figure 4.62**. Do you see how the wine bottle seems to be floating over the stone background? It was dropped into the new background and doesn't have a contact shadow. **Figure 4.63** shows the same bottle with a slight contact shadow that was created by stroking the bottom part of the bottle path with the Burn and Blur tools as described in the next exercise.

 **Ch4_winebottle.jpg**

 **Ch4_stonefloor.jpg**

figure 4.61

The contact shadow under the cup gives the cup a realistic visual weight.

figure 4.63

The addition of the slight contact shadow allows the bottle to rest visually on the stone background.

1. Make and name a path for the wine bottle. Activate the wine bottle path and convert it into a selection. With the Move tool, drag and drop the wine bottle onto the stone background.

2. Choose View > Rulers and drag a guide down from the top ruler to mark where the contact shadow will start and stop. Use the Pen tool to trace along the bottom of the wine bottle, as shown in **figure 4.64**, and name the path. In this instance, you do not need to close the path.

figure 4.64

Use a guide to help you judge where the contact shadow should end.

3. Add a new layer by clicking the New Layer button on the Layers palette, and name it *Contact Shadow*.

    Working on a separate layer is akin to working on clear acetate, allowing you to tone down specific areas without affecting the background layer or, in this case, the wine bottle.

4. To create realistic shadows, use the Eyedropper tool to sample a dark color from the stone floor. Select a small, hard-edged brush at 10% opacity and zoom in on the bottom of the wine bottle (**figure 4.65**).

figure 4.65

Setting the brush to 10% will let you carefully build up the shadow.

5. Click the Paths tab and activate the path of the bottom of the bottle.

6. On the Paths Palette fly-out menu, select Stroke Path and verify the Brush is selected as shown in **figure 4.66**.

    Note: Photoshop will reference the last painting tool you modified to be the tool in this window. You can always use the pull-down menu to select any of the other painting, toning, and focus options.

figure 4.66

Choosing the brush from the Stroke menu.

figure 4.67

The addition of the slight contact shadow lets the bottle visually rest on the stone background.

7. Click OK. Photoshop will stroke the active path with the tool you selected. Because you are working with a 10% brush, the effect will be very subtle. Repeat the stroking of the path two or three times until the shadow is visible. On the later strokes, I often reduce the size and hardness of the brush to make the center of the shadow darker than the edges of the shadow.

8. To see the effect, it is useful to hide the path by (Cmd + H) [Ctrl + H] to hide the extras—in this case the guide and the path. Return to the Layers palette and change the blending mode of the contact shadow layer to Multiply as shown in **figure 4.67** and notice how the shadow visually drops into place. Adjust the opacity to taste and if need be, use the Eraser tool to clean up any extraneous areas.

Tip

To stroke a path without using the Paths Palette fly-out menu, press the keyboard equivalent of the tool you would like to use and then press Enter or Return.

Creating Image Clipping Paths

You see images that are clipped all the time—the silhouetted washing machines or the bananas in the "two pounds for one-dollar" advertisements in the junk mail that fills your (analog) mailbox.

Figure 4.68 represents a photograph I took of a ship steering wheel at the South Street Seaport in New York City. The background is rather drab and distracting; I think the image would look better if the wheel were isolated on the page with a clipping path.

Image-clipping paths, commonly referred to as *clipping paths*, are vector-based information of the outline that is smoother than a pixel-based selection. Most importantly, image clipping paths are printed at the output resolution of the PostScript output device, so the edges will be very crisp.

Ch4_steerwheel.jpg

Original image

Selected with the Lasso tool.   With a clipping path.

figure 4.68

Selecting the steering wheel with the Lasso tool creates a ragged edge, while clipping the steering wheel with a path creates a crisp outline.

To create an image clipping path, follow these steps:

1. With the Pen tool, outline the object you want silhouetted, and name the path (**figure 4.69**).

2. Use the fly-out menu on the Paths palette and select Clipping Path.

3. Choose the path from the drop-down menu and type in a flatness value (**figure 4.70**).

   The higher the value, the straighter and possibly choppier the curves will be, but as David Blatner and Bruce Fraser explain in their essential book *Real World Photoshop*,

"You can almost always raise your flatness to between 3 and 5, never see the difference, and speed your printing times considerably." In the case of the steering wheel, I used a flatness setting of 4.

4. Save the file as a TIFF or EPS. When you import the file into InDesign, PageMaker, or QuarkXPress, the object will be perfectly silhouetted.

After converting a path into a clipping path, you can still use it just like a "normal" path and refine it, stroke it, fill it, and convert it into a selection.

figure 4.69

Creating the initial path.

figure 4.70

The image-clipping path isolates the steering wheel from the busy background.

COMBINING PATHS AND SELECTIONS

I love paths. I love their flexibility, small file size, gracefulness, and even the meditative mindset I get into as I focus in on the image with the Pen tool mantra of "click, hold, drag." But there are many times when I need the crispness of a path and the edge quality of a selection in one image.

Figure 4.71 illustrates an image with a variety of edge qualities. The sunglasses, arm and T-shirt are crisp, making them ideal Pen tool candidates. But the fluffy red vest and my hair blowing in the breeze are much too detailed, translucent, and random to be selected with the Pen tool. What is a Photoshopper to do? Combine paths and selections to take advantage of the best of both worlds.

ch4_katrin.jpg

1. I made three paths—one for each lens and one for the body (**figure 4.72**). Notice how I carefully followed the contour of the sunglasses frame and my arm but went inside of the fluffy vest and hair.

2. After converting the body path to a selection by dragging it down to the Load Path as Selection button on the Paths palette, I zoomed in on the vest, and using the Magic Wand Shift-clicked on the edge areas of the red vest to add them to the selection (**figure 4.73**). The crisp edges of the glasses and the arm and the fuzzy detail of the vest are now contained in one selection (**figure 4.74**).

3. I saved the selection as an alpha channel (**figure 4.75**) as explained in Chapter 3, "The Essential Select Menu."

figure 4.71

The original photograph has a variety of edge qualities that need to be taken into account when making selections.

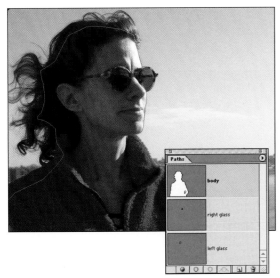

figure 4.72

Using a path as a foundation for an accurate selection.

figure 4.74

Shift-clicking with the Magic Wand to add the vest edges to the selection.

figure 4.73

After converting the path to a selection.

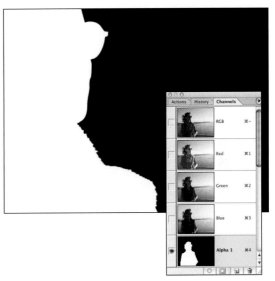

figure 4.75

The alpha channel created from the path and Magic Wand selection.

4. After adding the hair to the alpha channel as explained in Chapter 8, "Selecting Hair and Fine Detail," and loading the mask as a selection, I pasted a new sky into the image—but the image still doesn't look right. Take a look at the area on my sunglasses; the sky seen through the outermost sunglass lens is still the original sky and the new sky has oranges and reds. This is exactly the kind of image detail that can give away a composite (**figure 4.76**).

5. To fix this incongruity, I converted the right lens path into a selection, clicked on the layer mask of the sky, filled the selection with 50% gray, and painted in additional tonal variations on the mask to mimic how the tinted sunglass lenses vary in translucency (**figure 4.77**).

Combining soft and hard edges using the pixel-based selection tools (Lasso, Magic Wand, and Color Range) with crisp edges using the Pen tool is a fantastic method for creating convincing images.

figure 4.76

The original sky is still visible in the sunglasses—a dead give away of a shoddy composite.

figure 4.77

After converting the right lens path into a selection, I filled and painted it with shades of gray to let some of the new sky shimmer though.

Converting Selections to Paths

It makes sense that if you can convert a path into a selection, you can also convert a selection into a path. I'm not a huge fan of this technique, but it has helped enough people for me to include it here.

Ch4_cricket.jpg

1. Select Mr. Cricket with the standard or Magnetic Lasso tool (as shown in **figure 4.78** and as described in Chapter 2).

2. Open the Paths palette and click the fly-out menu; select Make Work Path, which will bring up the flatness dialog box (**figure 4.79**).

3. Because this is a method to create a work in progress path, use a Tolerance setting of 1.0, and click OK. The Tolerance setting determines how accurate the path will be—the higher the setting, the less accurate the path.

4. Use the Direct Selection tool (the white arrow) to refine the path (**figure 4.80**).

figure 4.78

The original carousel ride figure…when you wish upon a star.

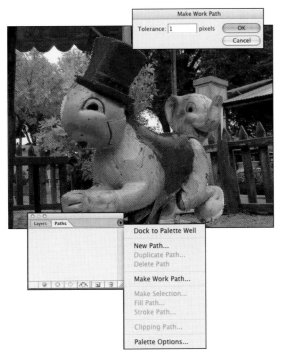

figure 4.79

Use a low tolerance to create a more accurate path.

figure 4.80

Name the work path and use the Direct Selection tool to refine the path.

Note

Paths add only 4Kb to 6Kb to a file, making them wonderfully efficient. But, because of their tiny file size, many people assume they should convert their alpha channels into paths to save file size. This is an urban myth that needs to be squelched wherever it raises its misunderstood head. Photoshop uses an efficient run-length encoding scheme to describe the masks, so when the file is closed, the masks hardly add anything to the file size. In addition, if you convert gradated alpha channels to paths you will lose the smooth edges and tonal transitions.

CLOSING THOUGHTS

I hope that by reading this chapter and practicing the techniques here you have banished the lurking Pen tool monster from your Photoshop list of things to learn. Throughout the rest of the book, you'll be using paths and the Pen tool to refine edges, create silhouettes, and make alpha channels that are elegant and precise.

Layers and Masks Exposed

II

5

MASKS ARE YOUR FRIENDS

Ask two New Yorkers how to get to JFK Airport and you'll probably get four different answers. For a first-time tourist, this same system with its many options can quickly become confusing and overwhelming. Likewise, working with Photoshop masks for the first time may feel like the deepest, darkest subway system you could find—especially when all you want to do is get back to your hotel room—I mean, create an image. One reason for the confusion is that just as you can get to the airport via many different routes, you can also achieve a particular result in Photoshop many different ways.

This chapter is your guide to the various types of Photoshop masks. It will help you understand the different approaches you can take to Photoshop masking by addressing the following:

- The essential masking concept
- Types of Photoshop masks
- Channel masks
- Vector masks

You may have noticed that this chapter, "Masks Are Your Friends," and the next chapter, "Layers Are Your Friends," have very similar titles. This has nothing to do with a lack of imagination (or my lack of sleep!)—it has to do with the fact that layers and masks work hand in hand. Considering both of them your friends will give you a larger Photoshop circle of friends to create images with.

TYPES OF PHOTOSHOP MASKS

All types of masks serve the same purpose—controlling which image areas you want to reveal or affect, and which image areas you want to conceal or not affect. The two most common masks are the layer and the channel mask, but many more features in Photoshop can act as masks, as you can see in **figures 5.1** through **5.13**. Although some of them may not fit the classic definition of a mask, I feel that any Photoshop control that reveals, conceals, or influences where an image effect takes place is just another type of mask. Most importantly, working with the following masks lets you combine images creatively and nondestructively, which encourages experimentation and discovery.

One last time—what do all masks have in common? They all hide and reveal image information and most importantly, using any of these masks lets you experiment, brainstorm, dabble, and create images without deleting, destroying, or changing pixels. Masks *are* your friends.

A Mask by Any Other Name Is a Mask

As discussed in Chapter 2, "Selection Strategies and Essentials," internally Photoshop sees all selections as grayscale images, which are commonly called *masks*, *alpha channels*, or *mattes*. Depending on the background or point of view of the person discussing masking, he or she may use the following terms interchangeably:

- *Mask* is the term often used by photographers, as it refers to the masks used in the traditional darkroom to block the enlarger light from exposing a specific part of the paper.

- *Alpha channels* is a term often used by longtime Photoshop users who worked with Photoshop before there were layers. In the dark ages prior to Photoshop 3, layers didn't exist, so the process of combining images relied very heavily on the alpha channels that reside below the image channels.

- *Mattes* is the term used by film and special effects professionals who use garbage and traveling mattes for compositing live action footage with background plates. In the film *The Matrix*, there's a classic shot in which Keanu Reeves is bending backward in slow motion to avoid a speeding bullet. The actor was shot in a blue screen environment and compositing artists used mattes to remove the cameras and studio rigging to replace them with the buildings seen in the final shot.

- *Frisket* is used by people with traditional airbrush or retouching experience and graphic designers who have done traditional paste-up. Now we're going way, way back to the pre-digital days!

Regardless of the term you use, they all accomplish the same thing: They let you work on images in a completely nondestructive manner. A mask doesn't make up the actual image data; rather, it is an adjunct component used to control where changes such as applying fills or filters and combining images take place.

Selection-Based Masks

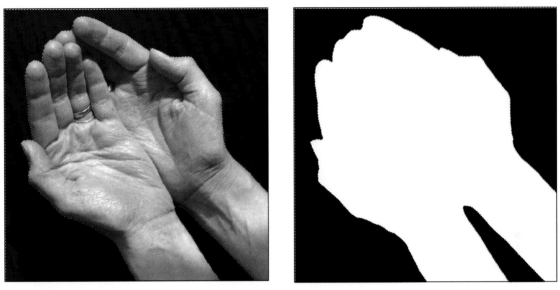

figure 5.1

The most fundamental of masks, an active selection is used to control where a change takes place or to establish a quick mask, layer mask, or alpha channel. The dancing ants—officially called the selection marquee—*signify the border between white (active) and black (inactive). For more information, see Chapter 2.*

Layer-Based Masks

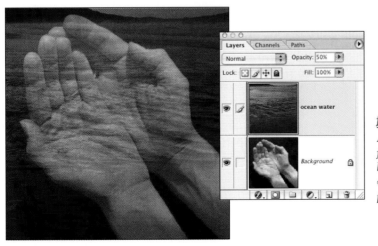

figure 5.2

Adjusting layer opacity is a straight-forward and often effective method to blend images. Layer opacity is controlled with the Opacity slider in the Layers palette.

Layer-Based Masks

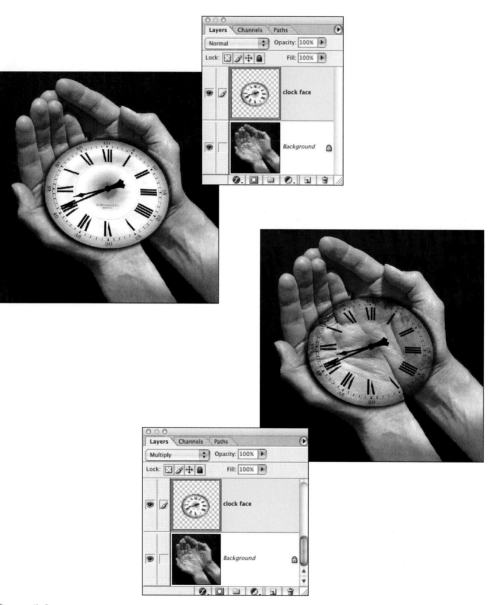

figure 5.3

As defined in Chapter 6, the blending modes mathematically compare and calculate pixel values for tone, color, and brightness to create both very useful and creative effects. Use the blending mode drop-down menu on the upper left of the Layers palette to select a blending mode.

Layer-Based Masks

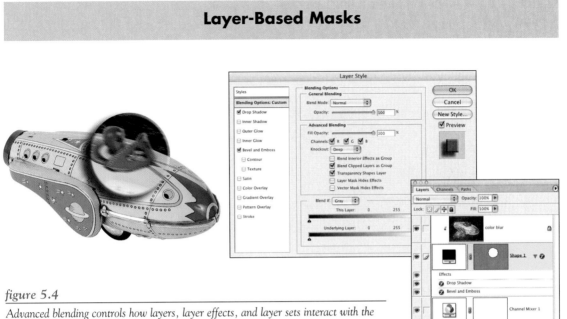

figure 5.4

Advanced blending controls how layers, layer effects, and layer sets interact with the rest of the image. In the Layers palette, use the fly-out menu to choose Blending Options to access the Advanced Blending options. Please see Chapter 6 for additional information.

figure 5.5

As discussed in Chapter 10, the Blend If commands are accessed by double-clicking on the layer icon and adjusting the four sliders to combine layers based on tone and color.

Layer-Based Masks

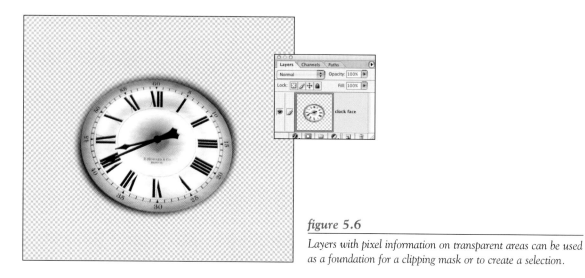

figure 5.6

Layers with pixel information on transparent areas can be used as a foundation for a clipping mask or to create a selection.

figure 5.7

In a clipping group, the transparent pixels of the layer mask out the content of layers above it. The name of the base layer in the clipping mask is underlined, and the thumbnails for the overlying layers are indented. The Blend Clipped Layers as Group option in the Layer Style dialog box determines whether the blending mode of the base affects the whole group or just the base layer.

Layer-Based Masks

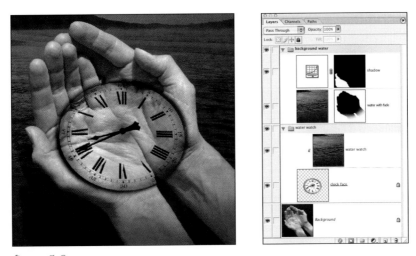

figure 5.8

Layer sets are folders used to organize multilayer composites. Changing the Layer Set blending mode from Pass Through to Normal treats the layer set like a separate image. It won't interact with the layers beneath it. This can be very useful when fine-tuning separate image elements of a composite.

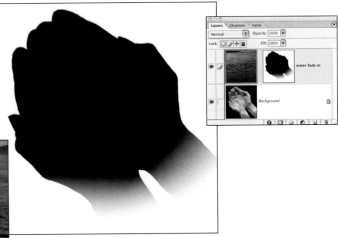

figure 5.9

Each layer can support a pixel-based mask, commonly called a layer mask, and a vector-based mask (discussed later in this chapter). Use the layer mask to hide and reveal parts of a specific layer when doing retouching, compositing (as shown here), and special effects. For an in-depth treatise on layer masks, see Chapter 7.

Raster-Based Masks

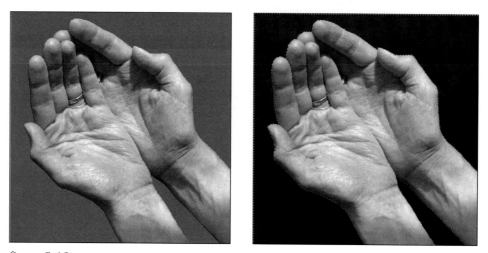

figure 5.10

Quick Mask mode is used to create, verify, and refine selections with painting tools and filters. Quick Mask lets you toggle between active selection and a transparent mask preview very quickly by pressing q whenever you have an active selection. Quick Mask is discussed in detail in Chapter 2.

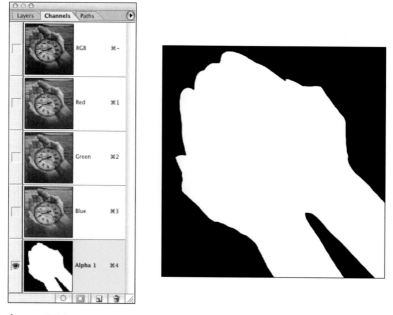

figure 5.11

The mother of all masks—alpha masks, also called channel masks—are grayscale file elements stored with an image, as long as you save the file in PSD, TIFF, or PDF file format. I recommend using PSD or TIFF when working on image composites. I'll cover alpha masks in depth in this chapter.

Vector-Based Masks

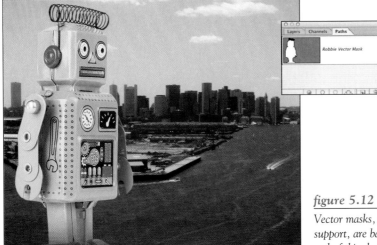

figure 5.12

Vector masks, the second type of mask a layer can support, are based on paths. I'll discuss them at the end of this chapter.

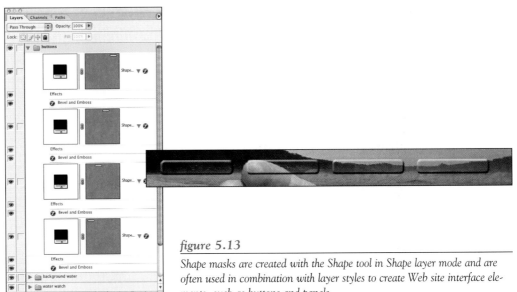

figure 5.13

Shape masks are created with the Shape tool in Shape layer mode and are often used in combination with layer styles to create Web site interface elements, such as buttons and panels.

The Rosetta Stone of Masking

Photoshop takes many different approaches to masking—from the straightforward active selection to the more involved alpha mask, the veritable Rosetta stone of masking. Alpha masking teaches that "white is active and black is inactive," which translates to "white reveals and black conceals." In other words, wherever you want to see an image or apply an effect, the mask needs to be white; wherever you want to hide an image or effect, the mask needs to be black, as illustrated in **figures 5.14** and **5.15**.

Shades of gray allow more or less image to show, with darker shades of gray hiding more than the lighter shades of gray.

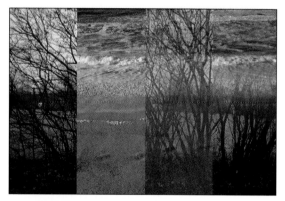

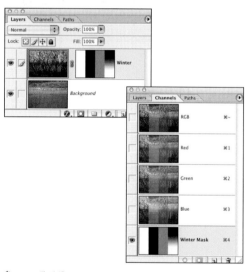

figure 5.15

The resulting image. In both layer and alpha masks, "white reveals and black conceals."

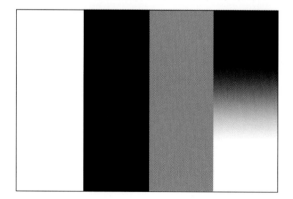

figure 5.14

The two source images and the layer mask.

WORKING WITH ALPHA CHANNELS

Every photographic image is made up of image channels—one for grayscale images, three for RGB (red, green, blue) and LAB (luminance and two color channels), and four for CMYK (cyan, magenta, yellow, and black)—and can support up to 56 channels, as listed in **table 5.1**.

table 5.1
Image and Alpha Channels

File type	Number of image channels	Number of possible alpha channels
Grayscale	1	55
RGB	3	53
LAB	3	53
CMYK	4	52

The image channels create the picture you see when you open a file, while alpha channels are added as needed and reside *behind* the image channels. Alpha channels are not visible unless you click on their name in the Channels palette or use (Cmd + [alpha-channel number]) [Ctrl + (alpha-channel number)], as shown in **figure 5.16**. Use (Cmd + ~) [Ctrl + ~] to return to viewing the image.

Adding alpha channels increases file size, but with Photoshop CS, the Adobe engineers have made alpha channels more efficient. Depending upon their complexity—from a simple geometric shape to the more complex fine-detail masks—each one can add between 10 percent and 25 percent to the file size. While this may still seem like a significant increase, the good news is that when you save and close the file, the channels are encoded very efficiently, and the file-size increase is negligible.

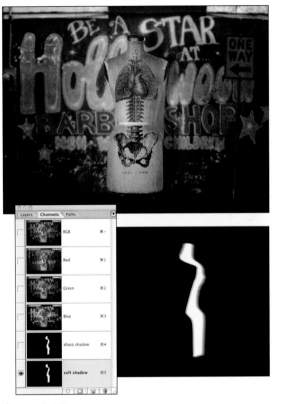

figure 5.16

To view the alpha channel, click on its name in the Channels palette.

Working in Hi-Bit

In 8-bit images, alpha channels have 256 shades of gray; in 16-bit files, they have over 65,000 shades of gray. The decision to work in 8-bit or 16-bit depends on whether your scanner or digital camera can capture a true hi-bit file and whether the additional image quality is required for your final output.

The cost of working in hi-bit is that the file is automatically double the file size of an 8-bit file, making every step in Photoshop slower and more processor intensive. It will also double your hard drive and storage requirements.

I work in hi-bit because maintaining the highest image quality for as long as possible into the imagemaking process is a good idea. You'll need to evaluate the benefits of hi-bit versus the file size and speed issue and decide if your final output truly requires a hi-bit workflow. In the future, printers will be able to print hi-bit files, so maintaining the highest quality information is a good idea.

When to Use Alpha Masks

With so many masking options to work with, choosing the best one may sometimes feel more like a toss of the die, rather than a precise decision. In fact, since layers and layer masks work so well together, many people have relegated alpha channels to the scrap bin of Photoshop history.

I use layer masks often. Seeing changes occur to the image as I work on the layer mask is essential in refining composites. But I also rely on alpha masks a great deal, especially when making complex selections. So use alpha masks in these situations (each of these will be addressed in Part Three of this book: "Selecting and Preserving Fine Detail").

- While making an involved selection, choose Select > Save Selection to save your selection in progress into an alpha channel. If you make a mistake, choose Select > Load Selection to reactivate the selection to the point you saved it as an alpha channel and continue working.

- After making an intricate selection, choose Select > Save Selection, especially if making the selection required a lot of time. This will save you from having to redo the selection the next time you open the document.

- Often building the best selection requires multiple steps, which is demonstrated in Chapter 10, "Selecting Translucency and Green Screen Techniques." When working with the Image Calculations command, saving the primary steps as alpha channels is essential in building the final mask.

- Use alpha channels to build luminance masks, as illustrated in Chapter 9, "Advanced Selection Techniques," to mask out hair and fine detail.

- Use alpha channels to save even simple selections if you plan to reuse the selection more than once.

In essence, save the alpha channel whenever you've spent more than a few minutes making a selection or when you are building professional masks based on image information. I've never regretted having a mask too many. Not having them when I needed them always resulted in extra work because I had to redo a previously made but not saved selection.

Layer Masks Vs. Alpha Masks

I am often asked when it is appropriate to use a layer mask versus an alpha mask. I distinguish the two as follows:

- Alpha masks are created and loaded *before* applying an image modification. Changing alpha masks after modifying the image has no effect on the image modification. Take, for example, **figure 5.17**: After creating the composite, I filled an oval selection on the alpha mask with white, but this didn't change the actual image at all.

- Changing a layer mask *after* applying a change affects the image, as demonstrated in **figure 5.18**. After making the composite, I filled an oval selection on the layer mask with white, which most definitely did change the image.

- A layer mask correlates to a specific layer; whereas an alpha mask correlates to the entire image. Although you can (Cmd-click) [Ctrl-click] on a layer mask to activate it and use it on a different layer, its influence is primarily dedicated to the layer with which it is associated.

- In the Channels palette, alpha masks are in plain text and are always visible, while layer masks are in italics and only visible when their specific layer is active.

In a nutshell, alpha masks are created and used before you make a change to the image and layer masks are used to interactively fine-tune the composite after a change or effect has been added. Use alpha masks to create complex selections before changing an image, as addressed in Part Three of the book. Use layer masks to refine images and composites, as addressed in Chapter 7, "The Power of Layer Masking."

Composite image

Composite image

Original alpha mask

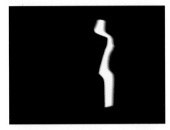

Original layer mask

Modified alpha mask

Modified layer mask

Unchanged image

Changed image

figure 5.17

Modifying the alpha mask does not change the image.

figure 5.18

Modifying the layer mask does change the image.

Managing Alpha Masks

Since each file can support up to 56 channels (although I've never seen anyone use all 56), I recommend giving your alpha channels descriptive names so that you can easily find what you're looking for in the Channels palette. Double-click on the channel name to rename it or double-click the Alpha Channel icon to open the Channel Options dialog box (**figure 5.19**), which gives you not only the ability to rename the channel but also to change mask indicators and behaviors.

figure 5.19

Open the Channel Options by double-clicking on an alpha channel icon.

Three options in the Color Indicates section of the dialog box control how the mask behaves in relationship to the masked areas:

- The default is Masked Areas, in which active areas are white and inactive areas are black. I strongly recommend using this default behavior.

- Choosing Selected Areas reverses the standard behavior of the mask. If your alpha mask is acting exactly the opposite of how you expect, this is a good place to verify that Masked Areas is selected.

- Selecting Spot Color adds channels to print additional colors other than the standard CMYK process colors. For example, you may use it to print a logo or graphic in specific premixed ink. Each spot color requires its own

plate on the press. To print an image with spot colors, you need to create spot channels to store the colors and save the file in the EPS or PDF file format. (Cmd-click) [Ctrl-click] on the New Channel button to add a Spot channel.

The Color and Opacity settings in the dialog box only determine the translucency when viewing the alpha channel though the image, as shown in **figure 5.20**. It does not impact how the alpha channels function.

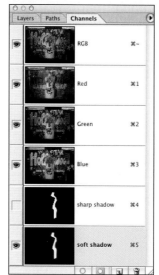

figure 5.20

Viewing the image through the alpha channel is helpful when refining the alpha channel with brushes or filters.

In the Save and Load Selection section, saving an active selection creates an alpha channel for saving the selection marquee (the dancing ants) as an alpha channel. To save an active selection without using the menu, open the Channels palette and click on the New Channel button (figure 5.21). Please see Chapter 3, "The Essential Select Menu," for more information on saving active selections and loading masks.

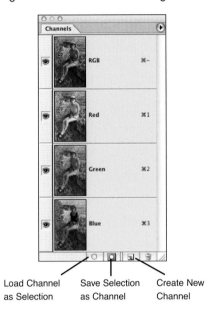

Load Channel as Selection   Save Selection as Channel   Create New Channel

figure 5.21

Clicking on the Save Selection as Channel button saves the active selection.

THE FIVE STEPS TO ALPHA MASTERY

Think of alpha channels like tools in a workshop or a kitchen drawer. The tools are there for you whenever you need them. When you do, you open the drawer, take one out, use it, and when you're done with it (as my father taught me), you put it back into the drawer. When you don't need it, it just "sits" there without affecting anything.

This is exactly how alpha masks function: They can be a part of an image and have absolutely no effect until you activate them. Working with alpha masks is a five-step process, done in the exact order outlined here:

1. **Make** the alpha channel: With an active selection, click on the Save Selection as Channel button or choose Select > Save Selection. Without an active selection, click on the Create a New Channel button or drag an image channel or alpha channel down to the Create a New Channel button.

2. **Target** where the change should take place: After making an alpha channel always activate the channel or layer to which you want to apply the change.

3. **Activate** the alpha channel: Select > Load Selection or (Cmd + Option + [alpha-channel number]) [Ctrl + Alt + (alpha-channel number)] to change the alpha channel into an active selection.

4. **Apply** a change: Apply the desired change such as adding an Adjustment Layer, running a filter, pasting in a new image element, etc.

5. **Refine** the composite: Depending on the image, this step requires more or less work and is most often done on the layer or the layer mask.

Keeping these five steps in mind—*make, target, activate, apply, and refine*—has helped me understand the masking process. The following examples reinforce these five steps.

Accentuating an Existing Sky

You can use any number of ways to improve skies—from simply accentuating the existing color, to adding new clouds, to changing the time of day or weather in a scene.

The photograph in **figure 5.22** is a tourist picture I took in Prague. It was a sunny day, but the sky is too dull. After making an alpha channel and activating it, I was able to bring out the natural sky with a Photo Filter Adjustment Layer, as shown in **figure 5.23** and outlined here:

Ch5_praguecathedral.jpg

figure 5.22

figure 5.23

Step One: Making the Alpha Channel

In most cases, the first step to improving the sky is to protect the parts of the scene—usually the buildings or landscape—from being affected.

1. To make a mask with all the fine detail of the cathedral spires, we need to take advantage of the mask within the image. Inspect the three image channels to find the one with the greatest difference between the building and the sky.

   In this example, the blue channel shows the greatest contrast between the sky and the cathedral. Drag the blue channel down to the Create New Channel button to duplicate it (figure 5.24).

2. Select Image > Adjustments > Curves (Cmd + M) [Ctrl + M] and increase the channel contrast by moving the white point to the left and the shadow point to the right (figure 5.25).

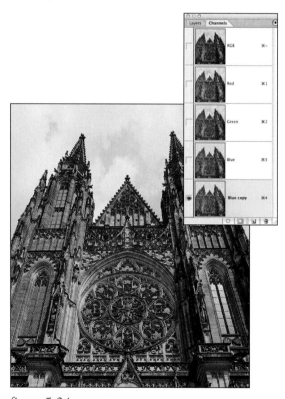

figure 5.24

Creating an alpha channel from an existing image channel maintains fine-edge information.

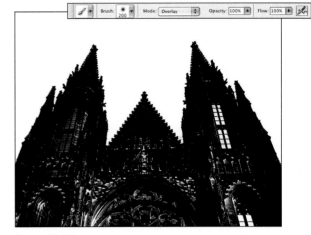

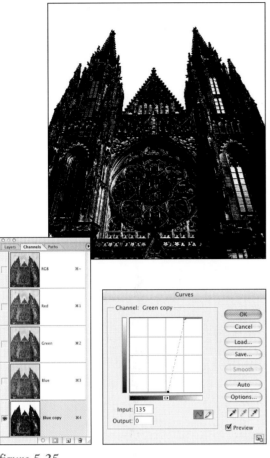

figure 5.25

Using Curves on the alpha mask to increase contrast quickly creates dramatic separation between the sky and the building.

figure 5.26

Painting with black in Overlay darkens the building without affecting the sky.

figure 5.27

Selecting just within the edge of the cathedral using the Polygon Lasso tool.

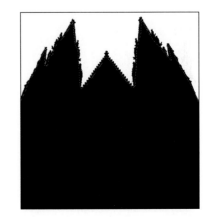

figure 5.28

Finishing the alpha mask by filling the active selection with black.

3. To separate the cathedral from the sky even more, use a hard-edged black brush, set to Overlay, and paint along the spire edges (figure 5.26).

   Using Overlay with black will ignore the white sky and let you quickly accentuate the separation. Don't worry about painting over the lower part of the building; we'll tackle that in the next step.

4. Use the Polygon Lasso tool with a zero feather to select just inside of the cathedral and the lower part of the building (figure 5.27). To quickly make straight-edged selections with the Lasso tool, press (Option) [Alt] to turn the freeform Lasso tool into the Polygon Lasso tool. Choose Edit > Fill > Use Black to create figure 5.28 and then deselect the selection.

Step Two: Targeting Where the Change Should Take Place

Now that the mask is done, you need to "tell" Photoshop where to work next. In other words, since the mask is done we need to return to the area that needs improvement, which in this example is the sky on the Background layer:

- To target the Background layer, click on the word RGB in the Channels palette (Cmd + ~) [Ctrl +~] to return to the photograph. If this image was a multilayered document, you would click on the specific layer you wanted to work on.

Step Three: Activating the Alpha Channel

As mentioned previously, you can have many alpha channels associated with an image, but for Photoshop to know which one you would like to use, you need to activate the correct alpha channel. Remember, alpha channels are like tools in a drawer—unless you take them out, or in essence, activate them—they won't do anything.

- To activate the alpha channel, which in this image is the fourth channel, press (Cmd + option + 4) [Ctrl + Alt + 4] to change the alpha channel into an active selection (figure 5.29).

figure 5.29

Activating the alpha mask creates an active selection.

Step Four: Applying the Change

Now for the fun part: actually seeing the results of the masking!

- Choose Layer > New Adjustment Layer > Photo Filter and use the Cooling Filter 82, as shown in figure 5.30. Notice how the active selection has been transferred into the Photo Filter layer mask and that only the sky is being accentuated.

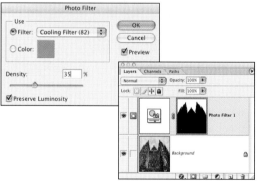

figure 5.30

Adding a Photo Filter Cooling filter is one way to make skies look bluer.

Step Five: Refining the Composite

To refine the image and make the day a bit sunnier, we can take advantage of the existing Photo Filter layer and layer mask to add a hint of sunshine to the façade of the cathedral.

1. Duplicate the Photo Filter layer by dragging it down to the New Layer button on the bottom of the Layers palette. Choose Image > Adjustments > Invert or (Cmd + I) [Ctrl + I] to invert the layer mask. Of course, this makes the building very blue (**figure 5.31**).

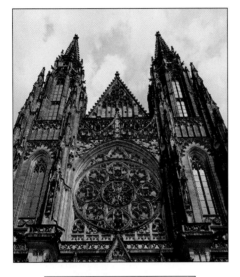

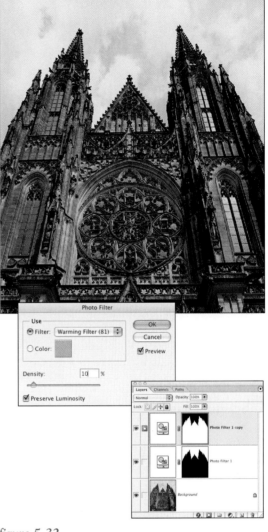

figure 5.31

Taking advantage of existing layer masks by doubling the layer is both easy and fast.

figure 5.32

Inverting the layer mask protects the sky and lets the Photo filter gently warm the building.

2. Double-click on the Photo Filter icon, choose Warming Filter 81, and reduce the density to approximately 10 percent. As you can see in **figure 5.32**, the building has a slight hint of sunlight, and my vacation picture looks much better.

Keep the five alpha making steps in mind—*make, target, activate, apply,* and *refine*—to work more confidently and efficiently.

Adding a New Sky

Sky replacements are a common task and are used to replace a drab sky with one that enhances the mood of the scene. In the following example, the golden guard in Bangkok (**figure 5.33**) could use a more dramatic sky to create the mood in **figure 5.34**. Following the five-step process of "make, target, activate, apply, refine," we'll replace the sky:

 ch5_bangkokguard.jpg

ch5_sunsetsky.jpg

figure 5.33

figure 5.34

Step One: Make

1. Inspect the three image channels to find the one with the greatest difference between the figure and the sky. In this image, the blue channel has the most tonal contrast (**figure 5.35**).

2. Drag the blue channel to the Create New Channel button, choose Select > All, Edit > Copy, Edit > Paste, followed immediately by Edit > Fade, and choose Color Burn (**figure 5.36**).

   Pasting and fading channels with blending modes increases contrast and is discussed further in Chapter 8, "Selecting Hair and Fine Detail."

Red

Green

Blue

figure 5.35

Inspect the image channels to find the one with the most contrast between subject and sky.

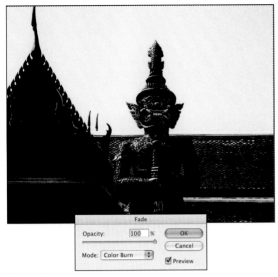

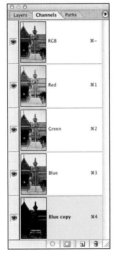

figure 5.36

Copy, pasting, and fading with blending modes quickly increases the contrast.

3. With the alpha #4 channel active, repeat the Select > All, Edit > Copy, Edit > Copy, followed by Edit > Fade, and choose Color Burn three more times to really punch up the contrast, as shown in **figure 5.37**.

4. To verify the integrity of the alpha mask, click on the view column next to RGB to see through the alpha channel to the image (**figure 5.38**).

figure 5.38

Viewing the image through the mask reveals that the roofline behind the figure needs to be added to the mask.

5. As you can see, the roofline behind the figure needs to be restored. Use the Polygon Lasso tool to select it and the lower portion of the image as shown in **figure 5.39**. Choose Edit > Fill > Use Black and Select > Deselect to create **figure 5.40**.

6. Paint in the details around the figure's head with a small, hard-edged black brush (**figure 5.41**).

The first step—making the mask—is done.

figure 5.37

After three copy, paste, and fade steps, the mask is almost finished.

figure 5.39

Selecting the roofline and spire with the Polygon Lasso tool.

figure 5.40

Filling the selection restores the correct roofline.

figure 5.41

Painting with a small black brush to refine the mask.

Step Two: Target

Target the Background layer, or activate the RGB composite channel (Cmd + ~) [Ctrl +~] to return to the unchanged photograph.

Step Three: Activate

Activate the fourth alpha channel (Cmd + option + 4) [Ctrl + Alt + 4] to change the alpha channel into an active selection (**figure 5.42**).

figure 5.42

Activating the mask creates an active selection.

Step Four: Apply

Applying the change is the most visible part of the process—it influences the final look of the image the most. Possible changes to apply include: using filters, adding Adjustment Layers, duplicating the selected area to a new layer, pasting in new image elements, or copying the active area to be used in a different image altogether.

1. Open the sunset picture, select All and Edit Copy, and then close the sunset file.

2. With the Bangkok guard image active, select Edit > Paste Into to replace the drab sky with the sunset sky. Once again, notice how the active selection that was based on the alpha channel has been transferred to the layer mask, as shown in **figure 5.43**.

3. Make sure the sunset is active by clicking on the layer icon. Use the Move tool to position the sunset sky wherever you want it (**figure 5.44**).

figure 5.44

Position the sunset with the Move tool.

Step Five: Refine

Zoom in to check the transition between the figure and sky. I see a slight white halo around the figure's head (**figure 5.45**).

It is very important to identify what is causing the halo before trying to fix it. Because the composite started with the alpha mask, you might think that it is causing the halo. But as illustrated previously with the example of filling the oval with white, after you activate an alpha channel and use it to create a new layer with a layer mask such as the sunset layer—it is the layer mask that is causing the halo. So it's actually the layer mask that needs to be refined to remove the halo.

1. Click the layer mask and select Filter > Other > Maximum to expand the white, which will show more clouds and reduce the halo effect. Use the lowest setting possible, which is 1 (**figure 5.46**). This resolves most of the problem very quickly.

figure 5.43

Pasting the sky into the active selection creates a new layer with a layer mask.

figure 5.45

The white halo around the figure's head needs correction.

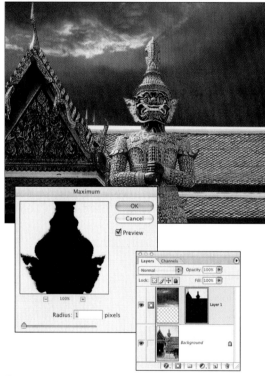

figure 5.46

The Maximum filter increases the white area of the mask, which in turn lets more clouds show and reduces the halo.

2. When you try this on your own images, using the Minimum and Maximum filters to expand or contract masks may leave transitions too harsh. I often follow them with a .5 Gaussian Blur to soften the edge ever so slightly.

CREATIVE TECHNIQUES USING ALPHA MASKS

Alpha masks are fantastic places to experiment with image luminosity, textures, and applying filters to interpret the edge quality of a saved selection. An alpha channel is an identically sized grayscale image of your original image. You can use all the painting tools and filters on the grayscale version to add textures and distortions.

Working with Image Luminosity

Every color image is made up of three or four image channels, and you can take advantage of these "images within the image" to create masks for re-choreographing the sense of light.

Loading the image luminosity by clicking on the Load Channel as Selection button (**figure 5.47**) translates an image or a channel's tonal values into an active selection based on all brightness values above 128. You can also use the command key combination (Cmd + option + ~) [Ctrl + Alt + ~] to do the same thing. In addition, you can load the brightness values of an individual channel, described in the following example.

ch5_facadebackdrop.jpg

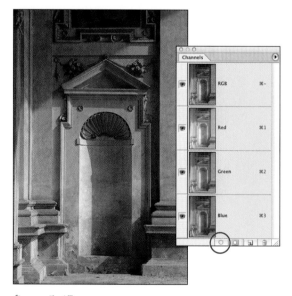

figure 5.47

Clicking the Load Channel as Selection button creates a selection based on image luminosity.

1. Inspect the color channels and activate the one with the smoothest tonal transitions. In most cases, this will be the green channel. You activate it by clicking on the word *green* in the Channels palette. (Cmd-click) [Ctrl-click] on the channel icon to create a rather abstract selection (**figure 5.48**).

figure 5.48

Saving the luminance selection of the green channel as an alpha channel.

2. Click on the Save Selection as Channel button and then choose Select > Deselect or (Cmd + D) [Ctrl + D].

3. Click on the newly created alpha channel and use Curves to increase the channel contrast (**figure 5.49**), which will make the following steps of re-choreographing the light more dramatic.

4. Target where you want to apply the change. In most cases, this will be the Layers palette. Activate the alpha channel (Cmd + option + 4) [Ctrl + Alt + 4] and add a Curves Adjustment Layer, which will automatically create an Adjustment Layer layer mask.

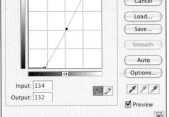

figure 5.49

Increasing the contrast of the alpha channel will make the creative image adjustments more dramatic.

5. Increase the contrast of the Curve with an S curve. This adds visual punch to the high-lights (**figure 5.50**).

6. By changing the blending mode to Soft Light, as shown in **figure 5.51**, I changed a pleasant day into a hot summer's day with harsh light.

7. You can continue experimenting with the layer mask. In **figure 5.52**, I inverted the Curve layer mask (Cmd + I) [Ctrl + I], adjusted the Curve, and changed the blending mode to Difference to create a more muted image interpretation.

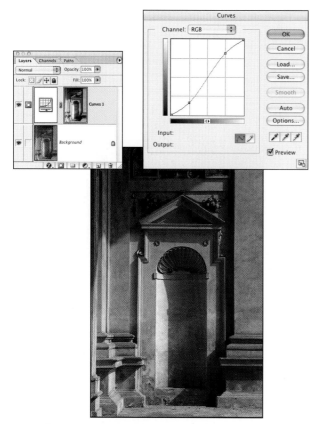

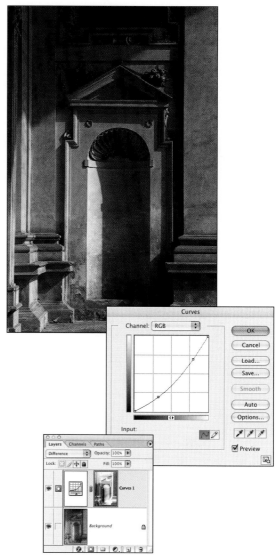

figure 5.50

The luminance mask has a greater effect on the lighter image areas.

figure 5.52

Experiment with blending modes and Curves to create new backgrounds.

There are practically no limitations to what you can do with these luminance masks to influence and interpret an image. I've spent many hours playing with this technique to create unique backgrounds for image composites. In **figure 5.53**, you see what happened when I duplicated the Difference layer and blurred the layer mask with a Gaussian Blur of 10.

figure 5.51

Experimenting with blending modes quickly adds creative interpretations.

figure 5.54

figure 5.53

Duplicating and blurring the luminance mask adds a diffuse glow.

Adding Textures to Images

We've all spent a lot of time cleaning up scans by cloning away dust or healing scratches. But it can be just as productive and often refreshingly creative to rough up an image, add imperfections, or give the image a weathered look. In fact, getting away from digital sanitary perfection (like the clock in **figure 5.54**) adds character to an image, which can be very appealing (**figure 5.55**).

There are many ways to add texture to an image, including using an alpha channel from one image to texturize another, as described in the following list.

ch5_clock.jpg

ch5_deserttexture.jpg

figure 5.55

1. Inspect the color channels of the image with the desired texture. In this example, the red channel has the clearest delineation of the cracks in the ground.

2. Duplicate the red channel by dragging it down to the "Create new channel" button on the bottom of the Channels palette.

3. Choose Image > Adjustments > Curves and radically increase the contrast (**figure 5.56**).

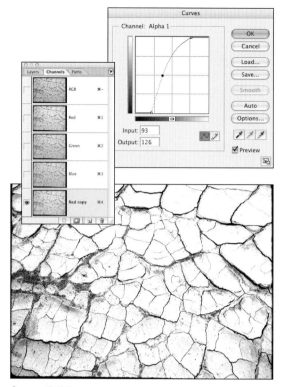

figure 5.56

Increase the contrast of the texture channel.

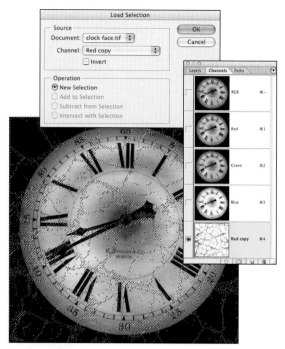

figure 5.57

Loading the texture channel creates an abstract selection.

4. Use the Move tool to drag the texture channel directly from the Desert Channel palette to the clock image. Dragging the channel to another image automatically creates a new alpha channel.

5. Target the layer to which you want to add the texture, choose Select > Load Selection, and choose Red copy (**figure 5.57**).

6. Add a Curves Adjustment Layer and increase the contrast, as shown in **figure 5.58**.

7. To accentuate the effect more, experiment with the layer blending modes. **Figure 5.59** shows the Multiply blending mode in use.

There are many ways to add variations to the effect, such as doubling the Adjustment Layer (**figure 5.60**), inverting the layer mask and changing the blending mode to Difference (**figure 5.61**), or using filters to interpret the textured layer mask, as I did in **figure 5.62**.

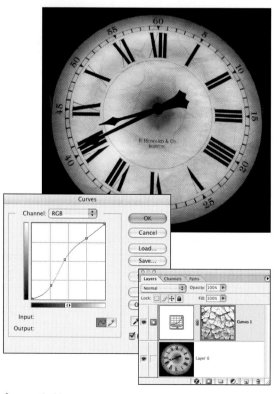

figure 5.58

Adjusting the texture contrast with an Adjustment Layer.

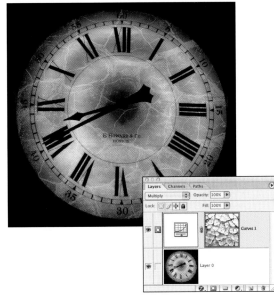

figure 5.59

The Multiply blending mode darkens the texture.

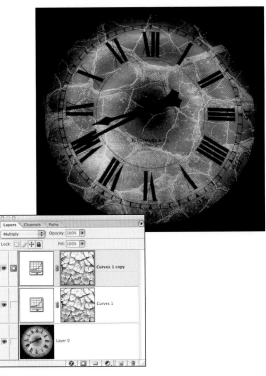

figure 5.60

Duplicating the Adjustment Layer doubles the effect.

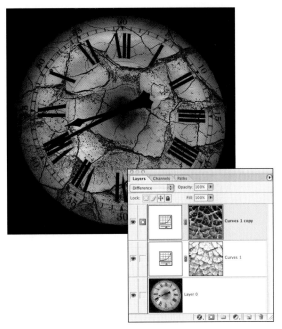

figure 5.61

Inverting the layer mask creates a different effect.

figure 5.62

Using the Sprayed Strokes filter adds even more character to the image.

So the next time you're out and about with your camera, take a few shots of that peeling paint, rusty metal, gravel driveway, or pockmarked telephone pole—you'll be happy to have your own image library of textures and inspiration to rough your images up with.

VECTOR MASKS

Vector masks let you mask image areas and layer styles using the flexibility and crispness of the Pen and Shape tools. Use them whenever you need a clean, sharp-edged design element.

Graphic designers use vector masks to isolate objects cleanly, and Web designers use Shapes to create Web buttons and graphics. With the addition of layer styles, they can easily create button states that change when the user mouses over the button.

Using Paths and Vector Masks

You can create empty vector masks on which you use the Pen or Shape tool to create the crisp outlines, or you can start with an existing Path or Shape and change them into a vector mask, as demonstrated here. In the following example, I isolated the violin and placed it on a soft background, as shown in **figure 5.63**.

⊕▷⟨ **ch5_violin.jpg**

⊕▷⟨ **ch5_reeds.jpg**

1. Double-click on the Background layer to turn it into a standard layer that will be able to support the vector mask.

2. Use the Pen tool to outline the subject—in this case the violin—and then close the path and name it, as discussed in Chapter 4, "Pen Tool Power."

3. Choose Layer > Add Vector Mask > Current Path (**figure 5.64**). If Current Path isn't available, you just need to return to the path and click on it to activate it before selecting the menu command.

4. The violin is now on a transparent background (**figure 5.65**), and you have a number of options. You could fine-tune the vector mask with the Direct Selection tool (white arrow) and/or use the Move tool and drag the violin to a new background. In this example, I dragged the violin over to the soft reeds photograph, which projects an evening mood (**figure 5.66**).

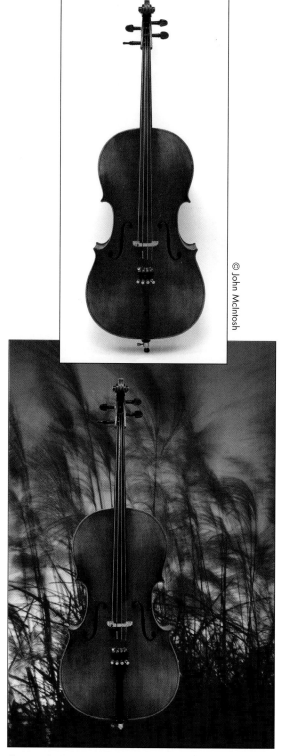

© John McIntosh

figure 5.63

The vector mask is flexible and precise.

figure 5.64

Adding the vector mask.

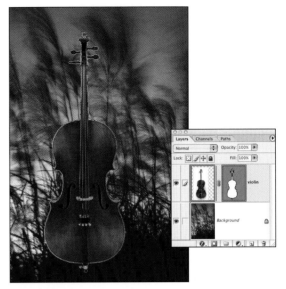

figure 5.66

Dragging the layer includes the vector mask.

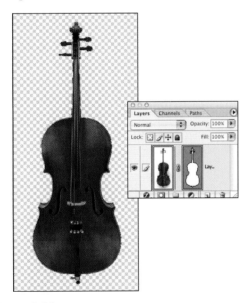

figure 5.65

The vector mask isolates the subject from the background.

5. (Option-click) [Alt-click] on the Image
    Adjustment button on the Layers palette and
    select Curves. Select Use Previous Layer to
    Create Clipping Mask and click OK. Enhance
    the tonality of the violin using an S Curve
    and click OK. To separate the violin from the
    background, change the blending mode to
    Soft Light (**figure 5.67**).

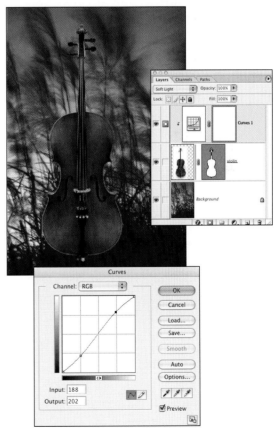

figure 5.67

*Using a clipping group to influence just the violin using
Curves.*

6. Zoom in on the edges of the violin. If you see any white remnants of the studio backdrop, refine the vector mask in the new file by hiding any parts of the original studio backdrop using the Direct Selection tool (white arrow).

The ability to refine the contours and edge of the mask with the precision of the Direct Selection tool is a fantastic feature.

7. If desired, you can have the violin blend into the reeds by adding a layer mask and using the Gradient tool with Black-to-Transparent to have the base of the violin fade into the reeds. In other words, you can combine the precision of the Pen tool with the softness of a pixel-based layer mask, as shown in **figure 5.68**.

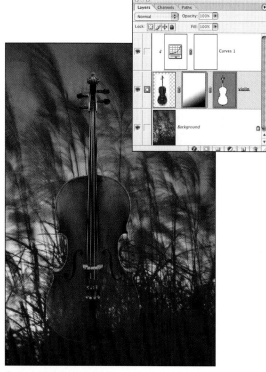

figure 5.68

Using a gradient layer mask to add a transition between the violin and the background.

 T i p

To maintain the crisp edge when printing to a PostScript printer, save the file as EPS or PDF and select Save Vector Data, which appears after you click the Save button.

Vector Mask Tips

- To work directly on the vector mask from the start, (Cmd-click) [Ctrl-click] on the Layer Mask icon and then use the Pen tool to outline the subject.

- Start to make the path and then (Cmd-click) [Ctrl-click] the Layer Mask icon at the bottom of the Layers palette. This will add a vector mask to the active layer based on the path that is visible.

- Choosing Layer > Rasterize > Vector Mask, changes the vector mask into a raster-based mask—into a standard layer mask onto which you can paint or use filters. But be forewarned: after rasterizing a vector mask, you loose its crispness and the ability to edit it.

Shapes and Vector Masks

The Shape tool draws vector outlines in geometric and custom shapes.

To create shape layers, make sure the Shape layer option is selected in the Options bar (**figure 5.69**). When you draw a shape, you'll notice that the Shape layer is created using the combination of a Color Fill layer and a vector outline. You can change the color by double-clicking on the layer icon and edit the shape with the Direct Selection tool, just as if it was a standard path, which it really is.

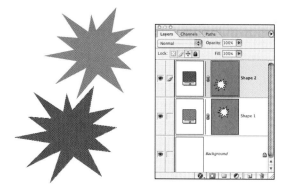

figure 5.69

Shape layers combine a Color Fill layer and a vector mask.

Photoshop comes with additional shapes, from ornamental, to nature, to Web graphic elements. Append them to the Shape picker, as shown in figure 5.70, and have fun experimenting!

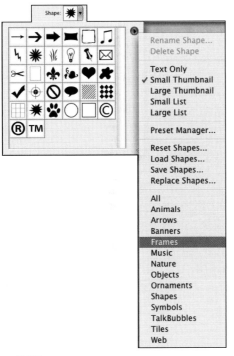

figure 5.70

Appending the additional shapes increases your choices.

CLOSING THOUGHTS

Photoshop provides many methods for revealing and concealing image information. Understanding the different types of masks, from adjusting layer opacity to creating sophisticated channel masks, can be an endless source of inspiration.

In the following two chapters we'll delve deeply into working with layers and layer masks. I hope you find them as exciting as I do.

6

LAYERS ARE YOUR FRIENDS

The four essential skills that dedicated Photoshop users need to understand are correcting and managing color, making selections, working with layers, and masking. Color correction is addressed in my previous book *Photoshop Restoration and Retouching*. In this book, Chapter 8, "Selecting Fine Hair and Detail"; Chapter 9, "Advanced Selection Techniques"; and Chapter 10, "Selecting Translucency and Green Screen Techniques" delve so deeply into how to make selections that ever since writing them I see dancing ants wherever I look. This chapter is dedicated to layers, layers, and layers. When working with layers, if you've ever experienced that sinking feeling of "I get it…I think I get it…well, I thought I got it…I'll never get it…," then you have opened to the right page!

This chapter will help you understand the fundamental principles and application of layers so that you can collage, montage, composite, and create the images that are in your mind's eye. In this chapter, you'll learn to

- Work with and manage layers
- Take advantage of layer sets and clipping masks
- Appreciate how layers provide control and flexibility
- Use Adjustment Layers effectively

Before we begin, I want to tip my hat to Lee Varis, a talented photographer and generous teacher, who coined the phrase "Layers Are Your Friends."

WORKING WITH LAYERS

Life without layers would be very one dimensional, static, inflexible, and just not worth getting out of bed for in the morning. Layers let you experiment, explore, and change your mind over and over again—all in an effort to perfect an image.

Layers are planes of image information you can move left, right, around, or up and down in the layer stack; change the density and effect of using layer opacity, blending modes, and advanced blending; vary the shape and size of; and fine-tune the visibility using layer masks.

An essential concept to understand when working with layers is the safety-feature factor—when you alter one layer, you are affecting only it and not the rest of the image. You simply activate the layer you want to change, apply the desired change, and evaluate the result before continuing.

When you view a layered document in Photoshop, you get a bird's eye view—Photoshop creates the image starting from the top layer and using all of the visible layers (**figure 6.1**). When you look at the Layers palette, you are looking at the image from the front (**figure 6.2**), and you control how layers interact based on their position in the layer stack and the use of opacity, blending modes, and masks.

TYPES OF LAYERS

Layers are basically slices of image information you assemble on top of one another to build an image. There are two general types of layers: image and effect. Image layers carry pixel and vector-image information (**figures 6.3** through **6.8**). Effect layers are used to add tonal, color, pattern, and texture effects (**figures 6.9** through **6.12**).

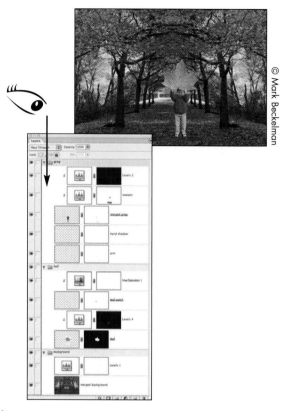

© Mark Beckelman

figure 6.1

Photoshop sees layered files from the top down.

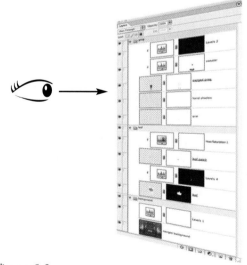

figure 6.2

You view the Layers palette from the front.

Image Layers

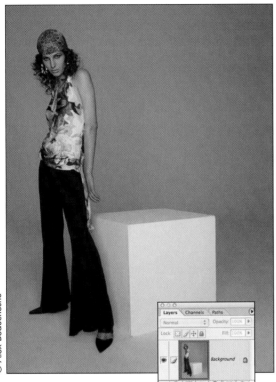

© Alex Beauchesne

figure 6.3

Background layer: *All images created with scanners or digital cameras come into Photoshop as a Background layer. Because the Background layer represents your original data, you should never work directly on it.*

Note

As long as the layer name contains *Background* in italics, it cannot support layer masks, blending modes, or opacity. To convert the Background layer into a standard layer, double-click on its Layer icon and rename it something meaningful. Of course, you should only do this on a duplicate file when you are absolutely sure the file is safely backed up.

Caution

Never—ever—paint, clone, or heal directly on the Background layer. Do I sound adamant about this? The Background layer is your original, your reference, your guide, and your image foundation. Do not touch it!

To maintain its integrity, either duplicate it by dragging it down to the New Layer button; do a Save As to backup the original file before undertaking any work; or work with layers and layer sets instead (a practice employed throughout this book).

Many compositing artists start each image with a blank document (File > New) and drag the image elements into the new working surface. This is a valid method for ensuring you don't inadvertently overwrite important image information.

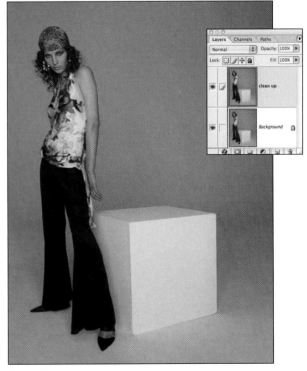

figure 6.4

Duplicate layers: *Duplicating any layer by dragging the layer to the New Layer icon creates an exact copy, in perfect registration, on which you can work without affecting the original data. Use the quick keys (Cmd + J) [Ctrl + J] to quickly duplicate a layer.*

Image Layers

figure 6.5

Merged layers: *As the number of layers increases, it is often easier to work on a Work in Progress (WIP) layer (in this example, named* refinement*), which is a flattened layer created using all visible layers.*

 T i p

After copying choose File > New, Photoshop automatically creates a new document the exact same size as the copied image information.

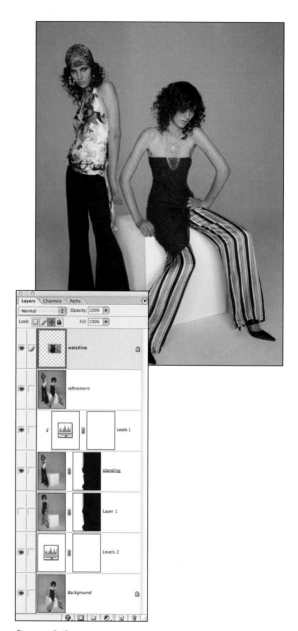

figure 6.6

Partial layers: *Many times you don't want or need to duplicate an entire layer. In these cases, select the part of the image you want to work on and then select Layer > New > Layer via Copy or press (Cmd + J) [Ctrl + J]. Photoshop will copy and paste the selected image information onto its own layer in perfect registration with the original data. When multiple layers contain the desired image information, select the area and choose Edit > Copy Merged followed by Edit > Paste to place the combined layers onto one layer.*

Effects Layers

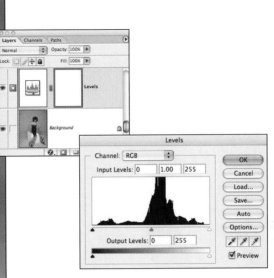

figure 6.7

Adjustment Layers: *Introduced with Photoshop 4.0, Adjustment Layers enable you to apply global and selective tonal and color corrections.*

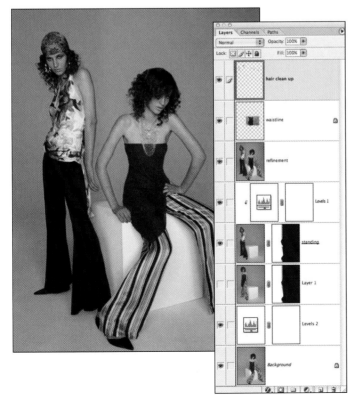

figure 6.8

Empty layers: *Photoshop represents empty layers with a grid pattern. Think of these empty layers as clear sheets of acetate on which you paint, clone, and heal without affecting the pixel data of the layers underneath.*

Effects Layers

figure 6.9

Neutral layers: *Empty layers filled with white, gray, or black that, in combination with a specific layer blending mode, are used to create lighting effects, sharpen files, and create film grain, as we'll do in Chapter 12, "Photorealistic Compositing."*

figure 6.10

Fill layers: *These let you add solid color, gradient, or pattern fills as a separate layer.*

Effects Layers

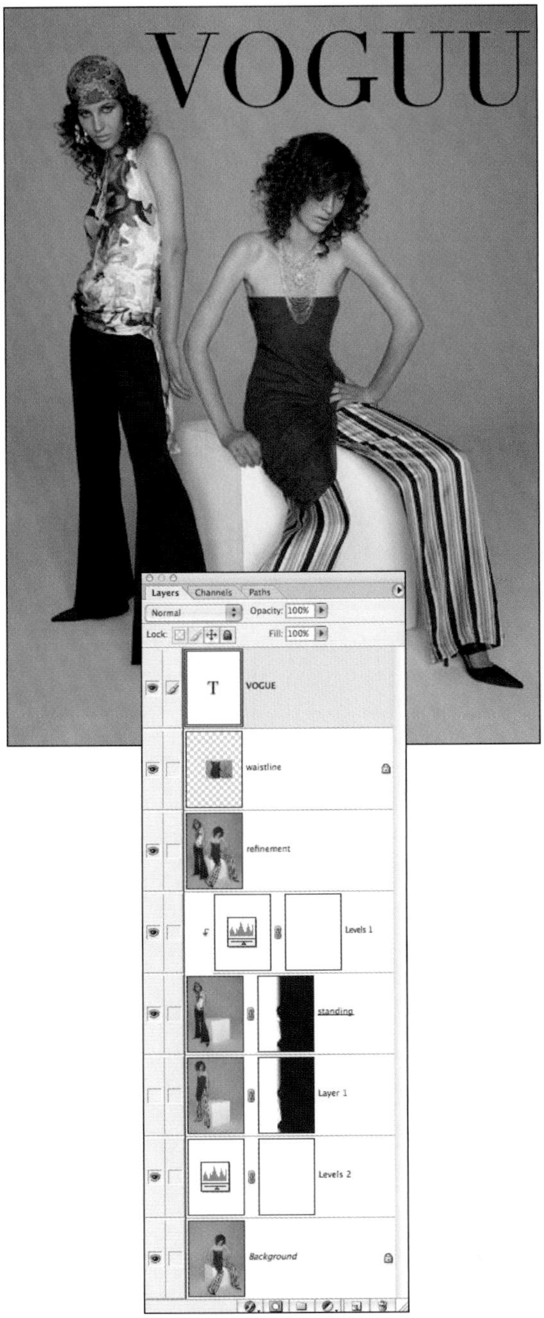

figure 6.11

Type layers: *Created by activating the Type tool and clicking anywhere on the image, type layers remain editable as long as the text is not rasterized. Photoshop automatically names the type layer after the text. It is signified by a large T on the Layer icon.*

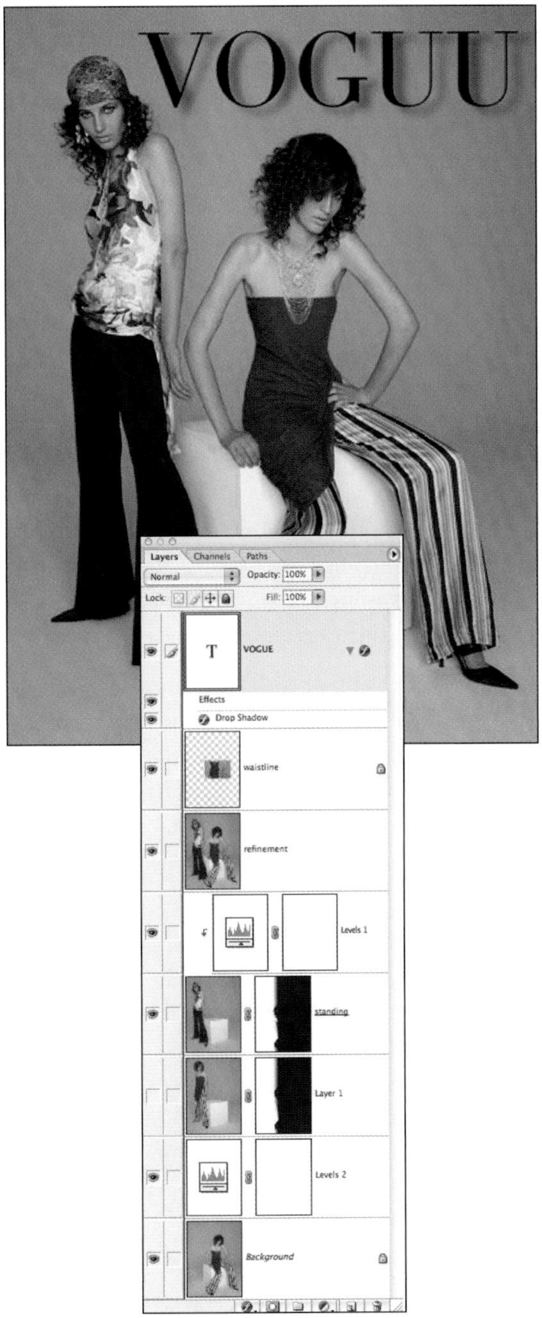

figure 6.12

Layer styles: *Although not considered a layer per se, Photoshop does count layer styles when calculating the internal layer count, which is limited, if you can call it that, to a total combination of 8,000 layers and layer styles.*

© Mark Beckelman

> ### Caution
>
> Rasterizing Type or Shape layers converts them into standard pixel-based layers, so you can apply filters and use painting tools on them. Because both Type and Shape layers are very small in terms of file size, duplicate them and turn off the visibility of the duplicate before rasterizing them. This duplicate layer will remain editable in case you need to rework the text or shape.

The best aspect of layers is that all of them (with the exception of the Background layer) support layer masks, blending modes, opacity and fill changes, and Advanced Blending Options—features you'll be working with to create fantastic images.

Layer Naming and Navigation

In many cases, a composite can require 5, 10, 20, or many more layers. Relying on the generic Photoshop name such as *Layer 1* or *Layer 1 copy* to identify layers is a sure path to confusion and frustration when you later try to find the one you need.

It only takes a split second, but naming your layers as you build an image lets you identify and activate the correct layer quickly and easily. Look at the difference between the two layer stacks in figure 6.13. On the left are the generically named layers; on the right the layers have useful names, making them much easier to use and navigate.

In addition, the context-sensitive menu of the Move tool gives you instant access to all the layers under your cursor that have pixel information. As shown in figure 6.14, (Cmd-clicking) [right-clicking] on any location shows all layers that have pixel information at that exact point. Best of all, you can then drag down to a specific layer name and activate it—even if the Layers palette is not open at the time.

To name a layer, simply double-click on the existing name of the layer in the Layers palette and type in a meaningful name. It only takes a split second to name a layer and it will save you countless minutes of frustration.

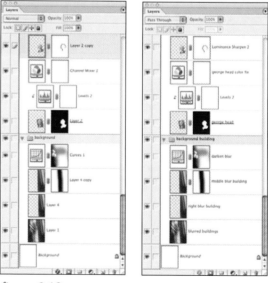

figure 6.13

The generic layer names in the palette on the left won't help you find your way through a complex image composite, but the ones on the right show that naming your layers is a good habit to establish.

figure 6.14

The context-sensitive menu of the Move tool shows you the layers that have pixel information at the cursor location.

Working with Layer Sets

In Photoshop CS, you can create up to a total of 8,000 layers and layer effects, something that requires a way to organize and manage layers more efficiently. Layer sets are folders in which you can place related layers. The folders can be expanded or collapsed by clicking on the small triangle next to the folder icon; the layers can be moved around within the set; and the layer sets can be moved around within the layer stack. You can have up to four layer sets nested inside a layer set.

Caution

Although you can have up to 8,000 layers and layer effects, Photoshop comes to a near-screeching halt if you use more than 800 layers.

You can create a layer set three different ways:

- Select New Layer Set from the Layers Palette menu, name the layer set, and then drag the desired layers into the set.

- Link all the layers you would like in a layer set, and then from the Layers palette fly-out menu select New Set from Linked. All the linked layers will be placed into the newly created layer set.

- Link the layers you need in a set and then drag any one of them down to the Layer Set button on the Layers palette to create a new layer set—my personal favorite.

You can delete a layer set three different ways:

- To delete the entire layer set without showing a warning dialog box, drag the layer set to the trash can on the Layers palette.

- Select Delete Layer Set from the Layers palette menu. The dialog box in **figure 6.15** then gives you choices to cancel the operation, delete the set (i.e., the folder) but not the contents, or delete the set and the set's contents.

- (Cmd-drag) [Ctrl-drag] the layer set to the trash can to delete the layer set folder without deleting its contents. The layers in the set remain in the document in the order they appeared in the set.

figure 6.15

You can delete the set (the folder) or the set and the contents.

As soon as you add a layer set, the blending mode is changed to Pass Through, which lets that layer set interact with the layers beneath it. Changing the layer set blending mode from Pass Through to Normal treats the layer set like a separate image, and it will not interact with the layers beneath it. This can be very useful when fine-tuning separate image elements of a composite.

Layer sets can have a mask, which masks out all of the layers in the set simultaneously. To add a mask to a layer set, click on the layer set folder and then click on the Layer Mask icon on the Layers palette. Use the painting and Gradient tools on this mask, exactly as you would use them on a standard layer mask as explained in the following chapter, "The Power of Layer Masking." Layer set masks can be pixel-based or vector-based, and they behave exactly as their layer counterparts.

Naming and Color-Coding Layer Sets

You can color-code layers and layer sets to quickly identify layer relationships and lock layers to prevent accidental edits to image data, transparency settings, and layer position. All in all, organizing, naming, or color-coding layers and layer sets takes only a moment, but it can save you a lot of time in hunting and searching for the layer you need. And if you work with a partner, on a team, or are part of a production workflow, organizing your layers and using layer names is particularly important.

Imagine you're working on a complicated composite, and for some reason you can't finish the image. If the layers are well named, someone else on your team can open the file, find the layers that need additional work, and finish the project. However, if the layers are scattered, generically named, or not in layer sets, it will take a while for someone else to determine where to even begin. In the worst-case scenario, a very important layer might be ruined or deleted. So enough said—name your layers!

Flattening and Discarding Layers

It's a good idea to practice being a conservative Photoshop user—that is, someone who doesn't throw away layers unless they're absolutely wrong or unnecessary—but who also has a large hard drive to accommodate all those extra files. Keep all production layers with a file because you never know if a mask or tidbit of information from a layer will be useful later on. By clicking on the eyeball in the view column on the left side of the Layers palette, you can turn off a layer whenever you like. The only time you need to flatten an image is just before sending a file to the printer or taking a file into a page layout program.

The Darker Side of Layers

As wonderful as layers are, they do come at a price, which is increased file size. Thankfully, when it comes to calculating file size for 8-bit images, Photoshop doesn't see all layers equally. Photoshop adds just the pixel information of the layers—meaning that if the layer only has a small percentage of pixel information, it will not add to the file size as much as a layer that is 100 percent pixel information.

The most efficient layers are Fill and Adjustment Layers (in which you do not use the layer mask), with each one only adding 4 Kbits to 6 Kbits to the file. The least efficient layers are duplicated and merged layers.

When calculating the file size of hi-bit images, Photoshop is less efficient. So adding any type of layers (except empty layers), including the miserly Adjustment Layer, doubles the file size. I hope that making layers more efficient in hi-bit files will be addressed in future versions of Photoshop.

Even though layers have a price, their advantages far outweigh their drawbacks. If working with a multi-layered file is slowing you down, consider the following options to improve Photoshop performance:

- Use the Photoshop Preferences to allocate as much RAM to Photoshop as possible. In my opinion, 512 RAM is the minimum amount you need for photo composites. More RAM lets you work not only faster, but also more efficiently, providing you more opportunity to experiment with creative variations. It is very stifling to think about doing something in Photoshop and then not do it, simply to avoid the progress bar or the spinning clock. Photoshop currently can address 2 GB of RAM. Hardware and operating system manufacturers, as well as Adobe Systems, will hopefully address this limitation soon.

  To determine whether you might benefit from adding more RAM to your computer system, do the following: With a document open, choose Efficiency by clicking on the black triangle in the Status bar on the lower left of the screen. For PC users, if the status is not visible, from the menu bar, select Window > Status Bar. If the efficiency dips below 100%, adding more RAM is recommended. RAM is like chocolate—you can never have too much!

- Adobe recommends three to five times the amount of RAM in relationship to your file size. When Photoshop has used all the allocated RAM, it writes the file information to a scratch disk. Adding a fast, dedicated hard drive reserved for Photoshop scratch disk can speed up Photoshop when the RAM is maxed out. I recommend keeping the computer system software and Photoshop on one hard drive and having a dedicated second hard drive as a scratch disk.

- Back up your files regularly, delete backed-up and unnecessary files, and use a maintenance program to defragment all of your hard drives.

- Only keep the files open that you need at the moment. Every open image is loaded into RAM, which reduces the RAM that Photoshop has for the image you're working on.

- To make your computer a speed demon, please see your computer documentation or contact local user groups or online resources for computer platform-specific recommendations.

Layers are the lifeblood of Photoshop. It was Diane Fenster, an imaging artist whose work appears in chapters 1 and 13, who mentioned that layers are akin to life: "The more you work, experiment, rearrange, and composite with them, the richer your image (and life) becomes."

LAYERS PALETTE ANATOMY

Divided into five distinct areas—attributes, visibility and linking, position and naming, buttons, and fly-out menu—the Layers palette (**figure 6.16**) is command central for image compositing. It's the first place to look to activate, change, affect, delete, or manage layers.

To make the following explanation of the various controls in the Layers palette more realistic, it would be helpful to have a layered file open.

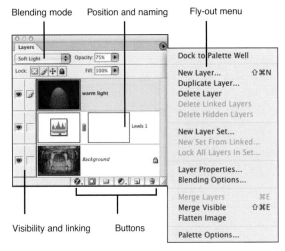

figure 6.16

The Layers palette is divided into five distinct areas.

T i p

To choose a Layer icon viewing size—from none to large—use the Layer fly-out menu to access the Layers Palette Options dialog box (**figure 6.17**). Throughout the book, I've used the large setting, but normally I use the medium setting for my own imaging projects.

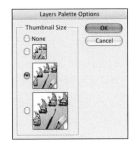

figure 6.17

Use Layer Palette Options to choose a Layer icon size.

Layer Attribute: Blending Modes

With just the Background layer active, none of the layer attributes are active. Click on any layer besides the Background layer to activate all four attributes. Starting on the upper left—the large button is a pull-down menu that controls which blending mode is applied to the layer (**figure 6.18**).

Every type of Photoshop layer, except for the Background layer, supports blending modes, which influence how a layer interacts with the layers below it. This happens on a channel-by-channel basis, so blending modes can in some instances create unexpected, yet pleasing results, as shown in **figures 6.19** through **6.42**.

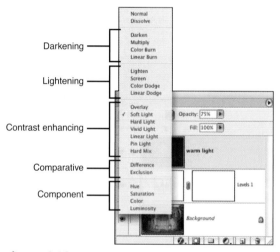

figure 6.18

The blending modes are organized into functional groups.

figure 6.19

Experiment with the blending modes to produce surprising image relationships, as shown in figures 6.20 through 6.42.

Combine

The effect of combining blending modes is influenced by layer opacity, as **figures 6.20** and **6.21** illustrate.

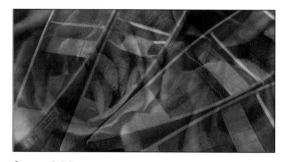

figure 6.20

Normal *is the default blending mode. The top layer dominates the layer below, unless the opacity is reduced as in this example to 50%, allowing the underlying layer to be visible.*

figure 6.21

Dissolve *is used to create stipple texture effects or paint-brush effects. Reducing the opacity changes the effect of the speckles. In this example, I reduced the layer opacity to 50%.*

figure 6.24

Color Burn *darkens the dark tones by increasing contrast.*

Darken

The darken modes (**figures 6.22** through **6.25**) create darkening effects when using colors darker than 50% gray:

figure 6.25

Linear Burn *is a combination of Multiply and Color Burn, which darkens by decreasing brightness.*

figure 6.22

Darken *replaces the lighter values with darker values and ignores values that are darker than the blend layer.*

Lighten

The Lighten modes lighten when using tonal values brighter than 50% gray, as illustrated in **figures 6.26** through **6.29**.

figure 6.23

Multiply *darkens all pixel values and is useful for adding density to highlights and midtones. This blending mode is commonly used to add scans of handwritten text to a composite when the artist wants the handwriting, but not the paper, to be visible.*

figure 6.26

Lighten *is the opposite of Darken; it replaces the darker values with lighter values and ignores values that are lighter than the blend layer.*

figure 6.27

Screen *is the opposite of Multiply; it lightens the entire image while reducing contrast.*

figure 6.28

Color Dodge *is the opposite of Color Burn; it lightens light tones and colors and increases contrast, but has no effect on dark image areas.*

figure 6.29

Linear Dodge *lightens by increasing brightness. Unlike Screen, it will clip the highlights to pure white and has a stronger lightening effect than either Screen or Color Dodge.*

Contrast

In the contrast group, all of the blending modes increase image contrast by changing the Highlight and Shadow values (**figures 6.30** through **6.36**).

figure 6.30

Overlay *multiplies the dark values and screens the light values, while maintaining the darkness and lightness of the base layer.*

figure 6.31

Soft Light *is a combination of Darken and Lighten and creates less dramatic effects than either Overlay or Hard Light.*

figure 6.32

Hard Light *is a mixture of Multiply and Screen and is useful for boosting image contrast.*

figure **6.33**

Vivid Light *combines Color Dodge and Color Burn to lighten and darken image values. Lighter areas are decreased in contrast, and darker areas are increased.*

figure **6.34**

Linear Light *combines Linear Dodge and Linear Burn, which decreases or increases in image brightness. Lighter areas are increased in brightness, and darker areas are decreased.*

figure **6.35**

Pin Light *is a combination of Lighten and Darken and is used to add special effects.*

figure **6.36**

Hard Light *is an extreme combination of Lighten and Darken. Reducing the fill opacity reduces the high contrast effect.*

Comparative

The Comparative modes (**figures** 6.37 and 6.38) mathematically compare and evaluate layers with one another.

figure **6.37**

Difference *compares layers—identical values are rendered as black, and values that are different are inverted.*

figure **6.38**

Exclusion *is a less contrasted version of Difference; the values that are different are rendered as gray.*

Image Component

The Image Component blending modes (**figures 6.39** through **6.42**) change the individual attributes of the layer.

The best thing about working with blending modes is that they are often surprising and completely reversible, which lets you experiment to create the desired results.

figure 6.42

Luminosity *is the opposite of Color and maintains the luminosity information of the active layer in relationship to the color underneath.*

 T i p

To cycle forward through the blending modes, press *v* to activate the Move tool, click on the appropriate layer, and use (Shift + the plus key) to cycle down the blending modes, or (Shift + the minus key) to cycle up the blending modes. See **table 6.1** for a complete list of the shortcut keystrokes you can use to access any blending mode.

figure 6.39

Hue *combines the luminance and saturation of the underlying layer with the hue of the active layer.*

table 6.1
The Blend Mode Shortcut Guide

Activate the Move tool, and then use the following shortcuts to change the layer blending modes. If a painting tool is active, then the shortcut will change the blending mode for the active tool.

Blending Mode	(Option + Shift) [Alt + Shift]	Blending Mode	(Option + Shift) [Alt + Shift]
Normal	N	**H**ard Light	H
Dissolve	I	**V**ivid Light	V
Dar**k**en	K	Linear Light	J
Multiply	M	Pin Light	Z
Color **Burn**	B	Hard Mix	L
Line**a**r Burn	A	Diff**e**rence	E
Lighten	G	E**x**clusion	X
Screen	S	H**u**e	U
Color **D**odge	D	Sat**u**ration	T
Linear Dodge	W	**C**olor	C
Overlay	O	Luminosit**y**	Y
So**f**t Light	F		

figure 6.40

Saturation *combines the luminance and hue of the underlying layer with the saturation of the active layer.*

figure 6.41

Color *reveals the color of the active layer and maintains the luminance values of the underlying layer.*

Layer Attribute: Opacity and Fill Opacity

When one layer is placed on top of or adjacent to another layer, the meaning of the separate image elements changes as a new relationship has been created. One of the easiest and often effective methods for creating, seeing, and responding to this changed relationship is to adjust the layer opacity, which determines the layer transparency.

A seemingly simple control, layer opacity is often the first parameter I adjust when I want to view the image relationships that are forming between layers. I can then refine them with blending modes, transformations, and masking, as illustrated in **figures 6.43** through **6.47**.

figure 6.44

At 100% opacity, the watch is completely obscured beneath the flowers.

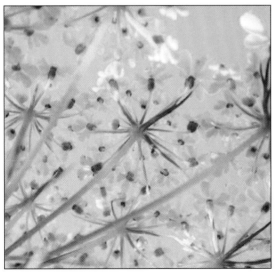

figure 6.43

The original source images.

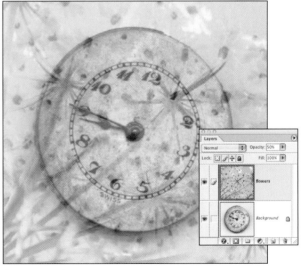

figure 6.45

The interaction of the layers at 50% opacity.

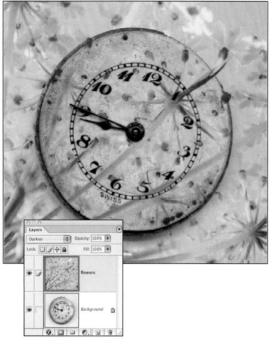

figure 6.46

Changing the blending mode changes the aesthetic interaction between the elements.

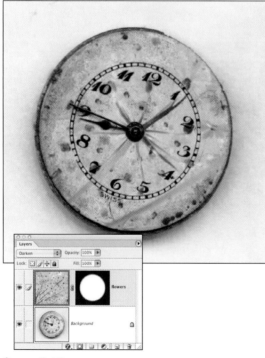

figure 6.47

The layer mask blocks the effect from being seen outside of the watch face.

Tip

To adjust layer opacity, make sure that the correct layer and the Move tool are active. Using the numeric keypad or keyboard, type the first number of the desired opacity, with *0* equaling 100%, *1* equaling 10%, and so on. Typing two numbers in quick succession adjusts the layer opacity to that value. For example, typing *45* reduces layer opacity to 45%.

Fill opacity is used primarily in combination with layer styles. Reducing fill opacity reduces the opacity of the layer while still maintaining the layer style. This is a fantastic feature to use with type for adding your copyright mark to images before posting them on a Web site as described here:

1. Activate the Type tool, and on the Options bar choose a straightforward font (the copyright notification should be legible, without distracting from the image). Use an easy-to-read, bold, sans serif font, and click in the center of the image.

2. Enter your copyright text, such as your name or URL. Press Enter (not Return) to enter the type.

   If you need to make the type larger or smaller, use Edit > Transform > Scale and press the Shift key while scaling the type to maintain the typeface proportions. Use the Move tool to position the copyright notice along the edge.

3. Choose Layer > Layer Style > Drop Shadow (**figure 6.48**) and adjust the Distance, Spread, and Size sliders as needed. Many people also add a Bevel & Emboss effect to emphasize the text even more.

4. Click OK and reduce the fill opacity to zero to make the text pixels invisible while maintaining the shadow effect (**figure 6.49**).

5. To apply this copyright notice to more than one image, open the other images and use the Move tool to drag the text from the Layers palette to the other images.

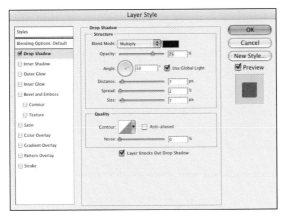

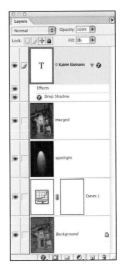

figure 6.49

figure 6.49

Reducing the fill opacity makes the type transparent, while maintaining the layer effect.

Tip

To adjust the fill opacity, press the Shift key and enter the first number of the desired opacity, with *0* equaling 100%, *1* equaling 10%, and so on. Pressing the Shift key and entering two numbers in quick succession adjusts the fill opacity to that value. For example, entering *65* reduces fill opacity to 65%.

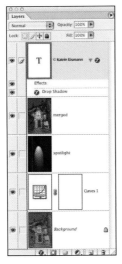

figure 6.48

Add a drop-shadow layer effect to the type layer.

Layer Attribute: Lock and Protect

Underneath the blending modes are four small icons that lock (or protect) Transparency, Pixels, Position, and All (**figure 6.50**). Click on one of the icons to activate it, and click it again to turn the protection off. As soon as any icon is clicked, a small lock is added to the Layers palette.

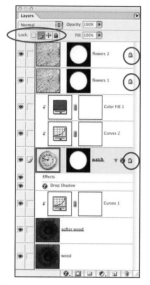

figure 6.50

The Lock buttons are a useful aid to protect layers and layer content.

On the Layers palette, from left to right, the layer attribute icons do the following:

- **Lock Transparent Pixels** is available for layers that contain transparency, such as partial image layers. Clicking it protects the clear areas of the layer. Protecting transparency is very useful when using filters such as Gaussian Blur to limit the effect to the actual pixels without changing the edge quality of the layer information.

- **Lock Image Pixels** is the exact opposite of clicking transparency. Clicking it will not let you paint or edit pixels but it does let you paint on transparent areas.

- **Lock Position** is a very useful control because it locks a layer into place and doesn't let you inadvertently move a layer. Believe me, I use this all the time to keep myself out of trouble.

- **Lock All** applies all three of the lock and protect functions to the layer.

Locking layer attributes is a quick, easy, and completely reversible method for protecting layers from mistaken moves or edits.

Visibility and Linking

To the left of the Layer icon are two columns—the view and activity columns. Clicking off an Eyeball icon temporarily hides that layer. (Option-clicking) [Alt-clicking] on a Eyeball icon reveals just that one layer. (Option-clicking) [Alt-clicking] on the Eyeball again turns back on all the layers that were previously visible. (Cmd-clicking) [Ctrl-clicking] on an Eyeball accesses a menu for hiding or showing just that one layer.

Next to the view column is the paint/mask/link column (this is my name for the column—I am not aware of any official term for it). Use this column to determine whether the layer pixels or layer mask is active and to link and unlink layers. When the layer is active, there is a Paintbrush icon next to the view column. When the layer mask is active, the paintbrush is replaced with a Mask icon (**figure 6.51**).

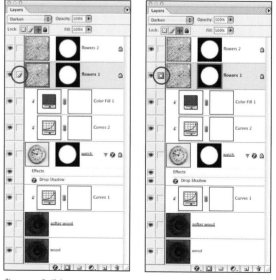

figure 6.51

The small paintbrush signifies the layer is active; the small Mask icon signifies the layer mask is active.

Linked layers are signified by a little chain (**figure 6.52**), which lets you to move and transform linked layers and paste layer styles to all the linked layers at once.

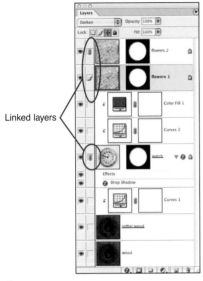

Linked layers

figure 6.52

Link layers that you need to move or transform.

Positioning and Naming

Grabbing the Layer icon with any tool, holding down your mouse button, and dragging up or down in the Layers palette changes the position of the layer in the layer stack. As you drag up or down, a heavier dark line appears between the layers when you've reached the position in the layer stack you want to the layer to be in—releasing the mouse button puts the layer into the new position.

To place a layer into an existing layer set, drag the layer to the Layer Set icon and, when the folder pops open, release the mouse. It is often easier and more precise to move and change layer activity with keyboard commands as listed in **table 6.2**.

Double-click on the text to the right of the Layer icon to activate the text and rename the layer. (Control-click) [right-click] to access layer styles and other additional controls (**figure 6.53**).

table 6.2

Layer Positioning Command Keys

To Do	Action
Move *layer up*	(Cmd + right bracket) [Ctrl + right bracket]
Move *layer down*	(Cmd + left bracket) [Ctrl + left bracket]
Activate *a higher layer*	(Option + right bracket) [Alt + right bracket]
Activate *a lower layer*	(Option + left bracket) [Alt + left bracket]

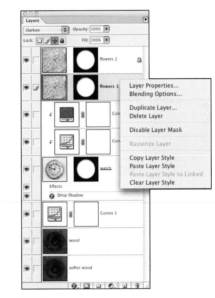

figure 6.53

The context-sensitive menu offers a quick way to duplicate and work with layer styles.

Layer Buttons

Along the lower frame of the Layers palette are six buttons (**figure 6.54**) that offer shortcuts to many of the commands contained in the Layer menu and Layers palette fly-out menu:

- **Add Layer Style:** Click and drag down to the desired layer style and open the Layer Style dialog box. Layer styles remain editable as long as you don't choose Layer > Layer Styles > Create Layers. Keeping layer styles editable lets you experiment, compare, and combine layer styles for creative effects.

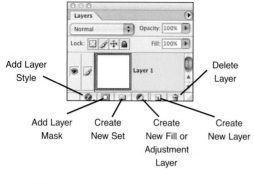

figure 6.54

The buttons are a quick way to work with layers.

- **Add Layer Mask:** Click once to add a white layer mask; (Option-click) [Alt-click] to add a black layer mask; and click again to add a vector mask, as discussed in Chapter 5, "Masks Are Your Friends." Layer masks are addressed in-depth in Chapter 7.

- **Create New Set:** Click to add an empty folder into which you can drag layers or drag one layer of a linked group of layers to the Layer Set icon.

- **Create New Fill or Adjustments Layers:** Here's a quick and convenient way to add Fill and Adjustment Layers. (Option-clicking) [Alt-clicking] on a Fill or Adjustment Layer opens the dialog box shown in figure 6.55 to name, group with, change color code, and select a blending mode before the layer is added. Selecting *Use Previous Layer to Create Clipping Mask* instructs the Fill or Adjustment Layer to only apply changes to the pixel information in the underlying layer and not affect the transparent areas or layers below the Clipping Mask layer. This is discussed later in this chapter.

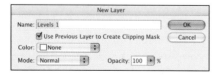

figure 6.55

Determining the layer behavior while adding it is very helpful.

- **Create New Layer.** (Option-clicking) [Alt-clicking] on it opens the same dialog box shown in figure 6.55. (Cmd-clicking) [Ctrl-clicking] it adds a new layer underneath the active layer.

- **Delete Layer.** This icon looks like a little trash can. To delete a layer, click the button and click the Yes button. To delete a layer without the warning, (Option-click) [Alt-click] on the trash can. Dragging a layer or layer set to the trash also deletes the content.

Dragging a layer mask to the trash can produces the dialog box shown in figure 6.56. Clicking the Discard button throws away the layer mask without applying it to the layer. This is a fantastic option to use when a layer mask is unnecessary or when you need to start the masking process over again. Use Apply carefully as it will apply its effect to the pixels, which in most cases permanently deletes pixels.

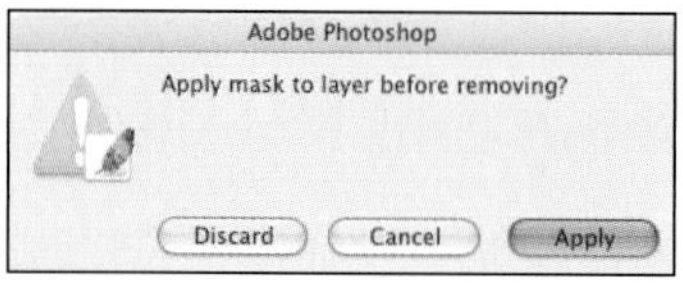

figure 6.56

Use the Delete Layer Mask option with care—often it is less destructive to Shift-click on the layer mask to turn it off rather than throw it away.

The Layers Palette Fly-out Menu

Click and hold on the small black triangle on the upper right of the palette to open the fly-out menu. Most of these controls are accessible via the buttons on the bottom of the Layers palette, which is where I prefer to access them. The controls unique to the fly-out menu include the following:

- **Delete Linked** is a quick method to delete more than one layer at a time. Link the layers you would like to remove and then choose Delete Linked.

- **Delete Hidden** is a very convenient command that lets you delete one or more layers that are not visible.

All of the other commands (except Palette Options) are available via the primary Layer menu, and are so important to understand that I'll include information about them here:

- **Merge Down** combines the active layer with the layer below it. You cannot merge down image layers containing pixel content into Fill, Adjustment, or Type layers. While Fill, Adjustment, or Type layers can be merged with underlying image layers, this should be used judiciously because merging these layers down removes the ability to edit and adjust them.

- **Merge Visible** should also be used with great care, because it combines all visible layers regardless of type into one pixel-based layer. Pressing (Option) [Alt] while selecting Merge Visible merges the layers to the active layer. Use this to create work-in-progress layers, as explained earlier in this chapter.

- **Flatten** is a command I use as rarely as possible because it flattens all visible layers into the Background layer with no options to adjust them. Of course, you'll often need a flat file to create JPEG files for Web pages or flattened TIFFs for page layout applications, but rather than choosing Flatten, select Flatten in the Save As dialog box.

✋ Caution

The most destructive functions in Photoshop are Erase, Delete, Merge, Flatten, and Rasterize. All of them delete pixels, throw away layers, or negate image or layer editability. If you have to use any of these functions, make sure you have a backup file or layer before doing so.

Moving and Transforming Layers

The only tool that moves pixel information is the Move tool. Press *v* or (Cmd-click) [Ctrl-click] with any tool on the image to change it into the Move tool. With the Move tool active, press the arrows on your keyboard to nudge a layer one pixel at a time. Holding the Shift key while pressing the arrow key nudges the layer in 10-pixel increments.

The Move tool options include:

- **Auto Select Layer** allows the Move tool to activate the layer that the mouse is hovering over, even if it's not active in the Layers palette. Because low-opacity layers easily fool the Move tool into selecting the wrong layer, I don't use this option.

- **Show Bounding Box** adds a thin dotted line around each layer (except for the Background layer), which looks similar to the Transform bounding box. The only time I turn this option on is when I need to find the exact center of a layer.

- **Align and Distribute Layers**, located to the right of the Show Bounding Box, are only active when layers are linked. Graphic, interface, and Web designers use these buttons to line up text or shape layers.

To move layers between images, you can grab the layer from the image or from the Layers palette. As you drag the layer to the destination image, you'll notice a faint outline around the destination image—release the mouse and the layer will fall into place. It is best to drag a layer with confidence—quickly and firmly—or Photoshop will warn you that the layer is locked.

To transform a layer, select Edit > Transform and choose the option you need to shape the layer information into size and position. Or better yet, use Edit > Free Transform, which lets you scale and rotate and access all the other controls by (Control-clicking) [right-clicking] inside of the image boundary. Because the Free Transform function gives me access to all the controls with less mousing movements, I use it exclusively.

🔍 Tip

The Transform commands use the interpolation settings in General Preferences. Before undertaking large up or down scaling, consider opening General Preferences (Cmd + K) [Ctrl + K] and changing the interpolation setting. Use Bicubic Smoother for scaling up and Bicubic Sharper for scaling down. For additional information on these preferences, see the "Photoshop Preferences" section in Chapter 1.

T i p

After applying a transform, you can apply the exact same transform to the same layer or a different layer again by choosing Edit > Transform > Again (Cmd + Shift + T) [Ctrl Shift + T]. To duplicate and repeat an image element transformation, use (Cmd + Option + Shift + T) [Ctrl + Alt + Shift + T].

Layer Foibles and Pitfalls

If you and the layers aren't getting along, stop what you are doing and answer the following questions to find the solution to the problem.

1. *Is the correct layer active?* Many times I am so enthralled with the image that I enthusiastically grab a tool and start to work, only to find that I'm working on the wrong layer. Always make sure the layer you need to affect is active. Click on the layer name in the Layers palette to activate it.

2. *Is it the layer or the layer mask that is active?* Before working on the layer or layer mask, make sure that the correct one is active. When the layer is active, it has a line around its icon and a Paintbrush icon is visible next to the view column. When the layer mask is active, the line is around the layer mask and the paintbrush is replaced with a Mask icon.

3. *Is there an active selection?* Many times when I make a selection, I automatically hide it using (Cmd + H) [Ctrl + H], which leaves the selection active but hidden and very easy to forget about. As soon as a tool is not working as expected, I automatically use the command key (Cmd + D) [Ctrl + D] to deselect a possible active selection. I won't tell you how many times this had tripped me up.

4. *Are you using the right tool?* This may seem obvious, but in the enthusiasm of working I have often grabbed the wrong tool or used the incorrect command key to activate a tool. Let's just say that it is difficult to clone with the Blur tool. On that note—the only tool that can move pixels or layers is the Move tool.

5. *Are you in Quick Mask mode?* Especially when working in Full Screen mode, it's not clear when you enter Quick Mask mode.

As long as you don't save a file, it's very difficult to get into irreparable trouble. If you feel you have backed your way into an image situation that you do not like, open the History palette and step backward by clicking on the history states (figure 6.57). Clicking on the topmost History icon reverts the file back to when it was originally opened.

figure 6.57

The History palette lets you step backward.

The final act of desperation is to choose File > Revert to bring the file back to the same state as when you first opened it. This is your final escape hatch—use it carefully.

If Photoshop is not behaving as expected or a tool is not responding, stop doing whatever you're doing, and with the help of this list identify the problem before you continue.

FINESSING LAYERS

Working with layers is more than just stacking them up in the order you want to see the image information. You can arrange, group, clip, and work with advanced blending options to create surprising effects quickly and efficiently.

Clipping Masks and Groups

Using a clipping mask is a fast and easy method for controlling how layers interact. A clipping group always starts with a base layer that has pixels on transparency. After adding an adjustment, fill, neutral, or image layer on top of the base layer, select Layer > Create Clipping Mask or (Cmd + G) [Ctrl + G] to group the upper layer with the lower.

Notice that the name of the base layer in the mask is underlined, and the thumbnails for the overlying layers are indented. You can also (Option-click) [Alt-click] on the thin line between layers to create a clipping group. Adding additional layers with a clipping group active will add them to that group.

Combining Text and Images

Clipping masks are commonly used to insert images into text, which is used on Web sites and in a lot of movie posters. It is incredibly easy:

1. To clip text with an image, open any image and use the Type tool to add your text. I recommend using a bold font that is very legible.

2. Drag the image you would like to be inside of the text into the file, which adds the image on top of the text—not what we were going for (**figure 6.58**).

3. With the top image layer active, select Layer > Create Clipping Mask to create the effect shown in **figure 6.59**.

4. You can move the layers individually or link them by having the text active and clicking on the Link button (**figure 6.60**) to move the layers together.

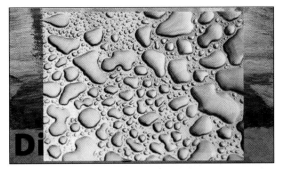

figure 6.58

Without clipping, the waterdrops layer covers the type.

figure 6.59

Clipping the top layer with the text.

figure 6.60

Linking the layers lets you move and transform layers together.

5. To separate the type from the image a bit more, I often add a slight drop shadow and a Bevel and Emboss layer effect (**figure 6.61**). Click on the Layer Style button on the lower portion of the Layers palette and experiment with these effects to create an image to your liking.

figure 6.61

Adding layer effects helps separate the type from the photographic background.

The best aspect of working with type layers is that you can re-edit the text and the layer styles and clipping groups remain active.

Compositing with Clipping Masks

Lyn Bishop is a very talented and insightful artist who has been working with digital tools and mixed media for many years to create wonderfully quiet, yet compelling images. **Figures 6.62** and **6.63** show how Lyn used a clipping mask with a Channel Mixer Adjustment Layer to remove some of the color from just the camellia flower while maintaining the color of the image background.

Use a clipping mask whenever you need to control an effect for a layer with transparency.

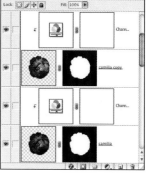

figure 6.62

With the clipping mask, just the flowers are slightly desaturated.

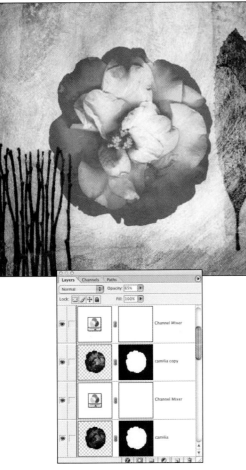

© Lyn Bishop

figure 6.63

Without the clipping mask, the entire image is impacted.

Creating Clouds with a Clipping Group

Replacing skies is a common task. It is addressed in Chapter 5, but I would like to show you a method for creating a faux sky that can be quite effective for those gray dreary days when a bit of blue would be perfect image improvement, as shown in **figures 6.64** and **6.65**.

1. Add a new layer. Click on the foreground Color picker and choose a sky blue. Activate the Gradient tool and choose the second gradient from the Gradient picker, which is Foreground to Transparent.

2. Draw the gradient from the top of the picture to the natural horizon, as shown in figure 6.66.

figure 6.64

figure 6.65

figure 6.66

Adding the blue-to-transparent gradient to a new layer.

3. (Option-click) [Alt-click] on the New Layer button and select *Use Previous Layer to Create Clipping Mask*, as shown in **figure 6.67**.

figure 6.67

Creating the clipping mask.

4. Make sure the foreground color is still sky blue and that the background color is white. Select Filter > Render > Clouds. You can rerun the filter as many times as you like until you get the results you want (**figure 6.68**).

figure 6.68

Use the Clouds filter to create clouds that suit your taste.

5. Add a layer mask to the gradient layer by clicking on the Layer Mask button on the bottom of the Layers palette and use a large soft, black brush to paint away clouds where they appear over the mountains (**figure 6.69**).

6. To give the clouds a truer perspective, select Edit > Transform > Perspective to pull out the top part of the clouds to widen them, as shown in **figure 6.70**, and use Edit > Transform > Scale to make them fit.

figure 6.69

The layer mask lets you hide unwanted areas.

figure 6.70

Transforming the faux clouds layer pushes the clouds back toward the horizon.

7. As a final touch of realism, we'll put simulated grain back into the clouds to hide the fact that they are computer generated. (Option-click) [Alt-click] on the New Layer button and select *Use Previous Layer to Create Clipping Mask*, choose Overlay, and select *Fill with Overlay Neutral Color - 50% Gray*, as shown in **figure 6.71**.

8. Choose Filter > Noise > Add Noise, check monochrome, and use a low setting to give the computer-generated clouds a hint of film grain, as I've done in **figure 6.72**.

The next time you're taking pictures on a less than perfect day, remember that you can add your own clouds in creative and inventive ways.

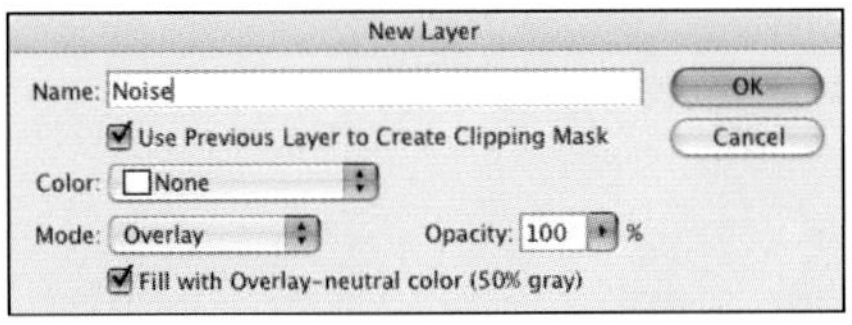

figure 6.71

Choosing a blending mode activates the Neutral Color checkbox.

figure 6.72

Adding noise to the neutral layer lets you fine-tune the effect.

Advanced Blending

Access the Advanced Blending features by double-clicking on the Layer icon to open the Layer Style dialog box (**figure 6.73**). There are a lot of things you can control here, but for now we'll focus on the Advanced Blending settings in the center.

- Fill opacity controls the opacity of the layer information while maintaining the visibility of layer effects.

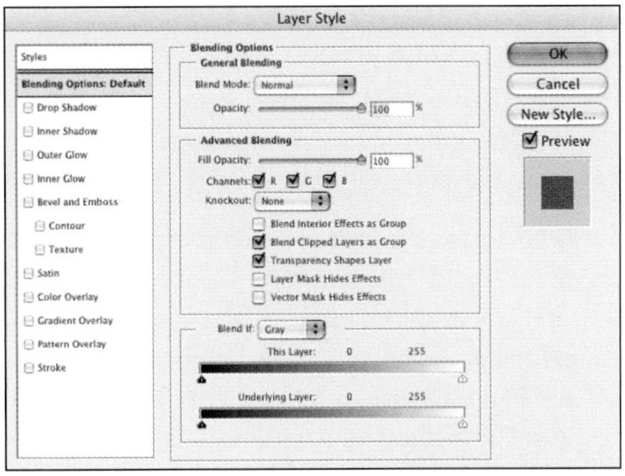

figure 6.73

The Layer Style dialog box.

- Deselecting any of the RGB channels hides that channel from the image.

- Knockout lets you *punch through* to reveal lower layers (shallow) or punch through deeper to the Background layer, which is demonstrated in the following section.

- Blend Clipped Layers as Groups (on by default) blends clipped layers as if they were one layer.

- Transparency Shape Layers determines that Layer Effects use the shape layer transparency as the basis for the shape of the effect.

- Layer Mask Hides Effects (off by default) is a very useful command. Often, when adding a layer style such as a drop shadow to a layer, you'll need to control exactly where it falls. When this is selected, you can use a layer mask to hide and reveal where the layer style takes place.

- Vector Mask Hides Effects (off by default) is the same as Layer Mask Hides Effects, but with a vector mask.

Knockout Effects

Knockout options let you specify which layers punch through to reveal content from other layers. For example, you can use a text layer to knock out a color Adjustment Layer and reveal a portion of the image using the original colors. To create a knockout effect, you need to decide which layer will create the shape of the knockout, which layers will be punched through, and which layer will be revealed. If you want to reveal a layer other than the Background, you can place the layers you want to use in a layer set.

I was asked to give a Photoshop presentation to a group of hand surgeons and needed to create a graphic for the opening of the presentation. I thought it would be fun to open with a photograph of my hand (**figure 6.74**) and use a faux lens to reveal a medical illustration, as if I was quasi x-raying my hand (**figure 6.75**).

⊕⊃⊱ **ch6_handphoto.jpg**

⊕⊃⊱ **ch6_handillustration.jpg**

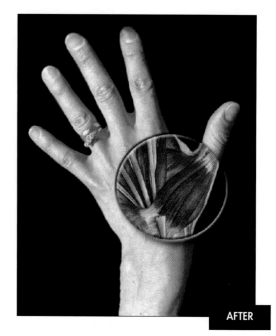

figure 6.75

1. To create a Knockout effect, start by deciding which layer will be revealed—in this case, the medical illustration. Drag the hand photo layer that is going to be punched through on top of the medical illustration and name it *hand photo* (**figure 6.76**).

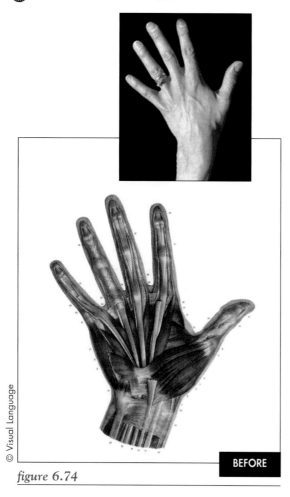

© Visual Language

figure 6.74

BEFORE

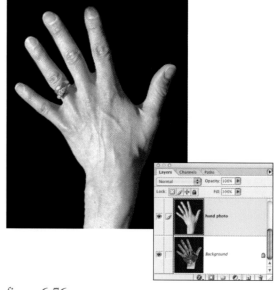

figure 6.76

Drag the layer on top of the layer that is going to be revealed.

2. Click on the Shape tool, select the elliptical shape, and make sure the Shape Layer is active in the Options bar (**figure 6.77**).

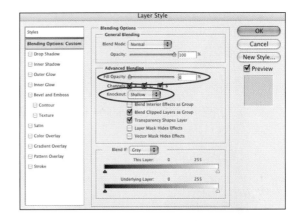

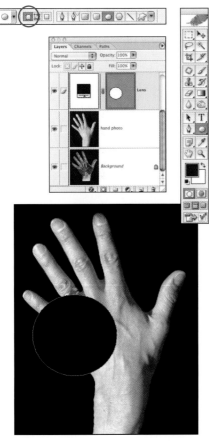

figure 6.77

Set the Shape tool to Shape Layer and use it to draw the "lens."

3. Hold the Shift key and create a perfectly round circle. It doesn't matter what color it is, as it will be adjusted with the layer fill in the Advanced Blending options in a moment.

4. Select Layer > Layer Style > Blending Options; reduce the fill to 0% and choose Knockout Shallow as shown in **figure 6.78** to reveal the illustration below the hand. If this composite had more than two layers, choosing Deep for Knockout would punch through all layers to the Background layer.

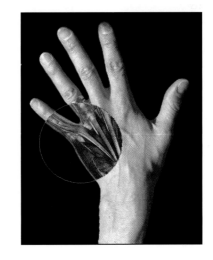

figure 6.78

Reducing the Fill and choosing Knockout Shallow reveals the layer below.

5. To make it look more like a lens, add a drop shadow, bevel, and emboss (**figure 6.79**) to give the lens shape a hint of dimension.

6. Use the Move tool to move the "lens" around the image to see through the skin to the muscles below.

For the medical presentation, I started with the lens layer completely off to the side and used the Move tool to bring it back into the canvas area to reveal the medical illustration—there was quite a positive and surprised reaction from the doctors.

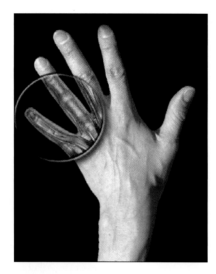

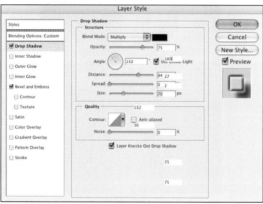

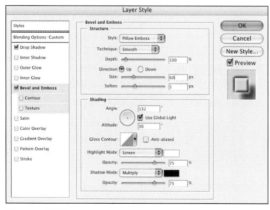

figure 6.79

Use layer styles to add a dimension to the lens shape.

WORKING WITH IMAGE EFFECTS LAYERS

Adjustment, fill, neutral and layer effects are all effect layers. They are used to add tone and color corrections, color fills and patterns, texture and light, and special effects to images.

- The Adjustment Layers are among my very favorite features in Photoshop and are fully supported in 16-bit in Photoshop CS, letting you maintain greater image quality well into the imaging workflow.

- Fill layers were introduced as a feature for Web designers, but as shown in Chapter 4, "Pen Tool Power," you can use them to add special effects and image patterns to photographic images.

- Neutral layers are a fantastic feature for adding texture, film grain, and lighting effects. Please see Chapter 12, "Photorealistic Compositing," and Chapter 13, "Creative Compositing," for additional uses of neutral layers.

- Layer styles are a flexible method for adding special effects to layers, most commonly used for type.

Adjustment Layers

Adjustment Layers are nondestructive layers that let you apply and change tonal and color adjustments as many times as needed without altering the underlying layer's original data until you flatten the image. Use Adjustment Layers when working with Levels, Curves, Color Balance, Hue/Saturation, Selective Color, Channel Mixer, Gradient Map, Photo filter, Invert, Threshold, and Posterize. I don't recommend using Brightness/Contrast because working with Levels and Curves offers better control and uses more sophisticated mathematics to apply the tonal changes. The benefits that working with Adjustment Layers offer include the following:

- They let you make tonal corrections without changing or degrading the source image data until you flatten the image.

- They support opacity; by lowering the Adjustment Layer's opacity, you reduce the strength of the tonal or color correction.

- They support blending modes, which mathematically change how layers interact with the layer below them. They are a great aid to quickly create stunning image effects or to improve image tonality.

- They are resolution independent, letting you drag and drop them between disparately sized and scaled images.

- They include layer masks with which you can hide and reveal a tonal correction with the use of any painting tool.

- They are especially helpful when making local tonal, contrast, and color adjustments to parts or smaller areas of an image.

- If you don't like an adjustment, you can reset it or just throw the offending Adjustment Layer into the Layers palette trash and start over.

Before compositing images together or applying creative changes, it is important that the image or images have the correct tone, contrast, and color balance. This is an issue that I addressed in great depth in *Photoshop Restoration and Retouching* and *Real World Digital Photography*, and rather than repeating all of that information here, the following section provides an overview of applying global and selective image corrections with Adjustment Layers.

Global Changes

Global tonal, contrast, or color adjustments affect the entire image equally. Global changes are best applied at the beginning of the imagemaking process to make the images you're going to composite look their best. For tone and contrast corrections, the two best options are Levels and Curves. For color correction, Photoshop offers a large number of choices including Levels, Curves, Color Balance, Hue/Saturation, Selective Color, and Photo filter.

Levels Settings

Using Levels (**figure 6.80**) you can influence three tonal areas of an image—the shadows, midtones, and highlights—by either moving the sliders or using black-point or white-point eyedroppers to define better black or white points. The gray eyedropper is used to define neutral areas in color images. Often, you can make an image come to life just by setting new white and black points and moving the Midtone Gamma Slider (to the left to lighten or to the right to darken the image).

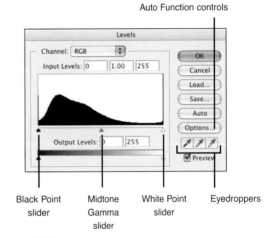

figure 6.80

The Levels interface.

The most important Level controls to enhance image tone include the following:

- **Eyedroppers:** Use the eyedroppers to set white and black points for both black-and-white and color images and the neutral gray eyedropper to define a neutral tone in color images.

- **Sliders:** Use the Highlight and black sliders to remap the black and white points. You prompt Photoshop to remap the points by moving the relevant slider to the area of the image that contains the majority of the light or dark information.

- **Auto button:** Use the Auto button to prompt Photoshop to set a light point to white and a dark point to black. How it determines which points to look at is configurable via the Options button directly underneath Auto.

To get the most out of Levels you will need to set the black-and-white target values before beginning. This tells Photoshop which values to use for black and white; it's called *targeting*. By targeting the Highlight and Shadow value for your printing process and paper combination, you ensure the image will remain within the reproducible range.

1. Open the Levels dialog box and double-click the white eyedropper. A Select Target Highlight Color label appears above the Color picker.

2. For printing to an inkjet printer, use the HSB scale and set the white target color to 96% brightness, or RGB 245, 245, 245, and click OK. For printing to offset, use the CMYK values of 5 C, 3 M, 3Y, and 0 K (**figure 6.81**).

3. Double-click the black eyedropper and set the shadow target color to 5% on the HSB scale, or 13, 13, 13 RGB (**figure 6.82**); and click OK.

By setting the white target color to 96%, you will hold slight tonality in your whitest whites, and the black target color 5% will hold shadow information in the darkest parts of the image.

The generic 96% highlight and 5% shadow values are a safe place to start to avoid printing highlights without tone (paper white) or shadows that are so dark with ink that you can't see any detail in them. Both values you set here are also referenced in the Curves settings, meaning you do not have to repeat setting these values in Curves. After changing the Shadow and Highlight eyedropper values, upon closing the Levels dialogue you will be prompted to save the new target colors as defaults. Click OK to apply these recommended settings

 T i p

Set the toolbar Eyedropper to 3 × 3 in the Options bar before entering Levels or Curves.

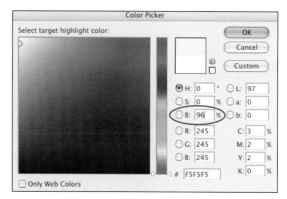

figure 6.81

Setting the white target color to 96% ensures you'll retain a slight tonality in the whitest part of your image.

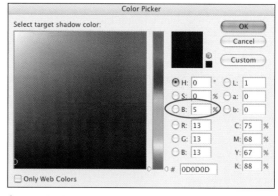

figure 6.82

The 5% Black Target Color setting maintains shadow information in even the darkest areas of the image.

Working with Levels

The Levels histogram is a great aid when doing tonal correction. It shows you where the tonal information is, so you can use it as a guide to apply corrections. In many cases, you can improve an image by adding a Levels Adjustment Layer and moving the Black and White Point sliders to where the histogram values start, as described in the following step-by-step example.

ch6_tilewall.jpg

1. After setting the white-and-black target values as discussed, select Layer > New Adjustment > Levels and move the black and white sliders to where the majority of image information starts (**figure 6.83**).

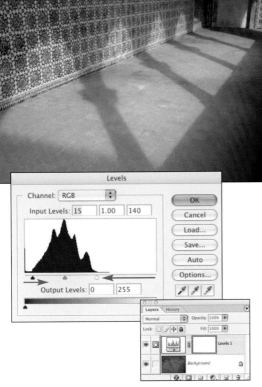

figure 6.83

Use the Levels Histogram to make tonal editing decisions.

2. Look at the image—is there anything in it that could be neutral? I decided the hint of wall on the background could be neutral, and by clicking on it with the gray eyedropper the image color popped into place (**figure 6.84**).

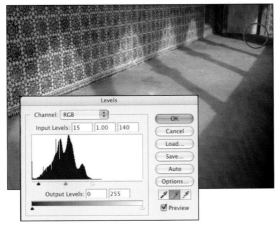

figure 6.84

The gray eyedropper removes colorcasts by defining them as neutral.

3. Depending on your image interpretation of the scene, moving the middle slider will make the image lighter or darker. In this example, I wanted to make the image more dramatic and strengthen the shadow areas, so I moved the Midtone slider to the right (**figure 6.85**).

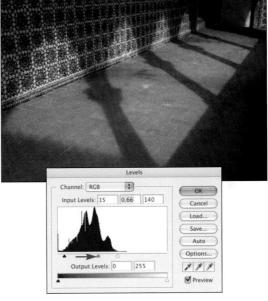

figure 6.85

Adjusting the Midtone slider makes an image lighter or darker.

You won't have to use all the tools in Levels for every image, but taking a few seconds to set a black, white, and neutral value can make a dull image pop to life.

Tip

To correct many images with a similar tonal character or colorcast, correct one representative image and then drag the Adjustment Layer from the Layers palette onto the other images one at a time.

Working with Curves

Identical to Levels, the Curves tool also has white, black, and gray eyedroppers, but the primary advantage of Curves is that you can adjust 16 tonal points versus 3 in Levels (highlight, midtone, shadow). This makes Curves the primary tonal and color-correction tool of professional imagemakers and prepress professionals. I'll show you how to make your photographs pop with a hint of contrast that is impossible to apply in Levels.

The Curves dialog box lets you work with either 0 to 100 dot percentages or 0 to 255 tonal values. Click the small triangles (**figure 6.86**) to toggle between the two. I've found that people with prepress experience prefer the 0% to 100% scale, while photographers prefer the 0 to 255 scale—the same values used in Levels. The 0 to 255 scale places the highlights on the shoulder (upper part) of the curve and the shadows on the toe (lower part) of the curve. This is how a photographer reads film curves and why I prefer to use the 0 to 255 scale. The 0% to 100% values are mapped exactly the opposite, with the highlights at the bottom left and the shadows at the upper right.

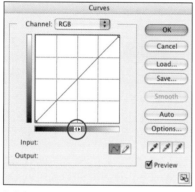

figure 6.86

You can choose to work in dot percentages or digital values by clicking the small triangles.

When you add a point to the curve and move it, you are changing the relationship between a pixel's input to output value. For example, if you move the midpoint 128 value up, you're telling Photoshop to remap the 128 values to a higher value, and the image will get lighter. If you are working with the 0% to 100% scale, moving the 50% point down will lighten the image. The best aspect of Curves is the control you have over the many points of tonal information.

Tip

(Option-click) [Alt-click] in the curves grid to toggle between a 4 × 4 quadrant and 10 ×10 10% increment grid.

Click the icon at the bottom right of the Curves dialog box to toggle between larger and smaller display sizes.

ch6_pigeons.jpg

With Curves you can quickly enhance image contrast by applying a classic S-Curve:

1. Add a Curves Adjustment layer, grab the Curve line at the 3/4 value point (**figure 6.87**), and pull down slightly.

2. Working in the same Curve, grab the Curve line at the 1/4 value point (**figure 6.88**) and pull up slightly. Notice how the highlights have more visual kick and the shadows are richer.

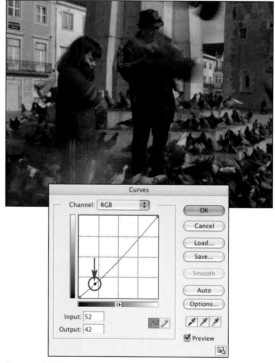

figure 6.87

Carefully darkening the shadows gives the image a stronger tonal foundation.

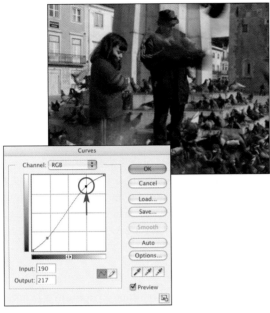

figure 6.88

Lightening the highlights plays into how our cerebral visual system processes tonal values.

3. Often I'll interpret the image midtones by moving them to the left or right and, as you can see in **figure 6.89**, by moving the midtone laterally to the left, the image midtones become lighter.

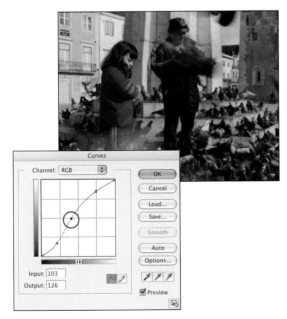

figure 6.89

Adjusting the midtones to the left or right changes the overall contrast.

4. In this example, the Curves adjustment improved the image contrast, but it also over-saturated the little girl's sweater (**figure 6.90**). By changing the Curves layer blending mode to Luminosity, the contrast correction is maintained while the false saturation problem is negated (**figure 6.91**).

figure 6.90

The image contrast is better now, but some areas are oversaturated.

figure 6.91

The Luminosity blending mode removes any false saturation that the contrast change may have added.

To Use or Not to Use Auto?

I was one of the many people who pooh-poohed any Photoshop feature with the word *magic* or *auto* in it, but beginning with Photoshop 7 the Auto feature in Levels and Curves has shattered my snobbishness. In either Levels or Curves, clicking Options produces the Auto Color Correction Options dialog box. It is here that you can cycle through the types of corrections or influence which values Auto Color applies to your images.

The Auto Color Correction Options Interface has six settings that let you control how the color is affected:

- **Enhance Monochromatic Contrast:** This is a quick way to add snap to an image by darkening shadows and lighting highlights. Photoshop clips all color channels at once, using identical values for each, making shadows darker and light areas brighter. This is the same as Image > Adjustments > Auto Contrast or moving the Shadow and Highlight sliders in Levels to where image information begins on the RGB or CYMK composite histogram.

- **Enhance Per Channel Contrast:** Quickly adds contrast and removes overall colorcast. Photoshop will adjust each channel separately. This is identical to moving the Shadow and Highlight sliders of the individual image channels to where the image information starts. This is how Image > Adjustments > Auto Levels works.

- **Find Dark & Light Colors:** Photoshop uses the lightest and darkest pixels in an image for the Shadow and Highlight values. This is the same as Image > Adjustments > Auto Color and may or may not introduce unwanted colorcasts.

- **Snap Neutral Midtones:** With this selected, Photoshop looks for nearly neutral colors in your image and then forces them to gray. Image > Adjustments > Auto Color uses this option.

- **Target Colors Clipping:** Enter values here to tell Photoshop the percentage of tones to ignore. For example, entering 0.02% for both Shadows and Highlights will skip the brightest and darkest 0.02% before starting calculations. If you want calculations to be based on non-neutral colors, clicking a color swatch will open the Color picker, where you can choose any color as the target Shadow, Midtone, or Highlight target.

- **Save as defaults:** Using this setting tells Photoshop that the current settings are the ones you want to use anytime you click the Auto button in Levels or Curves. If you select this option, the Clipping value you enter will also be the new defaults for the Auto Levels, Auto Contrast, and Auto Color menu commands.

Now that Adobe has added the ability to control the Auto Color Correction, I find myself adding a Levels or Curves Adjustment Layer and clicking through the options to see what is going to happen. Many times the results are very good, as demonstrated here:

 **ch6_castle_wall.jpg**

1. Open the castle wall image (**figure 6.92**) and add a Curves Adjustment Layer.

figure 6.92

The original image is murky.

2. Click on Options and cycle through the three choices to see which one suits your taste.

3. For this image, I prefer Enhance per Channel Contrast with Snap Neutral Midtones as shown in **figure 6.93** because it turned a murky image into one with snap with a minimum amount of work.

4. Click OK in the Options dialog box and, if necessary, adjust the Curves to fine-tune the image. In this example, I added a slight S Curve to increase the contrast and make the image a bit more dramatic (**figure 6.94**).

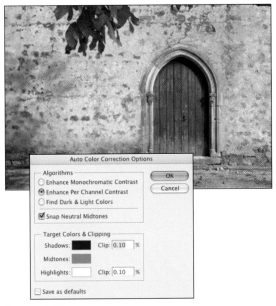

figure 6.93

Cycling through the Auto options is often a good starting point.

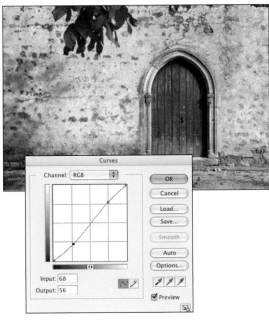

figure 6.94

After using the Auto feature, you can add your own interpretation to the image.

Correcting tone and color is a very important skill, and many books have been written about the topic. For additional information, please refer to *Real World Photoshop CS* by Bruce Fraser and David Blatner and *Photoshop Color Correction* by Michael Kieran.

Magical Shadow/Highlight

At first glance, the new Shadow/Highlight image adjustment may seem to accomplish similar results as Curves or Levels. Nothing could be further from the truth: Shadow/Highlight "looks" at an image in a similar way our eyes do. When we look at a scene, our eyes adapt, allowing us to see both the highlights and the darker areas. Shadow/Highlight adaptively compares and corrects each pixel, according to the surrounding luminance values. This enables image contrast to be increased in the shadows or highlights, or both, without significantly sacrificing contrast in the other tonal regions.

Shadow/Highlight is not an Adjustment Layer, and I highly recommend duplicating a layer before selecting Image > Adjustments > Shadow/Highlight. Moving the sliders in the simple interface to the left or right tells Photoshop how much correction to apply. Adjusting the Shadow slider lightens dark areas, and adjusting the Highlight slider darkens lighter areas. In **figure 6.95**, the ceiling is too dark and the walls are too light. By adjusting the Shadow and Highlight sliders as shown in **figure 6.96**, the important ceiling information is opened up, showing the wooden structure more clearly.

figure 6.95

The basic interface is very simple—and often produces very good results with little effort.

figure 6.96

Adjusting the sliders opened up the ceiling and toned down the walls.

To have more control over the Shadow/Highlight image correction, click on View More Options, which is broken up into three distinct areas: Shadows, Highlights, and Adjustments (**figure 6.97**):

In the Shadows and Highlights panes you have control over the following:

- **Amount:** Controls how much correction is applied.

- **Tonal Width:** Lower values restrict the adjustments to the darkest or lighter regions. Higher values include more tonal regions and will include midtones in the correction. Using a setting that is too high may introduce ghostly halos that add an undesired glow around dark subjects.

- **Radius:** Similar to the controls in the Unsharp Mask filter, the radius controls the width area around each pixel that is used to determine whether an image area is a shadow or highlight. Of course the optimum local neighborhood size depends on the image. I set the radius by looking at the image and eyeballing what percentage of the image is shadow and what percentage is highlight.

In the Adjustments pane you have control over:

- **Color Correction:** This is really saturation. I often reduce the standard value of +20 to +10 to offset any unwanted color shifts and saturation that changing exposure may introduce.

- **Midtone Contrast:** Lets you refine the middle values of the image, and in this case I reduced the midtone contrast to even out the exposure.

To work nondestructively, always duplicate the layer before selecting Image > Adjustments > Shadow/Highlights. Duplicating the layer or creating a merged layer also gives you the ability to fine-tune the image correction with layer opacity and layer masking.

figure 6.97

Reducing the Color Correction slider neutralizes the image.

Working with Neutral Layers

Neutral layers are black, white, or gray. Used in conjunction with blending modes (figure 6.98), they are invisible surfaces for employing a variety of Photoshop filters and effects to add film grain, abstract textures, tonal effects, and lighting effects.

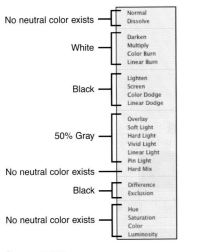

figure 6.98

The Layer blending modes with their neutral colors.

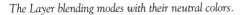 **ch6_churchfacade.jpg**

In the following example, I wanted to spotlight the church facade to create a more dramatic image background:

1. Choose Layer > New > Layer or (Option-click) [Alt–click] on the New Layer button in the Layers palette, which produces the New Layer dialog box (figure 6.99). As soon as you choose any blending mode except Normal, Dissolve, or the component blending modes (Hue, Saturation, Color, Luminosity), the *Fill with [name of blending mode] Neutral Color* option becomes available.

2. For lighting effects, I use Soft Light and select Fill with Soft-Light-Neutral Color (50% Gray), as shown in figure 6.100.

figure 6.99

(Option-clicking) [Alt-clicking] on the New Layer button opens the New Layer dialog box.

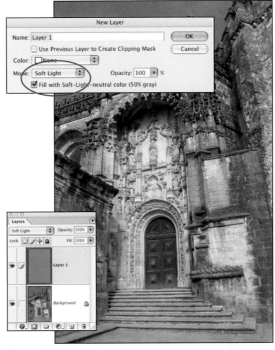

figure 6.100

Choosing Soft Light activates the Fill with Neutral Color check box.

3. Choose Filter > Render > Lighting Effects and use the soft directional spot (figure 6.101). The Lighting Effect filter doesn't just add light; it also makes the ambient environment darker, which you can control with the Ambient slider. Because you are working on an invisible layer, you need to "guesstimate" where the light will fall. In many cases, it won't "land" exactly where you need it, as it does in figure 6.102. You can fine-tune the position of the light as described in the following step.

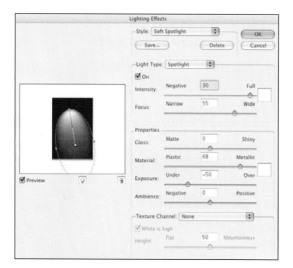

figure 6.101

Adjusting the lighting settings requires some guesswork.

4. Because the light is on a separate layer, you can move and transform the light into place, as I did in figure 6.103. If non-lit areas are revealed (figure 6.45), (Cmd-click) [Ctrl-click] on the Layer icon to make a selection of the lighting effect, choose Select > Inverse, and then Edit > Fill > Black (figure 6.104) to conceal the empty areas.

Adding lighting effects will be done frequently in the compositing process and will be explained in Chapter 12. Neutral layers are used to add film grain to digital composites to conceal possible textural differences between image elements, which we'll also tackle in Chapter 12.

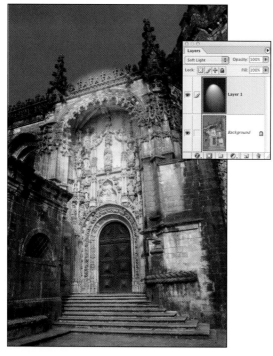

figure 6.102

Positioning lighting effects on a neutral layer requires a bit of guesswork and luck.

figure 6.103

Because the light is on a separate layer, you can move and transform it into place.

CLOSING THOUGHTS

If layers are the heart of Photoshop, then layer masks are the soul. If I had to choose one aspect of Photoshop to be my all-time favorite, it would be how layers and layer masks allow my imagination to run wild. In the next chapter, we will delve into how to use layer masking to combine images creatively and for production.

figure 6.104

Fill the transparent areas with black to complete the effect.

7

THE POWER OF LAYER MASKING

Some men have commitment problems—or so the cliché goes. Well, I've met quite a few Photoshop users with deep-rooted commitment problems, and yes, I count myself among them. We fear the commitment of making an irrevocable image-editing decision that we'll regret in the morning. In fact, if it wasn't for one essential feature in Photoshop—layer masks—I would be a nail-biting, sleep-deprived wreck.

Layer masks allow the commitment-wary and -weary the opportunity to try various approaches to their images without losing the flexibility to change their minds. In this chapter, you'll be introduced to the perfect partnership—layers and layer masks—and how they work hand in hand (or should I say pixel in pixel?). This chapter addresses

- How to work with painted, gradated, and selective layer masks

- When to use pixel or vector layer masks

- Why layer masks are powerful, flexible, and creative

- How to combine multiple image exposures

If I had to decide between giving up coffee or layer masks, I wouldn't think twice. I hear that tea has caffeine, too. So brew a cup of your favorite beverage and let's explore one of the most exciting and essential features of Photoshop.

WORKING WITH LAYER MASKS

Layer masks are the soul of Photoshop—the key to combining images in a completely nondestructive manner. They enable you to move, hide, blend, conceal, and experiment with image combinations to your heart's content—all without ever losing a single pixel.

Each layer can support a pixel and a vector layer mask. Pixel-based masks are used for blending photographs together, to gradually have images or tone and color changes fade in and out, and wherever painted or soft edge quality is desired. Vector-based masks are employed when Bézier accuracy and crispness is required. Both types are very useful, but the pixel-based mask is the true workhorse of the compositing artist.

Background and type layers do not support layer masks. Adjustment Layers automatically come with a layer mask. To add a layer mask to an image layer, either click on the Mask button in the Layers palette to add a white layer mask, or (Option-click) [Alt-click] to add a black layer mask. You can also choose Layer > Add Layer Mask > Reveal All to add a white layer mask, or Layer > Add Layer Mask > Hide All to add a black layer mask.

Just like Channel masks, pixel layer masks can be black or white with all shades of gray in between. Wherever the mask is darker, less image effect will show through; wherever it is lighter, more image effect shows through. In a nutshell, black conceals and white reveals—meaning that if you want part of an image to show through, then the corresponding mask must be light. If you don't want an image area to be visible, the mask must be black.

 T i p

Use the masking mnemonic, "White Reveals and Black Conceals" when working with layer masks.

Painted Layer Masks

When layers were introduced with Photoshop 3.0, I was having a problem adopting the new layered, dimensional approach to combining images. To understand how layers and layer masks worked, one night I opened two images that I liked (**figure 7.1**), literally plopped one on top of the other by dragging the Pegasus image over to the tree image, added a layer mask to the top one, and then started painting. If you, too, have struggled to grasp the concept of combining images using layer masks, following the same steps I did may help:

⊕▷⊱ **ch7_wintertrees.jpg**

⊕▷⊱ **ch7_pegasus.jpg**

figure 7.1

The two source images.

1. Open both images and decide which one will serve as the image background. I chose the winter tree branches image as the background, and the Pegasus image as the foreground subject.

2. Use the Move tool to drag the Pegasus over to the winter tree branches image and name the layer *Pegasus*.

3. Click on the Layer Mask button. Notice that nothing has changed in your image and that Photoshop has added a white layer mask to the Pegasus layer (**figure 7.2**).

4. Paint with a soft, black brush over those areas of the Pegasus layer that you do not want to see (**figure 7.3**). If by accident you paint over an area that you do want to see, press *x* to switch the foreground and background colors, and paint over the area you want to see with white. Keep in mind, white reveals and black conceals—meaning that if you paint with black on the layer mask, you will be hiding "Pegasus" pixels.

5. In a few minutes, you should have the image roughly combined. To fine-tune the image edges, zoom in on an area (**figure 7.4**) and paint with a smaller, harder brush. Press *x* to paint with black or conceal, or white to reveal the Pegasus layer. (Option-click) [Alt-click] on the layer mask to view it (**figure 7.5**).

figure 7.4

Zoom in and paint with a smaller, harder brush to fine-tune how the image elements come together.

figure 7.2

Adding a white layer mask does not alter the image in any way.

figure 7.3

Painting with a large, soft black brush quickly conceals areas of the Pegasus image you do not want to see.

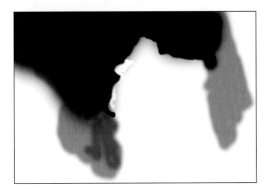

figure 7.5

Viewing the layer mask shows that white reveals and black conceals.

6. When you've finished, select File > Save As and save the file in the PSD or TIFF format (these are the two recommended formats that will maintain the layers). When you return to this image, you can readjust it any way you want by painting on the layer mask again.

Now you know how I learned layer masking—I spent an evening with these two images and kept painting back and forth to create the image shown in **figure 7.6**. It took me a few hours, but I finally got it and haven't looked back since.

White and Black Layer Masks

When you click on the Layer Mask button in the Layers palette, Photoshop adds a white layer mask, which reveals the entire image. Starting with a white layer mask is a subtractive mode of working. You see the entire image and paint away with black or gray the areas you do not want to see.

(Option-clicking) [Alt-clicking] the Layer Mask button adds a black layer mask, which hides the entire layer. You need to paint with white to add the image back—to work additively you bring the image back into view.

This technique is used very often in portrait retouching. Photographers will sharpen the entire portrait, and then by adding a black layer mask to the sharpened layer, they paint back in the sharpness only where it is needed—in most cases the eyes and lips (**figure 7.7**).

figure 7.6

The final image playfully reveals winter trees interspersed with a Las Vegas shopping arcade.

Without sharpening

Sharpened eyes

© Mark Beckelman

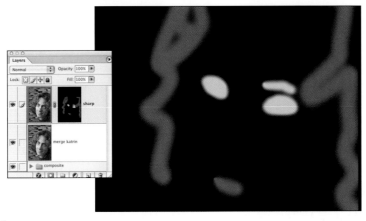

figure 7.7

The layer mask controls where the sharpening effect is applied to the original image.

Gradated Layer Masks

The largest paintbrush in Photoshop is the Gradient tool. You can use it on layer masks to control tonal and color effects and to seamlessly blend images together.

Darkening Image Edges

Adjustment Layers in combination with blending modes and layer masks offer a straightforward method for lightening and darkening (traditionally called *dodging* and *burning*) areas in an image where you want to draw attention. Light areas attract the viewer's focus, whereas dark areas are of less visual interest.

Traditionally, photographers often burned or darkened the edges of their prints to focus the viewer's attention on the center. If you employ this technique, you should do it as subtly as possible so that it's not noticeable. After finishing a composite, I often add a slight edge burn to darken the outer edges and keep the viewer's eyes focused on the center, as figure 7.8 illustrates.

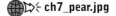 ch7_pear.jpg

figure 7.8

Framing the pear with a hint of darkness maintains the focus on the center of the image.

You can quickly create this darkening effect using an Adjustment Layer and the Gradient tool:

1. Activate the topmost layer of your composite or image.

2. Add a Levels or Curves Adjustment Layer—it doesn't matter which one you choose. As soon as the interface pops up, click OK without changing anything.

3. Change the blending mode to Multiply and reduce the opacity to 50%. The entire image will become darker (**figure 7.9**).

figure 7.9

Changing the layer blending mode to Multiply darkens the entire image.

4. Select Image > Adjustments > Invert or (Cmd + I) [Ctrl + I] to invert the layer mask, which will turn it black.

5. Activate the Gradient tool and select the second gradient from the Gradient picker—Foreground to Transparent (**figure 7.10**). Verify that white is the foreground color; if it isn't, press *x* to switch the foreground and background colors.

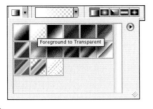

figure 7.10

You need the Foreground to Transparent gradient for this technique to work.

6. Press *f* to place the image into full-screen mode and zoom out to see the entire image. I prefer to start the gradient well outside the image (**figure 7.11**). Pull the first gradient from the upper left toward the center of the image, and then repeat on all four corners (**figure 7.12**). Continue as necessary to create an image to your liking, as I did in **figure 7.13**.

7. Turn the Image Adjustment Layer view column on and off to view the image with and without the darkening effect. If you like what you see, save the file. If you are not satisfied— maybe it's too light or too dark—adjust the layer opacity to create the desired effect.

figure 7.11

Working in full-screen mode and starting well outside the image lets you subtly darken the image edges.

figure 7.12

After one gradient pull from each corner, the image is more focused.

figure 7.13

Continue adding gradients to create an image to your liking.

8. If you are not at all happy with the effect, throw away the entire Adjustment Layer and start over.

Once you've darkened image edges like this a few times you'll be able to do it very quickly, giving your images a professional and subtle polish.

Balancing Image Exposure

Using the Gradient tool on a Levels or Curves Adjustment Layer is a quick and easy method for balancing exposure, as John Warner did with the panoramic image shown in **figure 7.14**.

To balance the image exposure, John used a Curves Adjustment Layer with a gradated mask as follows:

1. After scanning in the image, John added a Curves Adjustment Layer and lightened the entire image (**figure 7.15**).

2. By using a black-to-white gradient from right to left, he concealed the tonal change on the correct side of the image and let the change show through on the left, which lightened the left side and balanced the exposure perfectly (**figure 7.16**).

figure 7.14

The left side of the original image is just a little too dark.

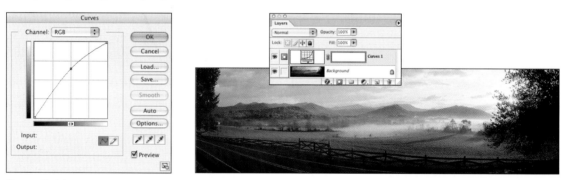

figure 7.15

Lighting the entire image using a Curves Adjustment Layer.

figure 7.16

The Gradient tool concealed the change on the right side of the image and revealed it on the left side.

Seamlessly Blending Images

Building image backgrounds by combining two or more images is a fantastic method for building up a stock of creative backdrops. The Gradient tool can help you achieve good results very quickly.

🌐⤳⚞ **ch7_sunset.jpg**

🌐⤳⚞ **ch7_reflection.jpg**

1. Open the two images you want to blend and determine which one will serve as the background and which one will be in the foreground. Drag the top image over to the bottom image with the Move tool. When dragging images—especially Background layers—it helps to do it with confidence or as I like to say, *with schwung.* Otherwise, Photoshop will pop up the polite yet irritating message: "Could not complete your request because the layer is locked." So drag quickly and with confidence. Pressing and holding the Shift key will place the top image exactly on the center point of the bottom image.

2. Add a layer mask to the top image and reduce the layer opacity to 50%. This helps you find the best position for the image, since you can see through to the lower image (see figure 7.17).

3. Click on the layer mask to make sure it is active, activate the Gradient tool, and choose the third gradient from the gradient library— black to white. Start the gradient where you want the bottom image to show through completely and draw up. Release the mouse when you reach the point in the top image that you want to see completely (figure 7.18).

4. Increase the layer opacity to 100% to see the results (figure 7.19).

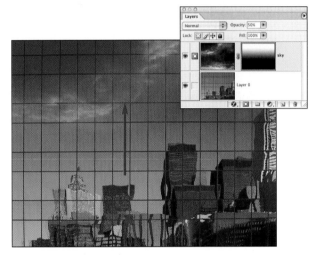

figure 7.18

Using a black-to-white gradient to reveal the buildings in the lower part of the image.

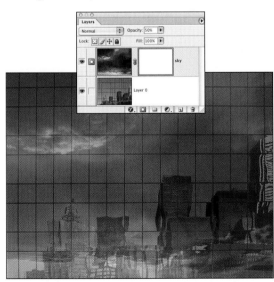

figure 7.17

After dragging one image onto another, reduce the layer opacity so that you can view the relationship between the two.

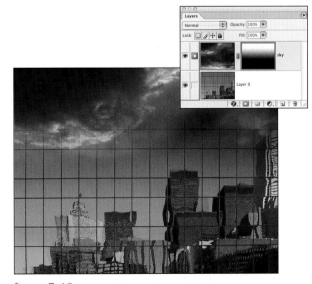

figure 7.19

Set layer opacity to 100% to see the image combination.

Adjusting Position

The layer and the layer mask can be moved together or independently of one another. To move the layer and mask together, make sure they are linked; to move either one independently, unlink them by clicking on the small chain between the layer and the Layer Mask icon.

To change the position of the sky:

- Move the sky with the layer mask (figure 7.20) by grabbing the top layer in the image and moving it using the Move tool.

figure 7.20

Moving the layer and the layer mask together.

- Move just the sky by unlinking the sky pixels from the layer mask. Click on the small chain between the layer and Mask icon (figure 7.21) and then make sure the layer is active before moving it.
- Move just the mask by unlinking the sky pixels from the layer mask. Click on the small chain between the layer and Mask icon, and then move the layer mask (figure 7.22).

figure 7.21

Unlinking the layer and layer mask by clicking the link icon lets you move just the layer or the mask.

figure 7.22

Moving the layer mask is very useful for fine-tuning the transition position.

There are many times when you want the mask to stay linked with the layer, but very often it is quite useful to move the layer mask—for example, when the steepness of the blend is perfect, but you want to change its position slightly.

Experimentation

The best thing about the Gradient tool and layer masks is that you can redo the blend over and over again to get the image exactly right. Take a moment to experiment with the Gradient tool—create very steep transitions by only drawing for a short distance; create a very long transition by drawing the gradient across the entire image. Try it going from right to left, or diagonally. I've provided a few variations in **figure 7.23**. Every time you draw a new gradient, the previous blend is overwritten, letting you experiment to your heart's content.

Long gradient

Right to Left gradient

Steep gradient

Diagonal gradient

figure 7.23

Experiment with the Gradient tool to create a variety of image effects.

Refining Blended Images

Many times an image combination requires more than a straight-line gradient to blend in a new background or sky, as shown in **figures 7.24** and **7.25**, in which I replaced the sky with a more dramatic one.

ch7_stormsky.jpg

ch7_pony.jpg

figure 7.24

figure 7.25

Combine the Gradient and Brush tools to refine layer masks to improve images as described here.

1. Open both images and drag the sky image on top of the pony image.

2. Add a layer mask to the sky image and draw a gradient from below the horizon to the top of the new sky to create the results shown in **figure 7.26**.

   Now the problem is that the new sky is covering the pony, which of course needs to be in front of the sky.

figure 7.26

The initial gradient on the layer mask adds the sky but covers the pony.

3. Click on the sky layer mask, and using a black brush with 50% hardness, carefully paint inside the pony to block the sky from being visible, as shown in **figure 7.27**.

4. (Option-click) [Alt-click] the layer mask to see exactly what is going on—the gradient is letting the new sky blend in, and the black areas are blocking the sky from affecting the pony (**figure 7.28**).

5. If by chance you paint into the sky and see a telltale halo (**figure 7.29**), (Option-click) [Alt-click] the gradient directly adjacent to the mistake. This samples the gray with the density of the gradient, and as you paint the sky will blend in without showing any density differences.

figure 7.27

Painting on the layer mask protects the pony from being affected by the sky layer.

figure 7.28

Viewing the layer mask is often a good way to catch errors.

figure 7.29

The lighter halo around the pony's head is a telltale sign of poor masking.

6. If necessary, (Option-click) [Alt-click] to sample darker or lighter density areas from the gradient as you work up or down the pony's head. You can see the detail work I did in **figure 7.30**.

figure 7.30

Sampling the density of the gradient lets you paint on the layer mask to remove halos.

Selective Changes

When you make a selection and then add an Adjustment Layer, Photoshop automatically transfers the active selection to the layer mask and the adjustments only take place within the active areas. Starting with a selection is demonstrated here to correct the backlit photograph of the golf course sign:

ch7_golfsign.jpg

1. Select the sign with the Polygon Lasso tool and feather the selection by 1 pixel to soften the edges ever so slightly (**figure 7.31**).

2. Add a Curves Adjustment Layer and raise the midtones (**figure 7.32**). As you can see, Photoshop has transferred the Lasso selection into the layer mask. The selected area—the sign—is white, so the Curves correction only takes place through the white areas of the mask, lightening the dark sign.

figure 7.31

Select the area you need to change.

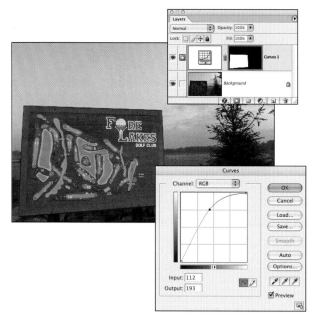

figure 7.32

Adding an Adjustment Layer with an active selection lets you work on the active area without affecting the rest of the image.

3. To soften the transition between the lighter sign and the background, choose Filter > Blur > Gaussian Blur and use a low setting of 1.

All active selections will automatically be transferred into the layer mask when you add an Adjustment Layer, allowing you to fine-tune images with great precision and care. You'll find lots more information on applying tonal and color corrections in one of my other books, *Photoshop Restoration and Retouching*.

MERGING PHOTOGRAPHIC EXPOSURES

Photographers are always looking for better tools and techniques to express their vision and not let the limitations of their tools negatively impact the quality of the final image. Some of the limitations they face include:

- The dynamic range of the scene is wider than what the digital camera or film can capture.
- The lens isn't wide enough to frame the full grandeur of the scene.
- The natural light doesn't illuminate the scene properly.
- The scene contains mixed color temperatures that conflict with one another.

Today photographers still face these challenges, but their tools have improved—they use professional digital cameras and can preview their images on laptops while on location or on set. The huge advantage of working with a professional digital camera is that a photographer can combine a series of exposures or acquire the file with multiple settings in Photoshop to achieve the following:

- Extend the dynamic range
- Expand the view of the scene
- Capture light over time
- Color balance a scene without having to gel or filter the lights or lens

Note that you can achieve similar results when working with film capture. However, the advantage of working with a high-quality digital *RAW file*—which is the native, unprocessed data as it was captured by the camera sensor—and the precision with which you can register the multiple files does give digital capture the definitive upper hand.

Adobe Camera RAW

Many prosumer and professional digital cameras produce RAW files, which offer a number of advantages, including hi-bit depth, lack of compression artifacts, and flexibility in image processing. Check your camera's documentation to determine if it will shoot RAW files.

I use the Adobe Camera RAW feature in Photoshop CS to process RAW files from my Nikon and Fuji cameras. In the example in the following section, we'll process the same RAW file twice to create a well-exposed image.

Luminance Masking

Very often a scene will have too much contrast. No matter how you adjust the camera exposure or tweak the file in software, either the highlights are too bright or the shadows are blocked. To create a file with detail in both the highlights and shadows, start by acquiring the same RAW file twice—once for the highlights and once for the shadows—so that you can capture the best of both images and create an image that has good shadow information and bright highlights with detail.

 ch7_helmet.nef

1. Working with RAW files in Photoshop CS opens the Adobe Camera RAW interface. Use the sliders to process the image so that it captures good highlight information. The shadows will look washed out, but that is fine. Make sure to keep the file in 16-bit (**figure 7.33**) and save it to your hard drive using the name *your subject_light.psd.*

2. Open the original image in Adobe Camera RAW again, but this time process it so that it captures good shadow information (**figure 7.34**). Now the highlights will be completely blown out and without detail—that is OK. Save the file to your hard drive using the name *your subject_dark.psd.*

3. Drag the light file on top of the dark file. Press the Shift key while dragging so that the file lands in perfect registration. Rename the layers to make it easier to keep track of which is which.

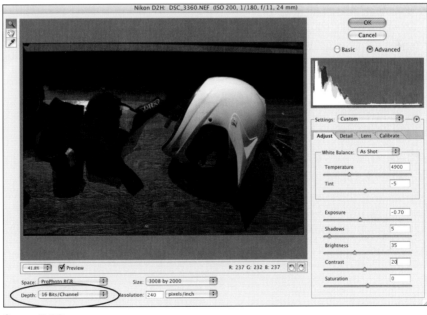

figure 7.33

Acquiring the file for the highlight values.

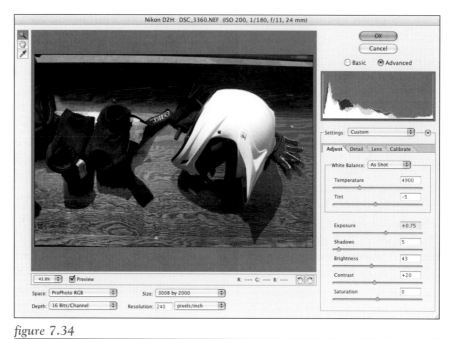

figure 7.34

Acquiring the file for the shadow values.

4. Turn off the highlight layer, click on the dark layer to activate it, and load the image luminosity by pressing (Cmd + Option + ~) [Ctrl + Alt + ~]. If your keyboard doesn't have a tilde key (~), (Cmd-click) [Ctrl-click] on the RGB icon in the Channels palette.

   Loading the luminosity activates the brightness values in each channel that are above 128, and the resulting selection is shown in figure 7.35.

5. Turn on and activate the highlight layer. Click on the Layer Mask button, which transfers the luminosity mask to the layer mask and seamlessly combines the images (figure 7.36).

6. To refine the layer mask, use Curves to darken the mask (figure 7.37). Keep an eye on the image highlights via the Info palette; you don't want them to go above 245. Make sure the helmet maintains subtle tonal detail in the highlights.

figure 7.35

Turn off the top layer and activate the Background layer before loading the image luminosity.

figure 7.36

Turn on the top layer and activate it. Clicking on the Layer Mask button transfers the active selection to the layer mask.

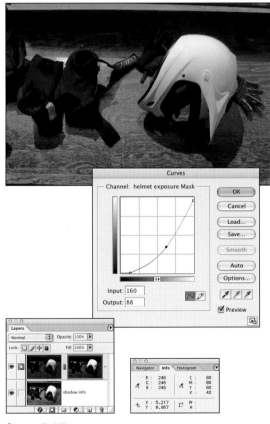

figure 7.37

Adjusting the layer mask using Curves lets you fine-tune the image combination.

7. Adjust the layer opacity for the desired effect. I often experiment at the same time with the layer blending modes to see if the effect is pleasing. To create the final image, I reduced the top layer opacity to 80%.

T i p

After acquiring a RAW file, duplicate it and close the original without saving changes. This lets you reopen the same RAW file without having to save the first one to your hard drive.

Once the images are combined and you've saved the new combination version, you can delete the saved files. All in all, this is a good technique to quickly help you bring image contrast within a printable range—special thanks to Stephen Johnson and Jeff Schewe for showing me this technique.

Emphasizing the Essential

Similar to the luminance-masking technique I just discussed, you can also extend an image's dynamic range to increase image drama by deciding which areas you want to reveal or conceal in creating the final image.

ch7_cloudtower.nef

1. Follow Steps 1 and 2 of the previous task to acquire the same image file twice—once for the highlights, in this example the clouds (figure 7.38), and once for the shadow information of the castle ramparts (figure 7.39). Remember to save the first file after you acquire it to your hard drive so that you can open the original RAW file again with different Camera RAW settings.

2. Drag the images into one file, add a layer mask, and use the Gradient tool to initially combine the images (figure 7.40).

3. Use a large soft, black brush to paint over the towers to complete the photograph, as shown in figure 7.41.

This technique is useful for accentuating specific image areas with the ability to paint information back and forth via the layer mask.

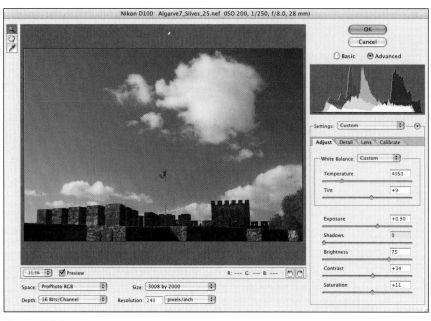

figure 7.38

Acquiring the file for the highlight values.

figure 7.39

Acquiring the file for the shadow information of the tower stone.

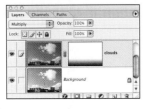

figure 7.40

Use the Gradient tool on the layer mask to create the initial image combination.

figure 7.41

Painting over the towers in the layer mask with a soft black brush allows the shadow information to show through.

Increasing Dynamic Range

John Warner is the consummate professional photographer—skilled, talented, creative, conscientious, and always ready to try new tools and techniques to produce better images. Having worked for over 20 years with film technology, John is now an avowed digital photographer who takes great pleasure in planning, composing, and compositing images. One of John's specialties is interior and exterior architectural photography—a field that brings many constraints and challenges with it. For example, it's pretty hard to move a building to face the light, or to close the window to control the exposure, when the client wants to simultaneously see the beautiful view and the interior of the room.

John photographs with high-end, digital cameras. After framing the image, he locks down the camera on the tripod and takes separate exposures for shadows, midtones, and highlights to create images that hold information from the darkest shadows to the brightest highlights.

Caution

When photographing multiple exposures, it is very important to set the camera to either manual exposure or Aperture Priority, both of which let the photographer set the f-stop (the aperture) and adjust exposure by changing the shutter speed. The slightest variation in f-stop will change the depth of field and the size of the subject in the image ever so slightly, making it more difficult to seamlessly combine the images.

Combining Exposures Using Layers and Masks

After photographing two exposures for the bedroom scene—one for the room (**figure 7.42**) and one for the exterior setting sun (**figure 7.43**)—John acquired and saved each file with the respective names *outside* and *inside*, and then blended them in Photoshop as follows:

Red

figure 7.42

John always exposes for the brightest values first, which in turn determine the ensuing exposures.

Green

figure 7.43

The exposure for the window light.

Blue

figure 7.44

The blue channel has the clearest window definition.

1. After bringing the two exposures into one file, John needs to mask the windows to combine the two exposures. He inspected the three channels of the inside layer and saw that the blue channel had the clearest window information (**figure 7.44**).

2. He duplicated the blue channel and increased its contrast with Curves (**figure 7.45**). He then selected all the nonessential image area—everything that is not window—and filled it with black (**figure 7.46**).

3. Returning to the Layers palette, John activated the window alpha channel using (Cmd + Option + 4) [Ctrl + Alt + 4]. He made sure the inside layer was active and clicked the Layer Mask button, which transferred the active selection to the layer mask (**figure 7.47**).

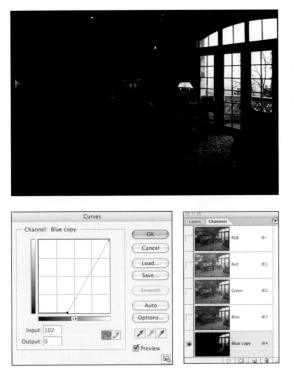

figure 7.47

After transferring the alpha mask to the layer mask.

4. John inverted the layer mask to reveal the room interior (**figure 7.48**).

5. Upon careful inspection, John refined the layer mask using a slight Gaussian Blur and a bit of painting to repair any unsightly seams to create the final image shown in **figure 7.49**.

figure 7.45

Increasing the contrast using Curves makes the alpha mask denser and better defined.

figure 7.46

Areas that don't contain window information are filled with black.

figure 7.48

Inverting the layer mask reveals the window exposure.

figure 7.49

The final image.

All in all, this technique works best with static subjects such as buildings and still lives. In the example shown in **figure 7.50**, the final image required three separate exposures: the room interior, the outside scene, and the fireplace. John then combined the three exposures and added a few additional flames to the fire to make the room even more inviting.

Combining Color Temperature

Photographing an interior scene with natural daylight coming in through the windows has always been a challenge for architectural photographers. This is because in most cases the room is lit with tungsten light, which has a color temperature of 3,400 degrees Kelvin and is inherently orange. The daylight coming through the windows is approximately 5,500 degrees Kelvin and is much bluer than the tungsten light.

To compensate for this, the photographer could either cover the windows with expensive gels (filters) to bring the color temperature down, or use daylight-balanced light to illuminate the interior, which in turn would conflict in color temperature with the room's lighting fixtures.

Working with a Canon digital camera, Mark Beckelman developed an elegant solution that requires him to photograph the scene only once as a RAW file, acquire the file three times in Adobe Camera RAW with different color temperature settings, and then combine the separate files as described here:

 ch7_kitcheninterior.jpg

ch7_kitchenexterior.jpg

ch7_kitchenstove.jpg

figure 7.50

After photographing the scene three times, John Warner combined the exposures to create this final image.

1. Mark shoots only in the RAW file format, which yields both higher image quality and greater creative interpretation upon acquiring the file. In this instance he acquired the same image three times (**figure 7.51**)—once with tungsten for the interior scene, once with daylight color balance for the exterior light seen through the windows, and once as a darker version that maintained the detail in the bright wall above the stove.

Interior exposure

Exterior exposure

Highlight exposure

figure 7.51

Acquiring the same exposure three times using different Camera RAW settings is the foundation of the composite.

2. Using the primary interior exposure as the Background layer, he Shift-dragged the window layer on top and named the layer *window*.

3. Mark outlined the windows with the Pen tool, turned the path into a selection, and clicked the Layer Mask button of the window layer, which added a layer mask. The mask reveals only the windows (**figure 7.52**) and now combines the daylight-balanced exterior with the interior.

figure 7.52

Combining the interior with the exterior exposures.

4. Mark noticed some daylight spill (**figure 7.53**) that was contaminating the scene. He removed it by painting on the window layer mask with a low-opacity, soft white brush to reveal the color-corrected layer.

5. After Shift-dragging the stove highlight file onto the composite, he (Option-clicked) [Alt-clicked] on the Layer Mask button to add a black layer mask that concealed the entire layer. He then subtly painted back the highlights with a low-opacity, soft-edged white brush (**figure 7.54**).

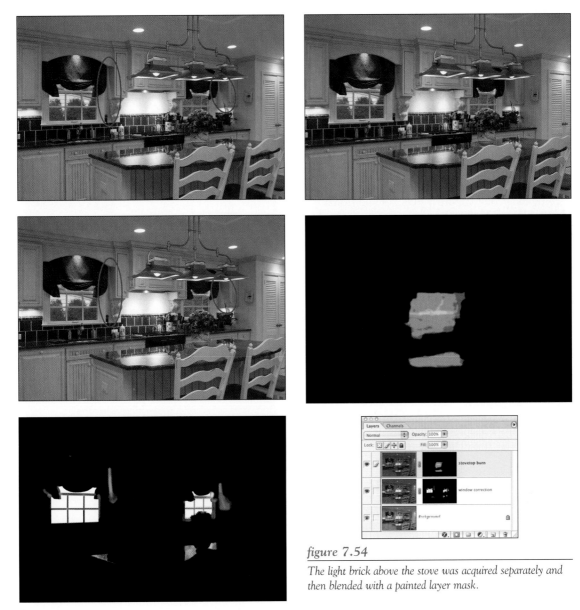

figure 7.54

The light brick above the stove was acquired separately and then blended with a painted layer mask.

figure 7.53

Light has a tendency to spread and spill, which can be corrected with layer masking.

Removing Color Contamination

Being the accomplished professional that he is, Mark noticed a few hints of blue, caused by the daylight that hit the reflective surfaces of the lighting fixtures and on the kitchen counters (**figure 7.55**). He used the following sophisticated technique to neutralize the color spill:

1. After zooming in on the blue, Mark added a Photo Filter Adjustment Layer, clicked on the square Color picker, and sampled the offending blue color (**figure 7.56**). For additional information on working with the Photo Filter Adjustment Layer feature, see Chapter 12, "Photorealistic Compositing."

2. To neutralize the blue, he needed the exact opposite color, which is only possible to calculate with the LAB values. *LAB* is a color mode that defines the image as Luminance and two color channels. It is used to calculate color relationships. If the A or B values are positive, making them negative, or vice versa, will flip the color values exactly to the opposite (**figure 7.57**). To neutralize the color completely, Mark increased the density of the color correction to 100%.

3. He then inverted the layer mask and painted over the offending blue with a small, soft-edged white brush to remove the color along the kitchen curtain and the chrome lights (**figure 7.58**).

figure 7.55

Paying attention to the smallest reflections and color details is part of being a professional photographer.

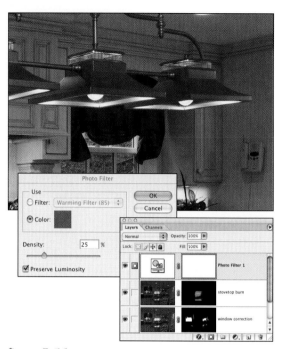

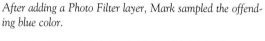

figure 7.56

After adding a Photo Filter layer, Mark sampled the offending blue color.

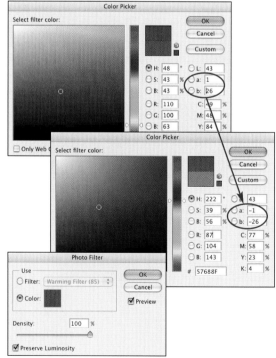

figure 7.57

Invert the A and B values to create the opposite color.

figure 7.58

Painting away the blue reflections polishes the image.

Creative Color Interpretations

Accentuating color temperature differences can add a beautiful creative twist to your images. Figure 7.59 shows the same camera RAW file acquired twice—once with daylight settings and once with interpretive color settings. As John Warner explains, "The first version is color balanced as if the light source were near tungsten, so the Blue Ridge Mountains become very blue. For the second version, I re-adjusted the Adobe Camera RAW settings to yield a smoky sepia and dialed down the exposure to keep the sky from burning out."

After acquiring and saving both files, John Shift-dragged the warmer file onto the blue file, and added a layer mask to the top file (the warmer file). He then used a large, soft brush to paint in the sepia tones. After changing the blending mode of the sky to Color, the image comes together (figure 7.60).

figure 7.59

Acquiring the same camera RAW file twice using different color balance settings.

figure 7.60

Combining the two color-interpreted files using a layer mask creates a hauntingly beautiful image.

Note

You can use the Mergenator script to automatically combine files that were acquired with different color temperature or exposure settings. Developed by Thomas Ruark and Julieanne Kost from Adobe Systems, Mergenator makes layered documents on which you apply layer masking to create the final image. To use the Mergenator, first install the script into the Presets/Scripts folder, make three folders (for example, Color 1, Color 2, and Done), and then select File > Script > Mergenator (figure 7.61) to create a new composite image without your having to open and drag the images manually.

⊕▷← **ch7_Mergenator.sit**

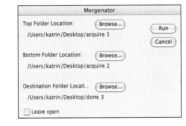

figure 7.61

To automatically combine the images, point the Mergenator Script at the two images containing the color-interpreted files and the composite folder.

Extending the Time of Day

For me, watching a sunset is as good as watching a thrilling Hollywood movie. But often when I photograph the scene, I'm disappointed by the results. In most cases, this is because either the sky looks good but the landscape is too dark, or the landscape looks good but the sky is washed out.

In the following example, John Warner set up his camera on a rooftop high above Asheville, North Carolina, and made two separate exposures—one for the cityscape, which required a longer shutter speed to capture the shadow detail, and one for the sunset. For a first-person commentary from John about the differences between getting multiple exposures using film versus digital, see the sidebar.

Obtaining Multiple Exposures Using Film and Digital: An Imagemaker Reflects

"When I worked with sheet film and a 4 × 5 Sinar view camera, doing double exposures on the same piece of film was tedious at best. It required exposing for the mountains and the sky at sunset, which left the city buildings looking like dark cardboard cutouts. After the sun went down, I had to keep the camera absolutely still for another hour until the sky was black and the city lights were gleaming. Then with a 40 magenta filter over the lens, I would re-photograph the scene for 8 minutes to 'burn' the city lights into the dark building shapes. Because the sky was black, no additional exposure would wash out the sunset, sky, and mountains. Of course, with this technique I had only one chance per sunset to get it right.

"Digital is far more forgiving. The approach is essentially the same as with film—it requires getting a good sunset shot that correctly exposes the sky and the mountains but leaves the foreground buildings as dark objects. About 45 minutes after sunset, I capture some additional shots exposing for the city lights (figure 7.62). Using Adobe Camera RAW, I can correct the color balance of the artificial lights away from their greenish cast, which eliminates the need for the 40 magenta filter. Shift-dragging the night exposure over to the sunset using the Lighten blending mode completes the composite. Another key advantage of digital is having multiple sunset frames to choose from, unlike the film example where you get one per session."

—John Warner

To combine the multiple exposures of the sunset scene, John did the following:

1. After Shift-dragging the city file onto the sunset file, John added a layer mask and used a large, soft-edged, black brush at 35% opacity to paint over the sky, which concealed the washed-out sky and revealed the properly exposed sky.

2. To boost the saturation of the sunset, he added a Hue/Saturation layer and increased the saturation by 30% to create the final image (figure 7.63).

figure 7.62

The proper sky exposure is on the top, while the proper city lights exposure is on the bottom.

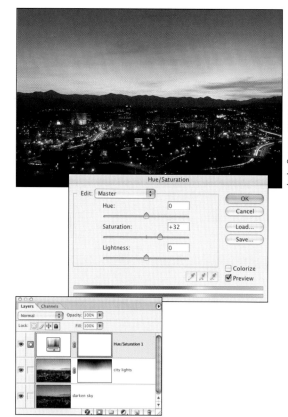

© John Warner Photography

figure 7.63

After blending the two exposures together, John used a Hue/Saturation layer to saturate the sky.

Modeling Architecture Using Light

One of the best aspects of working on a book like this is the opportunity to learn from many different imagemakers. Take a look at the home in **figure 7.64**. Now take a look at the seven separate photographs John took to capture the best light for the various aspects of the home, from the façade he lit with portable flash units; to the rooms where he used a warmer, more inviting light; to the exposures for the driveway, the sky, and the mountains in the background (**figure 7.65**).

figure 7.64

The final composite was created from seven separate exposures.

figure 7.65

The seven component images were shot over a three-hour time period.

John arrived a few hours before sunset to find the best angle to photograph the house and to plan the lighting. As he told me, "I always begin with the exposures of the exterior first, as they are the overall brightest elements in the image."

1. After downloading the files, John identified the best exposures for each element of the building. Starting with the initial exposure, he added the sky file and painted away the driveway with the layer mask and a soft-edged brush (figure 7.66).

2. He then added the lighter layers for the façade and room lights, all of which he set to the Lighten blending mode and adjusted the opacity to lighten the areas without overexposing them (figure 7.67).

3. John added the roof exposure and a layer mask and then painted away everything except the roof (figure 7.68).

4. He used two layers to enhance the driveway. Finishing touches included removing the distracting stripe of lights along the walkway and color correcting the stones on the right side of the frame to create the image shown in figure 7.69.

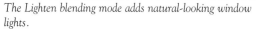

figure 7.67

The Lighten blending mode adds natural-looking window lights.

figure 7.66

Using the initial exposure as a guide, the sky is added.

figure 7.68

The roof was photographed earlier in the day.

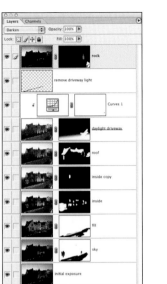

figure 7.69

The final composite.

Extending the Seasons

Photographing a large subject over time requires patience—but the results are certainly worth it as the photograph of the Biltmore Estate in Asheville, North Carolina, reveals. Taken over a period of a few months, the final composite combines a night shot with a late spring photograph in which the trees frame the estate (**figure 7.70**) to create the final composite shown in **figure 7.71**.

figure 7.70

Photographed over a period of a few months, the two images each carry important information.

© John Warner Photography

figure 7.71

The final composite is a stunning example of combined images.

Tip

To photograph the same subject over the course of days, weeks, or months, it is necessary to triangulate the tripod. After you set up the first shot, measure and write down the height from the tripod head to the ground. Then measure and note two vertical distances to fixed objects and the tripod head. If you use a zoom lens, also note the exact zoom setting you used. In the example of the Biltmore Estate, John was standing between two columns which he used as anchor points to triangulate the exact position of the tripod head so that he could return months later and set up in the same spot.

CLOSING THOUGHTS

Remember, if you want to conceal an area, paint the layer mask with black; if you want to reveal more of a certain area, the layer mask must be white. That's all there is to it—so grab a few files, stack them on top of one another, add some layer masks, and then start painting to hide, reveal, and conceal the image areas. I promise that if you do this a few times, you'll become a happy Photoshopper who can finally say, "I get it!" More importantly, you'll enjoy working with Photoshop more.

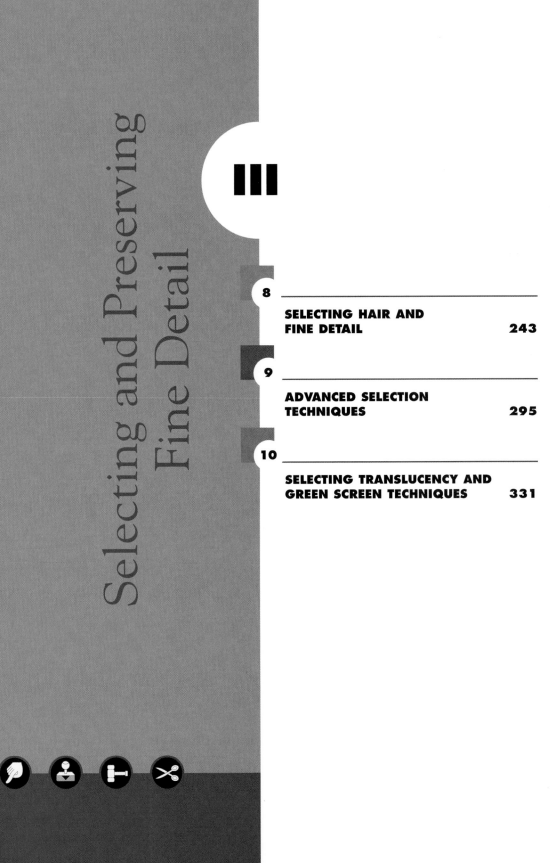

III

Selecting and Preserving
Fine Detail

   **8**

SELECTING HAIR AND FINE DETAIL

When it comes to silhouetting people with a full head of hair, animals with fur, or scenes with fine detail, I sometimes wish that everyone was as bald as Michael Jordan, that all animals were fish, and that I worked only with pictures of skyscrapers. But of course we don't live in a world where smooth selections play a key role in evolutionary development.

Making selections of fine details requires patience, practice, and creative thinking. One technique may work perfectly well on one type of image but not on another. You may need to combine techniques, and most of the time you'll need to fine-tune the mask with careful handiwork.

In this chapter you'll learn about

- Using Adjustment Layers to enhance a selection
- Discovering the mask in each image
- Using painting tools and blending modes to maintain detail
- Working with the Extract feature

When extracting fine details, sharp high-quality and high-resolution originals, in which the figure is in contrast to the background, yield the best results. If you plan on taking someone's picture for a composite, preparing the lighting, the point of view, and the background are essential to success (see Chapter 11, "Image Execution and Photography").

ACCENTUATING DIFFERENCES

The primary goal when separating images with fine detail from the background is to maintain as much detail as possible. The concept of preserving detail is so important that this chapter focuses solely on how to accentuate existing image information by separating light and dark areas, while maintaining subtle transitional tones. In the end it amounts to creating a silhouette that looks like it was precisely cut using a fine-edged scalpel rather than shredded with dull hedge clippers.

Thinking in Black and White

All Photoshop masks are black and white with shades of gray. When you make a mask based on a complicated subject, imagining the image in high-contrast black and white is very helpful. While making a fine mask, it may even look like you're ruining the image with excessive contrast, but as long as you use empty layers and Adjustment Layers, the original image will not be affected. In the following two examples, I'll show you how to use high-contrast Adjustment Layers to build a mask with fine detail.

Figure 8.1 shows an original studio photograph of a little girl by Mark Beckelman. One of the first steps in compositing this photo with a new background was to separate the girl from the studio background. A bad cutout job can really call attention to itself, as shown in figure 8.2—the telltale fringing and lack of detail attest to a poorly made silhouette. Figure 8.3 shows the same image with a silhouette that separates the girl from the background while maintaining the strands of hair.

The first selection was done with the Magic Wand tool, while the second selection was created with a combination of Adjustment Layers and painting. All in all, the second selection only took a few minutes more, but the results are certainly worth it (figure 8.4).

⊕▷← **ch8_water_girl.jpg**

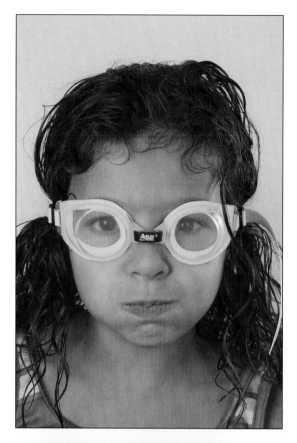

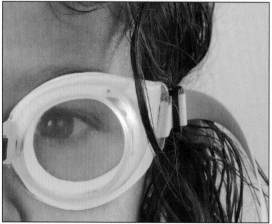

figure 8.1

The original photograph and a close-up of the hair.

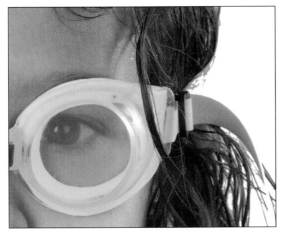

figure 8.2

The Magic Wand does not maintain fine detail.

figure 8.3

A good hair mask maintains delicate details.

figure 8.4

The final composite.

Although the little girl was correctly photographed with a simple, white background—separating her from it will require a number of steps. One way to approach such an image is to temporarily increase the tonal difference between the subject, in this case the little girl, and the background using a Curves Adjustment Layer to separate the subject from the background. The goal is to make a high-contrast black-and-white image that maintains edge transitions.

1. Add a Curves Adjustment Layer. To force the background to pure white, use the white eye-dropper and click on the studio backdrop.

2. Keep an eye on the tonal transitions of the hair along the side of the head as you move the shadow point to the right along the bottom of the Curve graph (**figure 8.5**). You can increase the contrast by moving the midpoint to the left. If your curve is too steep or you force the midpoint too far to the left or right, the delicate details and tonal transitions of the hair will be lost.

   As you work through these steps, it may look as if you are ruining the image. Don't worry—working with Adjustment Layers does not degrade actual image information. What you're actually doing is creating a false contrast so that you can focus on the transition details between hair and background to skillfully silhouette the girl.

3. Add a new layer by clicking on the New Layer icon on the Layers palette. This empty surface is the working surface for the upcoming steps, which involve making a simple selection with the Lasso and Pen tools and filling and painting to refine the mask in progress.

4. With the freeform Lasso tool, encircle the inside of the girl's head (**figure 8.6**), making sure you don't get too close to the edge of the head or include gaps in her hair where the backdrop shows through.

5. Select Edit > Fill > Use Black at 100% to fill the selection with pure black as shown in **figure 8.7**. Choose Select > Deselect (Cmd + D) [Ctrl + D] to drop the selection.

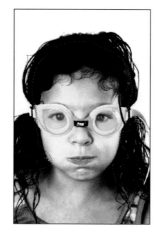

figure 8.6

When selecting the inside of the figure, be careful not to include important transition areas.

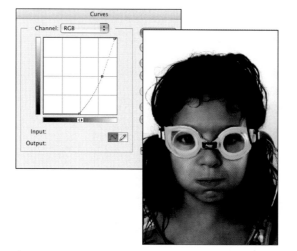

figure 8.5

Exaggerate the tonal contrast with Curves.

figure 8.7

Filling the selection with black.

6. To soften the transition between what was selected and the head, use a brush with 50% hardness and paint with black to create a subtle transition between the solidly filled area and the edges of the girl's hair (**figure 8.8**). It is important to stay inside of the head and not to paint over the hair detail.

7. The smooth-edged swimming goggles are ideal candidates for the Pen tool. Outline both the left and right side of the goggles and straps. Then after turning the paths into a selection, fill the active selection with black, as shown in **figure 8.9**.

figure 8.9

Select smooth-edged elements, such as the swimming goggles, with the Pen tool and fill with black.

8. Carefully inspect the transition areas between the head and the background. When I worked with this image, I noticed that the area on the lower-right side of the background was not completely white (**figure 8.10**). This problem can cause ghosting artifacts in a composite. To lighten up these delicate areas, create a new working surface that has all of the tones on it with the following technique. Add a new layer to the top of the layer stack. To merge all visible layers up, hold down (Option) [Alt] while selecting Layer > Merge Visible.

figure 8.8

Use a soft-edged brush to transition between the filled area and the edge of the hair.

figure 8.10

The background is not white, which will cause ghosting later in the process.

9. Now lighten up the telltale areas by using a soft-edged Dodge tool, set to Highlights and 5% to 10% exposure. Brush over the lighter areas once or twice to lighten just the background, as shown in **figure 8.11**.

   Now we have a black-and-white rendition of the image on a layer, but we need to transfer it into the layer mask to separate the girl from the background.

10. Open the Channels palette and (Cmd + Option-click) [Ctrl + Alt-click] the RGB icon or use the shortcut (Cmd + Option + ~) [Ctrl + Alt + ~] to load the layer luminosity as a selection (**figure 8.12**).

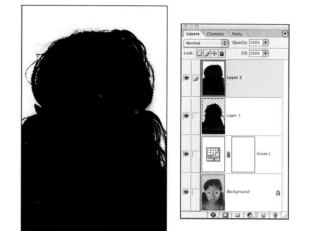

figure 8.12

Activating the layer so that it's a selection.

11. A background layer cannot support a layer mask, which is why you need to convert it to a standard layer. Return to the Layers palette, turn off all the layers except for the Background layer, and double-click the Background layer. Click OK and click on the Layer Mask icon to transfer the active selection into the layer mask (**figure 8.13**), which silhouettes the background but not the little girl. To invert the layer mask and silhouette the little girl perfectly, click the layer mask and select Image > Adjustments > Invert (Cmd + I) [Ctrl + I], as shown in **figure 8.14**.

12. If you are satisfied with the hair mask, delete the production layers you used to make the mask by choosing Delete Hidden Layers from the Layer palette fly-out menu. Choose File > Save As and use either the TIFF or Photoshop file format, which maintains the layer and mask.

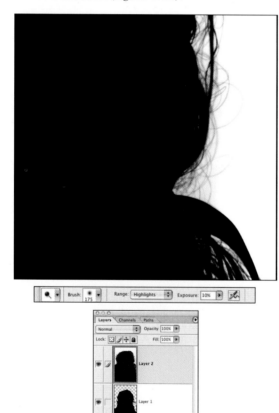

figure 8.11

To change light areas to white, paint with a low-exposure Dodge tool that is set to Highlight.

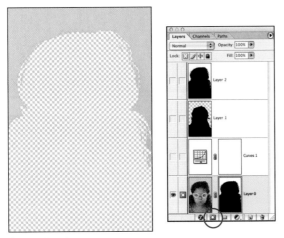

figure 8.13

After transferring the selection to the layer mask, you may need to invert it.

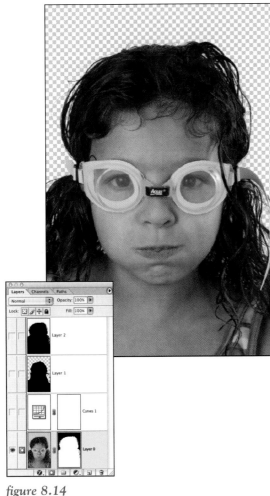

figure 8.14

Inverting the layer mask lets you see the little girl.

Exaggerating Differences Using Blending Modes

It would make my life a lot easier if all the portrait photographs I work with had an evenly lit, texture-free, contrasting background—but life has a tendency to be complex, and our snapshots reflect that.

Figure 8.15 is a classic snapshot of a happy mother with an even happier baby, standing in front of the family car. The challenges of this image are threefold—a busy background, a lack of contrast between the subjects' hair and the dark background, and the mother's fly-away hair. All of these factors make this a challenging, yet not impossible, mask to make. Rather than thinking about all the problems it presents—try thinking in black and white about separating image elements from one another to gracefully solve this challenge.

© Mark Beckelman

figure 8.15

The original photograph captures a candid moment.

In the following example, we will use a Channel Mixer Adjustment Layer and layer blending modes to boost contrast while maintaining edge detail. The idea is to quickly create as much contrast as possible and then use the fill and painting tools to refine the details. In the process, you'll add a number of nondestructive production layers to build up the mask. Finally, we'll take the family on a trip to a park and use the Lens Blur filter to defocus the trees, as shown in figure 8.16.

🌐⮑ **ch8_mother_child.jpg**

🌐⮑ **ch8_trees.jpg**

figure 8.16

Simplifying the background subliminally encourages the viewer to concentrate on the people in the picture.

Building the Initial Mask

1. Open the Channels palette and look at the individual channels. You can do this by clicking on each channel name or using (Cmd + 1, Cmd + 2, Cmd + 3) [Ctrl + 1, Ctrl + 2, Ctrl + 3]. Look for the channels with the most contrast and the smoothest tonality. In this image, both the red and the green channels contain contrast (**figure 8.17**) that we can take advantage of and accentuate to make a mask. Click RGB or (Cmd + ~) [Ctrl + ~] to return back to the color image.

2. To apply the "thinking in black and white" approach, add a Channel Mixer Adjustment Layer, select the monochrome box, and move the red and green sliders to the right. In this instance, I used the extreme values of +100 for red and +132 for green (**figure 8.18**).

3. To push the contrast even higher, take advantage of layer blending modes, which impact how the layers interact. The contrast-enhancing group is the largest group, beginning with Overlay. In this case, choose Hard Light as shown in **figure 8.19**, which screens the lighter areas, making them lighter, and multiplies the darker values, making them darker.

   The Channel Mixer layer is the foundation of the mask, but the contrast can be even stronger. In the next step, we'll experiment with additional blending modes to increase the effect.

Red channel

Green channel

Blue channel

figure 8.17

Look for the channel with the most contrast and smoothest tonal range.

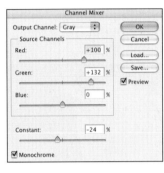

figure 8.19

Changing the Layer blending mode increases the contrast even more.

figure 8.18

To increase the difference between dark and light, use the Channel Mixer Adjustment Layer.

4. To create a new layer and merge all visible layers up, select Layer > New > Layer or (Cmd + Option + Shift + N) [Ctrl + Alt + Shift + N], followed by (Option) [Alt] Layer > Merge Visible (Cmd + Option + Shift + E) [Ctrl + Alt + Shift + E].

5. To increase the contrast, change the blending mode to Screen (**figure** 8.20), which will further accentuate the difference between the people and the background. Of course when you try this technique on your own images, a different blending mode may be more effective.

figure 8.20

Using multiple layers and experimenting with blending modes is an effective method for building contrast.

6. To make the entire background black and the people white, add a new layer and select areas of the image background with either the Lasso or Marquee tool (**figure 8.21**). Select Edit > Fill > Use Black to fill the selected area with black (Option + Delete) [Alt + Delete]. Continue selecting and filling with black, making sure that you don't select any hair or clothing.

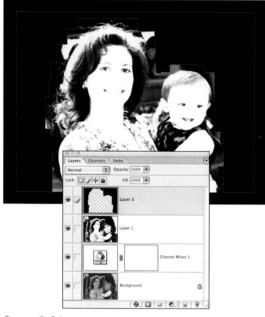

figure 8.21

Select the background area and fill with black.

7. Select the inside of the mother and child with the Lasso tool. Try not to get too close to the edge of the hair (**figure 8.22**). Press *x* to switch the foreground color to white and (Option + Delete) [Alt + Delete] to fill the selected area with white (**figure 8.23**).

8. To create a new layer and merge all visible layers up, (Cmd + Option + Shift + N) [Ctrl + Alt + Shift + N], followed by (Cmd + Option + Shift + E) [Ctrl + Alt + Shift + E].

Tip

To speed up the selecting and filling with black, press *d* to reset the Color picker to black and white and use (Option + Delete) [Alt + Delete] to fill with the foreground color.

figure 8.22

When making the selection, stay away from important edge detail.

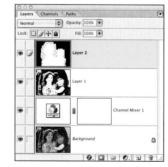

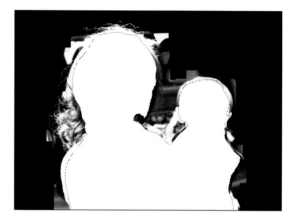

figure 8.23

Select the insides of the people and fill with white.

Tip

For the "add new layer and merge all visible layers up" technique to work, it is very important that the topmost layer in the layer stack is active before you add the new layer.

Fine-Tuning Transitions

Most of the work is done, but now we need to be a bit more careful as we blend between the filled areas and the fine-detail areas with the Dodge, Burn, and Paint Brush tools. The Dodge tool lightens and the Burn tool darkens image information. Although I rarely use them on a color image, I do use these tools all the time to enhance tonal information in masks.

Tip

All of the Photoshop painting tools, except for the Pencil tool, can have hard or soft edges. With any brush active, (Cmd-click) [right-click] opens the brush's context-sensitive menu to increase or decrease brush hardness. The 0% setting represents very soft, while 100% represents hard-edged. Use the hardness settings to match the edge quality of the subject you are working on.

Figure 8.24 shows the area by the little boy's head that needs greater tonal difference between him and the background. The lighter areas need to be even lighter and the dark areas need to be even darker.

figure 8.24

Refining the mask will maintain valuable edge information.

1. To lighten the boy's head, set the Dodge tool to Highlights and 5% to 10% exposure, and then use a soft-edged brush to gently dodge along inside his head (**figure 8.25**). When using the Dodge and Burn tools, it helps to release the mouse button or lift the Wacom stylus to start working on new areas.

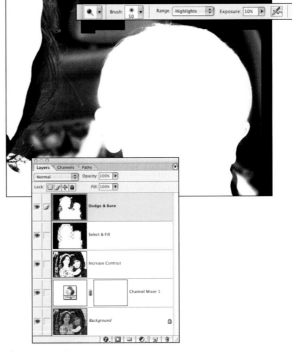

figure 8.25

Dodge the light areas.

2. Switch to the Burn tool. Change the range to Shadows and exposure to 5% to 10%, and then brush along the outside of the little boy's head to make the dark areas even darker (**figure 8.26**).

figure 8.26

To increase tonal difference, burn the dark areas.

3. Keep switching between the Dodge and Burn tools (O and Shift + O) to lighten the light areas and darken the dark areas, throughout the entire image.

4. Some areas of this image are not very well defined, such as the area by the boy's shoulders (figure 8.27). Use a white or black soft-edged brush to paint in the tonal transition (figure 8.28). If it is difficult to see where to paint, reduce the layer opacity to 50%, turn off the lower production layers to see through to the Background layer, and then trace along the contours (figure 8.29). Increase the layer opacity to 100% to see the results (figure 8.30).

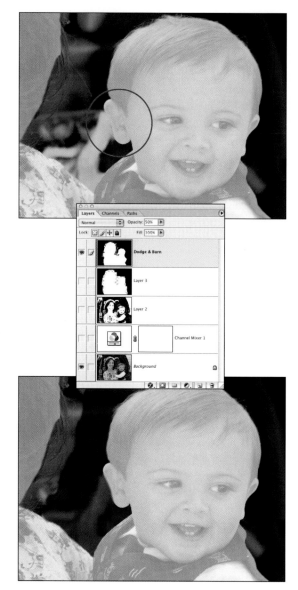

figure 8.29

Temporarily lowering the layer opacity to see through to the image is helpful when painting in edges.

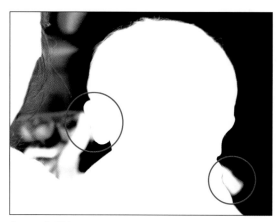

figure 8.27

Areas that are not clearly differentiated need to be hand-painted.

figure 8.28

The result of painting in the correct contour of the shoulder.

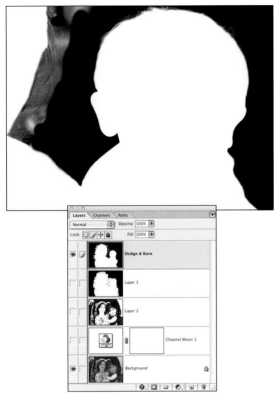

figure 8.30

Return to 100% opacity to see the results.

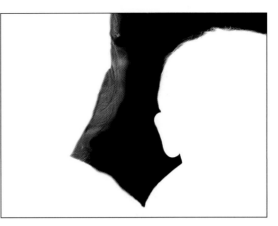

figure 8.31

A challenging area, which doesn't have very much tonal difference.

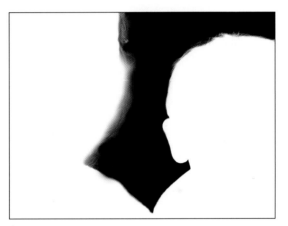

figure 8.32

Insinuating hair with a soft-edged brush.

5. The areas by the woman's shoulder offer a challenge, since the tonal difference isn't very great as shown in **figure 8.31**. In these cases, you can either opt to draw in every hair by hand or paint in a transition with a large soft brush, as I did in **figure 8.32**. Keep in mind, our task is to create a believable hair mask. Sometimes it's better to insinuate a transition than to use a lot of time on areas that may not be very important or that you can fix better later, when the new background is added.

6. After completing the mask as shown in **figure 8.33**, open the Channels palette and (Cmd + Option-click) [Ctrl + Alt-click] on the RGB icon. Or, use (Cmd + Option + ~) [Ctrl + Alt + ~] to load the layer as a selection.

figure 8.33

The completed mask.

7. Return to the Layers palette, turn off all the layers except for the Background layer, and double-click the Background Layer icon. Click OK and then click the Layer Mask icon to transfer the active selection into the layer. You should now see the family with a transparent background (**figure 5.34**). It is now safe to discard all the layers used to make the mask. Select Edit > Save As and save the file with a new name, such as *family with mask*, and choose the Photoshop or TIFF file format.

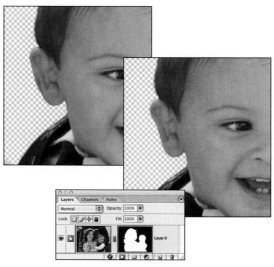

figure 8.35

Working on the layer mask refines the silhouette.

Working with Adjustment Layers and blending modes to build image contrast and then using the tonal and painting tools to define the differences helps in creating realistic masks.

Adding the New Background

By replacing the background, you change the environment and mood of the image, which is really where the creative fun begins. In this example, I opted to take the family on a trip to a park, but I could have used an abstract texture or a studio backdrop. This all depends on the look and feel you are trying to create. To unite the elements cohesively, it is better to try to replace the old background with a similarly toned one. This will reduce the need for cleanup later in the process.

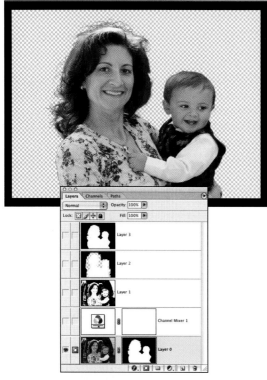

figure 8.34

After transferring the mask to the figure layer, the background is completely concealed.

8. **Figure 8.35** reveals I missed the correct contour of the little boy's right ear. To refine the mask, click the layer mask and paint with black—to hide more background—or with white—to reveal more layer information, in this case the little boy's ear.

1. Drag the new background—in this case the tree file—over to the family with mask file. Position the tree layer underneath the family layer by dragging it underneath the family in the Layers palette.

2. Press *f* to enter full-screen mode. Select Edit > Transform > Scale to size the trees up to fill the entire frame and position them as shown in **figure 8.36**. (I find scaling and transforming to be simpler to do when working in full-screen mode.)

figure 8.36

Scale and position the new background.

The trees are visually busy and distracting. By throwing them out of focus with the Lens Blur filter (available only in Photoshop CS), you can mimic the classic photographic technique of photographing portraits using a wide-open aperture to blur the background and focus attention on the people. When using the Lens Blur filter, a layer mask or alpha channel will create the most realistic results.

3. Activate the mother and child layer, click on the Channels palette, and drag the mother and child layer mask to the Mask icon to transfer it into an alpha channel (figure 8.37).

4. We need to protect the mother and child from getting blurred. Select Image > Adjustments > Invert (figure 8.38) to invert the channel mask, click on RGB, and then return to the Layers palette. With the trees layer active, select Filter > Blur > Lens Blur.

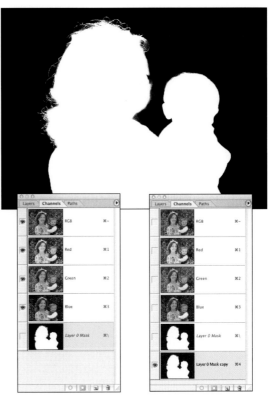

figure 8.37

Transfer the layer mask into the alpha channel.

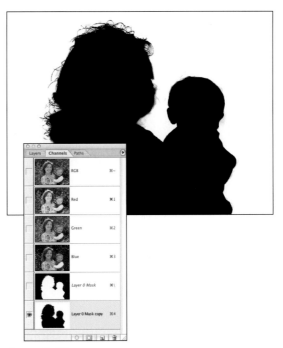

figure 8.38

Invert the layer mask, so that it is white where you need to see trees and black where the people are.

5. In the Depth Map Source section at the top of the Lens Blur dialog box, choose Layer 0 Mask Copy (**figure 8.39**). The Blur Focal Distance below this setting adjusts what is in focus and how large the orbs of light will be that you throw out of focus. In this instance, leave this setting at 0 for now.

6. Choose an Iris shape. I recommend hexagon or octagon. The other choices will seem unnatural because lenses usually don't have triangular or square blade configurations. The higher the Radius setting, the larger the aperture shape; the higher the Blade Curvature setting, the rounder the shape. Adjust these settings as desired, or as shown in **figure 8.40**.

figure 8.39

Select the alpha mask as the Depth Map.

figure 8.40

Choose an iris shape and radius amount.

7. The Specular Highlight settings are really where the Lens Blur magic takes place. The Brightness slider adjusts the brightness of the highlights; the Threshold slider tells Photoshop which highlight values to blur. By reducing the Threshold setting to 230, Photoshop creates aperture-shaped highlights on all brightness values above 230 and makes them as bright as the Brightness setting you choose (**figure 8.41**).

8. For the Noise settings, I recommend adding a hint of Monochromatic Gaussian Noise with a setting of 2 to avoid the overly smooth computer-blurred look. But all in all, how you use these sliders is really up to you and the effect you are trying to achieve. When you are finished, click OK and let Photoshop process the magic to create the image (**figure 8.42**).

figure 8.41

The Specular Highlights are controlled using Brightness and Threshold settings.

figure 8.42

The final image with a new background is perfect for framing and display.

9. To retouch any obvious edges, you have two choices: To clone over any visible edges, you can add a new layer above the woman and child layer, select the Clone tool, and select Use All Layers in the Options bar. To soften harsh transitions, you can refine the layer mask with the painting and blurring tools.

Making the mask, adding the new background, and refining the edges require patience and a caring eye. But when you see the look on your client's faces or family's surprise when you show them the new portraits, all the work is well worth it.

Masking with Shadow/Highlight

Introduced with Photoshop CS, Shadow/Highlight is a fantastic feature for correcting exposure and contrast problems. Lately I've been using it to create tonal difference on images. For instance, if I'm working on dark subjects on dark backgrounds, I'll use Shadow/Highlight as the first step in making the hair selection (figure 8.43). Again, this technique may make it seem as though you are ruining the image, but as long as you build the contrast using layers, the original image will not be altered in any way.

ch8_teenager.jpg

© Mark Beckelman

figure 8.43

The original image with a very dark background.

Creating the Silhouette

1. Duplicate the Background layer, select Image > Adjustments > Shadow/Highlight, and click Show More Options.

2. Because you are accentuating the shadow information of the background to separate the teenager's head, set the Highlights corrections to 0%.

3. Adjust the Shadows settings to lighten the dark background as much as possible. As you can see in **figure 8.44**, his hair is more visible now.

figure 8.44

Use Shadow/Highlight on a duplicate layer to lighten the shadow information.

4. Change the Layer blending mode to Color Dodge, which increases the contrast while preserving the black values (figure 8.45). In this example, I opted to add a Curves Adjustment Layer and increased the contrast further, which forces the dark values to pure black (figure 8.46). Remember, the goal is to make a high-contrast, black-and-white image.

5. Add a new layer and use the Marquee tool or Lasso tool to select large chunks of the background (after making the first selection, hold Shift to add to the selection) and select Edit > Fill > Use Black, to create the layer shown in figure 8.47.

figure 8.46

A Curves Adjustment Layer is used to make the whites whiter and the darks even darker.

figure 8.45

Changing the Layer blending mode to Color Dodge boosts the contrast even more.

figure 8.47

Filling the selection with black quickly blocks out large areas.

6. Use the Pen tool or Lasso tool to select inside of the teenager's head, and after converting the path to a selection (**figure 8.48**), fill with white (**figure 8.49**).

figure 8.48

Convert the path to a selection.

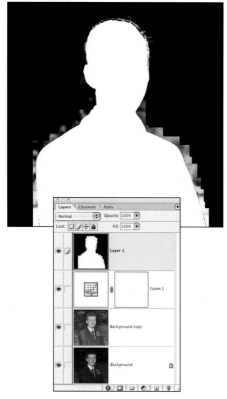

figure 8.49

Use the Pen tool or Lasso tool to select the interior of the figure.

7. Zoom in and use a small white brush to refine the selection edges inside the boy's head and a small black brush to refine the outside edges. Make sure not to paint over the hair detail information. You want a layer that looks like the one in **figure 8.50**.

8. (Cmd + Option + ~) [Ctrl + Alt + ~] to load the layer as a selection or open the Channels palette and (Cmd + Option-click) [Ctrl + Alt-click] on the RGB icon and return to the Layers palette.

figure 8.50

Carefully paint in the transitions using white.

9. Turn off all the layers except the Background layer and double-click the Background Layer icon. Click OK and then click on the Layer Mask button to transfer the active selection into the layer. You should now see the teenager with a transparent background (**figure 8.51**). It is now safe to discard all the layers used to make the mask. Drag them down to the Trash icon on the Layers palette and then choose Edit > Save As and save the file with a new name.

figure 8.52

The mottled, blue background adds a casual elegance to the portrait.

figure 8.51

After transferring the mask to the Background layer, the young man is silhouetted.

Adding an Abstract Background

Choosing an appropriate background is a creative decision; in this case, I added a mottled, blue backdrop (**figure 8.52**). The background I started with was a shot of a brick wall in an old train station (**figure 8.53**). When I took the photograph, I had no idea if I would ever use it. But because digital photography makes collecting images so inexpensive, I always shoot for my personal image library. I've never regretted having a file when I needed it—sometimes its just hours after shooting it that I need it, and other times it may be years later.

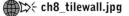 ch8_tilewall.jpg

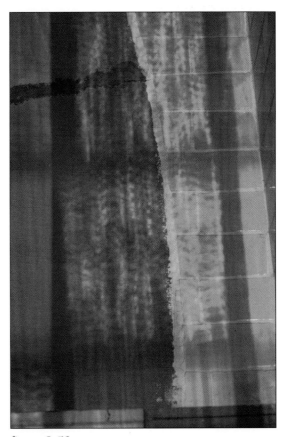

figure 8.53

The original tile wall.

After dropping in a new backdrop, you'll often need to refine the mask using blurring and painting. You may also need to adjust the color of the subject to better suit the environment. The following steps show you how.

1. Drag the wall file onto the teenager image and position it underneath the teenager layer. Choose Edit > Free Transform and scale the background to fit. Hold the Shift key while scaling to maintain the original aspect ratio.

2. Making the background softer gives it less visual interest. Use the Lens Blur filter to defocus the background ever so slightly. To change the color of the background, add a Hue/Saturation Adjustment Layer and select the Colorize option. I chose a blue tone by moving the Hue slider and adjusting the saturation (**figure 8.54**).

figure 8.54

Use a Hue/Saturation Adjustment Layer to create the color of your choice.

3. Darkening the background edges to mimic studio lighting is easy in Photoshop. Use the Elliptical Marquee tool to make a round selection behind his head (**figure 8.55**), and then choose Select > Inverse. Add a Curves Adjustment Layer and, without changing anything, click OK. Change the Curves Layer blending mode to Multiply and adjust the Opacity to approximately 50% (**figure 8.56**).

figure 8.55

Create a round selection for the spotlight.

figure 8.56

The Multiply blending mode darkens the background.

4. The circle is very apparent on the backdrop—click on the layer mask and use a high Gaussian Blur setting to soften the transitions. I blurred the mask by 25 pixels. As a result, the light transition is very subtle and effective (**figure 8.57**).

figure 8.57

A high Gaussian Blur creates a subtle transition and frames the subject's head with light.

5. Zoom to 100% view and inspect the transition areas of the hair to the background. If you see telltale white or black halos or the edges are too jaggy, you can modify the layer mask of the teenager using the Blur tool or Gaussian Blur filter to add very subtle transitions. Click on the teenager layer mask and select Filter > Blur > Gaussian Blur and use the lowest setting possible to soften the transitions. I used a .5 blur to add a hint of softness.

6. To refine individual strands of hair, use the Blur tool set to 10% pressure on the layer mask and gently brush over areas that need a slightly softer transition. I find it more effective to use less pressure and make several brush strokes rather than using more pressure and trying to get the softness right using only one stroke.

Taking someone out of one environment, in this case a very dark one, and placing him or her into a more colorful or lighter scene can leave telltale color spill on the subject, which is color contamination, or in this example, darkness around the teenager's face, as his original environment is reflected on his face.

7. To clean up the color spill, click on the teenager layer, select Layer > New Layer, choose *Use Previous Layer to Create Clipping Mask*, and change the blending mode to Color (**figure 8.58**). The clipping mask created by the underlying layer, in this case the teenager, will only allow areas of this layer to be affected that are directly over pixel information.

figure 8.58

To refine the tone, I used a clipped layer that was set to Color blending mode.

8. Select a soft-edged brush and (Option-click) [Alt-click] to sample the teenager's skin color from an area in his face that is not contaminated from the original environment. Now paint along the edges of the face and you'll see the skin color getting lighter and looking more skin-like. (Option-click) [Alt-click] the hair and paint over it to color it brown, as shown in **figure 8.59**, and then adjust the layer opacity to refine the color correction.

figure 8.60

The final composite.

Creative Backgrounds

There are many resources for backgrounds you can use, including CD stock images, online collections (www.ablestock.com, www.photospin.com, and www.liquidlibrary.com to name just a few), scanning in textures with a flatbed scanner, and my personal favorite—photographing your own. Whenever I can, I carry a digital camera with me and I'm always surprised by how many useful textures, walls, and skies I can photograph in a day. I use these files "as is" or I abstract them with Photoshop filters and coloring to create unique backgrounds whenever needed.

When photographing backgrounds, experiment with lens focal length, from wide to long, and focus. Although I love the Lens Blur filter, nothing beats an optically out-of-focus image, as **figure 8.61** shows. So the next time you're on vacation or have a few hours, grab a camera and take pictures to create a background library, as shown in **figure 8.62**. You'll be happy to have your own images, which will make your composites unique and let you offer your clients variations, as shown in **figures 8.63** and **8.64**.

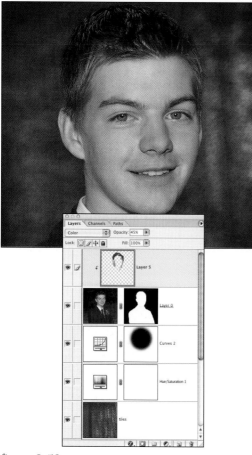

figure 8.59

Painting in natural skin and hair color.

The final image is something any parent would be proud to display (**figure 8.60**). As long as you maintain the layer mask, you can slip in additional backgrounds. Practice the idea of "thinking in black and white," and you'll be well on your way to solving many types of hair-masking challenges.

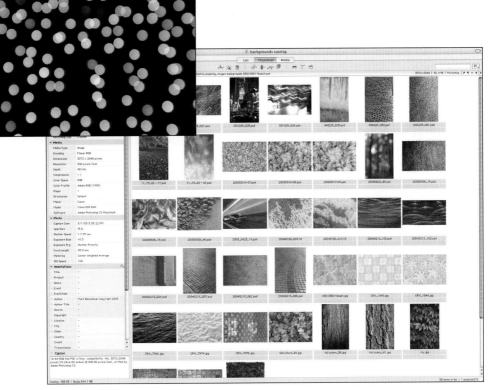

figure 8.61

Shoot both in and out of focus when collecting background material.

figure 8.62

Collect a variety of backdrop images.

figure 8.63

A wonderful backdrop from a stone sculpture garden.

figure 8.64

Believe it or not, scanning and blurring vegetarian sushi created this backdrop.

FINDING THE MASK WITHIN

Color images are most commonly made up of three RGB or four CMYK grayscale image channels, and each of these channels can serve as a foundation for a mask with fine-edge detail. The first step in finding the mask in any color image is to look at the channels individually, as we did earlier in this chapter with the photo of the mother and son, by opening the Channels palette and either clicking on the word red, then green, and then blue or (Command + 1, Command + 2, Command + 3) [Control + 1, Control + 2, Control + 3] to see the individual channels. Very often, this is the first thing I do when I open an image. I look for the channels with the most contrast, tonal differentiation, and smooth transitions. Or as my colleague Sean Duggan says, "every image has a hidden mask—you just need to find it."

 C a u t i o n

When inspecting channels, it is best not to click on the view column, commonly referred to as the eyeball column—this only turns views on and off and makes comparing channels more confusing. Use the command keys (Cmd 1, Cmd 2, Cmd 3) [Ctrl 1, Ctrl 2, Ctrl 3] or click on the name of the channel. To return to the composite channel, press (Cmd + ~) [Ctrl + ~] or click the word RGB in the Channels palette.

Take a look at the picture of the palm trees in **figure 8.65**. If I wanted to select either the palm fronds or the sky, I would be looking at a lot of work if I opted to use the Magic Wand or even Color Range. Now take a look at **figure 8.66**, in which I separated the three channels. Which one looks the most like a mask to you? Which one has the most tonal difference? The blue channel has the most contrast difference between black and white and already looks like a mask.

In the following section, you'll learn how to accentuate, tease, and enhance the hidden mask in each image to make masks that maintain fine detail.

figure 8.65

Snapshot of a palm tree.

Red

Green

Blue

figure 8.66

The individual channels—red, green, and blue.

Each image possesses unique characteristics, including film grain or digital camera noise, texture and amount of hair, lighting, and background color, that you need to consider when making a mask. The best originals to work with are properly exposed and in focus, fine-grained or low-noise, and include good tonal difference between the subject and the background.

Luminance-Masking Techniques

There are a variety of techniques for enhancing channels to make masks, including working with Curves, Paste and Fade, and creating masks with the Apply and Calculate commands, which is addressed in Chapter 9, "Advanced Selection Techniques."

No matter which technique you use, they all start with the same two steps: inspecting the channels to find the best channel to work with and transferring that channel into the alpha channel by dragging it down to the Create New Channel button on the Channels palette, shown in the following example. All of these techniques begin with an existing channel, which is a black-and-white image or the *luminance* of the image. These techniques are often referred to as *luminance masking*.

Working with Curves

The digital camera picture of Nora in **figure 8.67** is a perfect candidate for a new background, as shown in **figure 8.68**. A technique I've used quite often and very successfully to create a fine-edged mask is to duplicate the best channel and then use Curves to exaggerate the tonal contrast between light and dark tones for finessing the mask to pure black and white.

 **ch8_nora.jpg**

figure 8.67

The original digital camera photograph.

figure 8.68

With the new background, the image takes on a more angelic quality.

Building the Initial Mask

1. Before you begin, it is a good idea to get your working space in order. To see the details, it is best to view the file at 100% view (Cmd + Option + zero) [Ctrl + Alt + zero]. To help you monitor the tonal changes, make sure the Info palette is open and change the second readout to Grayscale by clicking and holding on the small triangle (**figure 8.69**) and selecting Grayscale.

figure 8.69

To monitor the tonal changes in the mask, read in black and white by setting the Info palette to Grayscale.

2. Inspect the three channels and decide which one has the finest detail and best contrast. In this example, the green channel has the best detail. Drag it down to the Create New Channel button (**figure 8.70**).

3. The goal is to make the light areas white and the darker areas as close to black without losing the subtle transitions of the hair. Select Image > Adjustments > Curves and make sure that the highlights are on the upper right and the shadows are on the lower left, as shown in **figure 8.71**. If your Curve values are flipped, click on the small switch button circled in the figure.

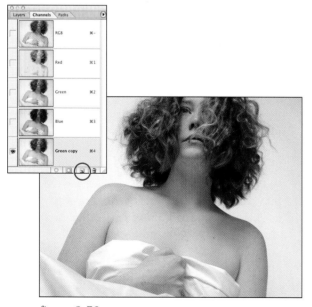

figure 8.70

Duplicate the channel with the most contrast to create channel #4.

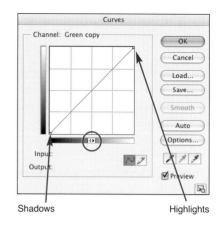

Shadows   Highlights

figure 8.71

Make sure the highlights are on the right, and the shadows are on the left.

4. Grab the highlight point on the Curve and move it along the top to the left until the light background areas are white. Grab the shadow point and move it to the right to deepen the dark areas of the image (**figure 8.72**). To monitor different parts of the image, press the spacebar to activate the Hand tool and scroll to see different areas of the mask.

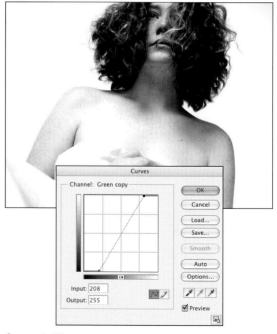

figure 8.72

Increase the contrast using Curves.

5. To add density, adjust the midpoint by grabbing in the middle of the Curve and moving the point to the right, as shown in **figure 8.73**. As you adjust the Curve, move the mouse throughout the image to verify the tonal values in the Info palette. The white areas should be reading zero and the black areas should read 100%.

I find it very useful to monitor these values, because the better the mask is now, the less retouching will be required later.

Correct contrast

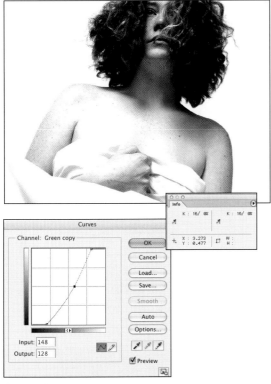

Too much contrast

figure 8.73

Darken the midpoint values, but make sure that the subtle transitions are not lost.

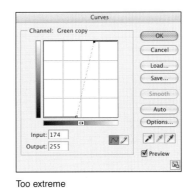

Too extreme

figure 8.74

Be careful not to overdo the contrast enhancement.

Caution

It is very important to keep an eye on the transition areas, because if you are too aggressive with highlight or shadow point moves, you will obliterate the fine detail and subtle transitions that are so important to maintain. See **figure 8.74** for examples of correct and overly contrasted images.

Fine-Tuning the Luminance Mask

The application of Curves accomplishes a great deal of the masking work, and in most cases you'll need to refine the mask with a combination of selecting and filling, painting, and dodging or burning to complete the mask.

1. Use the Eyedropper tool to check that the exterior, light areas of the mask are white and read 0% in the K readout. If any of the readouts on the white background don't (**figure 8.75**), paint over them with a soft-edged white brush until they read 0%, as shown in **figure 8.76**.

figure 8.75

The 7% K (grayscale) readout shows that the background isn't pure white.

figure 8.76

Painting with white cleans up the mask.

2. Use the Lasso tool to select the inside of the head and body and fill the selection with black. As you can see in **figure 8.77**, I stayed well away from the shoulders and the fine detail of her hair.

figure 8.77

The results of selecting and filling the body area with black.

3. Martin Evening showed me the following method to refine masks with brushes: To better define the shoulder areas, use a large, soft black brush that is set to Overlay and paint along the shoulders, as shown in **figure 8.78**. The Brush blending mode is very important, as it will let you paint over the dark areas with black and not affect the light areas. Conversely, if you need to lighten the lighter area on the other side of the shoulders, use white, and the dark values will not be affected.

figure 8.78

Painting with a black brush set to Overlay covers dark areas but doesn't affect the highlights.

Transferring the Mask

After making the mask you need to activate it to become an active selection that will be used as the basis of the layer mask.

1. In the Channels palette, click RGB or press (Cmd + ~) [Ctrl + ~] to return to RGB. Activate the mask by pressing (Cmd + Option + 4) [Ctrl + Alt + 4]. In the Layers palette, double-click the original Background Layer icon and click OK.

2. Click the Add Layer Mask icon (**figure 8.79**), which silhouettes Nora but leaves the background intact (**figure 8.80**). Because the mask is black where she is and white where the background is, you need to invert the mask by clicking on the layer mask and selecting Image > Adjustments > Invert (Cmd + I) [Ctrl + I] (**figure 8.81**).

Tip

On a layer mask, white areas reveal the layer contents, and black areas conceal the layer information.

figure 8.79

Activate the channel mask and convert the Background layer to a standard layer.

figure 8.80

On a mask, black conceals, which is why Nora isn't visible.

figure 8.81

After inverting the layer mask, Nora is visible and the background is hidden.

Creating the Composite

Now we can add a variety of backgrounds as desired. In this instance, I opted to use the Cloud filter to add an abstract sky backdrop.

1. Add a new layer and drag it underneath the layer containing Nora. Press *d* to reset the Color picker to black and white and then double-click the foreground color swatch. Select an attractive light sky blue.

2. Select Filter > Render > Clouds, which will create puffy clouds based on your foreground and background color choices. If you don't like the first version of clouds that Photoshop made, press (Cmd + F) [Ctrl + F] to run the Clouds filter again. I often run the Clouds filter a number of times until I'm happy with the rendition, like the one in **figure 8.82**.

3. View the image at 100% and inspect the edges of the hair and shoulders.

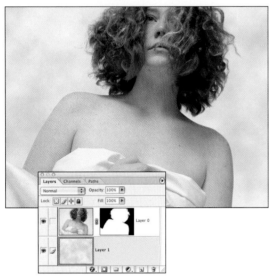

figure 8.82

Experiment with foreground and background colors and the Clouds filter.

Refining the Composite

Just as you refined the channel mask while creating the mask, you can also use the painting, toning, or blurring tools and filters on the layer mask to perfect it. I often make the channel mask as good as possible and then take my time refining the layer mask because it lets me see exactly how the elements are coming together as I work. For additional information on layer, channel, and other types of masks, please see Chapter 5.

1. Because the edge of the woman's shoulders is too sharp and she looks cut out, we need to soften the transition. To do this quickly, use a 5-pixel feathered Lasso tool to generously

select the woman from the neck down. Make sure the layer mask is active by clicking it in the Layers palette. Select Filter > Blur > Gaussian Blur and use as low a setting as possible to soften the transition. I used .5 Gaussian Blur (**figure 8.83**).

figure 8.83

A low Gaussian Blur softens the image transition ever so slightly and makes it more realistic.

2. If the edges of her hair need additional density, use a soft-edged Dodge tool, set to highlights, and on the layer mask gently stroke along the edges of her hair. The important concept to understand and utilize is that where the mask is white, Nora is visible; where it is black, the clouds are visible. In other words, white shows Nora and black shows the clouds. If you want more of her hair to show, those areas need to be lighter, which is why using the Dodge tool on the mask is useful.

3. To soften any possible jaggy artifacts, use the Blur tool at 10% to 20% pressure and brush over the jagged areas on the layer mask. This helps make the transition between clouds and hair more life-like.

Starting with the best channel to form the foundation of the alpha channel, which is used to create the layer mask, is one way to take advantage of luminance information. Refining the layer mask while viewing how the image pieces are coming together is a fantastic method to refine your composites. With some practice and patience, you'll be a hair-masking maestro in no time.

Using Paste and Fade Masks

Blending modes is one of the best Photoshop features that influence how pixels interact. They can be found throughout the program in the Layers Palette; Layer Styles; the Fill, Stroke and Fade commands; painting tools; and Apply and Calculate commands—but not in the Channels palette. Or are they? Shan Canfield introduced me to the following technique, and it taught me that channels can take advantage of blending modes, if you know where to look.

Figure 8.84 shows a high-school portrait in which the background is too dark and drab. By making a quick "paste and fade" mask, a studio backdrop was added and the photo was enhanced with an insinuation of greater depth (figure 8.85).

⊕↳⋇ **ch8_teenager_2.jpg**

1. Start by inspecting the three color channels to identify the one with the best contrast and tonal definition. In this case, the red channel is the best. Drag it down to the Create New Channel button (figure 8.86).

© Brent Shirk, Palmer Multimedia Imaging

BEFORE

figure 8.84

AFTER

figure 8.85

figure 8.86

Duplicate the red channel.

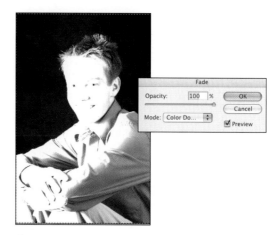

figure 8.87

Copy and paste the channel, and immediately choose Edit > Fade using Color Dodge blending mode.

figure 8.88

Repeating the copy and paste of the contrast channel and selecting Edit > Fade using the Color Dodge blending mode further exaggerates the black and white values.

2. With the copy of the red channel active, choose Select > All, then Edit > Copy, and then Edit > Paste. It will look as if nothing has changed in the image. Immediately after pasting, select Edit > Fade.

   Note: You have to select Fade immediately after pasting or else it will not be active. If your fade is grayed out, you must repeat the select, copy, and paste steps and then choose Fade.

   It is in the Fade command where the Shan Canfield magic happens. The Fade command includes the blending modes. By using a blending mode that builds contrast, you darken the darks and lighten the lighter areas to build a better mask.

3. On this image, use Color Dodge (**figure 8.87**) to effectively increase the contrast.

4. To exaggerate the contrast even more, repeat Steps 2 and 3 to copy the high-contrast channel 4 and paste it onto itself. Use Edit > Fade with Color Dodge to create a very high contrast mask, as shown in **figure 8.88**.

   When using this technique on your own images, you may not have to copy/paste the channel twice; the less aggressive blending modes may be more effective; and adjusting the Fade opacity may be helpful.

5. Verify the density of the mask using the Info palette. Make sure that the blacks are black and the whites are white. As shown in **figure 8.89**, the black density is not 100%. Choose Image > Adjustments > Levels and move the black slider to the right until the Info palette reads 100% (**figure 8.90**).

figure 8.89

Make sure that the black areas are really black—94% is not.

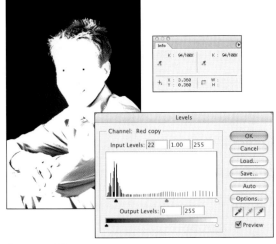

figure 8.90

Use Levels to force the dark values to true 100% black.

6. Select the inside of the boy using the Lasso tool and fill with white. Then choose Select > Deselect. Use a white brush set to Overlay to paint over his hair (**figure 8.91**) and to create a transition between the selected and filled area and the edges of the figure.

7. In the Channels palette, click RGB or use (Cmd + ~) [Ctrl + ~] to return to RGB. Activate the mask by pressing (Cmd + Option + 4) [Ctrl + Alt + 4]. In the Layers palette, double-click the original Background Layer icon, click OK, and click on the Layer Mask icon to transfer the active selection into the layer mask.

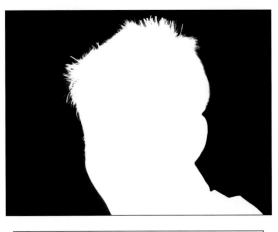

figure 8.91

Using a white brush that is set to Overlay, paint to enhance the edge details.

8. Add a new layer and position it underneath the teenager layer.

9. Press *d* to reset the Color picker to the default colors of black and white, and then press *x* to switch the colors so that black is the background color. Double-click on the foreground color swatch and choose a complementary color. I chose a rich burgundy to offset the blue of his shirt.

10. Select the Gradient tool and click the Radial button in the Options bar. Starting in the center of the image, click and pull towards the upper-right corner. **Figure 8.92** shows the desired effect. The longer you pull, the longer the transition between burgundy and black. If you don't like the first gradient you made, try again. The second gradient will overwrite the original. I often take four or five gradient pulls to get the transition just right.

11. To add a hint of texture to the gradient layer, (Option-click) [Alt-click] on the New Layer icon in the Layers palette and change the blending mode to Overlay. Then select Fill with Overlay-neutral (50% gray).

figure 8.92

Use a burgundy-to-black Radial gradient to draw in a new studio backdrop.

12. Select Filter > Noise > Add Noise and select Monochrome. The amount of noise you use depends on your personal taste, desired results, and file size. I used a setting of 5. Then choose Filter > Blur > Motion Blur and adjust the Angle and Distance settings as desired (**figure 8.93**). Experimenting and adding a bit of texture is helpful for avoiding the slick computer look.

13. If you see any telltale dark halos around the young gentleman (**figure 8.94**), tighten up the mask by judiciously using Levels and Gaussian Blur. Click on the layer mask to activate it, choose Image > Adjustments > Levels, and adjust the shadow point to the right to tighten the mask (**figure 8.95**). Use a very subtle Gaussian Blur of .4 to offset the hardness that Levels may introduce. You can repeat the Levels and Gaussian Blur two or three times with decreasing values to tighten the mask and produce a realistic-looking edge.

Now that I know how to take advantage of blending modes in the channels, I use this technique all the time. The blending modes help me achieve very good results, very quickly. For an excellent explanation of blending modes, visit www.adobeevangelists.com and download Julieanne Kost's article, "Blend Mode Magic."

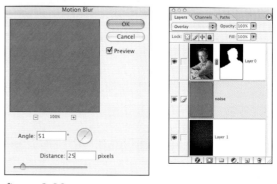

figure 8.93

After adding noise, use the Motion Blur filter to create a subtle brushed-aluminum texture.

figure 8.94

Study the image for telltale halos or artifacts.

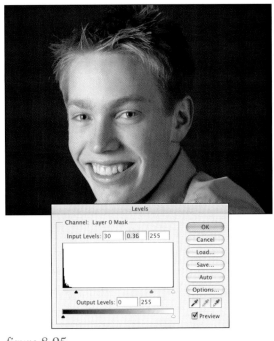

figure 8.95

Tighten the layer mask using Levels to remove halos.

WORKING WITH THE EXTRACT FILTER

The Extract filter separates soft-edged or finely detailed subjects from the image background. It also subtracts the color spill that the original background or environment reflected onto the object.

At first glance, the Extract filter interface may seem unwieldy, especially considering the fact that when you click OK, it deletes pixels—something that makes me very nervous. But if you provide the filter with the right definition of colors that you want to keep or delete, and transitional areas that contain both, it does a very good job. Better yet, if you take the time to prepare your file before entering the Extract interface, you can get even better results more quickly.

The most basic method of using the Extract filter begins by your outlining the subject with the Highlighter tool, which defines the transition areas. It is better to bias the Highlighter to the outside edge of the transition than to overspray the subject.

The second step is to select the Paint Bucket tool and click inside the outline to define the areas to keep. Anything outside of the highlight or fill is defined as colors to delete. But there is much more to achieving good results with Extract than outlining and filling, as discussed in the following section.

Selecting Shapes

Most people think that the Extract filter is only used to select hair or fine detail, but I've found it particularly useful for selecting shape-based subjects that have soft edges caused by a wide-open aperture (a low f-stop number). For example, I photographed the statue shown in **figure 8.96** in a museum where I was not allowed to use either a flash or a tripod. To get the shot, I had to shoot with a large aperture—wide open. As a result, the edges of the statue are not crisp or well defined.

ch8_roman_head.jpg

figure 8.96

The original digital camera snapshot of the Roman statue.

C a u t i o n

Since Extract deletes pixels, I always do two things before entering it: duplicate the layer and take a history snapshot. Duplicating the layer ensures the Background layer is not affected, and taking a history snapshot is helpful for refining edges after running the Extract filter.

1. Duplicate the Background layer and take a history snapshot as shown in **figure 8.97**. Then select Filter > Extract.

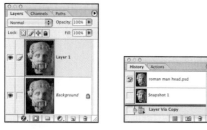

figure 8.97

Duplicate the Background layer and take a History snapshot before using the Extract interface.

2. Click the Highlighter tool in the upper left and outline the statue completely. The brush size should glide comfortably over the transition areas without being sloppy. When in doubt, bias the brush stroke to the outside area, because that is the area that Extract will delete. Areas that contain hard edges, like the top of the statue's head, should be highlighted with a smaller brush, and softer transitional areas, such as the lower right, should be highlighted with a larger brush. Press the left bracket ([) key to make the brush smaller, and the right bracket (]) key to make the brush bigger. Press (Option) [Alt] to change the Highlighter tool to the Eraser tool to erase unwanted highlighting.

3. Make sure to outline the entire head (**figure 8.98**) and then select the Paint Bucket tool. Click inside the outline to define the areas you want to keep.

4. After completing the highlight and fill, preview the extraction by clicking the Preview button. The checkerboard area (**figure 8.99**) shows what will be deleted. I often find it easier to view the extract on a black or white matte, which you can select on the lower right.

5. In this preview stage, you can refine the extract with the Cleanup and Edge Touchup tools. The Cleanup tool takes away more background area; press (Option) [Alt] to add information back (**figure 8.100**). The Touchup tool cleans up the outside edges (**figure 8.101**).

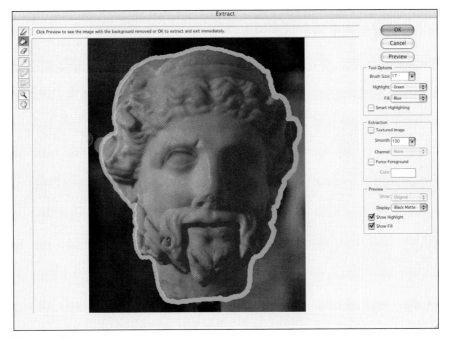

figure 8.98

Highlight the outside edge and fill the interior.

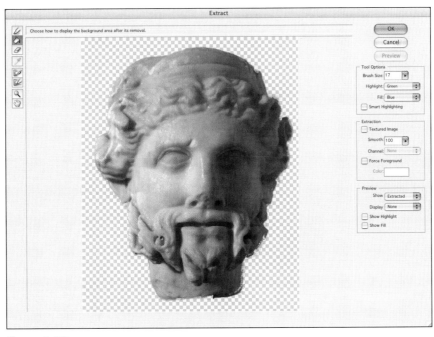

figure 8.99

Previewing the extract.

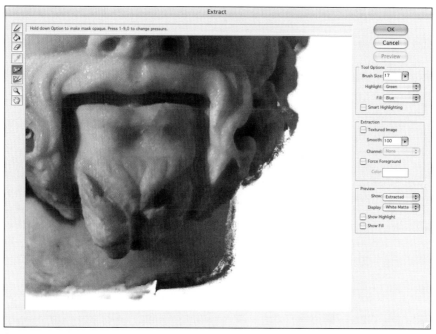

figure 8.100

Previewing on white lets you see ragged edges.

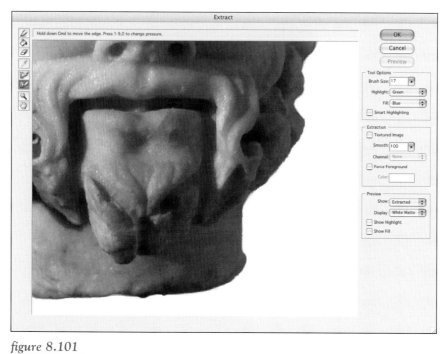

figure 8.101

Clean up the edges and transitions before exiting Extract.

6. Click OK and Photoshop extracts the subject. Turn off the view column of the underlying layer to study the edges. If they need refining, as shown in **figure 8.102**, activate the History brush, click on the history snapshot, and paint back the missing areas (**figure 8.103**). When you are satisfied, drag the statue to another file (**figure 8.104**) or add a new background to the statue file.

Tip

Change the Tool Option colors for the Highlight and Fill tools to contrast the subject you are extracting.

figure 8.103

Refine the edges of the extract using the History brush.

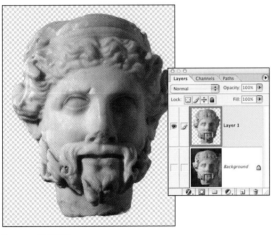

figure 8.102

The extracted head.

figure 8.104

The transition areas are maintained when the layer is moving to a different file.

Using Advanced Settings

When you're comfortable with the basic Extract functions, use the Smart Highlighting, Force Foreground, and Texture options to achieve even better results.

Smart Highlighting

Smart Highlighting is ideal for clearly defined subjects, such as the Kewpie doll in **figure 8.105**. At first glance, it looks like a simple selection to make, but the similarity of tones is actually quite challenging.

Smart Highlighting applies a highlight that is just wide enough to cover the edge regardless of the current brush size. To get the best results, switch between the Standard Highlighter and the Smart Highlighing as needed. For example, to outline the car in **figure 8.106**, I used Smart Highlighting (**figure 8.107**) on the front of the car, and then I deselected Smart Highlighting (**figure 8.108**) and used the Standard Highlighter on the softer, out-of-focus area in the back of the car. **Figure 8.109** shows the result.

ch8_kewpie_doll.jpg

ch8_red_car.jpg

figure 8.105

The clearly defined edges of the Kewpie doll are ideal candidates for using the Smart Highlighting.

figure 8.106

The original car has both crisp and soft edges.

figure 5.107

Turn on Smart Highlighting to paint over clearly defined contours, such as the front of the car.

figure 8.108

Turn Smart Highlighting off to paint over the softer contours in the back of the car.

figure 8.109

The silhouetted toy car.

Force Foreground

Force Foreground is useful when the area to be selected is either too fine or too diffuse to outline and fill with the Paint Bucket. For example, selecting flames like those in **figure 8.110** is always challenging. Russell Brown posted a very useful "Extracting Flames" PDF on his Web site www.russellbrown.com, which I am respectfully paraphrasing here.

ch8_flames.jpg

1. Duplicate the Background layer, take a History snapshot, and select Filter > Extract.

2. Use a large highlighter to paint over all of the flames (**figure 8.111**).

3. Deselect Show Highlight in Preview Options, select Force Foreground, and select the Eyedropper tool. Use the Eyedropper tool to select an average color of the flames. Click Preview and increase smoothing to reduce edge artifacts (**figure 8.112**).

4. If not enough flames are selected, choose a darker color with the Eyedropper and click Preview again. As Russell explains, "The lighter the foreground color you choose, the lighter the selected value is. However, if you choose a midtone, it includes both dark and light shades."

© Mark Beckelman

figure 8.110

Flames have always been a challenge to select appropriately.

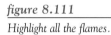

figure 8.111

Highlight all the flames.

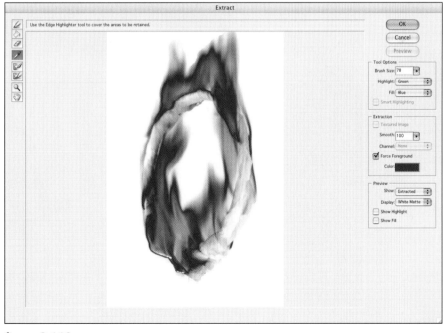

figure 8.112

To base the extraction on color, use Force Foreground.

5. Click OK to extract the flames (figure 8.113). Set Snapshot 1 as your History brush source and brush away any telltale gaps (figure 8.114).

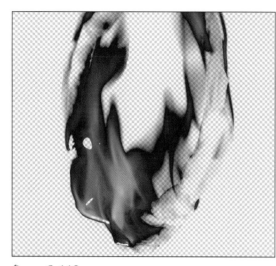

figure 8.113

The original extraction has a few gaps.

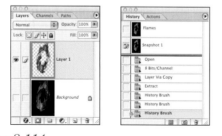

figure 8.114

Refine the extraction using the History brush.

Texture and Smooth

The texture option lets you separate subjects from backgrounds that have similar colors but different textures or when the texture is an essential component of the image. For example, to separate the brown Easter bunny from the brown wall in **figure 8.115** looks challenging, but by selecting Texture and increasing the smooth amount, I was able to separate the bunny from the store environment rather quickly.

figure 8.115

The brown rabbit in a brown environment can be extracted, if there is enough textural difference.

Preparing a File for Extract

Doing the initial highlighting before entering Extract results in noticeably better extractions. I also find it easier to do the initial work in Quick Mask or in an alpha channel versus using the Highlighter tool in Extract.

Working with Quick Mask

When you highlight the outline of a subject, you're defining the transition areas for the Extract filter. The problem for me is that painting within the Extract interface feels cramped. I can do a better job painting in Photoshop. Images with curves and hollow areas, such as the pacifier in **figure 8.116**, are ideal candidates for the Quick Mask pre-treatment before creating the final mask (**figure 8.117**) with the Extract filter.

⊕▷ **ch8_schnuller.jpg**

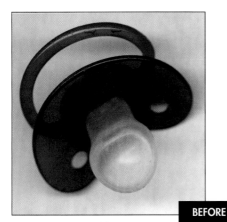

figure 8.116

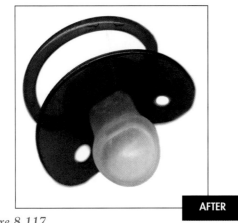

figure 8.117

1. Duplicate the Background layer and take a history snapshot.

2. Press *q* to enter Quick Mask mode and select a hard-edged black brush.

3. Draw along the edges of the pacifier (**figure 8.118**).

4. After completing the outline, press *q* to exit Quick Mask mode. Open the Channels palette and select Save Selection as Channel (**figure 8.119**). In the alpha channel, you should see a black line outline of the pacifier. If you see a black channel with white lines, choose Image > Adjustments > Inverse.

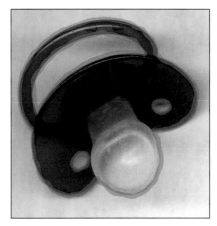

figure 8.118

Paint over the contours in Quick Mask mode.

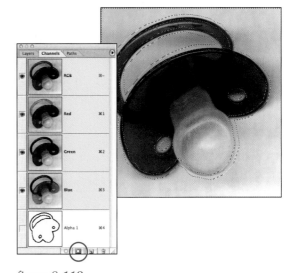

figure 8.119

Click on Save Selection as Channel.

5. Select > Deselect and Filter > Extract.

6. So far, nothing seems to have changed. But if you click on the Channel pull-down menu on the right side of the Extract interface, you will see and then can select the newly created channel, most likely called Alpha 1, as shown in **figure 8.120**.

7. Voilà—instant outline. Select the Paint Bucket and click in the center of the pacifier to fill the areas you want to keep (**figure 8.121**). Click Preview and use the Cleanup and Edge Touchup tools to refine the extraction (**figure 8.122**).

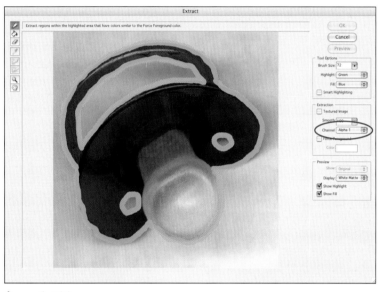

figure 8.120

Select Alpha 1 to define the highlight.

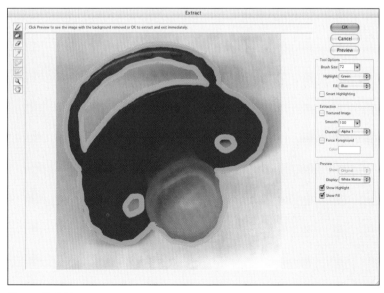

figure 8.121

Fill the interior area.

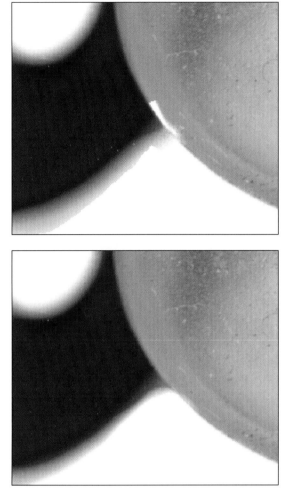

figure 8.122

Refine the details using the Edge Touchup tool.

Working with Alpha Channels

The following technique is ideal for subjects that are photographed against contrasting backgrounds in which you can use the Magic Wand or the Marquee tool to make the initial selection.

I was interested in using an antique watch face in a composite, and at first glance, I figured selecting it would be simple—just use the Elliptical Marquee tool to select the watch and I'd be done. But upon careful examination, I discovered that its uneven edges are an essential part of the watch's character and needed to be maintained (**figure 8.123**).

 ch8_watch.jpg

figure 8.123

The irregular edges of the watch are integral to its character.

1. Duplicate the Background layer and take a history snapshot. Activate the Elliptical Marquee tool and hold down (Option + Shift) [Alt + Shift] on the center of the watch and draw out a perfectly round selection. Draw slightly into the background to encircle the ragged edges (**figure 8.124**).

2. Select the Magic Wand tool, reduce its tolerance to 16, and make sure that Contiguous is selected, which will ensure that only the light areas where you click will be deselected. Press (Option) [Alt] and click on the extraneous background areas, as shown in **figure 8.125**.

3. Click on the Channels palette and click the Create New Channel button (**figure 8.126**). You should now see a black mask with the modified circular marching ants.

4. Select Edit > Stroke and stroke the selection by setting Width at 6 pixels, Color on white, and Location at Center (**figure 8.127**) to draw a white line around the selection. Select > Deselect and then Image > Adjustments > Inverse or (Cmd + I) [Ctrl + I] to invert the mask and make a black line that will serve as the foundation of the extract.

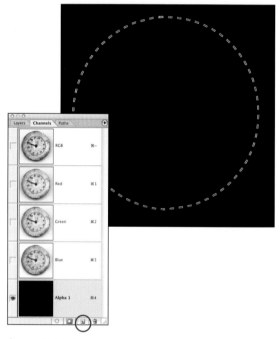

figure 8.124

Use the Elliptical Marquee tool to select the watch face.

figure 8.125

Lower the Magic Wand Tolerance and select Contiguous
before subtracting from the Elliptical Marquee selection.

figure 8.126

Click on Create New Channel.

figure 8.127

Stroke the selection with white.

5. Return to RGB and enter the Extract interface. Use the Channel pull-down menu to choose the newly created channel, most likely called Alpha 1. Select the Paint Bucket and click in the center of the watch to fill the interior (**figure 8.128**). Click Preview to verify the extraction (**figure 8.129**) and clean up the watch edges if necessary.

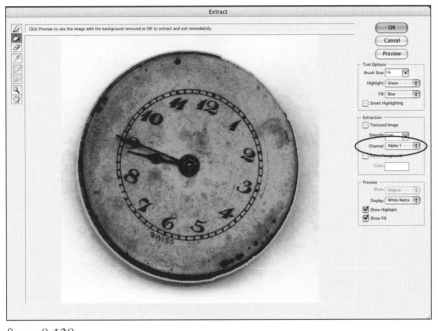

figure 8.128

Select Alpha 1.

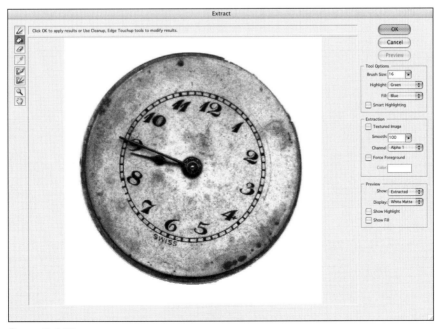

figure 8.129

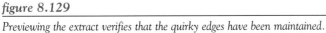
Previewing the extract verifies that the quirky edges have been maintained.

Starting the extraction with an alpha channel is a fantastic method for getting better results from Extract, faster.

Although Extract is sometimes demonstrated for selecting hair, I have rarely achieved acceptable, professional results using it. The luminance-masking techniques in the beginning of this chapter and the advanced techniques in the following chapter create better hair masks than Extract does. As you've seen, I do use Extract to select shapes and soft-edged subjects, but for hair I rely on the other, more effective techniques.

CLOSING THOUGHTS

Selecting hair shouldn't be a hair-raising experience. If you think in black and white and take advantage of the channel that possesses the most contrast, you can create amazing selections, masks, and composites. But remember, when you're selecting hair, a one-stop button that does a perfect job does not exist. A high-quality mask is always one that you invested time and care into. Believe me, it's worth it—the better the mask in the first place, the less retouching you'll do later on in the compositing process.

9

ADVANCED SELECTION TECHNIQUES

It used to be that when I needed to make a fine-edged selection, I often wasn't sure which technique to use. But over the years, with a little patience, curiosity, and experimentation, I've added various techniques and approaches to my repertoire for making professional selections of hair, delicate cloth, and intricate landscape scenes. I've also learned that every mask I make teaches me valuable skills for the mask I'll make tomorrow.

In this chapter, you'll learn how to

- Take advantage of image differences
- Combine masks to silhouette challenging subjects
- Harness the power of the Apply Image and Calculate commands
- Add texture to images for creative effects

When extracting fine details, you'll obtain the best results if you use high-quality, high-resolution originals—ones in which the figure is in sharp contrast to the background. So if you plan on taking someone's picture for a composite, preparing the lighting, the point of view, and the background is essential. (For more information on photography for compositing, see Chapter 11, "Image Execution and Photography.")

OPPOSITES AND DIFFERENCES ATTRACT

Having a positive outlook on life is a good thing, but when you're using Photoshop, having a negative outlook can be very beneficial. Thinking in negative values—light to dark or dark to light—can make selecting finely detailed or soft-edged subjects, such as the lupines in **figure 9.1**, much easier. The following technique accentuates the difference between the flowers and the sky and creates a mask that maintains the details of the flowers, so that you can insert a new sky, as shown in **figure 9.2**.

figure 9.2

The new sky frames the flowers wonderfully.

🌐▷⳹ **ch9_lupines.jpg**

🌐▷⳹ **ch9_storm_sky.jpg**

Use the following technique with images that have a tonal difference between the subject and the background.

1. Set the eyedropper to 3 by 3 Average and sample the color of the sky.

2. Add a new layer and choose Edit > Fill > Use Foreground Color or (Option + Delete) [Alt + Delete] to fill the layer with the sampled color.

3. Change the colored layer's blending mode to Difference to get the results shown in **figure 9.3**.

figure 9.1

The flowers are very beautiful, but the drab sky detracts from the image.

© Dynamic Graphics, Inc.

figure 9.3

The Difference blending mode reveals everything that is not the same color—in this case, it's the flowers.

figure 9.4

Use a Levels Adjustment Layer to increase the difference between the light and dark areas.

4. Accentuate the difference using a Levels Adjustment Layer to deepen the black and lighten the white areas (**figure 9.4**). Use Levels judiciously, as increasing the contrast too much can obliterate important image detail.

5. Add another new layer and use the Marquee tool to select the lower part of the picture. Choose Edit > Fill, use White, and then choose Select > Deselect (**figure 9.5**).

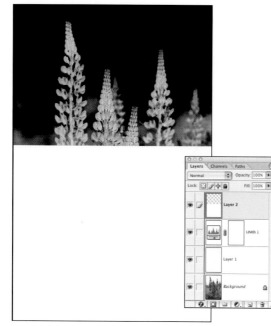

figure 9.5

Building up the mask requires a variety of layer types.

6. On the layer with the white fill, create a transition along the horizon line (**figure 9.6**) by painting with white using a soft brush. Then clean up the black sky areas (**figure 9.7**) using a black brush.

figure 9.6

Paint in a soft transition with a white brush.

figure 9.7

Cleaning up the sky with a black brush.

7. To differentiate the flowers from the sky, turn the flowers to grayscale using a Channel Mixer layer, set to Monochrome. Then add the red and green channels to remove the gray values (**figure 9.8**). The results look very much like a mask, with black-and-white areas and shades of gray in the transitional areas.

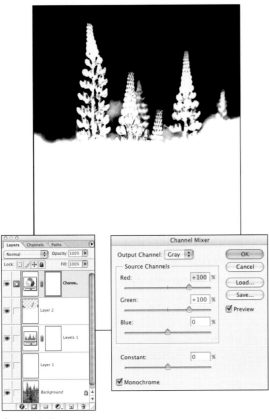

figure **9.8**

The Channel Mixer layer with Monochrome selected removes the color information.

figure **9.9**

After loading the layer's luminosity as a selection, add a layer mask to isolate the flowers from the original background.

8. The secret to getting this quasi-mask information into the flower layer lies in the black-and-white luminosity. With the top-most layer active, press (Cmd + Option + ~) [Ctrl + Alt + ~] to load the image luminosity.

   If your keyboard doesn't have a tilde key, open the Channels palette and (Cmd-click) [Ctrl-click] on the RGB icon.

9. Double-click on the original flower Background Layer icon to change it to a standard layer. (Option-click) [Alt-click] its eyeball to hide all the other layers. Click on the Layer Mask icon in the Layers palette. You should see the flowers masked onto a transparent checkerboard, similar to **figure 9.9**.

10. You can either delete the layers used to make the mask or just ignore them for the rest of the project. To delete them in one fell swoop, use the Layers palette fly-out menu and drag down to Delete Hidden Layers.

11. Open the sky background and use the Move tool to drag the background to the lupine image. Move the sky layer underneath the lupine layer (**figure 9.10**). To add a sense of realism, blurring the new background with the Lens Blur filter may be helpful to match the depth of field of the flowers with the sky.

figure 9.10

Positioning the sky layer underneath the flowers replaces the original sky.

12. Click on the lupine layer mask and use black and white soft-edged brushes to refine the edges of the lupines. If you see any slight white halos, paint on the layer mask using a small, black brush. If parts of the lupines are hidden (figure 9.11), paint using white to reveal them. In some cases, I also use the Blur tool on the mask to carefully soften edges that are harsh or jagged.

figure 9.11

Painting with white on the layer mask reveals the missing tip of the flower.

Selecting Layer Masks

When refining layer masks, it is very important to first click on the layer mask to activate it before working on it. I would rather not tell you how often I have started painting, thinking that the layer mask is active, only to find out later that I'm affecting the layer information instead. Figure 9.12 shows how easy it is to overlook this very important detail. On the left, the layer is active; on the right, the mask is active.

There are two clues for figuring out which of the two is really active. The first is the icon that appears to the left of the layer thumbnail. If it is a small brush icon, the layer is active. If it is a mask icon, the mask is active. The second clue is the border around the thumbnail—the active component has a thin double border. Chapter 7, "The Power of Layer Masking," addresses working with layer masks in greater detail.

 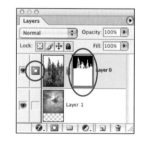

figure 9.12

[Left:] The layer is active. [Right:] The layer mask is active.

THE MULTI-PASS TECHNIQUE

In an ideal world, isolating a subject would be a simple matter—a click here, a click there, and the mask would be done. But in the real world, making a fine-edged mask often requires a variety of approaches to create the best results. Take a look at the image in figure 9.13. How do you approach this image, with its three distinct masking challenges? The smooth boots and pants would be best selected using the Pen tool. The red jacket would be a perfect candidate for a luminance mask (or a Vivid Light layer, described in the steps that follow). And the hair would be best masked by painting in the mask.

figure 9.14

Mark Beckelman replaced the distracting garage scene with a cloudscape background.

No one masking technique exists that can isolate all three areas at once and equally well. In cases like this, you can use a multi-approach technique to build the best mask for each area and, after combining the separate masks into one, you can replace the background to create a scene similar to **figure 9.14**.

I usually begin this process with the easiest part to select. In the case of the little girl, I'll begin with the boots, pants, and red jacket. The initial time I spend with the file lets me familiarize myself with it and think about how I'm going to approach the more difficult aspects. The interim result of the multi-pass technique is a multi-layered document that uses contrasting color layers to show how the mask is forming. The final step combines the layer masks to create one layer with the isolated subject.

The three considerations I take into account when approaching a complex image are:

- How can I get the most work done with the least amount of time and effort?

- What details need to be maintained?

- What details can be ignored?

© Mark Beckelman

figure 9.13

The original photograph contains a variety of masking challenges, from the smooth boots and pants to the strands of hair.

For example, it may sound like a great idea to maintain every strand of hair, but as you can see in **figure 9.15**, this makes Rachel look like Dennis the Menace plagued by some serious static electricity. If you look at the final image, you'll notice that I ignored a number of the fly-aways to simplify the image and focus the viewer on Rachel's beautiful face. It is best to do what will make the file look its best, which varies from file to file.

 ch9_rachel.jpg

figure 9.15

Trying to maintain every single hair can work against you.

Masking the Smooth Contours

1. As I already mentioned, it's best to begin with the easiest part of the image, which in this case means "Pen tooling" the boots and pants. After completing the path, you need to name it. I used *Boots & Pants*.

2. To see how the mask is going to work, you can use a technique I learned from one of my students at the School of VISUAL ARTS in New York City: Convert the Boots & Pants path to an active selection and inverse the selection (Select > Inverse). Then add a solid Color Fill layer and choose a very noticeable color that contrasts with the image. The color contrast between the bright blue and the photograph (**figure 9.16**) is so apparent that you can easily tell what is masked and what isn't.

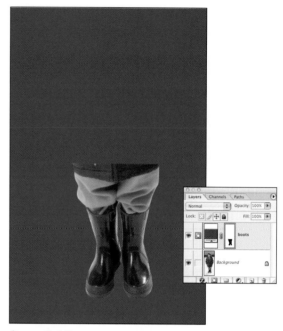

figure 9.16

Use a contrasting color that clearly shows you what is and what isn't selected.

3. Zoom in on the feet and you'll notice that I've overlooked two nubs in her boots. By painting with a small hard-edged white brush on the layer mask, you can follow the correct contour of the boots, as shown in **figure 9.17**.

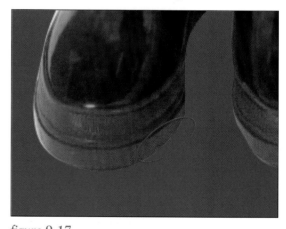

figure 9.17

Paint on the Color Fill layer mask to fine-tune the mask. In this case, the mask was obscuring the tread on the boots.

4. Before moving on to the red jacket area of the image, turn off the Boots & Pants Color Fill layer. Then drop down to the Background layer and duplicate it. Afterward, change the blending mode to Vivid Light, which will increase the image contrast dramatically.

5. Use the Lasso tool to roughly encircle the red jacket (**figure 9.18**) and (Option-click) [Alt-click] with the Magic Wand on the white areas to subtract them (**figure 9.19**). This is a quick technique that I learned from Lee Varis, a Los Angeles-based photographer and digital imaging expert, and it makes child's play of isolating subjects on solid-colored backdrops.

6. Invert the selection and add a Color Fill layer (**figure 9.20**). You can use the same color or a different one than you used previously.

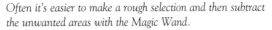

figure 9.19

Often it's easier to make a rough selection and then subtract the unwanted areas with the Magic Wand.

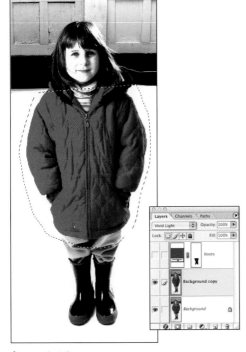

figure 9.18

The Vivid Light layer adds a false contrast that you can use to make a quick selection of subjects on white backdrops.

figure 9.20

Use the second Color Fill layer to mask out the jacket.

7. Upon careful inspection, you'll notice a slight white halo around the little girl (**figure 9.21**) that needs to be removed by slightly tightening the layer mask. Use Filter > Other > Maximum of 1 to expand the black part of the mask, which removes the white halo, and Filter > Blur > Gaussian Blur, with a setting of .5, to soften the edge of the mask ever so slightly. The results are shown in **figure 9.22**.

   For additional information on using filters to refine layer masks, see Chapter 3, "The Essential Select Menu," and Chapter 5, "Masks Are Your Friends."

figure 9.21

Zoom in to verify the edge quality; in this case, the slight white halo needs to be removed.

figure 9.22

After expanding and softening the mask, the white halo disappears.

8. To help avoid confusion, it is a good idea to name the most important layers. I named them *Boots & Pants* and *Jacket*.

Isolating the Hair

The hair is a challenge in this image because three distinct tonal areas need separated: the left side in front of the driveway, the top part by the garage, and the highlight on the right side.

1. Turn off all the layers created so far so that only the Background layer is visible. Open the Channels palette to inspect the three channels; concentrate just on the left side of her head by the driveway. The green channel shows the best separation between her hair and the driveway. Drag the green channel down to the Create New Channel button on the Channels palette.

2. With the new alpha channel active, choose Select > All, and Edit > Copy. Then choose Edit > Paste, followed by Edit > Fade. Select Color Dodge to boost the contrast of the separation (**figure 9.23**).

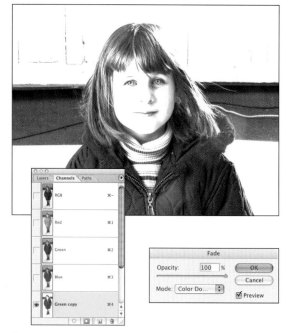

figure 9.23

Fade with Color Dodge quickly builds mask contrast and separation.

3. Use a soft-edged brush, set to Overlay at 25% to 50%, to paint with white over her hair and with black over the driveway. This will take a few passes and some patience to create the separation shown in **figure 9.24**.

4. While I was working on the left side of the mask, I noticed that the highlight on the right side also had good separation, so I painted it with the Overlay brush to add the separation, as shown in **figure 9.25**. You may want to do the same.

5. To see how the mask is coming together, invert it (**figure 9.26**). This technique helps me better visualize the mask. Paint out the face using the Brush tool, set to Normal with black at 100%. Select the areas to the girl's left and right using the Lasso or Marquee tool and fill with white (**figure 9.27**). To see where to paint, click on the view column next to RGB so that you can see through the file (**figure 9.28**).

figure 9.25

Enhance as much contrast as possible.

figure 9.26

Invert the mask so that you can visualize it more easily.

figure 9.24

Painting with Overlay lets you lighten the whites and darken the black areas.

figure 9.27

Select and fill exterior sections.

figure 9.28

Looking through the file to the RGB image lets you view the image while refining the mask.

6. To select the top part of the head, inspect the three channels and notice that the blue channel has the best separation. Duplicate it and choose Select > All. Then choose Edit > Copy, Edit > Paste, and Edit > Fade. Select the Hard Light blending mode to darken the hair and lighten the garage door (**figure 9.29**).

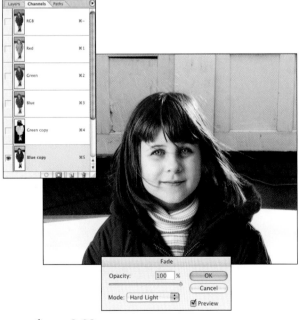

figure 9.29

In separating the top part of the head, the Hard Light blending mode brings out the hair very quickly.

7. Use a soft-edged brush, set to Overlay at 100%, and paint with white over the garage and with black over her hair. This will take a few passes and some patience to create the separation shown in **figure 9.30**. Change the brush back to Normal and clean up any artifacts.

8. Use the Lasso or Marquee tool to select the large areas behind the little girl and fill with white (**figure 9.31**).

figure 9.30

To separate the girl's head from the garage, paint with black and white.

figure 9.31

Selecting and filling the background with white helps you see how the mask is coming together.

9. The next step combines sections of the two alpha channels to create one mask for her hair. Select the channel named Green Copy and encircle the part of the mask that is responsible for the center portion of her hair (**figure 9.32**). Then select Edit > Copy.

10. Select the channel that encompasses the top part of the head (Blue Copy) and choose Edit > Paste to paste the selected channel information into the Blue Copy channel (**figure 9.33**). Since the initial selection is still active, Photoshop will paste the section of the mask precisely over the same area in the Blue Copy Channel, even though you've switched alpha channels. Use a large white brush to clean up the background (**figure 9.34**). You can ignore the jacket and boots, because they're already masked out.

11. To help avoid confusion, it is a good idea to name the most important channels. I named the channel that has the girl's head information in it *head*.

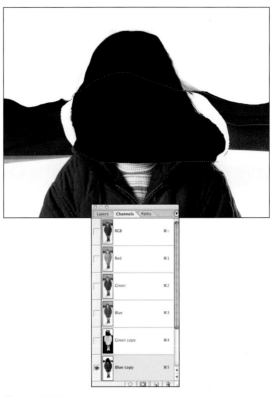

figure 9.33

Pasting one part of the mask into another combines the masked areas.

figure 9.34

After combining the masks, use a black-and-white brush to clean up any details.

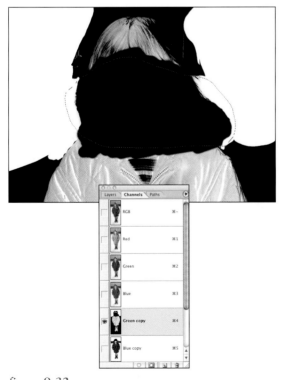

figure 9.32

Selecting and copying the center portion of the mask.

Combining the Masks

Now the boots and pants are in one layer mask, the jacket mask is in another layer mask, and the head is in an alpha channel. They all need to be combined to separate the girl from the cluttered background.

1. Return to the Layers palette, double-click the Background layer, and name it *little girl*. Choose Select > Load Selection and choose Head (**figure 9.35**). This will load the alpha channel as an active selection.

2. Click on the Boots Color fill layer, choose Select > Load Selection, and then choose Boots Mask. Choose Intersect with Selection, as shown in **figure 9.36**.

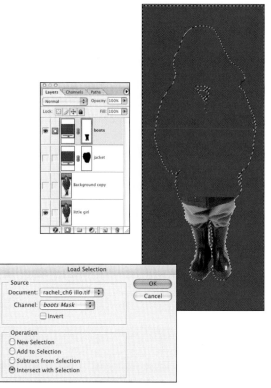

figure 9.36

Intersecting the boots mask with the active selection.

3. Click on the Jacket Color fill layer and choose Select > Load Selection. Choose Color Fill 2 Mask and select Intersect with Selection (**figure 9.37**).

4. Turn off all layers except the little girl layer and click the Layer Mask button. Now the little girl is hollow and you can see the garage. Select Image > Adjustments > Invert (Cmd + I) [Ctrl + I] to invert the layer mask to silhouette the little girl (**figure 9.38**).

5. If necessary, paint refinements onto the girl's layer mask to fine-tune the silhouette.

6. After you've finished silhouetting the little girl, drag her onto a new document to replace the drab garage with a more fantastic scene.

figure 9.35

Using the Load Selection command to activate the alpha channel with the head mask.

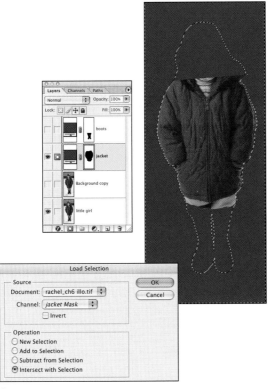

figure 9.37

Intersecting the jacket mask with the active selection.

figure 9.38

After combining and inverting the masks, the little girl is perfectly silhouetted.

Would it have been better to photograph the little girl with the white background without the garage door showing? Of course. But as it happened, Mark was setting up for a photo shoot and his neighbor's daughter wandered over. She asked to have her picture taken. As you may know, it's often easier to take the picture than to explain to a seven-year-old that it won't work out. Much to Mark's surprise, he really liked the little girl's expression. But he swears that next time the seamless paper will be mounted higher to cover the entire garage door!

Will you always need to use so many masks and steps to separate a subject from the background? I certainly hope not—but keep this multi-step technique in mind the next time you face an image that has a variety of tonal or edge qualities you need to mask out. Treating each area separately lets you use the best (and fastest) method for each area.

IMAGE CALCULATIONS

Under the Image menu you'll find two useful commands—Apply Image and Calculations. Before the introduction of layers in Photoshop 3.0, image compositing and controlling effects relied heavily on channel masking. The most advanced method to create fine-edged masks was to use the Image Calculation commands to combine and refine images and channels. Today—with the use of layers and blending modes—many of their results can be achieved more easily. However, these commands still offer useful methods for creating image composites and for building masks that maintain fine tonal and edge detail. Because Image Calculations use interchannel math that compares channel values to create the results, they are often called *chops* (**ch**annel **op**eration**s**).

> **Note**
>
> A discussion of Calculations would not be complete without a sincere tip of the hat to John Knoll, Kai Krause, David Biedny, Bert Monroy, and Bryan Guignard. It is with great appreciation that I learned from all of their lectures, books, articles, and online tutorials.

The Apply Image and the Calculate commands have similarities and differences that make them more daunting to understand than they really need to be.

The two commands share the following requirements:

- Images you want to calculate need to be open. You can't navigate to a closed file on your hard drive to use it during a calculate session.

- Images you want to calculate together need to be the exact same width and height (to the very pixel). With the booming popularity of digital cameras, this requirement is becoming easier and easier to meet.

- You can mix and match RGB, LAB, CMYK, and grayscale images using the Calculate command.

- Both commands can be used to move selections between files.

- In addition to the standard blending modes, both Apply Image and Calculate include the Add and Subtract blending modes (see "Blending Mode Guide" for more information).

The primary differences are:

- The Apply Image command uses the composite color image or single channel as its source to create color images or channels. It cannot create a new document, channel, or layer.

- Because the Apply Image command overwrites the active source, I recommend you either duplicate the file before using Apply Image or make certain you're working on a copy of your original file.

- The Calculate command lets you choose a source from any open image with the same image resolution, but it only uses a single grayscale channel. Calculate creates a new channel, black-and-white document, or an active selection, but never a color file.

To be completely accurate, the Duplicate command is also a calculate function, and it is the fastest way to duplicate a file—especially one with many layers and channels. Holding down (Option) [Alt] while selecting Image > Duplicate bypasses the duplicate window. You also have to keep your mouse button down during this maneuver; if you release the mouse when the menu drops down, while holding the Alt key, the menu disappears.

Blending Mode Guide

The Calculate commands apply the math of the blend to the layer, channel, or composite to create the desired effect. It is essential to remember that *0* is the equivalent of black, *128* is the equivalent of gray, *255* is the equivalent of white, and that all blends compare pixel values to calculate the result.

- **Normal:** Combines the two sources based on opacity.

Darkening Group: Neutral to white; will have no effect on light areas; the effect will be progressively stronger as the tones become darker.

- **Darken:** Dark pixel values replace light values.
- **Multiply:** Multiplies values less than 50% gray times each other, resulting in darker values, while light areas are not affected.
- **Color Burn:** Results in a darker channel with increased contrast.
- **Linear Burn:** Is a strong combination of Multiply and Color Burn and forces dark values to pure black.

Lightening Group: Neutral to black; will have no effect on dark areas; the effect will be progressively stronger as the tones become lighter.

- **Lighten:** The opposite of darken, it compares the two sources and replaces the darker pixels with lighter pixels.
- **Screen:** The opposite of multiply, results in a lighter channel while dark areas are not affected. Also reduces contrast.
- **Color Dodge:** Increases contrast of areas lighter than 50% gray while preserving black values.
- **Linear Dodge:** Is a combination of Screen and Color Dodge and forces light areas to pure white.

Contrast Group: Neutral to 50% gray; will have no effect on 50% gray areas; and are all good for adding contrast—specifically, for making the dark values darker and the light values lighter.

- **Overlay:** Multiplies dark values and screens light values, which increases contrast but without clipping to pure white or black.

- **Soft Light:** A combination of dodge, which lightens the light values, and burn, which darkens the dark values. Adds less contrast than Overlay or Hard Light.

- **Hard Light:** Multiplies the darks and screens the light values and increases contrast dramatically.

- **Vivid Light:** Lightens the values above 50% gray by decreasing the contrast, and darkens the values below 50% gray by increasing contrast.

- **Linear Light:** Combining linear burn and linear dodge, this blend mode lightens the values above 50% gray by increasing the brightness, and it darkens the values below 50% gray by decreasing brightness.

- **Pin Light:** Combines darken and lighten to replace pixel values. Always very contrasty. Used for special effects and more infrequently to create masks.

- **Hard Mix:** Lighter values lighten and darker values darken to the point of threshold and posterization.

Combination Group: Found only in the Apply Image and Calculate commands.

- **Add:** Adding light values results in lighter-to-bright white values. Black-value areas remain black (0+0=0). The Scale factor is any number between 1.000 and 2.000. The Offset value lets you lighten or darken the pixels in the destination channel by any brightness value between -255 and +255. Negative values darken the image; positive values lighten the image.

- **Subtract:** Subtracts the pixel values from the corresponding pixel values and uses scale and offset as in Add.

Comparative Group: Neutral to black.

- **Difference:** Reveals identical pixel values as black, similar values as dark and opposite values as light to white values.

- **Exclusion:** Similar to Difference but with less contrast. Blending with black produces no change and white inverts the compared values.

Have I memorized all of these blending modes? No. But I do know which general group to start with to darken, lighten, enhance contrast, and so on. Often just getting into the tonal ballpark makes for a good start, and then you can choose a related blend to see if the effect is creating the desired effect.

The Apply Image Settings

Apply Image is the smaller of the two commands. It always uses the active image as its target, meaning the image that is active when you select Image > Apply Image will always be on the receiving end of the Apply Image command. Before we use Apply Image to make masks, an overview of the terms shown in **figure 9.39** will be helpful.

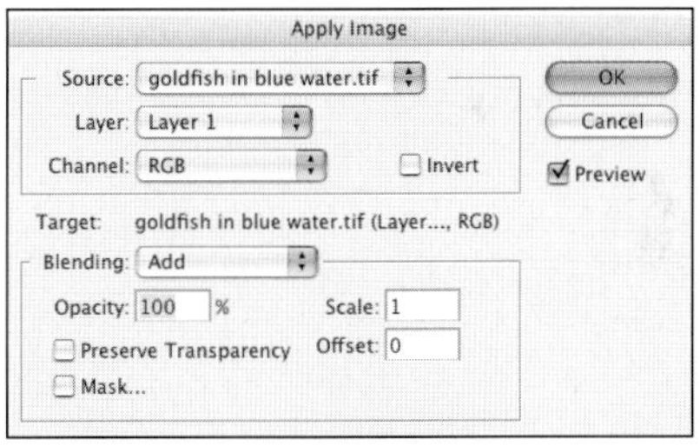

figure 9.39

The options in the Apply Image dialog box.

- **Source:** Pull-down menu used to select from the other open images to be processed with the active image.

- **Layer:** Determines which individual layer or merged layers of the source will be used. Merged is only available if both files are in the same color mode.

- **Channel:** Determines if the results will go into the merged color file or into one individual channel. If the layer you choose has transparency (such as a text layer), transparency will also be a choice.

- **Target:** Is always the document that was active when you invoked the Apply Image command. When making masks (as we will do later in this section), the name of the active channel will appear here.

- **Blending:** The mathematical formulas used to combine the layers or channels.

- **Scale and Offset:** Only active when Add or Subtract are chosen in the Blending option. The Scale factor is any number between 1.000 and 2.000—a higher Scale value darkens the image. The Offset value lets you lighten or darken the pixels in the destination channel by any brightness value between +255 and −255. Negative values darken the image; positive values lighten the image.

- **Opacity:** Controls the percentage of the source used in the calculation process. The lower the percentage, the more the target is used.

- **Preserve Transparency:** If the target layer has transparency, use this checkbox to protect it from being affected.

- **Mask:** Lets you control where the calculation takes place, with a mask from any open image that has the same pixel resolution.

- **Invert:** Switches tonal values from within the Apply Image command.

- **Preview:** Lets you monitor the effect of all the above settings. Thank goodness!

In a nutshell, before using the Apply Image command, make sure the image, layer, or channel you want to composite or make a mask for is active. Use the pull-down menus to create the desired results.

Using the Apply Image Command on One Channel

Can you imagine trying to outline the fine details in Big Ben? Even just thinking about it makes me nervous. But the Apply Image command can separate the tower from the clouds in no time at all, as shown in **figure 9.40**.

Close-up of the original

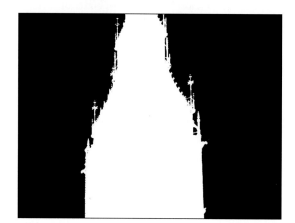

Close-up of the mask

Close up of the isolated tower with all the details intact

figure 9.40

Masking out the clouds while maintaining the filigree and gargoyles is a perfect task for the Apply Image command.

🌐⤵ ch9_bigben.jpg

1. Before entering the Apply Image command, inspect the image color channels (Command + 1, + 2, + 3) [Ctrl + 1, + 2, + 3]. In this example, the blue channel reveals the most tonal difference between the tower and the clouds (**figure 9.41**).

Red channel

Green channel

Blue channel

figure 9.41

Inspect the image channels to identify the one with the most tonal contrast.

2. Duplicate the blue channel by dragging it down to the Create New Channel button on the Channels palette.

3. With the blue channel copy active, select Image > Apply Image. Since the blue channel had the most tonal difference, we will blend the blue channel into the blue channel copy, which is the source shown in **figure 9.42**. By changing the blending option to Color Burn, the contrast is greatly increased.

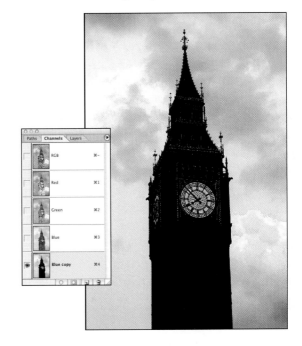

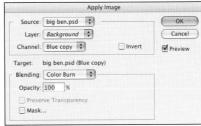

figure 9.42

Blending the channel possessing the most contrast with itself using Color Burn increases the contrast dramatically.

4. Very often, I'll repeat Apply Image with the same channels but experiment with the blend to create even whiter whites and darker darks. Choose Image > Apply Image with Source: Blue Channel of Merged Layer, and select Hard Light. As you can see in **figure 9.43**, the tower is very dark, and the clouds are getting lighter and lighter.

5. To boost the contrast even more, use Levels and move the shadow value to the right, the Highlight slider to left and the Midtones slider to the right to force the remaining light areas to white and the dark areas to black, as shown in **figure 9.44**.

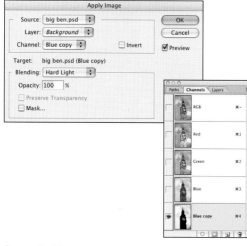

figure 9.43

Repeating the Apply Image command creates more contrast for separating the tower from the clouds.

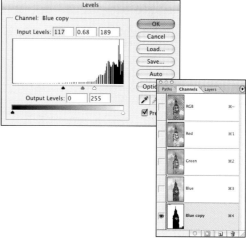

figure 9.44

Use Levels to make the white areas pure white and the dark areas pure black.

6. Use the Polygon Lasso tool to select the interior of the tower and fill with black to remove the inside filigree from the mask. Choose Select > Deselect, and then paint with white to clean the sky (**figure 9.45**).

7. Now the tower is black and the clouds are white. For the mask to select the tower, choose Image > Adjustments > Invert (Cmd + I) [Ctrl + I] to flip the tones. Return to the Layers palette and choose Select > Load Selection > Blue copy. Select > Feather with 1 and choose Edit > Copy. Select File > New and click OK. Choose Edit > Paste to drop the silhouetted Big Ben onto a blank file (**figure 9.46**).

figure 9.46

The isolated Big Ben.

All in all, isolating Big Ben with all of its wonderful gargoyles and gothic filigree was accomplished quickly and easily with the Apply Image command. Using Apply Image to combine identical channels into themselves is a good place to start to learn how the Apply Image command works.

figure 9.45

Clean up the mask to remove the vestiges of the clouds and block out the remains of the clock.

Using the Apply Image Command on Multiple Channels

I wanted to replace the drab studio background in **figure 9.47** to place the young woman into a more interesting sunset scene, as shown in **figure 9.48**. The Apply Image command can be used to mathematically blend the one channel into itself, or, as in this example, to blend two channels to make a mask.

🌐⤳⊱ **ch9_wavy_hair.jpg**

🌐⤳⊱ **ch9_sunset.jpg**

figure 9.47

The studio backdrop doesn't do the woman justice.

figure 9.48

Replacing the background makes the image more interesting.

Isolating Soft-Focus Hair

1. Before entering the Apply Image dialog box, inspect the color channels of the portrait to see which ones have the best tonal information. In this example both the red and the green channels contain valuable tonal information (**figure 9.49**). Because the green channel offers the best tonal differentiation, duplicate it by dragging it down to the Create New Channel button on the Channels palette.

Red channel

Green channel

Blue channel

figure 9.49

Inspect the color channels to identify the channels with the best tonal contrast for building the mask.

2. The red channel contains good tonal separation in the highlights between the studio backdrop and the model's hair, which we can take advantage of by combining the red channel with the green. With the green channel copy active, select Image > Apply Image and set the source to red channel. To increase the channel contrast, blend the red channel using the Hard Light blending mode, as shown in **figure 9.50**, to create the initial mask.

3. If needed, you can repeat the Apply Image command with the same or a new setting to enhance the mask even more. In this case, I used Apply Image again to blend in the red channel of the merged layer with Overlay (**figure 9.51**). In no time at all, I have a very good start for a mask that maintains the hair detail.

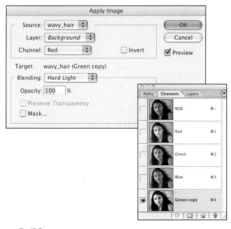

figure 9.50

Blending the red channel into a duplicate of the green channel using the Hard Light blending mode increases the contrast.

figure 9.51

Repeating Apply Image increases the contrast even more; in just two steps, you're very close to a perfect mask.

4. Open the Info palette and add Color Samplers (nested under the eyedropper in the toolbar) to the white area on the upper-left and upper-right corners (**figure 9.52**). I changed my readout to Grayscale by clicking on the small triangle under the eyedropper in the Info palette. *K* stands for black and is the clearest readout for verifying masks. *0* equals pure white, and 100 equals pure black.

figure 9.52

Measuring the white areas using the Info palette.

5. With a low-pressure setting and a large soft-edged brush, use the Dodge tool, set to Highlights, to lighten the background to pure white (**figure 9.53**). Lighten gently and avoid destroying delicate hair information at this stage. You will have a chance to refine the mask when the images come together in the composite, which has the advantage of seeing the effect of the mask in combination with the new background.

6. Select the interior of the woman (**figure 9.54**) and fill with black to create the results in **figure 9.55**.

T i p

When selecting large areas of a mask with the Lasso or Marquee tool, make sure the feather is set to 0 before making the selection. Using a feathered selection tool may impact the edge quality of the mask in unexpected and undesired ways.

figure 9.53

The Dodge tool, set to Highlight, cleans up lighter areas of masks very quickly.

figure 9.54

Without going too close to the edge of the hair, select the interior portion of the figure and carefully draw down along her shoulder.

figure 9.55

To block out the woman's face so that it isn't affected in the composite, fill with black.

Compositing the Woman into the Sunset

1. Return to the RGB channel. Choose Select > Load Select and choose Green copy (**figure 9.56**).

2. Open the sunset image and use the Move tool to drag the sunset over to the woman image (**figure 9.57**) and click the Add Layer Mask button to create the initial composite (**figure 9.58**). The image doesn't look too bad for a preliminary composite. But the light halos caused by the lighter studio backdrop around her hair are distracting, and the sunset is too strong, which distracts from her.

figure 9.57

Dragging the new background to the woman's image maintains the active selection.

figure 9.58

Clicking on the Layer Mask button transfers the selection into a layer mask.

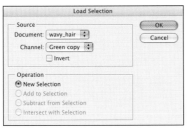

figure 9.56

Loading the green copy mask changes it into an active selection.

3. By adjusting the opacity of the sunset layer to 65%, its color dominance is reduced, which allows the focus of the image to be the woman and not the sunset (**figure 9.59**).

figure 9.59

Adjusting the layer opacity of the sunset mutes its garish color and helps blend the images together.

The Apply Image command works extremely well on large files. Once you've tried it a few times and become familiar with the terms and effects, you'll find yourself using it often. Of course, you'll need to experiment with the channels and blending modes that work best for your own images.

Working with the Calculations Command

The Calculations command processes single channels to create a new channel, a black-and-white document, or an active selection, but never a color file. As you can see in **figure 9.60**, its interface is divided into four primary sections—Source 1, Source 2, Blending, and Result. In addition, if you click on the Mask button in the Blending box, the interface contains a total of 12 pull-down menus and 3 invert checkboxes to create practically innumerable possible combinations. No wonder people shy away from Calculations!

figure 9.60

The options in the Calculations dialog box.

As described previously, many of the parameters for Apply Image and Calculations are identical. Working from top to bottom, here they are:

- **Source 1 and 2:** A source is an individual channel or grayscale merged channel from an open image's layer, layer transparency, channel, or selection. Imagine it as Source 1 being applied on top of Source 2.

- **Blending:** Is divided into three areas—blending, opacity, and mask. Blending works exactly the same way as Apply Image. Opacity controls the opacity of Source 1. The mask option lets you control the calculation through an alpha channel, an image channel, and an active selection to protect parts of Source 2 from being affected by the calculation.

- **Result:** This option indicates where the result should go—a new alpha channel, a new document, or an active selection.

Remember, Source 1 is processed through Source 2 via the blend and mask options to create the result.

Using the Calculations Command on One Image

To separate the woman from her environment in figure 9.61, I used the Calculations command to create the start of an alpha channel. I then enhanced the alpha channel with selections and the brush tools to make the mask in figure 9.62 and produce the final composite (figure 9.63). Would it have been better to have the model photographed in a studio on a white seamless backdrop? Of course. But a lot of clients use existing stock images, and removing or replacing the background is a common request.

ch9_sports_woman.jpg

ch9_water.jpg

figure 9.61

figure 9.62

The mask created using the Calculations command.

figure 9.63

This image has three primary areas that need to be masked: her body, her hair, and the water bottle. The body is clearly defined, but her dark hair is on a dark background. You might lose a bit of your own hair if you don't use Image Calculations to tease out as much image information as possible. The challenge with the bottle is that the translucency needs to be maintained to make the composite more convincing and refreshing.

Calculating Fine Details

1. Inspect the color channels of the sports_woman file. Notice that both the red and the blue channel display useful tonal contrast to take advantage of.

2. Choose Image > Calculations and set Source 1 to Red, Source 2 to Blue, and Result to New Channel. Because we need to increase the contrast—make the dark values darker and the light values lighter—use one of the contrast-enhancing blending modes. I chose Hard Light (figure 9.64). The tonal definition distinguishing her face and arm is striking. Now name the channel *bottle*.

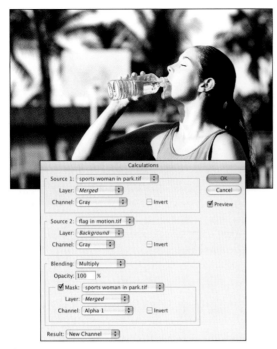

figure 9.64

Blending the red and blue channels together using the Hard Light blending mode boosts the contrast appreciably.

figure 9.65

Creating a separate mask for the ponytail, which has different tonal characteristics than the majority of the image.

3. To create a mask for her ponytail, choose Image > Calculations and set Source 1 to Red and Source 2 to Red using the Hard Light blending mode. Choose New Channel from the Result pull-down menu (**figure 9.65**) and name the channel *hair*.

Using Calculations requires experimenting with the variety of possible combinations. Thankfully, the preview is accurate.

Combining and Completing the Mask

Now we have two masks, one in which the bottle and woman are well defined, and one where her ponytail stands out well.

1. Her dark hair is still a problem, which is solved by duplicating the Hair channel and inverting it (**figure 9.66**). Now we have three masks, each responsible for specific areas. The masks need to be combined into one mask to separate the woman from the background. Our goal is to make the woman white and the background black.

figure 9.66

Inverting a duplicate of the ponytail mask lets me see the contrast that is available to take advantage of.

2. Click on the hair alpha (#5) and select the interior portion of the woman using the Lasso tool. You don't need to select the entire figure at once; often I'll select a section of the image and fill with white, deselect, and move on to the next segment (**figure 9.67**).

3. Use the Pen tool to follow the smooth contours along her leotard and arms (**figure 9.68**). When using the Pen tool, stay approximately 2 pixels inside of the figure to maintain the natural edge quality of the photograph. Convert the path into a selection and fill with white.

4. Use the Marquee or Lasso tool to select large portions of the background and fill with black (**figure 9.69**).

figure **9.68**

Use the Pen tool on the smooth contours to make precise selections.

figure **9.67**

Selecting smaller parts of the image is easier than trying to select the entire figure at once.

figure **9.69**

Use the Marquee tool to select tile-like chunks of the background before filling with black.

5. Use a 50% hardness brush, set to Overlay, to make the outside edges black and the interior edges white (**figure 9.70**). On more critical areas such as by the bottle and mouth, you may need to use a smaller, harder brush to paint in the separation.

6. Pen tool the bottle and use the path, which you can load and invert to protect the bottle as you paint (**figure 9.71**). The areas under her chin require you to switch the brush back to Normal to paint along the contour of her throat. The more care you use in making the mask now, the less time you'll need to repair the composite later.

figure 9.71

To protect the bottle while painting on the mask, convert the Bottle Pen path to a selection.

T i p

When painting with an Overlay brush it is often helpful to paint a few strokes, release the mouse button or lift the pressure-sensitive stylus, and then start painting again to "tell" Photoshop to start a new brush stroke.

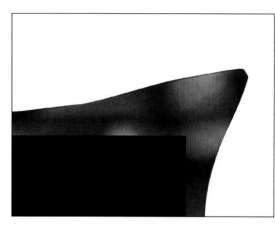

figure 9.70

Using the Overlay blending mode in conjunction with a black or white brush lets you paint without affecting the opposite tones.

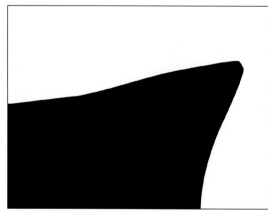

7. If you're not sure which areas to paint, hide the Bottle and Hair Copy channels (**figure 9.72**). The Calculate mask renders the bottle details so well that you'll only need to paint over the areas in her hands, which should have no translucency. By painting with black and white, you should create results similar to those shown in **figure 9.73**.

figure 9.72

To see where to paint, view the mask through the RGB information.

figure 9.73

The mask is almost done. Now all that needs to be added is the ponytail information.

7. To add her ponytail to the mask in progress, select the Hair Copy layer and roughly select the back of her head (**figure 9.74**). Choose Edit > Copy, click on the Hair channel, and select Edit > Paste. The results are shown in **figure 9.75**.

figure 9.74

Selecting and copying the best ponytail information.

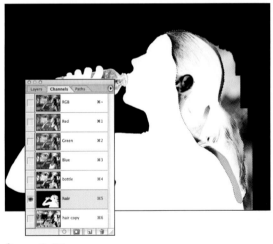

figure 9.75

Pasting the ponytail information into the Hair channel adds the fine details needed to maintain believability.

8. Refine the back of her hair by painting to create the final mask (**figure 9.76**).

9. To add the bottle into this mask, turn the Bottle path into a selection and then use Calculations (**figure 9.77**). The Lighten blending mode will only lighten darker areas without affecting the white areas of her hands.

figure 9.76

After refining the ponytail by painting, the mask is coming together beautifully.

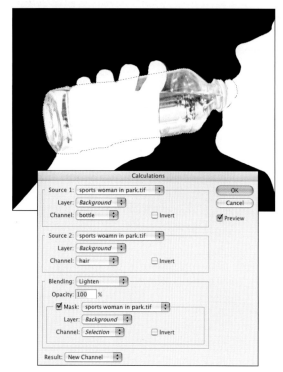

figure 9.77

Calculating the better bottle into the mask.

10. When the mask is complete, return to the Layers palette and drag the water image onto the woman document. Activate the hair mask (the fifth alpha channel) using (Cmd + Option + 5) [Ctrl + Alt + 5]. With the water layer active, click the Layer Mask button and select Image > Adjustments > Invert to reveal the woman (**figure 9.78**).

figure 9.78

After changing the background and refining the layer mask, the water really looks refreshing.

Remember, you can paint on the layer mask using any painting tool to refine how the images come together and view the results at the same time (we discussed this in Chapter 7, "The Power of Layer Masking"). In this case, I used small black and white brushes to refine the edges and transitions to create the final image.

Using the Calculations Command on Two Images

Many years ago, when computers were much slower and 256 MB of RAM was worth a king's ransom, Calculations were used to move channels and selections between two images. Now that hard drives are so much larger and computers are faster and more powerful, this aspect of Calculations isn't used as often. But the ability to mathematically combine channels between images can be very creative. In the following example, I added the cracked texture to the torso (**figure 9.79**) by creating a texture map and using a Curves Adjustment Layer to adjust the tones, which tattooed the texture into the skin.

 ch9_torso.jpg

 ch9_cracked_texture.jpg

Tip

For the Calculations command to recognize multiple files, all the files need to be identical in size. If the files are close in size and aspect ratio, and maintaining exact proportions is not important, try this tip to match file size:

1. Open all images on which you would like to use the Calculations command. Of the group that needs resizing, make the least important one active by clicking on it.

2. Select Image > Image Size. With this dialog box open, choose Window from the main menu and drag down to the name of the most important file you need to match. Photoshop will automatically resize the active file to the exact size of the chosen file.

You can match file, image, and canvas size between images when the File > New, Image Size, and Canvas Size dialog boxes are open by selecting Window > *name of the open file*. Photoshop will transfer the referenced file's size to the open dialog box.

figure 9.79

Calculations let you blend images together in surprising ways.

The goal is to create a channel mask that combines the torso tonal contours with the cracked texture. To isolate the torso from the background, we'll use a combination of Calculations and the Pen tool.

1. Start by inspecting the color channels to see which one has the best tonal information. In this file, the red is the best black-and-white version of the file, as shown in **figure 9.80**.

Red channel

Green channel

Blue channel

figure 9.80

You'll have better results if you begin by using the best black-and-white version of the image.

2. Select Image > Calculations and set Red as both Source 1 and Source 2. Use the Add blending mode and adjust the Offset and Scale to enhance the contrast without forcing the highlights to pure white and the blacks to pure black. I used −32 offset and a scale of 1.55 as shown in **figure 9.81**. The result should be set to New Channel.

figure 9.81

To create an alpha channel with a well-defined tonal range, Calculate the red channel with itself.

3. Use the Pen tool to select the four negative areas of the image. I find it easier to select one at a time, convert that path to a selection and fill with black, and move on to the other areas. For example, I started by selecting the small hollow area under his arm, changed the path to a selection, and filled with black. Choose Select > Deselect and select the second area and so forth, as shown in **figure 9.82**.

figure 9.82

Selecting and filling the four background areas using black.

4. Open the texture image and make sure that it is the exact same size as the torso image. Then choose Image > Calculations and set Source 1 to torso alpha 1 and Source 2 to the cracked texture. Choose a texture channel that creates a striking effect. Red will give a contrasty version and green a slightly more muted version, I used the Multiply blending mode but Hard Light works very well too. The result should be a new channel, as shown in **figure 9.83**.

5. The best aspect of Calculations is the ability to experiment as I did in **figure 9.84**—by changing channels and blending modes, you can quickly create intriguing images.

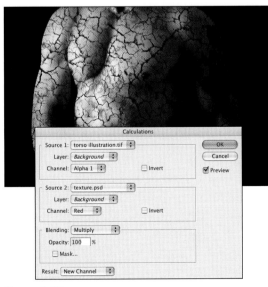

figure 9.83

Combining the texture with the torso to create an unusual combination.

6. Return to the Layers palette and choose Select > Load Selection Alpha 2. Add a Curves Adjustment Layer and click OK without changing any settings. Experiment with the blending mode of the Curves layer—I used Screen to add the cracked texture to the torso shown in **figure 9.85**.

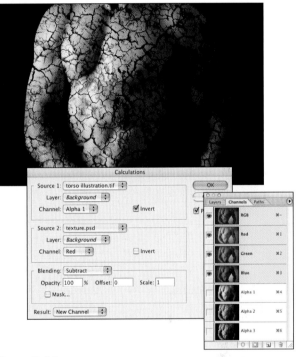

figure 9.84

Experiment by changing the source and blending modes.

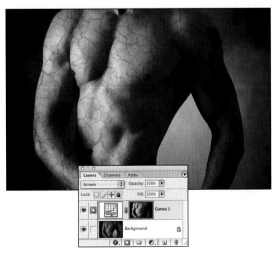

figure 9.85

The Curves Adjustment Layer, set to Screen, applies the texture of the rock to the torso.

7. The options to add and manipulate the texture are only limited to how long you can stay awake! I doubled the Curves layer, blurred the mask with a 5-pixel Gaussian Blur to soften the texture, and changed the blending mode to Soft Light to make his skin glow with texture, as shown in **figure 9.86**.

figure 9.86

Doubling the Curve and blurring the layer mask causes his skin to glow.

CLOSING THOUGHTS

There are many ways to accomplish similar effects in Photoshop, but it is important to not always do the same thing day after day. Apply Image and Calculations are not the user-friendliest features in Photoshop, and at first they intimidated me very much because the name reminded me of advanced mathematics. Now that I understand the differences and similarities of the two, I use them more and more. We'll be using both to separate delicate subjects such as water and smoke in the following chapter.

10

SELECTING TRANSLUCENCY AND GREEN SCREEN TECHNIQUES

Imagine trying to hold a strand of smoke, the shimmer of water, a transient shadow, or a bit of motion blur. Selecting translucent subjects requires extracting the subject from the original photograph while maintaining the most delicate details. The nuances of reflections, translucency, and fine detail in a scene are among the most beautiful aspects of photography, adding dimensionality and delicacy to an image that is barely tangible, yet vitally important.

You can work with Photoshop to preserve the finely detailed translucency of your subjects, or you can turn to dedicated masking plug-ins, such as Corel KnockOut, Human Software AutoMask, and Extensis Mask Pro, many of which offer downloadable try-out versions. In the first part of this chapter, we'll use Photoshop to mask translucency, motion blur, and delicate tonality. In the second part, we'll venture into working with green screen photographs, both with and without third-party plug-ins.

In this chapter you'll learn to

- Select translucent subjects, including glass and motion blur
- Mask out wedding veils and flowing cloth
- Work with flames, fireworks, and smoke
- Understand green screen photography and extraction

GLASS AND TRANSLUCENCY

When I studied still-life photography, my instructor dedicated a month to photographing glassware. We learned how to do white line and black line photos, which in essence are the difference between using white or black reflector cards to define the shape of the subject. In other words, photographs of glass and lighter-colored liquids are defined by the environment, which includes lighting and reflections used to portray and define them.

In most cases, selecting glassware usually starts with making a precise Pen tool path of the subject to define the outer contours of the object. The second step can include a variety of techniques, such as creating a luminance mask of the translucent areas, using the Image Calculations command to combine the hard-edged path with the translucent image information, or using layer blending modes and layer masks to create the illusion of transparency in the composite.

Working with Glass and Color

The goldfish in **figure 10.1** needs nicer water, so I decided to give it a vacation (**figure 10.2**). I wasn't trying to make the water completely realistic, but I did want to maintain the feeling of the glass bowl and the effect the blue water would have on the table.

My strategy was to outline the goldfish bowl with the Pen tool, use the Image Calculations command to combine the crisp outline with the best tonal information while maintaining the feeling of the glass bowl, and then refine how the water and the fishbowl interacted to make the goldfish happy in his new home.

🌐▷← **ch10_goldfish.jpg**

🌐▷← **ch10_water.jpg**

Defining Shape and Translucency

1. Outline the fishbowl with the Pen tool and name the path *Bowl*.

figure 10.1

BEFORE

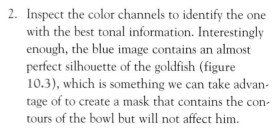

figure 10.2

AFTER

2. Inspect the color channels to identify the one with the best tonal information. Interestingly enough, the blue image contains an almost perfect silhouette of the goldfish (**figure 10.3**), which is something we can take advantage of to create a mask that contains the contours of the bowl but will not affect him.

Red channel   Green channel   Blue channel

figure 10.3

Viewing the image channels reveals the blue channel is a mask waiting to be used.

3. Convert the bowl path into a selection and click on the blue channel in the Channels palette. Choose Edit > Copy, which will copy just the interior of the fishbowl from the blue channel.

4. Create a new channel (**figure 10.4**), and select Edit > Paste. This drops the interior of only the blue channel into the alpha channel (**figure 10.5**). Name the alpha channel *Fish*.

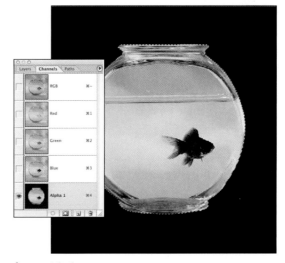

figure 10.5

The blue channel information has been copied into the new alpha channel mask.

5. The fish isn't perfectly black, but it needs to be to protect this part of the image. Use a 50% hardness black brush to paint over the body (**figure 10.6**). To maintain the translucency of the fins, I reduced the opacity and hardness of the brush and painted on the tail in the direction it is moving.

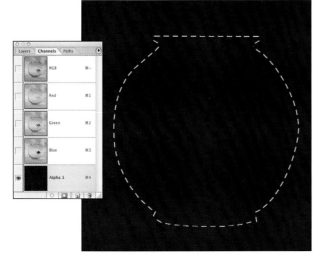

figure 10.4

The path outline of the fishbowl guarantees the contours are precisely selected.

figure 10.6

Painting the fish black will protect it from being overwritten by the new water.

Brush Tips:

When refining layer or alpha masks with the Brush tool:

- Pressing the left bracket key ([) reduces brush size; pressing the right bracket key (]) increases brush size.

- Shift + left bracket makes the brush harder; Shift + right bracket makes the brush softer.

- Refine brush size and hardness by (Ctrl-clicking) [right-clicking] on the image to open the Brush picker.

- On the Options bar, reducing opacity weakens density. Reducing flow slows down how quickly the brush builds to the designated opacity.

- With a brush active, typing in a single digit sets the brush to that percentage of opacity *times 10*. For example, typing *2* sets the brush to 20%. However, if you type two numbers in rapid succession, such as *65*, the ×10 factor disappears and the brush is set to 65% opacity. (If you type the two digits too slowly, you'll get the opacity of the first number you typed times 10.) If you need a single-digit opacity, such as 2%, you can get that by quickly typing a leading *0* before entering the *2*. You can also change the flow rate of the brush using the Shift key with the same digits that control opacity.

6. Return to the RGB composite channel. Open the water file and drag it onto the fish file. Choose Select > Load Selection and choose the Fish alpha channel; with the water layer active, add a layer mask to create the results in **figure 10.7**.

7. In this example, I simply reduced the opacity of the water layer to 65% to diminish its intensity, as seen in **figure 10.8**.

figure 10.7

The layer mask controls where the new water shows.

figure 10.8

Reducing opacity is a simple, yet effective method for blending images together.

T i p

To move or scale image layer information independently of the layer mask, it is very important to unlink the layer from the mask and activate the image layer, not the layer mask, before moving or scaling.

Refining the Image

There are a number of details to attend to here—the water shouldn't be above the original water line, the fishbowl walls and base need to be more visible through the water, and the blue color of the water needs to be reflecting onto the table and the top of the fishbowl.

1. Use the Gradient tool on the layer mask to make sure water only shows below the original waterline. Press *d* to reset the Color picker to black and white. Activate the Gradient tool, and from the Gradient picker on the Options bar, choose the second gradient, which is always Foreground to Transparent.

2. Click on the layer mask, and start the gradient by the upper waterline and draw it to the lower waterline (**figure 10.9**). Using the black-to-transparent gradient lets you add a gradient without overwriting the entire mask in the same way that a standard black-to-white gradient would.

figure 10.9

The shorter the length of the gradient line, the quicker the transition will be.

3. The image is looking better and the fish is happier, but the water is too dense along the thicker edges and base of the fishbowl. Because the following step requires us to paint intuitively on the layer mask, it's a good idea to duplicate the layer to ensure you have a backup copy of the layer to fall back onto in case you make a mistake. Duplicate the water layer and turn off its visibility.

4. Select a soft-edged black brush, set to 50% opacity. Click on the original layer mask and brush over the base and edges of the bowl to hold back some of the water (**figure 10.10**).

figure 10.10

Using the soft black brush, set at 50% opacity, on the layer mask lets some of the fishbowl shimmer through.

T i p

When refining soft transitions on layer or channel masks, use only the outer edges of a large soft-edged brush to subtly paint in the transitions.

Adding Tinted Reflections

If the water was really this blue, it would be reflected on the tabletop and the upper ring of the fishbowl. Therefore, a hint of blue needs to be added to better incorporate the fishbowl into the environment.

1. Activate the fish layer, sample the blue of the water with the Eyedropper tool, and add a Solid Color Fill layer, which will automatically be blue.

2. As you can see in **figure 10.11**, the entire image is solid blue. Select the layer mask and press (Cmd + I) [Ctrl + I] to invert the mask to black (**figure 10.12**) and to reveal the image again.

3. In the Paths palette, drag the Bowl path down to the Make Selection button. Return to the Layers palette. Choose a large, soft-edged white brush with a low opacity of 15% and brush along the top of the fishbowl (**figure 10.13**) to add a just a hint of color reflection.

4. To paint in a touch of blue under the bowl as I have in **figure 10.14**, choose Select > Inverse, increase your brush size, and paint in a hint of blue on the table. (Option-click) [Alt-click] on the layer mask to view it (**figure 10.15**). (Option-click) [Alt-click] again to return to Normal view.

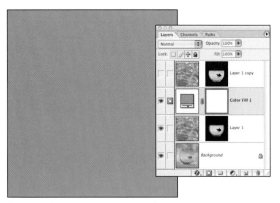

figure 10.11

The blue color will add a sense of realism.

figure 10.12

Inverting the layer mask hides all the color.

figure 10.13

Painting in a hint of blue on the top of the fishbowl.

figure 10.14

Follow the contours of the natural reflections to paint in a hint of blue.

figure 10.15

Viewing the layer mask can be very instructive; wherever it is light, the color shows through.

The steps used to control and finesse how the water and the original image interact will of course vary depending on your taste. When applying this technique to your own images, it is more important to transfer the concept rather than to follow the exact steps. Look for the tonal details, enhance them, and enjoy mimicking light and color to mirror and reflect your own reality.

The Hourglass in Twilight

To create *Twilight* (figure 10.16), Mark Beckelman used layer masks and blending modes to combine a clouds background with photographs of an old gentleman and an hourglass (figure 10.17), giving the hourglass a sense of translucency and light.

© Mark Beckelman

figure 10.16

Twilight *by Mark Beckelman.*

figure 10.17

The hourglass and the gentleman were lit and photographed with the final image in mind.

1. After Pen tooling the glass section of the hourglass, Mark copied it into the clouds image. Of course, it was completely opaque (**figure 10.18**). By reducing the layer opacity and adjusting the Lighten blending mode, the hourglass begins to interact with the clouds (**figure 10.19**).

figure 10.18

The studio backdrop in the hourglass ruins any sense of realism.

figure 10.19

The Lighten blending mode and the layer mask let the clouds show through the hourglass.

2. Often duplicating a layer with translucency and adjusting the blending mode and opacity lets you build up image density. **Figure 10.20** illustrates that by duplicating the hourglass layer in Normal mode, set at 50% opacity, the shape and contours are developing well. Mark painted on the layer mask with a soft black brush to control where the clouds show through.

3. To add a hint of blue color to the hourglass, Mark sampled the blue from the sky and added it to a new layer underneath the hourglass layers using the Soft Light blending mode. Having separate layers for the top and bottom color glazes (**figure 10.21**) gave him complete control over the effect of the blue.

4. **Figure** 10.22 shows the layers Mark used to build up the image. Please see Chapter 12, "Photorealistic Compositing," to learn how Mark added lighting effects to complete the image.

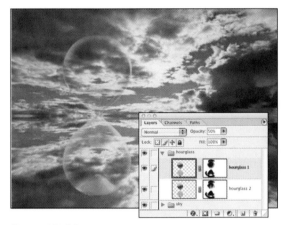

figure 10.20

Duplicating the hourglass layer and adjusting the blending mode and opacity adds visual depth to the hourglass.

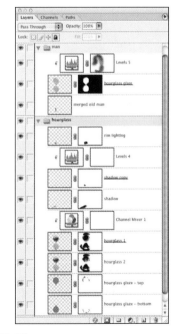

figure 10.22

Each layer is responsible for a specific aspect of the composite, which lets Mark adjust and refine the image.

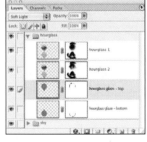

figure 10.21

Placing the blue underneath the hourglass layers, set to Soft Light, subtly colors the clouds and glass.

As Mark explains, "The background was created first, followed by the hourglass and the color and lighting effects. Then I added the gentleman and refined the sand and shadow at his feet."

SELECTING MOTION BLUR AND CLOTH

I love to photograph motion blur and drag shutter effects, which are created using a camera shutter speed of one-quarter of a second or slower in low-light situations. The painterly effects are surprising and refreshing—sadly, selecting them can be less invigorating.

The flag in figure 10.23 was photographed in the studio, but it really needs to be outside, as shown in figure 10.24. My strategy was to use the channel with the best contrast in combination with the Pen tool to select both the solid and the blurred parts of the flag. As often happens when you mix studio photos with environmental ones, the color of the light doesn't match, as shown in the interim image in figure 10.25.

ch10_motion_flag.jpg

ch10_clouds.jpg

In the following steps, I'll show you how to select the motion blur and re-create the actual blue color of the clouds to make the pieces fit together more realistically.

1. Outline the solid parts of the flag with the Pen tool, convert the path to a selection, and then save the selection as an alpha channel, as shown in figure 10.26.

2. Inspect the three channels to find the one with the best tonal information; in this example, it's the red channel. Duplicate it by dragging it down to the Create New Channel button in the Channels palette. To enhance the motion of the flag, boost the contrast by using Levels on the copy to darken the blacks and lighten the whites (figure 10.27).

3. Combine the crisp outline and the motion blur channel using the Image Calculations command (figure 10.28). Set Source 1 to the Red copy channel and Source 2 to the Alpha 1 channel. Using the Add blending mode, the two channels are combined perfectly. As soon as images have more than one or two channels, name them to avoid possible confusion. Name the combined channel *Motion Flag*.

© Dynamic Graphics, Inc.

BEFORE

figure 10.23

AFTER

figure 10.24

figure 10.25

Combining disparate image sources that reflect different lighting without correcting the different colors can produce a glaring error.

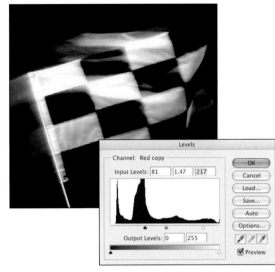

figure 10.27

Increasing the contrast of the red copy using Levels separates the motion from the background.

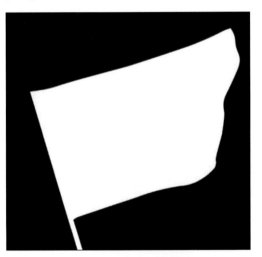

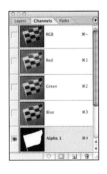

figure 10.26

The alpha channel created from the active Pen Tool path.

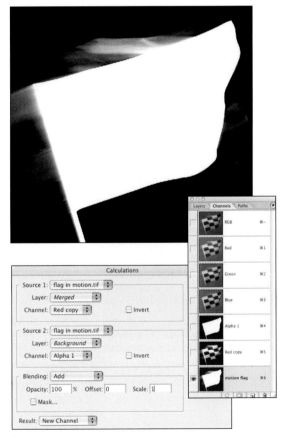

figure 10.28

Combining the crisp Pen tool outline with the motion channel.

4. Target the RGB composite channel by click-ing on the word RGB in the Channels palette or press (Cmd + ~) [Ctrl + ~]. Click on the Layers palette and choose Select > Load Selection, and then choose Motion Flag. Choose Layer > New > Layer via Copy (Cmd + J) [Ctrl + J] to place the selected flag onto its own layer (figure 10.29).

5. Open the clouds image, drag it to the flag image, and position the cloud layer under-neath the isolated flag layer. As you can see in figure 10.30, the warm color of the studio lights conflicts with the blue of the clouds.

6. Sample the blue color of the clouds and activate the flag layer. Select Layer > New Fill Layer > Solid Color, then select *Use Previous Layer to Create Clipping Mask*, and then change the blending mode to Color (figure 10.31). Click OK.

Photoshop adds the new Solid Color Fill layer, clips it with the flag layer, and sets the blending mode to Color—all of which ensure that the color will be applied only to the flag pixels (figure 10.32).

7. The solid part of the flag is too blue for my taste. You can control this by modifying the Solid Color layer mask. To hold back half of the blue, load the Alpha 1 channel as an active selection, click on the Solid Color layer mask, and choose Edit > Fill > 50% Gray (figure 10.33).

figure 10.31

Adding the Solid Color layer using clipping and the Color blending mode.

figure 10.29

The isolated flag.

figure 10.32

The flag is too blue, while the motion areas look fine.

figure 10.30

Placing the clouds underneath the flag reveals the disparate-ness of the original light sources.

figure 10.33

Holding back 50 percent of the blue on only the flag better melds the colors.

Separating motion shots that were taken in the studio with a solid background, such as the flag, are often easier than extracting motion shots taken outside like the one in figure 10.34.

To separate the football player and place him on the blue clouds (figure 10.35), I used the Image Calculations command as described previously to create the initial mask and then did a lot of handwork on the mask to paint out the background. Subjects shot on a solid background are easier to separate, and if you can control the background while taking the picture, you'll always be one step ahead of the game (this is discussed in more detail in the following chapter, "Image Concept and Execution").

BEFORE

figure 10.34

AFTER

figure 10.35

Veils and Cloth

Veils and flowing cloth are classic masking challenges. You may have already been called upon to replace the backgrounds of brides with veils, which requires you to maintain the illusion of translucency so that the new background shimmers through. In the following example, a young girl was photographed in a studio on Confirmation Day (figure 10.36), but wouldn't it be nice to have her outside the church, as shown in figure 10.37?

🌐↳⊱ **ch10_confirmation.jpg**

🌐↳⊱ **ch10_church.jpg**

Before you dive into masking an image with a veil, take a moment to identify which areas need to be 100-percent protected or black (usually the person), which ones need to be completely active or white (usually the background and any hollow areas, as circled in figure 10.38), and which parts need to be translucent. Start by masking out the solid areas and then proceed to the translucent areas, as described in the following list.

Creating the Initial Outline

1. Use the Pen tool to outline the entire figure, including the veil. It's critical that you not miss isolating the hollow areas, which need to be treated just like the image background (figure 10.39) and will be replaced with the new background image.

figure 10.36   **BEFORE**

© Mark Beckelman

figure 10.37   **AFTER**

Translucent   Solid white

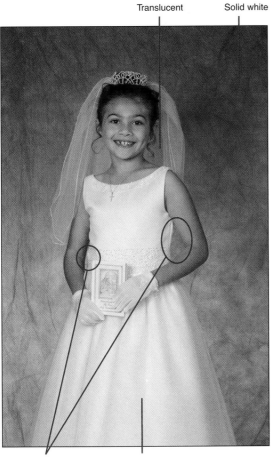

Hollow white   Solid black

figure 10.38

Identify the areas that need to be maintained (black), replaced (white), and translucent.

figure 10.39

Defining the exterior contour using the Pen tool.

2. Convert the path to an active selection, save the selection as an alpha channel, name the channel *Girl*, and press (Cmd + D) [Ctrl + D] to deselect the active selection (figure 10.40).

3. Click on the eyeball next to the Girl channel in the Channels palette to verify the quality of the outline. Use a small hard-edged black or white brush to refine any edges that aren't just right (figure 10.41).

figure 10.40

Saving the Pen tool selection as an alpha channel.

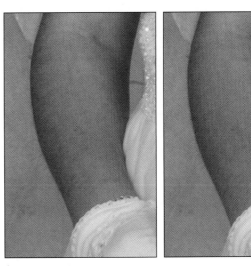

figure 10.41

Refining the alpha mask will result in a better composite.

4. Because the girl needs to remain 100% solid, invert the mask (Cmd + I) [Ctrl + I] (**figure 10.42**).

5. Pen tool just the veil, name the path and convert it to an active selection (**figure 10.43**). I opted to soften the crispness of the active selection with a feather of one pixel.

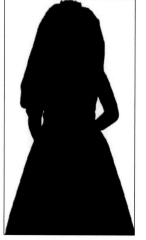

figure 10.42

Inverting the alpha mask to protect the little girl.

figure 10.43

Use the Pen tool to outline the veil.

6. Keeping the selection active, inspect the three image channels and notice the clarity of the green one. Choose Image > Calculations, and set Source 1 to Green and Source 2 to Girl. Then in the bottom section of the dialog box, make sure you specify the mask that will control where the image combination takes place by selecting the checkbox beside Mask and choosing Selection in the Channel drop-down box (**figure 10.44**). In this example, you can use either Screen or Add as the blending mode—they do the same thing in this case.

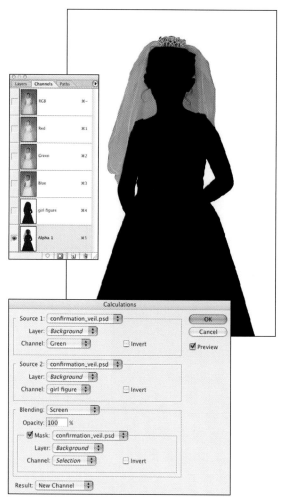

figure 10.44

Use the Image Calculations command to combine the alpha channel of the little girl with the veil information.

7. Return to RGB and click on the Layers palette. Open the church image and drag it on to the girl file. Choose Select > Load Selection and load the channel named *Alpha* as a selection (Cmd + Option + 5) [Ctrl + Alt + 5]. Click on the Add Layer Mask button in the Layers palette, and the church should be behind the little girl (figure 10.45).

8. Unlink the Church layer from its layer mask so that the mask is not transformed in the following step. Click on the Church Layer icon and choose Edit > Free Transform to scale the church into position, as shown in figure 10.46. Be sure to hold the Shift key when transforming to maintain the aspect ratio.

figure 10.46

After scaling the church, the image is coming together very nicely.

◯ T i p

When images are destined for the background and will be blurred, you can scale the background image without negatively impacting image quality. Scaling the background will make it softer, and blurring with Gaussian or Lens Blur will conceal any scaling artifacts.

figure 10.45

The initial placement of the church image.

9. To fine-tune how the two images come together, zoom to 100% view and refine the layer mask. Paint with black or white to clean up edges or use the Blur tool, set to 25% strength, to smooth out any harsh or jaggy edges (figure 10.47).

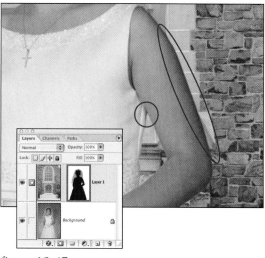

figure 10.47

To soften the transitions, refine the layer mask using the Blur and Paintbrush tools.

Refining the Background

The background of an image should be, well, in the background, and its role is to make the foreground of the image stand out. Three effective methods to reduce the importance of the background are: darken, blur, and desaturate. I rarely do all three on one image, but in this example blurring and darkening the background lets the little girl stand out.

1. Blur the background with Filter > Blur > Gaussian Blur, with a setting of 3, to soften the church (figure 10.48).

2. To darken the background, press (Option) [Alt] and select Layer > Adjustment Layer > Curves. Select *Use Previous Layer to Create Clipping Mask* and change the blending mode to Multiply. Without changing the curve, click OK and adjust the layer opacity (figure 10.49).

figure 10.48

Blurring the background diminishes its visual importance.

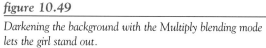

figure 10.49

Darkening the background with the Multiply blending mode lets the girl stand out.

3. Before saving the final image, select All and then Image > Crop to delete the extraneous church information. To save the flattened file as a separate file, Choose Layer > Flatten Image and then File > Save As.

Transformation Tips

Here are a few points to remember when transforming images:

- Press (Cmd + T) [Ctrl + T] to enter Free Transform.
- Press Shift while dragging to maintain the aspect ratio.
- Press (Option) [Alt] to apply the same transform on both sides of the image.
- Press (Option-Shift) [Alt-Shift] to apply the same transform on both sides of the image and maintain the aspect ratio.
- (Cmd-click) [Ctrl-click] on any transform handle to bring up other scale options.
- (Cmd-click) [Ctrl-click] on a corner transform handle to enter Distort.
- (Cmd-click) [Ctrl-click] on a center transform handle to enter Skew.
- Press (Cmd + Z) [Ctrl + Z] to undo the last transformation.
- Press the Esc key to exit the transformation and return the image to its original state.
- To avoid degrading image quality unnecessarily, it's better to apply all transformations (scale, rotate, perspective, etc.) at once.

When masking out veils, start by identifying the solid background and the solid figure and what needs to be translucent. Between you and me—the first time I tried masking out the little girl, I needed seven alpha channels and a lot of time. After thinking through what really needed to be masked, I accomplished the same task in less time and with only two alpha channels. **Figure 10.50** shows variations of the same image created by the students in my Advanced Photoshop class at the School of VISUAL ARTS.

figure 10.50

A variety of solutions created by students at the School of VISUAL ARTS.

Working with Flowing Cloth

Not all masks are used for compositing or to replace image backgrounds. In fact, I make just as many masks to control color and tone corrections.

Figure 10.51 is a stock photography image that is simply too saturated to reproduce well. **Figure** 10.52 is the same image, but by reducing the image saturation in the fabric, the image will reproduce much better and, interestingly enough, the face is clearer. I created the mask using the Image Calculations command and reduced the excessive color saturation using a Photo Filter Adjustment Layer and Selective Color Adjustment Layers.

ch10_veil_dancer.jpg

To check if your images are oversaturated or if specific colors fall outside of the printable color gamut of your printer, select View > Gamut Warning. The downside of Gamut Warning is that it does not show you how far outside of your printers' capabilities a certain color is. In the following example, almost the entire image is oversaturated, so it needs to be corrected to reproduce accurately.

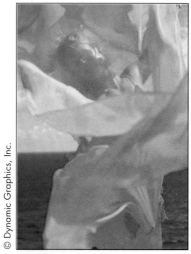

© Dynamic Graphics, Inc.

Original Image

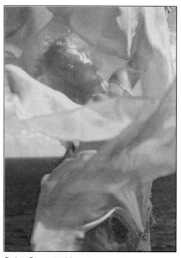

Color Corrected Image

With Gamut Warning

figure 10.51

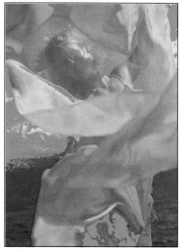

With Gamut Warning

figure 10.52

1. By inspecting the three channels (figure 10.53) it is clear why the image is oversaturated. The red channel has too little image information and the blue channel is too dense, creating a saturated nightmare to print.

2. Choose Image > Calculations and set Source 1 to Red and Source 2 to Blue. Because the red channel is so thin in density, I selected Invert.

After trying all of the contrast enhancing blending modes, I used the Vivid Light blending mode (figure 10.54) to create a mask that quickly isolated the woman from the scene.

3. The mask needs to be inverted so that the woman and veil areas are white and the background is black. Return to RGB by pressing (Cmd + ~) [Ctrl + ~], choose Select > Load Selection, and choose Alpha 1.

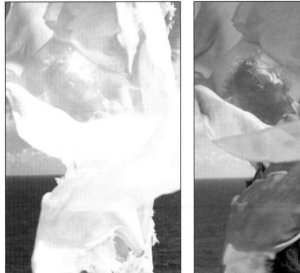
Red channel

Green channel

Blue channel

figure 10.53

Inspecting the three color channels reveals that the red channel has almost no tonal information and that the blue channel is too dense.

figure 10.54

Combining the red and blue channels to create an alpha channel.

4. Choose Layer > New Adjustment Layer > Photo Filter and choose the Cooling Filter 82. I increased the density to 45%. As you can see in **figure 10.55**, Photoshop transfers the active selection into the Photo Filter layer mask and the correction effect only takes place where the mask is light. You can use Photo Filters Adjustment Layers for image correction and creative image enhancements.

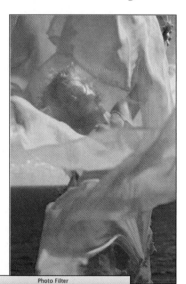

figure 10.55

The Photo Filter Adjustment Layer effectively removes the color cast.

5. You can stack image adjustments to refine your images with a great deal of control. Choose Select > Load Selection and choose Alpha 1 to reactivate the alpha mask, or (Cmd-click) [Ctrl-click] on the Photo Filter

layer mask to create an active selection. For this image, I adjusted the yellow ink components with Selective Color Adjustment Layer (**figure 10.56**). Selective Color lets you refine color components with great finesse and is very useful when an image is oversaturated.

I face a variety of color problems every day, and very often the problem isn't the wrong color—it's simply too much color. By using a mask to control where the color correction takes place, an image will reproduce better.

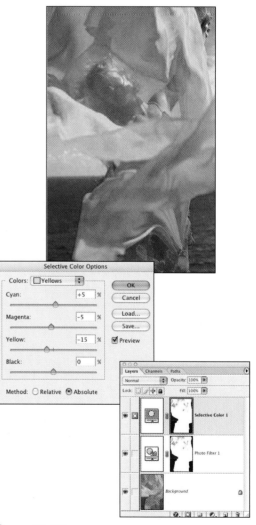

figure 10.56

Selective Color reduces the color saturation in the yellows.

PLAYING WITH FIRE, SMOKE, AND FIREWORKS

One way to select flames is to use the Extract filter, as we already discussed in Chapter 8, "Selecting Hair and Fine Detail." Later in this chapter, you'll learn to separate a delicate wisp of smoke from a green studio backdrop. One of the easiest methods of selecting flames and fireworks is to not select them at all, but to use the Blend If command to conceal the backdrop while revealing the flame or fireworks.

Working with the Blend If Command

The Blend If command, located in the Layer Styles dialog box, is one of my favorite features in Photoshop. I use it to sketch, brainstorm, or simply be surprised by how images come together. The Blend If command is ideal for combining images that have a wide tonal difference between dark and light.

Before we use Blend If to combine images, an overview of the terminology used in the Layer Styles dialog box (**figure 10.57**) and how it functions will be helpful. You can access the dialog box by double-clicking on the layer thumbnail in the Layers palette, by choosing Layer > Layer Style > Blending Options, or by using the Layer palette fly-out menu to access Blending Options. For the examples used in the discussion that follows, I used a layer with a black-to-white gradient.

- In the bottom center of the dialog box, *This Layer* refers to the layer you double-clicked on or that was active to produce the Layer Styles dialog box. Use the corresponding sliders below it to specify the range of pixels that will not appear in the final image. For example, if you drag the white slider to the left to 200, pixels with brightness values higher than 200 will not be blended and will not be visible in the image (**figure 10.58**).

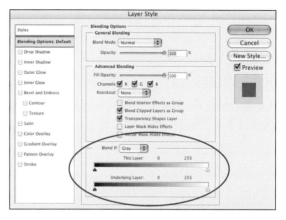

figure 10.57

The Layer Style dialog box and the original source images.

figure 10.58

Moving the Highlight slider to 200 conceals all values above 200.

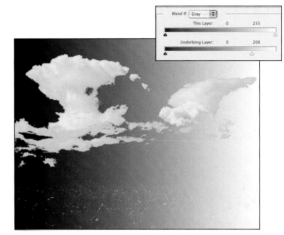

figure 10.59

Moving the Shadow slider to 200 reveals all values above 200.

- *Underlying Layer*, located beneath This Layer, is the layer underneath the active layer. Use the corresponding sliders to specify the range of pixels that will be visible in the final image. For example, if you drag the white slider to 200, pixels with brightness values higher than 200 will show through the active layer (**figure 10.59**).

- To create a transition between what is blended and what isn't, (Option-drag) [Alt-drag] one half of a slider triangle to the left or right (**figure 10.60**). The two values that appear above the divided slider indicate the partial blending range.

- Push the sliders back together to lessen the transition.

- If you drag the black slider beneath This Layer to the right and then stop at 35 pixels, for instance, brightness values lower than the place at which you stopped—in this case, 35 pixels—will not be blended, and therefore, will not be visible in the image (**figure 10.61**).

- Use the Underlying Layer sliders to specify the range of pixels that will be visible in the final image. For example, if you drag the dark slider to 70, pixels with brightness values lower than 70 will show through the active layer (**figure 10.62**).

figure 10.60

(Option-drag) [Alt-drag] to create a transition.

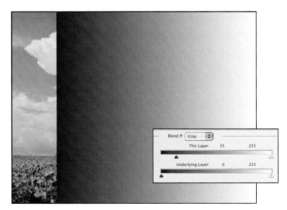

figure 10.61

Moving the Shadow value to 35 conceals all tones lower than 35.

- Experiment using all four sliders with and without the (Option-drag) [Alt-drag] technique to combine the images in surprising ways (**figure 10.63**).

🔍 **Tip**

When working with the Blend If command: Adjusting the This Layer sliders conceals image information; adjusting the Underlying Layer sliders reveals image information.

For one of my projects, I needed to add the fireworks to the bridge scene in **figure 10.64**. Can you imagine trying to select either the bridge or fireworks? The Blend If command made it possible to create the image variations in **figure 10.65** in a few moments. Granted, the masking may not be perfect, but often the possibilities trigger new ideas and approaches.

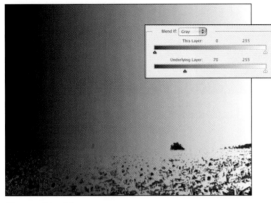

figure 10.62

Adjusting the Shadow value of the underlying layer reveals tonal values.

© Dynamic Graphics, Inc.

figure 10.63

(Option-dragging) [Alt-dragging] creates a transition for both the Shadow and Highlight values.

© Dynamic Graphics, Inc.

figure 10.64

The original bridge and fireworks photographs.

figure 10.65

Creating variations on an image combination is easy.

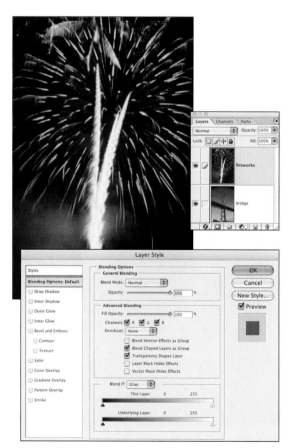

figure 10.66

Double-click on the Layer icon to open the Blend If command.

ch10_fireworks.jpg

ch10_bridge.jpg

1. To center the fireworks on the bridge image, use the Move tool and hold the Shift key while dragging the fireworks onto the bridge image. To access the Blend If option, double-click on the Fireworks Layer icon (**figure 10.66**).

2. The bridge is completely hidden. Use the Underlying Layer sliders to pop it through the fireworks.

   When I work with the Blend If option, I grab the appropriate slider—the black one for shadow information and the white one for highlight information—and make a gross move to the right or left. In this instance, the bridge is dark, so I moved the Underlying Layer Shadow slider to the right to see if the effect is roughly working (**figure 10.67**).

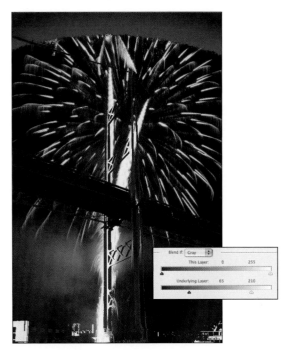

figure 10.68

Adding a hint of underlying highlights gives off a sense of light that the fireworks would normally contribute to the scene.

figure 10.67

Make a gross move to see if the effect is working.

3. To show some of the bridge highlights, move the Underlying Layer Highlight slider to the left (**figure 10.68**).

4. Starting with the Shadow sliders, (Option-drag) [Alt-drag] one half of the Shadow slider triangle to the left. To add a highlight transition (Option-drag) [Alt-drag] one half of the Highlight slider to the right (**figure 10.69**).

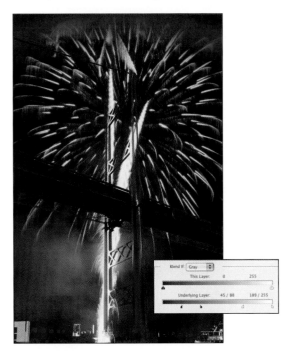

figure 10.69

(Option-dragging) [Alt-dragging] separates the sliders and adds effective transitions.

5. It's a good idea to always experiment with blending modes. In this instance, I changed the blending mode to Hard Light to add a hint of contrast and let the fireworks pop a bit more (**figure 10.70**).

figure 10.70

Experimenting with blending modes can add impact.

The Blend If command is a fantastic feature, which lets you combine and merge images without having to make complex masks. **Figure 10.71** shows an image I made in 1997 with an earlier version of Photoshop. Even back then, I used the Blend If command to combine the doll's face with the water. **Figure 10.72** shows how dull the image would be without Blend If controls.

I hope that the Blend If command is as exciting to you as it is to me. Best of all, as long as you save your files in either Photoshop or the TIFF file format with layers enabled, you can return to the file and adjust the Blend If sliders to your heart's content.

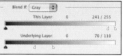

figure 10.71

Using the Blend If command, I was able to sink the doll's head into the water.

figure 10.72

Without the Blend If command, the image is flat, and would require complex and time-consuming masking to achieve similar effects.

Creative Smoke

If you are going to photograph flames or smoke, use a black velvet backdrop. To separate the smoke from the backdrop, light it from behind. As you can see in **figure 10.73**, Mark Beckelman used a stick of incense as the smoke source and within an hour had dozens of beautiful and abstract smoke patterns he used to create the composite in **figure 10.74**.

⊕↝⌇ **ch10_smoke.jpg**

1. Mark doubled-clicked the Background layer and named it *Original*, rotated the original file counterclockwise, and used Image > Canvas Size to add 200 percent more canvas on the left side (**figure 10.75**).

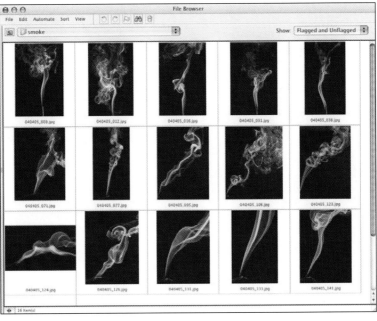

figure 10.73

Photographing the smoke with a black background will simplify the compositing process.

© Mark Beckelman

figure 10.74

By duplicating, flipping, and blending one image, Mark created this smoky Rorschach image.

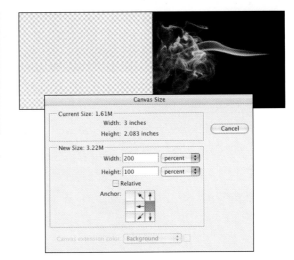

figure 10.75

Extending the canvas.

2. He then duplicated the original layer and chose Edit > Transform > Flip Horizontal and moved the copy to the left (**figure 10.76**). Much to his surprise and pleasure the image had an inherent beauty. He used the command keys (Cmd + Option + Shift + E) [Ctrl + Alt + Shift + E], followed by (Cmd + Option + Shift + N) [Ctrl + Alt + Shift+ N], which added a new layer and merged the visible layers onto it.

3. To lighten the lower part of the smoke figure, Mark added a Curves layer and raised the midtones, as shown in **figure 10.77**, which lightened the entire image overall.

figure 10.76

After duplicating and flipping the original layer, the image pops into place.

figure 10.77

Using a Curves Adjustment Layer to lighten the image.

4. Mark used Image > Adjustments > Invert to change the Curves layer mask to black, and then he used a large white soft brush to paint in the lightening effect exactly where he wanted it in the lower part of the smoke creature (**figure 10.78**).

Figure 10.79 shows another variation of Mark's smoke portraits. I enjoy their abstract beauty very much. When I look at them I see animal faces; Mark sees insects.

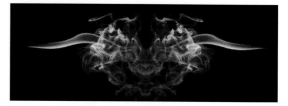

figure 10.78

After painting in selective lightening, the image is more dramatic.

figure 10.79

Endless variations are possible.

Note

When photographing smoke, the air needs to be very still. And if you're photographing fire, don't forget to have a working fire extinguisher close at hand!

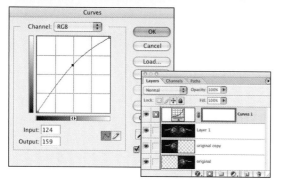

BLUE SCREEN AND GREEN SCREEN TECHNIQUES

A local TV weather forecaster, Forrest Gump shaking President Kennedy's hand, and the hordes of warriors in *Lord of the Rings: The Return of the King* all have one thing in common: Not one of these examples exists as we see them on TV or in the movies, although we like to believe they do.

The weather forecaster is standing in front of a pure blue screen, which is then chroma-keyed out of the scene and replaced with the weather map, making it look as if the weather forecaster is interacting with the image. Have you ever noticed how weather forecasters constantly look off camera as they're pointing at the map? They are actually watching themselves on a monitor to see where they're pointing.

For the *Lord of the Rings* trilogy, Weta Digital (www.wetadigital.com), the special effects production house in New Zealand that created the innumerable computer-generated and computer-enhanced shots, built a huge outdoor blue-screen backdrop. To create the thousands of warrior soldiers, five rows of soldiers in full costume marched in front of the blue screen. After one take, the five rows would be mixed up and moved further away from the camera and they would march by again. This was repeated a number of times. The digital compositing department pulled masks (also referred to as mattes) based on the blue channel, and the receding rows of masked soldiers were composited together to create an unbelievably large army.

Because blue is rarely found in skin tones, it's the default color used for blue-screen studio backdrops. Green is being used more and more, because green paint reflects more light than blue. In addition, video and digital cameras capture the best detail and luminance information in the green channel. The drawback to using either a blue screen or a green screen is that the color can contaminate the subject with color spill, which is undesired, as blue or green tinges on people don't look healthy or natural.

Blue Screen and Green Screen Photography

Issues to consider when photographing using blue screen or green screen:

- The background should be evenly illuminated to create an even surface from which to *pull the key*, the digital video artist term for making the mask.

- The lights that illuminate the background should be behind the subject.

- Keep the subject as reasonably far away from the backdrop as possible to reduce unwanted color spill.

- Light your subject with a dedicated set of lights. You can light the subject as dramatically as you normally would in a photography studio. Many people think that lighting for blue screen or green screen photography needs to be very flat—that is true for the backdrop, but not for the subject. As you can see in **figure 10.80**, the background is lit with three FluoTec 650 daylight balanced lamps, and we used daylight balanced studio strobes and reflectors to light the subject (**figure 10.81**).

© Samuel Oh

figure 10.80

A green-screen studio at the School of VISUAL ARTS with a well-illuminated backdrop.

figure 10.81

You can light the subject creatively with continuous light sources, flash, and reflectors.

- Make sure your subjects aren't wearing the same color as the backdrop, or else they will suddenly have holes where their clothes used to be. For example, a green blouse is masked out along with the green backdrop. Or as you can see in **figure 10.82**, the green in the flower stems has been removed, making the flowers look dead.

- You can build a green-screen studio with bright green seamless paper. Light the backdrop with two lights (preferably studio flash heads) on either side at a 45-degree angle to the seamless paper. Use Rosco #389 colored gels over each background light to intensify the green.

Professional photography suppliers sell blue-screen and green-screen cloth backdrops, and in larger cities you can rent them for daily use. You can achieve similar results with almost any solid-colored background. White, gray, or black do not work as well because most subjects also have those tones.

figure 10.82

Avoid having green in the subject when using a green backdrop.

© Mark Beckelman

Working with Digital Anarchy Primatte Chromakeyer 2.0

Green-screen photography is a very useful tool for compositing artists. The third-party plug-ins or programs available to do masking in conjunction with green screen photography do more than just pull a mask based on the background color; they also remove the offending color spill very well. Digital Anarchy Primatte Chromakeyer 2.0, Nova Design Cinematte, and Ultimatte's AdvantEdge are available for both Mac and PC. In the following section, I use Primatte 2.0 (visit www.digitalanarchy.com to download a trial version of Primatte 2.0) and Photoshop CS to pull some amazing masks with translucency and detail.

⊕▷⤙ **ch10_green_glass.jpg**

1. Primatte 2.0 is a Photoshop plug-in that works with either RGB or CMYK 8-bit files. When I work with Primatte, I like to see how the green-screen subject and the background are interacting—so I start by dragging the green-screen photo on top of the background image.

2. Choose Filter > Digital Anarchy > Primatte to enter the interface (figure 10.83) views— Composition, Mask, Foreground, and Background.

3. Use the Select button to circle a sample of the green background color, and in a few seconds the first rendition of the image extraction is displayed (figure 10.84).

4. I find it very useful to view the mask to look for artifacts and density by clicking the Mask button and using the Clean BG (background) tool to add density to the mask, which will yield a cleaner extraction (figure 10.85).

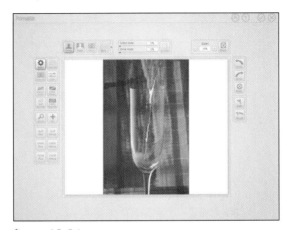

figure 10.84

Circle a sample of the background color to achieve these results.

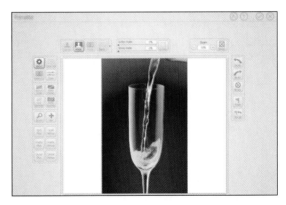

figure 10.85

View the mask to verify and adjust density.

© Mark Beckelman

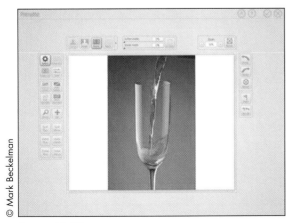

figure 10.83

The initial Primatte interface.

Without very much work at all, I achieved the results shown in **figures** 10.86 and 10.87.

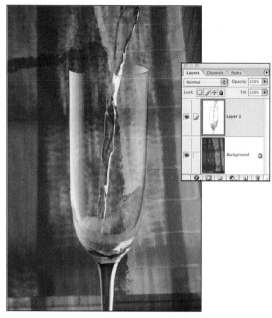

figure 10.86

Removing the green background took about 45 seconds.

figure 10.87

Viewing the isolated glass.

Green Spill Removal

Green-screen software does more than pull a mask—it also removes the green spill. **Figure 10.88** shows a figure in which I did my best to mask out the green background using Color Range, which works rather well—but the green in the smoke is horrific. By removing the green in the smoke with a Hue/Saturation layer, the smoke looks lackluster (figure 10.88). If the image is as delicate as these wisps of smoke or as sparkling as the champagne glasses, working with dedicated green screen software will result in better results, more quickly. **Figure 10.89** shows how well Primatte removed the green from the smoke.

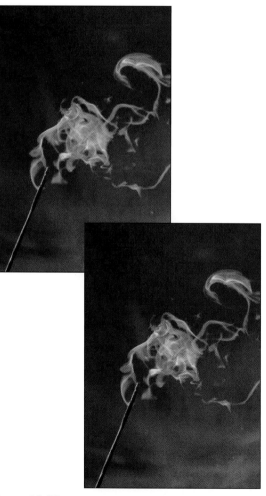

figure 10.88

Working with just Photoshop leaves too much green spill in the smoke, shown on the left. By desaturating the green, the smoke loses any sense of delicacy.

© Mark Beckelman

figure 10.89

On the left, the original green-screen photograph. On the right, the green-screen composite using Primatte.

Green Screen with Photoshop CS

Can you achieve very good results by shooting on green screen or a contrasting color and using Photoshop to make the mask? Yes, if the subject isn't translucent and if the green spill is minimized as much as possible.

Mark Beckelman photographed his niece Julia to show off her wonderfully curly hair, using both white and green backgrounds. As Mark explains, "I made sure that the lighting on the background was completely even and exposed properly (approximately the same f-stop reading as the foreground) and that the background was far enough away from Julia to avoid spill."

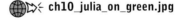 **ch10_julia_on_green.jpg**

ch10_julia_on_white.jpg

ch10_flag.jpg

In the following example, you have a unique opportunity to work with Photoshop CS to compare compositing a green-screen photo with a similar image that was photographed on a white background.

Making the Mask from the Green-Screen Image

1. Inspect the three channels to find the one with the best tonal separation. It comes as no surprise that the green channel has the best separation (**figure 10.90**). Use Image > Image Calculations and set both Source 1 and Source 2 to Green using the Hard Light blending mode (**figure 10.91**).

Red channel

Green channel

Blue channel

figure 10.90

Inspecting the color channels reveals that the green channel serves as the best foundation with which to build a mask.

2. Choose Image > Adjustments > Levels and force the light background to white and darken the shadow information (**figure 10.92**).

figure 10.91

Using the Image Calculations command to create the initial alpha channel.

figure 10.92

Using Levels to make the light areas white and the dark areas black.

3. Select the interior of her body and head with the Pen tool, convert the path to a selection, and fill with black (**figure 10.93**).

4. Use a large, soft-edged black brush to paint over the hair (**figure 10.94**).

5. Return to the Layers palette and press (Cmd + Option + 4) [Ctrl + Alt + 4] to activate the alpha channel and choose Select > Feather of 1. Drag the girl over to the flag background. It is rather apparent how much green is still in her hair (**figure 10.95**).

figure 10.93

Pen tooling the interior of the figure.

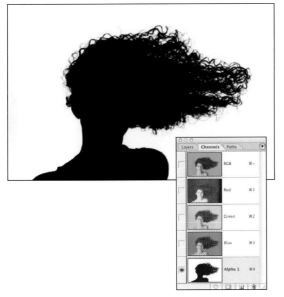

figure 10.94

Filling and painting with black to protect the girl.

figure 10.95

After dragging the girl onto the flag image, the green is very visible.

Removing Green Spill

1. To remove the green, hold (Option) [Alt] and select Layer > New Fill Layer > Solid Color Fill. Select *Use Previous Layer to Create Clipping Mask* and change the mode to Color. Click OK and use the Color picker to choose a hair color to create the results shown in **figure 10.96**.

figure 10.96

The Solid Color Fill layer replaces all color.

2. Use (Cmd + I) [Ctrl + I] to invert the Solid Color layer mask and paint over the green spill with a large white brush (**figure 10.97**).

3. To remove the last vestiges of green along her shoulder and face, add a new layer and change its blending mode to Color. With a brush active, (Option-click) [Alt-click] to sample the color (for example, from her shoulder) and paint away the green (**figure 10.98**).

Figure 10.99 shows the same image with the key pulled using Primatte, which took me about 30 seconds to accomplish.

Am I suggesting that everyone run out and buy a blue screen or green-screen backdrops and software to go with it? Not at all. But if you need to do a lot of background replacements, I strongly recommend you consider it. The time saved in making masks and removing green spill will quickly make up for the costs in the backdrop, lights, and learning curve.

figure 10.97

After inverting the layer mask, paint with white to reveal the brown and remove the green spill from her hair.

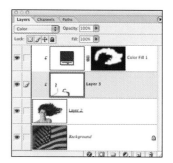

figure 10.98

Layer 3 removes the green spill along the shoulders.

figure 10.99

The same image, but I used Primatte to pull the key and remove the green spill in about 30 seconds.

figure 10.100

Julia photographed using a white background.

© Mark Beckelman

Working with a White Backdrop

If you don't have a green-screen backdrop, try using a white one (**figure 10.100**). Just as with a green-screen or blue-screen background, it is important to have enough distance between the subject and the backdrop to avoid color or light spill (**figure 10.101**).

The Double Hair-Masking Technique

The following technique is ideal for pulling masks from images that were photographed with a simple studio backdrop. It requires you make two masks—one of which is a hint smaller than the other to fine-tune the edges of the hair. I learned this technique from Colin Woods, publisher of *Design Graphics*—one of the best and certainly most beautifully produced digital techniques magazines available.

figure 10.101

There needs to be enough distance between the model and the background to reduce color or light spill.

1. Inspect the three channels and duplicate the one with the darkest hair, which in this image is the blue channel (**figure 10.102**).

2. Use Levels to dramatically mask the light background white and the dark areas black, without making the background dirty (**figure 10.103**).

figure 10.102

To create the initial alpha channel, duplicate the channel containing the darkest hair.

figure 10.103

Using Levels to make the light areas white and the dark areas black.

3. Paint in the remaining areas of the mask (**figure 10.104**).

4. Duplicate the alpha channel and name it *Alpha #4 Large* and *Alpha #5 Small*.

figure 10.104

Painting in the interior of the girl using black.

5. Activate the Small channel. To shrink it ever so slightly, choose Filter > Other > Maximum and use a low setting of 1 (**figure 10.105**). Now you have two alpha channels—one is 1 pixel smaller than the other. **Figure 10.106** shows you how precise the difference is.

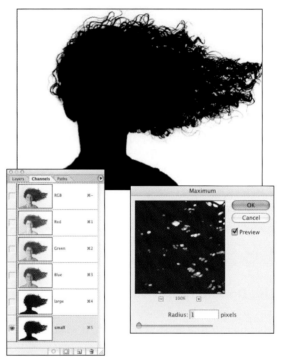

figure 10.105

Duplicate the alpha channel, name one Small *and one* Large, *and then use the Maximum filter on the Small alpha channel to shrink it by one pixel.*

figure 10.106

There's a one pixel difference between the two alpha channels.

6. Press (Cmd + ~) [Ctrl + ~] to return to RGB, double-click on the Background layer to convert it to a standard layer, and duplicate it (**figure 10.107**).

7. Drag the flag file to this image and position it underneath both layers of Julia (**figure 10.108**).

8. Choose Select > Load Selection and choose Large.

9. Click on the Add Layer Mask button and change the blending mode to Multiply (**figure 10.109**).

10. Activate the topmost layer, choose Select > Load Selection, and choose Small. Click on the Add Layer Mask button (**figure 10.110**).

figure 10.107

Duplicate the layers.

figure 10.109

Changing the layer blending to Multiply increases the density of the hair.

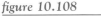

figure 10.108

Dragging the new background underneath the girl layers.

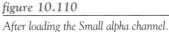

figure 10.110

After loading the Small alpha channel.

11. To refine the hair mask, use a low Gaussian Blur of 1 on the Multiply layer. I opted to duplicate the Multiply layer and reduce its opacity to 70% to strengthen it (**figure 10.111**).

figure 10.111

To fine-tune the composite, soften the Multiply layer mask slightly and duplicate it.

CLOSING THOUGHTS

Creating masks is an essential skill. If you've made it this far without ripping out your own hair, then you are well on your way to being a true Photoshop meister. Just remember, each image you toil over is an opportunity to perfect your own masking techniques, which can only serve you better as you tackle your next image.

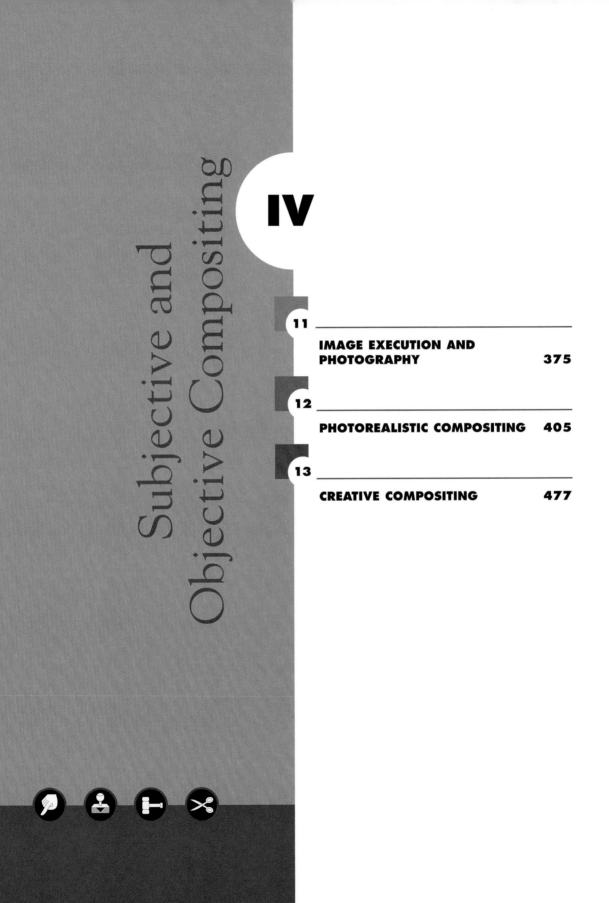

Subjective and
Objective Compositing

IV

11

IMAGE EXECUTION AND PHOTOGRAPHY

Commercial photographers and illustrators are often hired to express someone else's ideas and, depending on the client, they may get explicit sketches and directions or be given free reign to develop the concept. Fine artists express their own ideas and concerns. Both fine artists and commercial Photoshop users benefit greatly from planning the image, which includes everything from concept, to photography, to working in Photoshop, and finally to outputting the image.

Chapter 1, "The Creative Process and Configuring Photoshop," and Chapter 13, "Creative Compositing," discuss inspiration and ideas. This chapter concentrates on the execution of the concept in terms of planning and photographing for compositing. In this chapter you will learn about

- Planning and executing the image
- Photography for compositing
- Essential photography issues
- Appreciating light and shadow

The following three chapters concentrate on showing how professional photographers and artists are using many of the techniques explained in the previous chapters to create fantastic and inspiring images.

EXECUTING THE IMAGE

After the concept is developed as discussed in Chapters 1 and 13, the next step is to plan and execute the image. This is a very practical and important stage of image creation as you make decisions to accomplish the goal within the time, location, budget, and talent constraints you've been allotted or have allotted to yourself. Being creative within limitations is often more rewarding and productive than unfettered daydreaming about what isn't feasible or achievable. Don't regard limitations as negative—instead see them as parameters to work with rather than against.

Planning the Image

Before you go on a long trip, you plan it. Depending on where you're going and for how long, you pack differently. And if you're like me, you might make a checklist: passport, tickets, amount and type of clothing, photography equipment, and so on. I do this to be safe, prepared, and comfortable, which lets me concentrate on and enjoy the trip.

Planning an image is just as important as planning for a long trip to an exotic or remote location. More importantly, the more you plan the imaging process, the fewer compromises you will have to make later. Good planning always results in better images.

The primary question to address when planning your image is, "What will it take to achieve the image goal?" The practical aspects of this answer include all of the various constraints that are part of the project. Let's take a closer look at those now.

Look, Feel, and Style

What will the final image(s) look like? The subject and look of the image needs to express the concept. Some issues I consider when planning my final images include the following:

- Will the image be in color or black and white?
- How stylized will the image(s) be?
- What size and format will the final image have?

- What type of output will I employ?
- Will the image be a single image or part of a series?

All of these are very important decisions to make, and they are best made before you begin shooting or gathering your image elements.

Ansel Adams and Edward Weston developed the idea of *previsualization*, which entails envisioning what the final print will look like before the shutter is released. The look and feel of the final print guided camera exposure, development times, and print manipulation.

In filmmaking, previsualization is an essential component of the production schedule. Often referred to as *previz*, it is the process where film scenes are rendered beyond the simple descriptions in a script or in storyboards. Previz enables the director, cinematographers, and CG artists (computer generated) to plan and experiment with camera angle and motion, subject matter, and point of view to develop the look and feel of the scenes. Of course, it is easier and less expensive to brainstorm and refine the shot before crew, location, and a possible cast of thousands are standing around waiting for the director and cinematographer to make up their minds.

In film post-production, the compositing artist needs to be able to previsualize the scene, as complicated scenes can have well over 200 elements that all need to be masked out and interact in the framework of the specific scene and the entire story.

For example, Neo Afan produced his thesis project at the School of VISUAL ARTS in Photoshop and After Effects. Each frame (approximately one-fifteenth of a second) had up to 120 layers and masks, all of which were simultaneously moving and changing, as shown in **figure 11.1**. To manage the project, Neo Afan needed to visualize the assets in After Effects (**figure 11.2**) and envision how they would work before actually sitting down at the computer. Needless to say, he didn't sleep very much in his final semester.

figure 11.1
_____

Working in After Effects requires exacting organization and planning.

figure 11.2
_____

Each element is on its own layer, which is constantly moving and interacting with other assets in the frame.

Models, Props, and Locations

Does the image include people? Models need to be cast, booked, photographed, and, of course, they need to be compensated according to how the image will be used—editorial, commercial, stock, fine art, and so on. If you're just starting out, contact local acting and modeling schools to find people who are also beginning their careers and are hoping to secure headshots and photographs for their books. Actors and models are usually less inhibited about striking a requested pose or portraying an emotion or attitude. You'll need a signed model release that states you have the right to their likeness. I've posted links to model, property, and location releases on this book's Web site.

Does your image require props? If so, do you already have them or do you need to borrow, rent, or buy them? Will you need additional insurance or security for the props?

Will the image(s) be photographed in the studio or on public or private property? There are numerous rules and regulations to photographing in all of these situations, and I find it better to research the rules. When in doubt, ask permission first and photograph second. Does the shot require travel, immunizations, or visas? This all has to be addressed before you pack your toothbrush and camera bag.

Format, Resolution, and Equipment

Film comes in a number of standard formats from 35 mm to large-format film. The type of photography you're doing will influence the film format used. For example, 35 mm and medium format are much faster to work with than large format film, while in skilled hands the large-format film will increase the final image quality.

Working with digital cameras requires that file size and image resolution be considered before you start taking pictures. Sporting from 3- to 22-megapixel image sensors, digital cameras are quickly surpassing film quality. Image resolution depends on the size and type of your final output (this is discussed further in "The Business of Imagemaking," an appendix to this book that is available on the book's Web site). If a job doesn't require hundreds of megabytes of image data, consider yourself lucky. If you do require the highest image quality, consider renting the camera equipment, whose cost is added to the final bill as a line item.

Don't let perceived camera-format limitations hamper your photographic style. John Warner photographs with the Canon 1Ds, an 11-megapixel digital camera with the classic rectangular 2:3 35mm format. But take a look at the interior architecture shots in **figure 11.3**. John uses a Canon TS-E 24mm shift lens that permits simultaneous depth of field and perspective control. Obviously not shot in the standard 35mm format, John photographs three to four frames with 20-percent overlap and uses Photomerge in Photoshop CS to seamlessly combine the images to portray the grandeur of the vaulted ceilings. When I asked him if he starts photographing at the top or the bottom or left or right side for horizontal images, he told me, "My preference is to begin in the center where no shift corrections are required and work outward toward the top and bottom or left and right outer frames."

Do you have the equipment to do the job? Or will you need to buy or rent additional camera bodies, lenses, lights, or backdrops? No professional photographer goes on an important shoot with just one camera body—equipment fails and you have to keep on shooting. All of this needs to be considered. The more often you do it, the better you'll become at the entire process.

figure 11.3

After shooting three to four frames, John Warner used Photomerge to stitch the interior scenes together.

Roles and Responsibilities

Who will take the pictures and who will do the retouching and compositing? Working collaboratively lets team members work within their strengths. Sadly, I've seen a number of photo studios go out of business because the photographer thought he needed to do it all—from capture, to Photoshop, to output. If you do wear many hats—photographer, compositing artist, and general manager—planning ahead is even more essential, as you're responsible for the entire process.

When shooting fashion, you'll need a makeup artist (**figure 11.4**), hair stylist, and clothing stylist. Hire a food stylist when doing high-end food photography. These people are experts in their field, and the better they are, the better you will look.

 T i p

> Photograph what you know. Your expertise of the subject or location will give you valuable insights that other, perhaps even better, photographers just don't have. Always form a solid foundation by researching your concept and subject as much as possible.

All in all, the better the planning, the better the production, the better the final image(s) will be. There is nothing worse than getting to a location and not having a piece of equipment or shooting permission that you need to do the job.

figure 11.4

Working with professional makeup and clothing stylists will result in a more professional end product.

PHOTOGRAPHY FOR COMPOSITING

Mechanically speaking, photography is the act of rendering three dimensions onto a two-dimensional surface. The decisions a photographer makes influence whether that flattening process is successful or not. These decisions include what lens, shutter speed, and f-stop are used, where the camera is positioned, the quality of light, and the environment the picture is taken in.

Photoshop is a 2D application in which you are working on the X (horizontal) and Y (vertical) axis of an image. The third dimension, which is not in Photoshop, is the Z dimension—the depth dimension in which camera, light, and position can be changed. Once an image is photographed and is in Photoshop you cannot change a great many of these important visual properties. So you need to carefully plan and photograph with these considerations in mind before launching Photoshop.

Planning the image and choreographing the photography for the masking and compositing process will result in easier files to work with and more successful final images. Understanding the fundamental photographic issues to consider when planning a composite, which include the types of backgrounds, lenses to use, your point of view, and lighting considerations, will make your composites better. In fact, the advantage of doing the photography for a specific composite rather than trying to finagle existing files into place is almost immeasurable.

Please note, this book isn't an all-inclusive photography book and the dedicated space cannot replace the numerous books, lectures, and classes that address photographic issues. If you are interested in improving your photography skills, I sincerely recommend taking photography and studio lighting classes at your local community college.

The Deciding Factors

Before you get your camera out and clean the lens, you have to identify the deciding factors—the ones you have little or no control over and will have to match as best as possible. As Mark Beckelman explains, "Start with the attribute you have the least control over, such as location, perspective, props, and lighting." Once you've identified the limiting factors, you'll need to match them with regard to perspective, lighting, point of view, focal length, scale, and so on.

Matching Location

Who doesn't like building paper airplanes and seeing them glide through the room? Well, Mark took this childhood memory one step further when he decided to have children glide around Manhattan on homemade paper airplanes, as shown in **figure 11.5**. As soon as he had the idea, he knew what he had to do first—go to the top of the Empire State Building and take the deciding location shot (**figure 11.6**).

© Mark Beckelman

figure 11.5

The final image is a composite of three separate photo shoots: the location, the children, and the paper airplanes.

figure 11.6

The location and point of view are the deciding factors in this scene, which is why it needs to be photographed first.

When he returned from the city, he acquired the files and made a guide print, and it was to this guide print that he photographed the paper airplanes with a variety of interesting angles and perspectives (**figure 11.7**).

As Mark explains, "It was essential that the planes were established first, as the camera angle of the kids on the plywood plane was dependent on those previous shots. I had made it a point to make the plywood plane the same proportion as the paper version so that I could match perspective later on. By doing it in this sequence, I didn't have to over-shoot the kids in angles that were unnecessary for the composition—I could instead concentrate on shooting a variety of expressions and clothing variations" (**figure 11.8**).

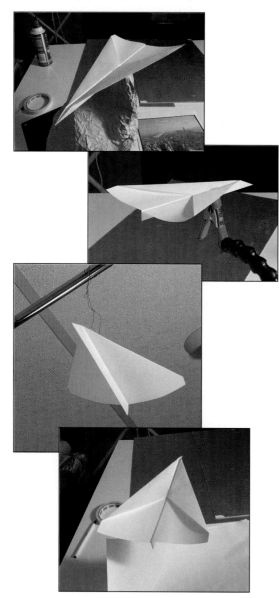

figure 11.7

Planning the position and angle of the planes ahead of time saves time later in the compositing process.

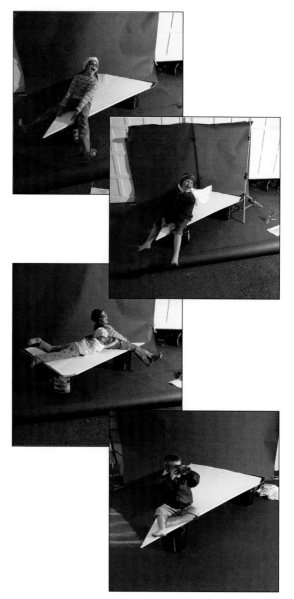

figure 11.8

Photographing the children with lighting and perspective that matches the planes will make the final image more believable.

1. With the photography done, Mark got down to work in Photoshop. He started by dropping in the airplanes, as they would provide the surface for the children (**figure 11.9**).

2. To create the blurred effect, Mark duplicated the airplane layer and ran the Motion Blur filter to blur the entire plane. By reducing the layer opacity, and adding a layer mask on which he painted with black, the sense of motion is more apparent in the nose and tail of the plane (**figure 11.10**).

3. After adding the children, Mark selected parts of them and pressed (Cmd + J) [Ctrl + J] to create a new layer so that he could apply Motion Blur and adjust layer opacity without blurring the entire child (**figure 11.11**).

4. The final step was to warm the entire image with a Color Fill layer to give it a closer to sunset feeling and add grain to tie the entire image together. (Adding grain is discussed further in Chapter 12, "Photorealistic Compositing.")

All in all, the image may look like the child's play that it portrays—but the success of the image relies on the idea and the execution to work as well as it does.

figure 11.10

Adding a hint of motion blur to each plane.

figure 11.11

With the children on board, the image is coming together.

figure 11.9

The paper airplanes for the children.

Matching Perspective

The image in **figure 11.12** is a poster for a fictitious City of Books festival in downtown New York. The image represents how literature makes up the city. Because the buildings were the part of the poster Mark couldn't control, he started the project by photographing a variety of buildings and street locations (**figure 11.13**). The next step was to pho-

tograph old books (**figure 11.14**) and the woman reading in the same perspective and with similar lighting as the buildings. For greater flexibility when compositing the image, Mark photographed each book twice—once in perspective of the building, and once straight on to capture the spine. To see how the books were added to the buildings with the proper perspective, see Chapter 12.

figure 11.12

The final composite for the City of Books festival.

figure 11.13

Scouting and shooting a variety of shots can trigger new ideas.

figure 11.14

Photographing the books from a low perspective will be helpful in matching them to the buildings.

Matching Props

Thinking Outside the Box was one of 12 winners of the 2003 Adobe International Digital Imaging Competition. Sponsored by Adobe Sytems, Inc. and `Photoworkshop.com`, Mark's image (**figure 11.15**) was selected from more than 3,000 entries. Great care was taken when photographing and composit-ing the men so that their perspective meshed believ-ably. The deciding factor of this image was the cube (**figure 11.16**), which Mark photographed first and used as a reference when lighting and photographing the variations of the man (**figure 11.17**) to fit with the surface he was placed on.

figure 11.15

Thinking Outside the Box is an award-winning image.

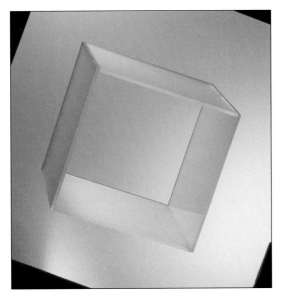

figure 11.16

The translucent cube played a crucial role in deciding how the man had to be lit and photographed.

figure 11.17

Propping up the man made it possible for him to look as though he were floating.

PHOTOGRAPHIC ESSENTIALS

Before making a single exposure, a professional photographer makes numerous decisions regarding camera equipment, lighting, studio considerations, and style. These decisions influence the look, feel, and quality of the image and can make or break the final composite. Planning ahead and making the right equipment choices and shooting decisions will always result in a better image.

Lenses

A lens is measured in terms of focal length, usually in millimeters, and light strength, which is how wide the diaphragm can open to work in low-light situations. The higher the focal length, the narrower the angle of view, the greater the magnification, and the larger the background is in relationship to the foreground, making the relationship between background and foreground more compressed.

Figure 11.18 shows the same model of the World Trade Center photographed in front of the New York skyline with four different focal-length lenses: 18mm, 35mm, 70mm, and 300mm. Keeping the size of the model approximately the same, you can see how far away the city is in the 18mm shot and how it becomes larger and closer as the focal length increases, until the background looms behind the model in the 300mm image. As the focal length increased, I needed to move further away from the model to maintain the relative size of the model in the frame.

Because the lens affects the angle of view and the size relationships in the image, lens focal length is a very important consideration to take into account before you start taking pictures. If you want the background to appear far away, shoot it with a wide-angle lens. If it needs to be closer, either crop the wide-angle image to narrow the perspective or, better yet, shoot it with a longer (higher focal-length number) telephoto lens.

18mm

35mm

70mm

300mm

figure 11.18

The focal length of the lens determines the angle of the view and the degree of magnification.

Note

I am not a fan of cropping an image to fake longer focal length because cropping throws away information, and the resulting blow-up may be too poor in quality to be worth the effort.

Consider using the cinematographic technique of *forced perspective* to make objects larger or smaller than they really are. You can do this by placing objects closer or further away from the camera, as was often done in Hollywood B-movies, in which the dinosaur was really just a papier-mâché model that was placed incredibly close to the camera to make it appear really huge and threatening. More recently, in *Lord of the Rings*, Ian McKellan was often positioned closer to the camera to make his character, Gandalf, appear taller than the actor really is.

Using the appropriate focal length is an important aesthetic decision. If you have a zoom lens, always compose the photograph first by positioning yourself closer or further away from the subject, and then use the zoom to fine-tune the angle of view and relative relationship of the background to the foreground. In other words, a zoom lens is not a substitute for walking closer or further away from your subject.

Exposure

Photographic exposure is determined by the combination of aperture size (f-stop), shutter speed, and film or CCD ISO rating (International Standards Association). The faster the shutter speed, the wider the aperture has to be to let enough light hit the film or sensor to create an acceptable exposure. The slower the shutter speed, the smaller the aperture can be.

The third component used to calculate exposure is the ISO rating of the film or sensor. The lower the rating, the more light is needed to create a good exposure. So if you're photographing in low light, you would use a higher speed film—perhaps a 400 or 800 ISO—or increase the ISO setting on your digital camera.

The drawback is that the film grain or camera noise may become more noticeable, which will negatively impact the final image quality. Unless you are trying to achieve creative grain effects, shoot at the lowest possible ISO film or digital camera setting possible. It is easier to add grain texture in Photoshop (see Chapter 12) than it is to take it away, which is always a slippery compromise between blurring the grain or noise while maintaining image detail.

Proper exposure always results in higher image quality. Of course, you can take a dark picture and make it lighter in Photoshop, but doing so will degrade the image information. Make the best image in front of the lens and don't rely on Photoshop to fix bad images.

Most 35mm cameras and digital SLRs have a program or automatic mode to calculate an exposure combination that yields good images. Get to know your camera and use the program mode when you need to work quickly and want the camera to do the thinking for you. That way you can concentrate on the subject in the viewfinder and don't have to be the exposure calculator. Use manual mode when you have the experience, time, or a light meter to set the desired shutter/aperture combination to create the photographic effects described in the following two sections on shutter speed and depth of field.

Shutter Speed

Fast shutter speeds freeze motion and slow ones blur motion (**figure 11.19**). Slow shutter speeds also create interesting effects if the subject is moving (**figure 11.20**). The still shot was a 4-second exposure when the Ferris wheel was stopped, and the second image was a four second exposure when the Ferris wheel was moving.

There are numerous plug-ins and techniques to add motion blur to an image, but optical motion blur is always more authentic looking than motion blur that is synthetically induced via software. If you plan on adding motion blur to a composite, try to take a few frames with the subject blurred to use as an image asset or reference (**figure 11.21**). If you use Shutter Priority mode, you set the shutter speed and the camera selects the aperture. This is a good mode to use when you need to either freeze or blur motion.

© Seán Duggan

figure 11.19

The crisp water was exposed with a very fast shutter speed of 1/320 of a second. The velvety water was exposed with a slow shutter speed of 3 seconds.

figure 11.20

Using a tripod during long exposures lets you experiment with combining crisp image elements and motion in the same frame.

figure 11.21

Viewing images on a digital camera LCD screen lets you learn while photographing and experiment with shutter speed and depth-of-field effects.

Depth of Field

The depth of field determines how much of the image is sharp. Smaller apertures increase depth of field, while a larger aperture decreases the depth of field. Small apertures have high numbers such as 11, 16, and 22, while large apertures that let in a lot of light have low numbers such as 4, 2.8, and 2. As you can see in **figure 11.22**, the three dolls were photographed with varying depth of field, letting the photographer focus in on the front, back, or all three of the dolls.

In Aperture Priority mode, you set the aperture and the camera selects the shutter speed. Use this mode to control what is sharp and what isn't. Portraits are often photographed with a shallow depth of field to throw the background out of focus, while keeping the person in focus.

© Mark Beckelman

figure 11.22

Adjusting the depth of field lets you define which planes of the image are sharp.

Let There Be Light

Based on the word *phos*—Greek for light— photography is appreciating, working with, and enjoying light. Light changes over the course of the day and seasons, as figure 11.23 illustrates.

Photographed over six weeks, the scene changes dramatically as the time of day shifts from early morning to late evening, from calm to stormy, and from clear to hazy.

figure 11.23

The play of light is constantly changing—during the day, the weeks, and the seasons.

Quality of Light

Based on the sun and how it changes over the course of the day, the quality of light is a mesh of the following attributes:

- **Intensity**: From overpowering bright midday sun to a delicate twilight, the intensity and strength of the light determines camera exposure and sets the overall mood of the image.

- **Size and distance**: Think of a cloudy day and a sunny day—the cloudy sky is the largest, softest light source possible, causing shadows to be very soft and diffuse. The noonday sun is the smallest possible light source, and it is a harsh pinpoint of light creating well-defined shadows. The closer the light to the subject, the larger it is in relationship to the subject, which makes the light and shadows softer (figure 11.24). Moving light further away from the subject causes it to become smaller and harsher, as the well-defined shadows in figure 11.25 attest to.

figure 11.24

The closer the light is to the subject, the larger the subject, and the softer the shadows.

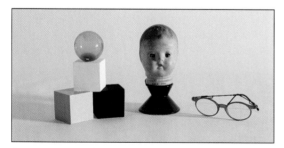

figure 11.25

The further the light is from the subject, the smaller the light source and the harsher the shadows.

- **Direction**: From low and raking, to high and flattening, the angle and direction of the light control dimensional rendering and shadow length and position. A low angle accentuates texture and casts long dramatic shadows, as the shadows in figure 11.26 illustrate, while a high light source flattens the subject and creates shorter, harsher shadows.

- **Color**: From the welcoming pinks of an early summer morning to the intense blue of midday sun or the spectacle of a winter sunset, the color temperature of light ranges from orange to blue to white, and is measured in degrees Kelvin. The environment also adds color to an image, as the light bounces from the environment onto the subject, as shown in the studio still life in figure 11.27.

- **Number**: How many lights are used to illuminate the scene? In most cases, professional photographers will use at least three lights— main, fill, and backlight. The main light is the primary light; it determines the proper exposure setting. The fill light lightens the side of the subject that is not illuminated by the main light and is often a white or silver piece of cardboard that reflects light back into the scene. The backlight separates the subject from the background.

The quality of light is also influenced by altitude, relative humidity, air quality, season, and local geographic factors such as mountains, bodies of water, and flora. Light can caress or crush the subject, and planning for it is an essential aspect in the previsualization and planning of a composite. When matching a deciding factor such as an environment or a prop, study the light in the image and match it while photographing the elements that will be added.

Low backlight

High backlight

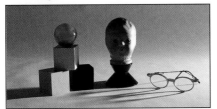

Low sidelight

High sidelight

Low three-quarter light

High three-quarter light

Low straight-on camera

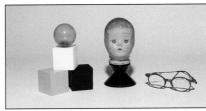

High straight-on camera

figure 11.26

Light direction and angle determine the size and position of the shadows.

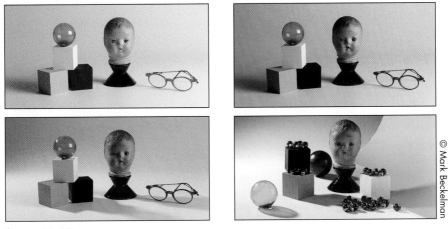

© Mark Beckelman

figure 11.27

Gelling the lights adds color and interpretation—from warm to cool—to mixed lighting. Notice how the blue paper tints the doll's face blue and that the shadows also have color.

✍ *Successful Lighting*

Figure 11.28 shows the result of combining five exposures to create the peel-away effect of an Apple G5 computer. The challenge of this image is twofold: lighting the solid and translucent surfaces and creating the peel-away look. Figure 11.29 shows the progression of the lighting, in which each exposure is responsible for a specific element of the G5. Studio lighting is part adding, part subtracting, and part bending light, which is what the pieces of reflectors and cardboard referred to as *flags* and *gobos* (go between) are doing.

The second aspect of the photo shoot was to create the peel-away effect, which is of course not how an Apple G5 opens. After removing the side panel, Mark curved and taped a sheet of white artist cardboard into position (figure 11.30), which he airbrushed in Photoshop to match the look and feel of the actual computer. The advantage of photographing the cardboard in position with the computer is that the natural play of light and shadow was established by the subject and just needed to be accentuated in Photoshop, not re-created, which may not be as successful as doing the photography correctly from the onset.

To add the flipped Apple logo to the peel, Mark used the original establishing photograph. He flipped it, rotated it, masked it, and used the Color Burn blend mode (figure 11.31). The final finesse was the addition of a high-tech background and reworking the lighting behind the G5 (this is described further in Chapter 12). Do not try this at home—I mean do not try to open your computer like this! Please do try the photography and the compositing!

figure 11.28

Peeling away the G5 to see the interior.

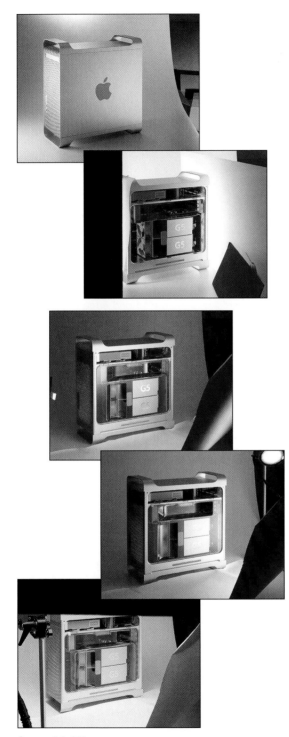

figure 11.30

A curved piece of cardboard serves as the stand-in for the peel-away effect.

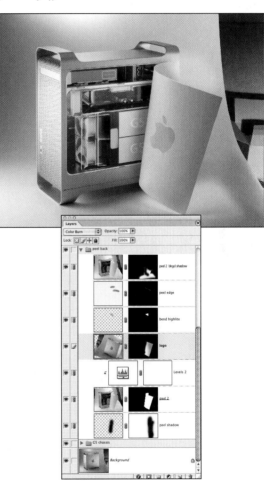

figure 11.29

Each aspect of the G5 needed to be lit separately.

figure 11.31

Flipping the original photograph and adjusting the blending mode reveals the Apple logo.

Shadow

Where there is light, there is shadow. The shadows sculpt the subject and underscore the emotion of the scene. The lower the light, the longer the shadows. Shadows are at their longest in the wintertime and shortest in the summer, and the closer to the equator you are the less this differential is.

For a compositing artist, understanding how light creates shadow is very important. It is always better to plan for and photograph real shadows versus using Photoshop to create faux shadows.

As you can see in figure 11.32, Mark Beckelman stuck two markers into a small pile of sand to create the shadows for the man in figure 11.33. Photographers also use Rosco Cinefoil, a flexible foil used to modify light. It can be cut into any shape needed and lit to cast the required shadows.

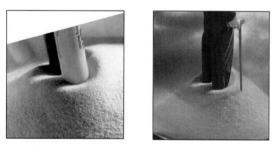

figure 11.32

Use appropriate props to cast realistic shadows.

figure 11.33

The final composite.

Successful Shadows

In early 2002, the Enron and Arthur Anderson accounting debacle was just starting to surface in the news. *Business Week* asked Mark Beckelman to create a photographic illustration for the cover article, *Accounting in Crisis: What's to Be Done?* Based on M.C. Escher's image *Drawing Hands*, Mark proposed having one hand writing in an accounting ledger and the other erasing what had just been entered. His sketch for the art director is in figure 11.34.

Mark broke the image down into four distinct elements—the ledger, the background, and the two hands. To create realistic shadows, the quality and direction of the light had to be consistent. The main light was a Chimera light bank, which is a rectangular light box that produces a soft wrap-around light with diffuse shadows. The fill and edge lighting was adjusted to shape the hands (figure 11.35).

By photographing each hand in the correct position and on white, Mark had more options than if he had photographed the hands on the ledger itself. By placing the hands and their shadows on separate layers, Mark was able to use the Multiply blending mode for the shadows (figure 11.36) and Normal for the hands. A gradated layer mask lets the hands blend into the ledger, and a green layer, set to color, matched the color of the hands to the ledger (figure 11.37).

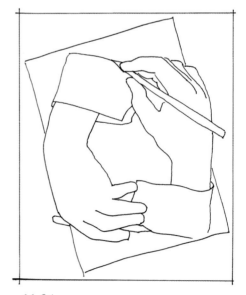

figure 11.34

Often a simple sketch is all that is needed to convey the concept.

figure 11.35

Maintaining the identical camera position and adjusting the fill and edge lighting to create the correct shadows.

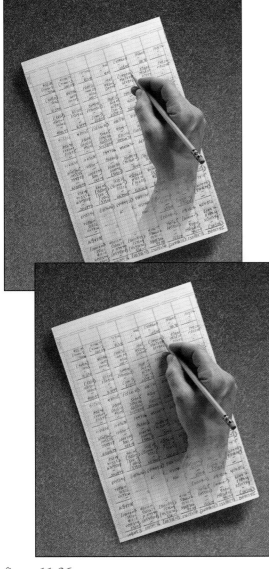

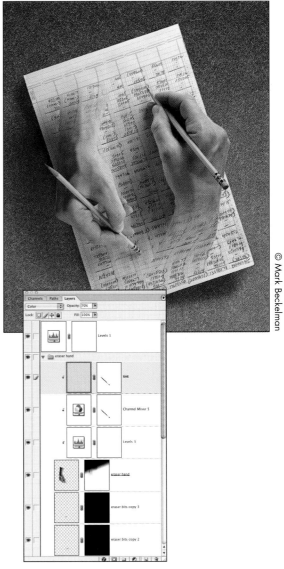

© Mark Beckelman

figure 11.36

Keeping the shadows and the hands on separate layers allows greater control.

figure 11.37

Tinting the hands ledger-green adds to the absurdity of the Enron corruption.

Background Considerations

The nature of the subject matter (surface, shape, and edge characteristics) and the environment in which the final piece will be dropped into determine the best background to photograph, as listed here:

- The background should contrast the subject without contaminating it with color or flare.

- Smooth-edged, light subjects can be photographed on white, gray, or the color of the environment they will be dropped into.

- Dark subjects can be photographed on white or gray, but you need to be careful not to over-light the background or else too much light will produce bleed around the dark subject and make masking and compositing problematic.

- Reflective and translucent subjects should be photographed on a color of the final environment that they'll be placed in, as the color of the environment is always reflected in the subject.

- The finer the detail you need to maintain, the more important it is to carefully backlight the subject to create separation between it and the background.

- When working with fine hair, smoke, and fluids, use green screens and third-party plug-ins to extract the subject from the scene, as explained in Chapter 10, "Selecting Translucency and Green Screen Techniques."

- Avoid backgrounds with texture or uneven lighting, both of which will make the silhouetting process more difficult.

- Avoid positioning the subject or model too close to the background.

The larger the final print and the more critical the viewer, the more important all of the photographic considerations are.

Additional Equipment Recommendations

I cannot emphasize enough the value of a solid tripod to ensure that the camera doesn't move, which is particularly important when photographing multiple exposures like the previous G5 peel-away shot.

If you are working in a studio, having lighting equipment is a given. The first decision you'll need to make is whether to use hot light (tungsten, continuous light source) or strobe (high-intensity flash), which depends on how you work and what your subject matter is. The majority of studio photographers use flash equipment. Take a studio lighting class or visit a number of photography studios before making your decision.

Photography studios are usually half photo studio and half woodshop. In fact, some of the best compositing photographers are either model makers themselves or they work with excellent model makers. Photographers are tinkerers by nature—they build solutions in front of the camera using models and physical sets, which is always better than trying to do it in Photoshop.

Run, do not walk, to buy a Macbeth ColorChecker (8 1/2-inch by 11-inch or 3.25-inch by 2.25-inch), as shown in **figure 11.38**, which is a checkerboard array of 24 scientifically prepared colored squares. Many of these squares represent natural objects of special interest, such as human skin, foliage, and blue sky. These squares are not only the same color as their counterparts, but also reflect light the same way in all parts of the visible spectrum. Because of this unique feature, the squares will match the colors of natural objects under any illumination and with almost any color reproduction process. This means you can shoot under a variety of lighting situations and always color balance your images on the Macbeth ColorChecker.

When working with digital camera images and shooting in the RAW format, photograph the ColorChecker in the same lighting as your subject and open the file in Adobe Camera RAW (**figure 11.39**). Use the White Balance eyedropper tool and click on the second light gray square (**figure 11.40**) to color balance your image to neutral. Adjust the additional settings to further process the image appropriately.

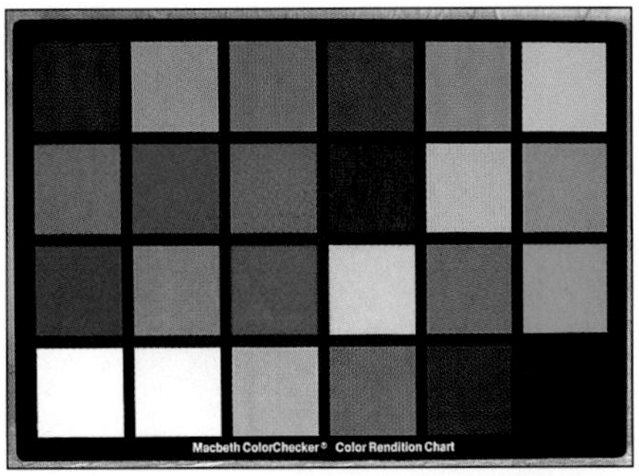

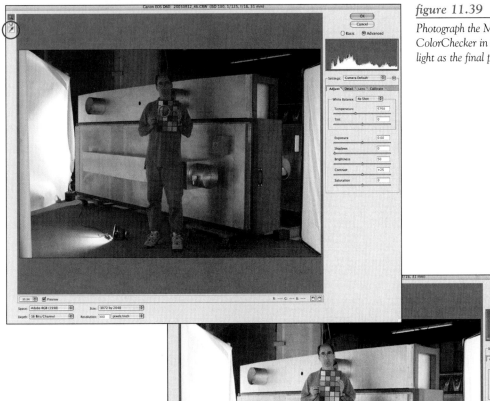

figure 11.38

A Macbeth ColorChecker is an important piece of professional equipment.

figure 11.39

Photograph the Macbeth ColorChecker in the exact same light as the final photograph.

© Mark Beckelman

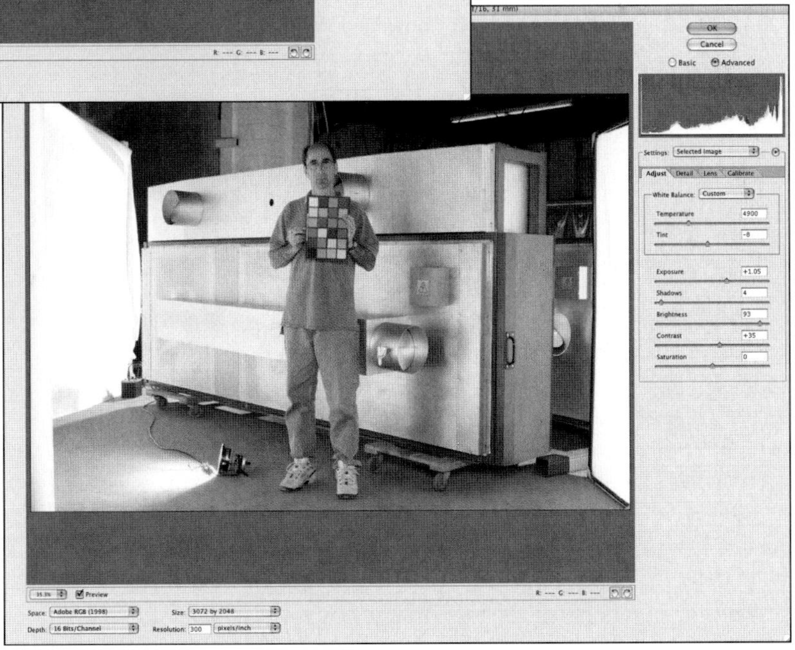

figure 11.40

The White Balance eyedropper tool neutralizes the color temperature, letting you create a very good image quickly and easily.

To apply this setting to the rest of the images taken under the same light, click on the small triangle to the right of the Settings pull-down menu and save the settings with a meaningful name. When you open the rest of the photo shoot, use the Settings pull-down menu to select the appropriate setting for the shoot at hand.

You can also apply the Camera RAW settings via the File Browser > Automate > Apply Camera RAW settings to update the images in the File browser. For additional information on working with Adobe Camera RAW, refer to *Real World Camera Raw with Adobe Photoshop* by Bruce Fraser (Peachpit Press).

A photographer always has a wish list of new lenses to try, light modifiers to experiment with, and filters to interpret. For additional information on a wide variety of important photographic issues, including determining exposure, camera equipment, image composition, digital darkroom techniques, and color management from capture to print, see my book *Real World Digital Photography*, *Second Edition* (Peachpit Press).

How Is That Possible?

One of the things Nick Vedros is known for are his images that make people stop and say, "How did he do that?" Nick loves challenges and solving so-called problems. When the studio received the layout for an ad featuring surfing frogs, Nick had to put on his thinking cap. He hired set builder Dale Frommelt to build a synthetic polyester wave that stood approximately 3 feet wide and 2 feet high. When he was setting the mold, Dale placed the surfboard into the wave (figure 11.41).

Nick took some image captures of water spraying on the model to create the mist behind the board (figure 11.42), carefully and patiently placed a tree frog on the board (figure 11.43), and tried to capture a frame before the little guy jumped off. He also captured a few frog frames to serve as the swimming frog (figure 11.44). Because Nick shoots digitally, he was able to see when he had the perfect shot. Mike McCorkle, the in-studio digital artist, then compiled all the images together to create the final image (figure 11.45).

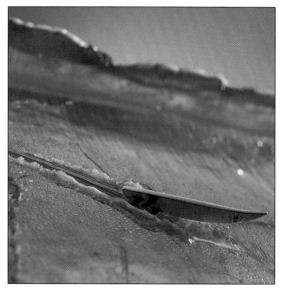

figure 11.41

The wave and surfboard model.

figure 11.42

Spraying water on the model adds an important sense of realism.

figure 11.44

Capturing a different point of view of the same frog.

figure 11.43

Hanging ten.

figure 11.45

The final composite is believably nonbelievable, which is exactly why it is so much fun.

CLOSING THOUGHTS

Photographers are creative problem solvers who combine physics and creativity to create fascinating images. You don't need a lot of expensive equipment to take a great picture—you need heart, vision, and empathy to create a great image. Enjoy the light and the adventure—your camera is your license to explore the world in and outside of you.

12

PHOTOREALISTIC COMPOSITING

To see the best examples of photorealistic compositing, you need to go to the movies. Recent examples of excellently executed special effects include the launch sequence in *Apollo 13* and the compositing of environments and live-action footage in the *Lord of the Rings* trilogy. The special effects in *Apollo 13* were so well done that after a screening for the actual astronauts and their families, Director Ron Howard was asked where he had found the footage and why NASA hadn't seen it before.

On the other hand, going to see a high-budget movie and being distracted by poor effects shatters our suspension of disbelief. Without it, we don't enjoy the movie because we view it as false, making it difficult to relate to the story and characters.

Many of the same issues that special-effects artists pay attention to when working on films are the same ones that Photoshop artists need to be aware of. In this chapter you will learn how to

- Find and follow perspective
- Enhance image focus
- Work with light and shadow
- Match film grain and image texture
- Create shape and dimension

Get ready to create fantastic realities that are so good your viewers will believe every single detail!

PHOTOREALISTIC COMPOSITING DETAILS, DETAILS, DETAILS

Photorealistic composites don't have to portray an actual event or scene. Rather, photorealistic composites reference reality and are so well done that the viewer agrees to accept them as real, although many times what is being portrayed is an impossibility. For example, you may love a glass of beer after a long hot day, but I doubt that you've ever seen a heart in the bubbles as shown in figure 12.1. Or perhaps you have a Palm Pilot to keep track of addresses and appointments, but I hope it isn't like the one in figure 12.2.

© Valentine Ale. Computer Graphics: Robert Bowen. Photography: Steve Bronstein

figure 12.1

Dozens of layers were used to create the heart and make the beer more inviting.

The more time and attention you put into the planning and photography, the more effectively the image will come together, as I discussed in Chapter 11, "Image Execution and Photography." Once the images are in Photoshop, you'll carefully combine them so that no telltale signs of the compositing process remain. If the viewer catches mistakes, such as color mismatches or lighting inconsistencies, then the composite has failed, and you've lost their trust.

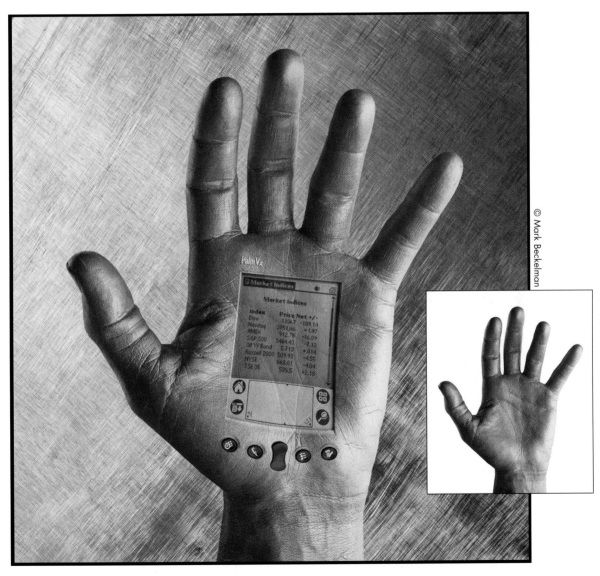

© Mark Beckelman

figure 12.2

The original hand was photographed with silver makeup, which adds realism to an improbable image.

The following list points out critical issues to consider when making both photorealistic and creative composites. Many of the techniques to resolve these issues are addressed later in this chapter.

- **Perspective and point of view**: The position of the camera determines the appearance and relationship of the elements to one another. Matching the planes of perspective when adding new elements starts with determining the vanishing point in the primary image (discussed later in this chapter). Examples of point of view include high (birds eye), low (ants view), or your own eye level. Determining the point of view before photographing will make combining image elements easier.

- **Size relationships**: Elements in the foreground need to be larger than image elements in the background, and the scale of image elements needs to be consistent with one another. Our visual system understands that when objects overlap, the object in front is closer.

- **Lens issues**: As illustrated in Chapter 11, lens focal length determines the angle of view and the relationship of the background to the foreground, size, and compression. The depth of field in an image can be shallow, in which only a narrow plane is in focus, or deep, in which the entire image from front to back is in focus. You can create a false lack of depth of field with the Lens Blur filter, but it is impossible to refocus an image with a shallow depth of field.

- **Color and contrast**: Image elements need to match each other in terms of color, tone, and contrast. Use Image Adjustment Layers to globally color balance and correct the tone and contrast of the individual elements before bringing them together. After the pieces are in the composite file, fine-tune the color and contrast to create a harmonious image.

- **Light and shadow**: The quality, color, strength, and direction of the light are essential attributes of an image, as I discussed in Chapter 11. Light and the thrown shadow need to be consistent throughout the image. Light bounces

from the environment onto the subject, causing the subject to be tinted with the colors of the environment and vice versa. This effect is more visible on light and shiny surfaces.

- **Reflections**: Shiny surfaces, such as glass, chrome, and metallic subjects, need to reflect the light and environment. Objects on shiny surfaces, such as a marble floor or glass tabletop, also need a reflection.

- **Texture and film grain**: Each film type and format has a characteristic film grain structure, so haphazardly mixing film stock should be avoided. Digital cameras have their own image characteristics to consider when combining images. Adding a Film Grain Noise layer at the end of the compositing process (as discussed later in this chapter) conceals texture and grain inconsistencies.

- **Edges and edge quality**: An image is made up of edges and transitions. Before dropping in new elements or changing a background, study the original edges in the image and use your selection and layer masking skills to mimic and maintain those edges.

- **Artifacts and patterns**: As the modernist architect Mies van der Rohe said, "God is in the details." The details we all need to pay attention to when compositing include masking out studio backdrops from the hollow areas between models' legs and arms; removing incongruous artifacts such as a hand that was on someone's shoulder from the original picture; preventing poorly cloned background extensions that create a noticeable patterned effect; and—my personal favorite—avoiding repeating obvious image elements such as duplicating the same fish over and over again, or repeating the same clouds or flowers to create a new environment.

The next time you're flipping through a magazine or watching a movie, take a moment to study the compositing details of the image or scene. The more images you look at, the better your own work will be. If you discover additional issues that should be added to this list, please send them to me and I'll post them on the book's Web site.

MATCHING PERSPECTIVE

Early Renaissance artists including Alberti, Brunelleschi, Donatello, and Masaccio had an appreciation for the beauty of mathematics, and they developed the concept of perspective to compose and organize images. They understood the picture plane as a transparent window through which the viewer looks into the scene from a fixed standpoint. Prior to the use of perspective, paintings looked flat and figures were stacked on top of one another as if they were paper cutouts without any form or substance.

Types of Perspective

The three types of perspective are one-point, two-point, and three-point perspective. One-point perspective renders only one vanishing point and all vertical and horizontal lines without perspective (figure 12.3). The classic example of one-point perspective is the road that winds its way toward the distant horizon. Two-point perspective rotates the viewer's point of view to a corner perspective, with parallel lines that have two vanishing points. Often the vanishing points are outside of the actual image plane (figure 12.4). The closer the vanishing points are to the center of the image, the larger and more dramatic the subject will be. Three-point perspective, often used by architects, designers, and computer special-effects professionals, renders the additional vanishing point well above or below the horizon to add dramatic volume to the subject (figure 12.5).

figure 12.3

One-point perspective is signified by one vanishing point, which in this photograph is behind the chapel.

figure 12.5

Three-point perspective has dramatic vanishing points that are well above and below the horizon line.

figure 12.4

Two-point perspective is signified by two vanishing points whose center points determine the horizon line.

Determining Perspective

Matching the perspective of an existing photograph starts with determining the vanishing points, which in turn determine the horizon line. The horizon line is at the viewer's eye level; it can be high or low depending on where the photographer took the picture or on the effect you are trying to achieve. Running parallel to the horizon is the ground line; parallel lines between the ground and the horizon are called *transversals*.

Drawing Perspective Lines

Finding the perspective lines is an important first step, especially when adding new elements to the image that need to maintain proper perspective and scale. In the following example, we will find the true perspective and add additional windows to the building. Use the Shape Line tool to draw perspective lines onto your images as described here:

🌐⮞⤵ **ch12_NYstreets.jpg**

1. The vanishing points are often outside of the image, so it is useful to increase the horizontal image canvas size by 300% to give you enough room to pull the parallel lines out to the vanishing points.

2. The Line tool is nested in the Shape tool. Activate it and set its options to Shape Layer, a 3-pixel width, and choose a bright contrasting color. I used red, which will contrast with the buildings and the blue sky very well as seen (**figure 12.6**).

3. Use the Line tool to trace the top-right roofline of the tallest corner building. Activate the Direct Selection tool (white arrow) and click and drag over the two anchor points on the right side (**figure 12.7**). Using the Direct Selection tool, pull the line down and to the right (**figure 12.8**).

4. Use the Line tool to trace along the lower line of the building and pull until the first line intersects to establish the first vanishing point (**figure 12.9**).

5. Repeat on the left side of the building (**figure 12.10**).

figure 12.6

Extend the canvas size by 300% and select the Line tool's Shape Layer option.

figure 12.7

Trace along the first roofline and use the Direct Selection tool to activate the two handles on the right side of the line.

figure 12.8

Use the Direct Selection tool to pull out the first perspective line.

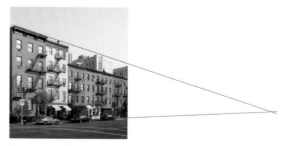

figure 12.9

To determine the first vanishing point, trace along the lower perspective line and pull to the right to intersect the first line.

6. I am planning on adding an additional row of windows to the left side of the building, which requires tracing the perspective lines of the top and bottom of the existing windows (**figure 12.11**). Link the perspective lines and from the Layer palette fly-out menu, select New Set from Linked to place them all into one layer set.

Using Perspective Lines

Once the perspective lines are in place you can confidently add image elements in proper scale and perspective.

1. Activate the Background layer and generously select the largest column of windows with the Polygon Lasso tool. Press (Cmd + J) [Ctrl + J] to place the selected windows onto a new layer; name it *New Windows*.

figure 12.10

Determining the top and bottom perspective lines on the left side of the building.

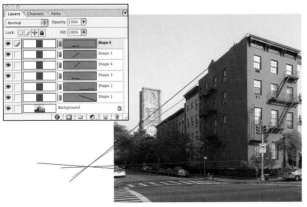

figure 12.11

All perspective lines meet at the vanishing point.

2. Use the Move tool to position the windows to the right and align the top window frame with the upper window perspective line. Select Edit > Transform > Scale while pressing Shift to maintain aspect ratio and pull the lower-right transform handle down and to the right to align the lowest window frame with the lower window perspective line (**figure 12.12**).

3. Add a layer mask and paint away any telltale artifacts, such as the piece of fire escape, to create the final image (**figure 12.13**).

figure 12.12

Scale the additional windows with the perspective lines to ensure proper scale.

figure 12.13

The layer mask hides extraneous image information and lets the pieces blend together.

Compositing Using Perspective

For the Book Festival poster that Mark Beckelman created for this book, Mark began by photographing the city scene and the books (see Chapter 11 for details). To fit the books into the buildings, Mark determined the perspective of the three primary buildings to which the books would be added and then added them using the following method:

1. Mark traced the perspective and contours of the three buildings that would be replaced with books (figure 12.14). To make the perspective line layers more manageable, Mark placed them all into a layer set.

2. After outlining the first book with the Pen tool and turning the path into a selection, Mark dragged the book into the building image. By positioning the book underneath the Perspective Lines layer set, he could clearly see how the book needed to be transformed to fit the building (figure 12.15).

3. Mark chose Edit > Free Transform (Cmd + T) [Ctrl + T] and (Control-clicked) [right-clicked] to access the context-sensitive menu of the Free Transform tool. By using a combination of skew, scale, and distort, Mark shaped the book cover into place (figure 12.16).

4. He then brought in the spine of the book and positioned it into place to match the front of the building (figure 12.17).

5. To have the book interact with the building, Mark changed the blending mode to Multiply, which also revealed the overlap between the two photographs (figure 12.18). By (Cmd-clicking) [Ctrl-clicking] the Spine Layer icon, the transparency was loaded. Mark activated the Book Cover layer and (Option-clicked) [Alt-clicked] the Layer Mask button to add a layer mask that would conceal the active area (figure 12.19).

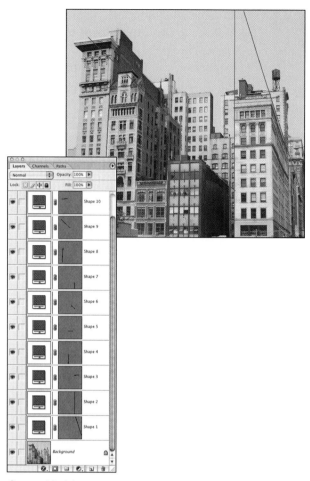

figure 12.14

Finding the perspective of the buildings is the first step to adding new image elements.

figure 12.15

The perspective lines will help transform the book into place.

figure 12.16

Using Free Transform to distort and skew the book cover into place.

figure 12.18

The Multiply blending mode lets the book and building interact, but also reveals extraneous book cover information.

figure 12.17

Treating the book cover and spine separately helps produce a better fit.

figure 12.19

The transparency of the spine serves to mask out the unneeded book cover information.

6. To strengthen the effect of the book on the building, Mark duplicated the Spine layer and set it to 25% opacity. He also duplicated the cover and set that layer to 50% opacity. Since it was on the darker side of the building, he felt that it could be darker and used a 50% layer opacity.

7. Now the building is interfering with the legibility of the book (**figure 12.20**). To resolve this, Mark came up with an effective method for blocking the building so that the wording would be legible. He sampled a lighter color from the original building, added a new layer underneath the book pieces, and painted over the book title and anywhere he thought that the book and building interaction appeared too busy (**figure 12.21**). Since the book layer is in Multiply mode it became more visible by applying a lighter color underneath it.

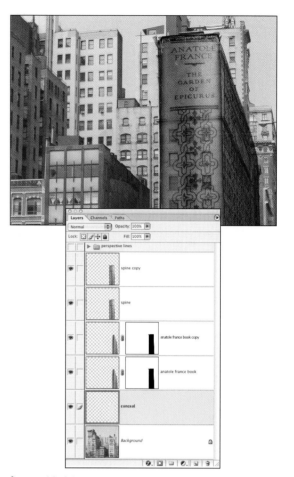

figure 12.21

The conceal layer makes the title more legible.

8. After placing the other two other books onto their respective buildings, Mark added a new layer and merged all active layers up by doing the following: He pressed (Cmd + Option + Shift + N) [Ctrl + Alt + Shift + N], followed by (Cmd + Option + Shift + E) [Ctrl + Alt + Shift + E]. He then made the perspective even more dramatic by choosing Edit > Transform > Perspective (**figure 12.22**).

9. Mark then duplicated the merged layer and retouched details with the Clone Stamp and Healing Brush tools and then added the sky (**figure 12.23**).

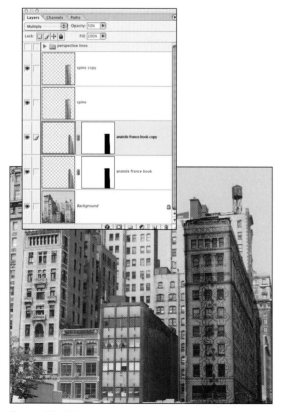

figure 12.20

Duplicating the layers and adjusting opacity to balance the image exposure.

figure 12.22

Exaggerating the perspective gives the buildings a greater visual presence.

10. The original foliage photograph was in Mark's personal image stock collection. He selected the tree using Color Range and layer masked, duplicated, and flipped to create a frame for the image (**figure 12.24**). Using the same tree five times is a quick and effective method to have all the branches match in terms of color and density, which adds to a sense of realism.

figure 12.24

The foliage is created by duplicating one tree five times, which helps keep the viewer's eye in the center of the frame.

figure 12.23

Adding the new sky.

11. Mark then added the woman (**figure 12.25**). Being the consummate professional that he is, he placed an antique book in her hands to match the look of the books used on the buildings in the background. Paying attention to subtle details like this gives the image important visual integrity.

12. To finish the image, Mark added a hint of warmth with a Photo Filter Adjustment Layer and subtly darkened the top of the image using a Levels Adjustment Layer to create the final image (**figure 12.26**).

Starting the poster with a strong concept and planning the photography made it easy to bring the images together smoothly and convincingly.

figure 12.25

Mark added an antique book to cover the contemporary book the woman was holding that better matched the books on the buildings.

figure 12.26

Darkening the top of the image reduces its visual importance.

Perspective and Scale

Perspective lines can also be used to add elements to an image in the correct scale. Nick Vedros was asked to create a campaign for the Smithsonian Museum that highlighted transportation equipment, including a steam locomotive, a Model-T, and a trolley car. The assignment involved taking the collection pieces out of the museum environment and integrating them into contemporary scenes. Of course, the equipment couldn't actually be moved out of the museum, so Nick had to photograph the museum displays in the Smithsonian, shoot the environments on location, and then photograph the models in proper position and period costume (**figure 12.27**). After all the elements were photographed, the studio's digital imaging expert, Mike McCorkle, was charged with combining the pieces into one very effective and believable image (**figure 12.28**).

figure 12.27

The source materials were photographed in three separate locations.

figure 12.28

The final composite combines the historical trolley with a contemporary environment.

1. The element that determines the correct perspective is the background plate, in this case the contemporary train station, which Nick had photographed first. Mike drew in the perspective lines and then added the trolley car (**figure 12.29**).

2. Mike then added the passengers by using the Pen tool to outline the trolley windows, made the path into an active selection, and copied and pasted the people into the trolley. He used separate layers for the primary passengers so that he could better control their brightness and color using clipped Adjustment Layers (**figure 12.30**).

3. To refine the image, Mike turned on the trolley's headlight, added light and reflections to the ground, and added a hint of yellow reflection to the modern train in the background (**figure 12.31**).

All of the images that Vedros and Associates created for the Smithsonian Museum are all perfectly executed. I can almost hear the call, "All aboard!" and the trolley's bell clanking in the distance.

figure 12.29

Fitting the trolley into the correct perspective.

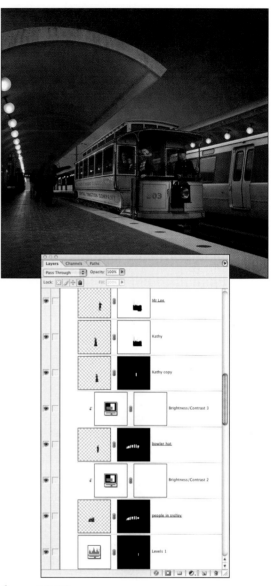

figure 12.30

Each person was added individually and fine-tuned with dedicated Adjustment Layers.

figure 12.31

Curves Adjustment Layers are used to build up and turn on the light and reflections.

Perspective Cropping

Photographers use a variety of camera formats and types of equipment, including large format view cameras and shift lenses that allow them to swing, shift, and tilt the lens in relationship to the film plane and subject. This is especially useful when photographing architecture, as the camera movements correct the falling-backward feeling that photographing buildings without the specialized equipment have (**figure 12.32**). To correct for this tipping backward, you can either use the Crop tool with Perspective enabled, or, as I prefer, use guides to fine-tune the perspective (**figure 12.33**), which is described in the following list:

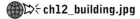 **ch12_building.jpg**

1. Since this technique works directly on the background layer, select Image > Duplicate and save the file to your hard drive. Press *f* to enter full-screen mode. Choose View > Rulers and drag out two vertical and two horizontal guides from the ruler to frame the subject—in this case, the Rock and Roll Hall of Fame and Museum in Cleveland (**figure 12.34**).

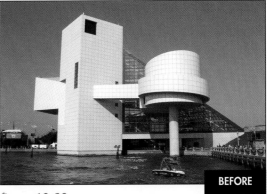

figure 12.32

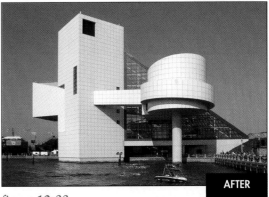

figure 12.33

figure 12.34

Add guides to serve as correct vertical and horizontal references.

T i p

Try to do all of the transformations in one session of the Transform tool, rather than applying, for example, a scale, clicking OK, and then assessing the next Transformation command. Applying all transformations at once is less destructive and will result in better image quality.

2. Double-click the Background Layer icon and click OK to the New Layer dialog box, which changes the background layer to a standard layer. Choose Edit > Free Transform (Cmd + T) [Ctrl + T]. (Control-click) [right-click] to access the individual transformation controls. To pull out the individual corners of the image, start with Distort (**figure 12.35**). I started in the upper-left corner and then pulled out the upper right.

figure 12.35

Distort lets you fine-tune perspective corrections caused by less than perfect image framing.

T i p

When accessing the Transform context-sensitive menu, you have to (Control-click) [right-click] the actual image and not the gray area around the image.

3. Align the vertical lines of the building with the vertical guides using additional transformations. The Skew command is very useful for shifting the upper or lower part of the building to the left or right. In **figure 12.36**, you can see how I skewed the building to the left by grabbing the lower-center transform handle and moving it down ever so slightly to the left.

4. Continue pushing and pulling the image plane to straighten out the building. Once you are satisfied with the correction, click OK. As you can see in **figure 12.37**, correcting perspective often reveals empty transparent corners that are easily concealed by cloning scene information—in this case, additional water—to complete the image.

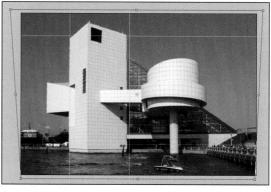

figure 12.36

Use skew to align vertical lines very quickly.

figure 12.37

Perspective cropping often leaves empty areas.

5. Pulling out image corners causes unnecessary image information to fall outside of the image frame. To remove it and reduce the file size, choose Select > All and Edit > Crop to delete the extraneous image information.

Tip

Avoid extreme wide-angle lenses when photographing a subject that needs to be in correct perspective. The distortion, especially visible at the edges of the image, will make finding the correct perspective more difficult.

Photographing buildings and landscapes without a professional view camera or a shift lens often causes the subject to fall backwards; use perspective correction to straighten the world out.

ENHANCING FOCUS AND ATMOSPHERE

When looking at the real world, our eyes can only focus on one image plane at a time, making whatever we're not looking at the moment soft and diffuse. When we photograph with small apertures, entire scenes can be in focus from front to back, as illustrated in Chapter 11. Although this is often quite effective, it can be just as effective to soften image areas to insinuate a shallower depth of field. By defocusing image areas, you are also making them less interesting for your viewer and they will therefore look at the more important image areas. In the following section, you will learn to add depth of field, image softness, and fog to enhance photographs.

Enhancing Depth of Field

Enhancing the depth of field is an ideal method for diminishing distracting or unimportant backgrounds. In the original photograph of the baseball player in **figure 12.38**, the busy background draws the attention away from the player at bat. In the edited image (**figure 12.39**), the player is fully in focus and the background is a mere memory. Here's how to do it:

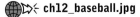 **ch12_baseball.jpg**

BEFORE

figure 12.38

AFTER

figure 12.39

1. Outline the baseball player with the Pen tool and name the path *Batter*.

2. Having the most control over what is in and out of focus requires a dedicated layer for sharp and soft image information. Duplicate the Background layer and name it *Blurred*.

3. Select Filter > Blur > Lens Blur and adjust the blur amount to throw the background suitably out of focus. In this example, I also brightened the highlights by reducing the Threshold slider to 235 and setting Brightness to 4 (**figure 12.40**).

4. Add a layer mask to the blurred layer, convert the Batter path to an active selection, and press (Option + Delete) [Alt + Delete] to fill the active selection with black (**figure 12.41**).

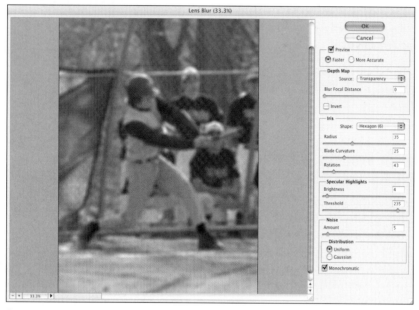

figure 12.40

Adjust the focus and image highlights using the Lens Blur filter.

figure 12.41

The layer mask conceals the blurred batter and reveals the in-focus batter underneath.

5. Now the player looks as if he is floating unnaturally. To add a transition between what is in and out of focus, use the Gradient tool, set to Black-to-Transparent, and draw a gradient from the grass to the player's feet (**figure 12.42**).

Blurring destroys image detail and texture. You'll need to re-create it as described here and discussed later in the chapter. When you zoom in, the difference in image texture between the in-focus player and the blurred background is very apparent (**figure 12.43**).

1. To add noise to just the blurred background, (Option-click) [Alt-click] the New Layer button in the Layers palette. Starting at the top, name the layer *Noise*, select Use Previous Layer to Create Clipping Mask, change the blending mode to Soft Light, and select Fill with Soft Light Neutral Color, set to 50% gray.

2. Choose Filter > Noise > Add Noise and use a setting that adds noticeable noise without making the image look over-speckled. Make sure to select monochrome to avoid adding color sparkles the image (**figure 12.44**).

Too smooth

figure 12.43

The blurred image area is too smooth in comparison to the original image texture.

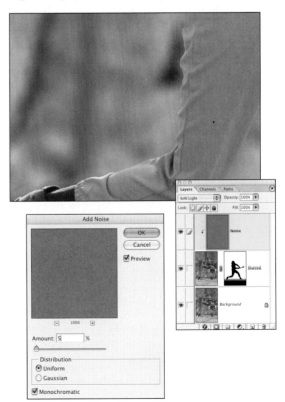

figure 12.42

Adding a Black-to-Transparent gradient onto the layer mask brings the ground back into focus.

figure 12.44

Adding monochrome noise to a Soft Light layer reduces the smooth appearance of the blurred layer.

3. If the noise is too crisp, use Filter > Noise > Median to make the noise clumpier (**figure 12.45**). Since the noise is on a separate layer, you can adjust the opacity to fine-tune the texture. I reduced the layer opacity to 75%.

4. To reduce the visual importance of the background even more, add a grouped Hue/ Saturation layer. (Option-click) [Alt-click] the Adjustment Layer icon while choosing Hue/Saturation. This brings up the New Layer dialog box. Select the option Use the Previous Layer to Create Clipping Mask. Reduce the saturation by 25% (**figure 12.46**).

Tip

When working with neutral gray layers to create film grain you can erase the entire effect by selecting Edit > Fill and filling with content of 50% gray to replace the less than perfect film grain. The original layer blending mode will remain intact, allowing you to rebuild the film grain with the Noise, Median, and Blur filters.

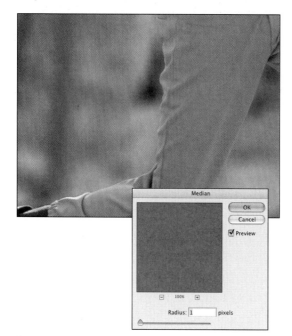

figure 12.45

The Median filter clumps the noise to make it look more like film grain.

By blurring the background and reducing the color slightly, the background is less distracting and your eye remains on the baseball player. Play ball!

figure 12.46

Desaturating the background reduces its visual importance.

Focusing the Viewer's Eye

Defocusing less important image areas encourages the viewer to linger on sharper areas. For example, the original photograph taken at a Society for Creative Anachronism celebration is a pleasant portrait (figure 12.47). But by reducing the visual interest of the busy background, Lee Varis encourages the viewer to focus more on the women (figure 12.48).

figure 12.47

figure 12.48

1. Lee enhanced the image exposure and tonality using a Curves Adjustment Layer. He made adjustments to lighten the image and remove the slight yellow color cast (**figure 12.49**).

figure 12.49

Correcting exposure and removing the slight yellow cast using Curves.

2. He duplicated the Background layer and used the Gaussian Blur filter on the Background layer to soften the entire scene.

3. On the duplicate layer, Lee selected the group of women using a slightly feathered Lasso tool and added a layer mask, which let the blurred background be visible behind them.

4. To add a natural transition from sharp foreground to soft background, Lee used the Linear Gradient tool, set to Black to White (third choice in the Gradient picker), and changed the Gradient tool's blending mode to Lighten. Starting at the top of the layer mask,

he drew the gradient three-quarters down the image (**figure 12.50**). The Lighten blending mode causes the white attribute of the gradient to affect only the dark areas of the mask and not the white part that is responsible for the women.

5. To enhance the timeless atmosphere of the image, Lee added a new layer, sampled the color of the earth and, with white as a background color, used the Clouds filter to create an abstract dusty texture (**figure 12.51**).

6. By reducing the layer opacity to 64% and transferring and inverting the layer mask to the dusty cloudy layer, the image gains in both atmosphere and apparent focus (**figure 12.52**).

figure 12.50

Using the Lighten blending mode with the Gradient tool creates a subtle transition between sharp and soft.

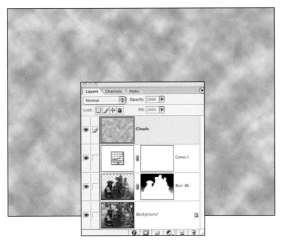

figure 12.51

The Clouds layer will serve to create a dusty atmosphere.

figure 12.52

Masking the Clouds layer and adjusting the opacity creates a sense of depth.

Tip

To transfer a layer mask from one layer to another, activate the target layer you want to add the mask to and drag the desired layer mask down to the Layer Mask button.

7. To enhance the group of women a bit more, Lee needed to sharpen them without sharpening the background. With the topmost layer active, Lee (Cmd-clicked) [Ctrl-clicked] the women's layer mask to turn the mask into an active selection. He then selected Edit > Copy Merged to copy all of the visible layers and then selected Edit > Paste which pasted just the women onto a new layer.

8. Lee used Filter > Other > Highpass, with a setting of 2, to find the image edges and turn the layer neutral gray (figure 12.53). By changing this layer's blending mode to Overlay, only the enhanced contours remain visible, and the women are sharper. Additional information on sharpening appears later in this chapter.

Enhancing image focus lets the photographer re-choreograph an image to guide the viewer's eye to the more important areas of the image.

figure 12.53

The Highpass layer is an effective sharpening technique.

Adding Atmosphere

Standing at the edge of a quiet body of water to gaze, ponder, and dream is one of the most relaxing pleasures I know. In the original image of Mono Lake, the dramatic calcium-carbonate tufa towers dwarf the Sierra Mountains in the distance, and the lake is peacefully calm (**figure 12.54**). In the enhanced rendition (**figure 12.55**), Lee Varis has accentuated the blues in the sky and more dramatically added wisps of morning fog. Lee told me fog is very rare at Mono Lake—well, rare until Photoshop is added to the weather forecast, as Lee has described in the following steps.

⌖ ch12_monolake.jpg

1. To accentuate the blues in the sky, add a Solid Color fill layer (Layer > New Fill Layer > Solid Color) and choose an appealing, vibrant blue. To allow the blue to interact more naturally with the sky, change the blending mode to Overlay (**figure 12.56**).

2. To limit the blue enhancement to the sky areas, use gradients on the layer mask. Make sure black is the foreground color and choose the second gradient from the Gradient picker, which is always Foreground to Transparent. This gradient allows you to add multiple

© Lee Varis

BEFORE

Figure 12.54

AFTER

Figure 12.55

gradients to an image or mask. Using the black to transparent gradient, start a bit under the horizon and pull up to just above the mountaintops. Add an additional gradient from the left corner toward the center (figure 12.57).

3. To create the tone and color for the fog, add a Curves Adjustment Layer and lighten and colorize the entire image. Pulling up the shadows on both the RGB composite curve and red channel and removing all blue information creates a delicate sunrise fog (figure 12.58).

figure 12.56

To enhance the blue values, use a bright-blue Color Fill layer and the Overlay blending mode.

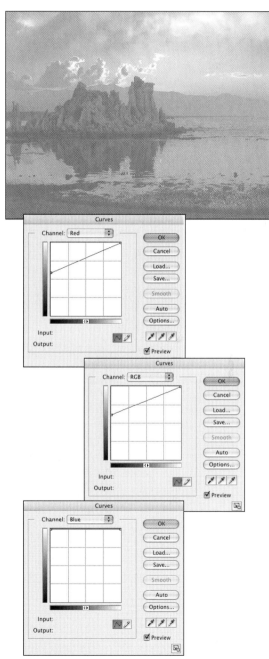

figure 12.58

Use Curves to light and influence the color of the fog.

figure 12.57

Use a Black-to-Transparent Gradient tool to limit where the blue enhancement takes place.

4. To create the Fog effect in the background, start by running the Clouds filter on the Curves layer mask. To limit the fog to the horizon area and not on the tufa towers, paint using a soft black brush to conceal the fog (**figure 12.59**).

5. To create a hint of wispy fog in the foreground, repeat the Curves procedure but don't adjust the red and blue curves, so that the foreground fog will be more neutral, and thus, more effective (**figure 12.60**).

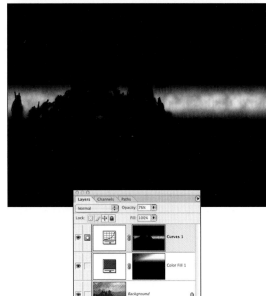

figure 12.59

Use the Clouds filter and a soft black brush on the layer mask to create the fog effect.

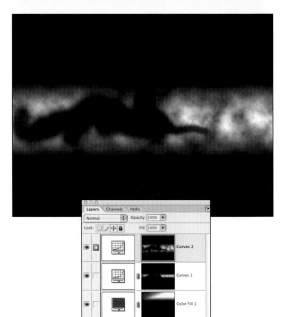

figure 12.60

An additional layer with neutral fog finishes the scene perfectly.

Experimenting with softness and fog to create the perfect image atmosphere can often transform a good photograph into a "wow" photograph.

HARMONIZING LIGHT AND SHADOW

Beautiful light is an inspiring element to work with, but often the quality of light isn't ideal, as seen in the original photograph by Lee Varis (figure 12.61). Not one to be satisfied with the initial capture, Lee transformed the low-contrast, backlit scene into a striking image (figure 12.62) using the technique Lee calls *digital chiaroscuro*, in reference to the Renaissance painters who used dramatic light and shadow contrast to add dimensionality to their work. Masters of chiaroscuro include Rembrandt, Leonardo da Vinci, and Caravaggio.

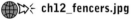 ch12_fencers.jpg

figure 12.61

figure 12.62

Creating light and atmosphere starts by imagining how dramatic you would like the lighting to be. In the following example, Lee added rays of light that seem to cut through the dusty haze:

1. Outline the figures using the Pen tool. (Please note: to save you some time the Web file ch12_fencers.jpg has the path intact.)

   As Lee explains, "I like doing the hard things, like making selections and masks first—the rest is much more fun if you don't have to stop the creative process to make a complex outline or mask."

2. The auto exposure of the camera over-compensated for the bright background that resulted in the underexposed foreground figures. To remedy this, duplicate the Background layer and choose Image > Adjustments > Shadow/Highlight and use a setting of 35% for the shadows and 0 for the highlights to correct the image (**figure 12.63**).

3. Add a Curves Adjustment Layer to lighten the image and add a bit of contrast (**figure 12.64**). At this point the initial exposure has been corrected, but the atmosphere of the image doesn't express the action of the image.

4. To create a new working surface, use (Cmd + Option + Shift + N) [Ctrl + Alt + Shift + N), followed by (Cmd + Option + Shift + E) [Ctrl + Alt + Shift + E] to add a new layer and merge the visible layers up.

5. On the Paths palette, select the path and click the Load Path as Selection button to create an active selection. Return to the Layers palette and, with the merged layer active, click the Layer Mask button (**figure 12.65**). It will look as if nothing in the image has changed since the merged layer is an exact duplicate of the layers below it.

figure 12.64

Enhancing image contrast using Curves.

figure 12.63

Always use a duplicate layer when using Shadow and Highlight to correct image exposure.

figure 12.65

Creating a new working surface may not make it appear as if anything has changed.

figure 12.66

Placing the Clouds layer underneath the fencers makes the dust appear as if it's in the background.

6. To create the smoky atmosphere often used in the background of chiaroscuro paintings, add a new layer underneath the merged Fencers layer and name it *Dust*. To create realistic dust and smoke, use the Eyedropper tool to sample a light color from the dirt in the picture. Also with the Eyedropper, (Option-click) [Alt-click] to sample a darker color from the scene. This will place the darker color into the Background Color Picker swatch.

7. With the empty dust layer active, select Filter > Render > Clouds and adjust the layer opacity to approximately 75% to allow the background to shimmer through (**figure 12.66**).

8. Add a layer mask to the dust layer and use the Black-to-Transparent Gradient tool to reduce the dust visibility on the bottom and top of the picture (**figure 12.67**).

figure 12.67

Using a Black-to-Transparent gradient to refine the Dust Clouds layer.

Adding Light Beams

Now the image is much improved, and in the following steps you'll add beams of light to the scene and enhance the highlights on the two fencers.

1. Duplicate the Dust layer, name it *Beams of Light*, and discard the layer mask without applying the changes (**figure 12.68**).

2. (Option-click) [Alt-click] the Layer Mask button to add a black layer mask to the Beams of Light layer, and use the Polygon Lasso tool with a feather of 30 to draw in the beams (**figure 12.69**).

3. Fill the active selections with white and change the layer blending mode to Screen (**figure 12.70**). The combination of the Dust layer and the Beams of Light layer adds a very attractive visual depth to the image. When working with your own images, you may need to experiment with the layer opacity to create pleasing results.

figure 12.69

Drawing in the beams of light onto a black layer mask.

figure 12.68

Creating the surface for the beams of light.

figure 12.70

Using the Screen blending mode and adjusting layer opacity to create the beams of light.

Fine-tuning the Figures

Lee added a hint of highlight contrast to the fencers, giving them an effective visual kick:

1. Click on the fencer layer and (Cmd-click) [Ctrl-click] the layer mask to create an active selection. Press (Cmd + J) [Ctrl + J] to lift just the fencers onto a new layer and then use Image > Adjustments > Desaturate to remove all of the color (**figure 12.71**).

2. Press and hold (Option) [Alt] on the Adjustment Layer icon as you drag down to Curves and select Use Previous Layer to Create Clipping Mask. Adjust the curve to remove all shadow information and increase the highlight contrast (**figure 12.72**).

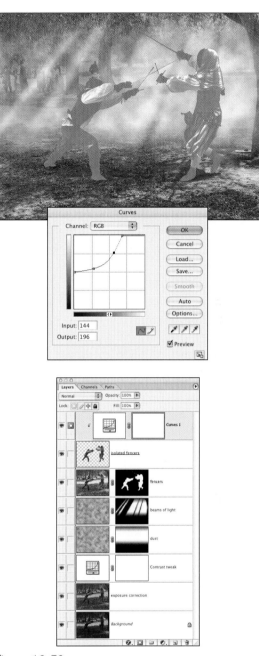

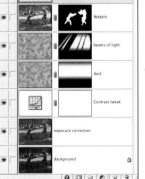

figure 12.71

Creating an isolated and desaturated Fencer layer.

figure 12.72

Using a clipped Curve removes all tonal values from the shadows and increases contrast in the highlights.

3. Click the isolated Fencer layer and change the blending mode to Overlay to pop the fencers off the foreground (figure 12.73).

Working with layers, blending modes, and masks lets you apply magical corrections and enhancements. Thinking like a painter in these situations can often bring new life to a photograph. I'm sure these techniques will help your images leap off of the page.

figure 12.73

Changing the desaturated Fencer layer to Overlay lets the fencers literally pop out of the dust.

Enhancing Studio Lighting

In studio lighting, just as much time is dedicated to adding light as it is to blocking, softening, and filtering it. Photographers use the oddest sounding contraptions to create lighting effects, including gobos to block light, cookies to create a mottled effect, barn doors and snoots to focus light, and scrims to diffuse the light. Our eyes are naturally attracted to lighter areas, so by darkening less important image areas and lighting more important ones, you can more easily guide a viewer's eye through the image.

In Chapter 11, I showed you the shot breakdown used to create the composite in progress shown in figure 12.74. In the following section, you'll learn how Mark Beckelman polished the image using neutral layers to create subtle, yet effective lighting effects (figure 12.75).

© Mark Beckelman

BEFORE

figure 12.74

AFTER

figure 12.75

Refining Studio Lighting

Modeling the light in a scene with shadow, shape, and dappling adds dimension and visual interest as explained here:

1. To bring the G5 forward, Mark opted to darken the background, by adding a new layer and changing the layer blending mode to Multiply. He used the Eyedropper tool to sample a gray from the shadow under the computer and chose Edit > Fill with Foreground Color to create the very dark image shown in figure 12.76.

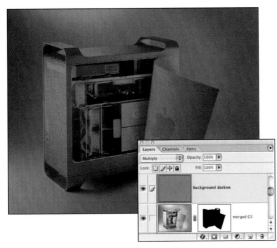

figure 12.76

Darkening the overall image using a layer set to the Multiply blending mode.

2. To keep the darkening effect off of the G5, Mark used an existing path to create a selection and added a layer mask (figure 12.77). By reducing the layer opacity to 24%, the background remains a hint darker, which makes the lighter G5 more prominent.

3. The next step was to add a touch of back lighting behind the computer to create visual separation between it and the background. Mark (Option-clicked) [Alt-clicked] the New Layer button to create a new layer, changed the mode to Soft Light, and selected Fill with Soft-Light-Neutral Color (50% gray). Mark transferred the layer mask from the darkening layer to this layer by dragging the desired layer mask to the Mask button.

4. He then used a very large soft white brush to daub in two soft backlights (figure 12.78). Mark adjusted the layer opacity to 80%.

figure 12.77

The layer mask keeps the Darkening effect from impacting the computer.

figure 12.78

An 80% Soft Light layer adds a hint of backlighting, which separates the computer from the background.

Darkening Image Edges

Photographers often darken image corners to encourage the viewer to focus on the center of the image. I described one method to achieve this effect in Chapter 5, "Masks Are Your Friends." Another method darkens the image corners by multiplying a duplicate layer of the image with itself and using a layer mask to control the effect:

1. Mark added a new layer and merged all visual layers up to it by pressing (Cmd + Option + Shift + N) [Ctrl + Alt + Shift + N], followed by (Cmd + Option + Shift + E) [Ctrl + Alt + Shift + E]. He changed the blending mode to Multiply and reduced the opacity to 40% (figure 12.79).

2. To apply the Darkening effect only in the corners, he (Option-clicked) [Alt-clicked] on the Layer Mask button to add a black layer mask and used a White-to-Transparent Gradient tool to fade the corners in (figure 12.80).

Tip

When you try this on your own images, it is easier to add delicate blends in full-screen mode and draw the gradients in from far outside of the image (figure 12.81).

figure 12.79

The Multiply blending mode darkens the entire image.

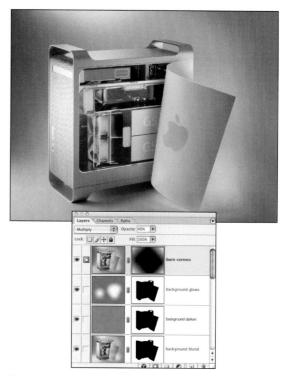

figure 12.80

A White-to-Transparent gradient is used on each corner to subtly darken the corners.

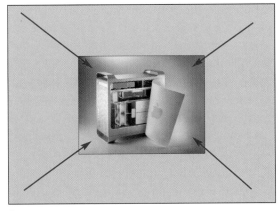

figure 12.81

Zooming out and starting the gradient well outside of the image allows for a more delicate effect.

3. Once he was finished with the lighting effects, Mark added a brushed aluminum backdrop (**figure 12.82**) and changed the layer blending mode from Normal to Soft Light. After adjusting the layer opacity, the texture was incorporated into the background perfectly (**figure 12.83**).

figure 12.82

The brushed aluminum background plays on the computer's metal casing.

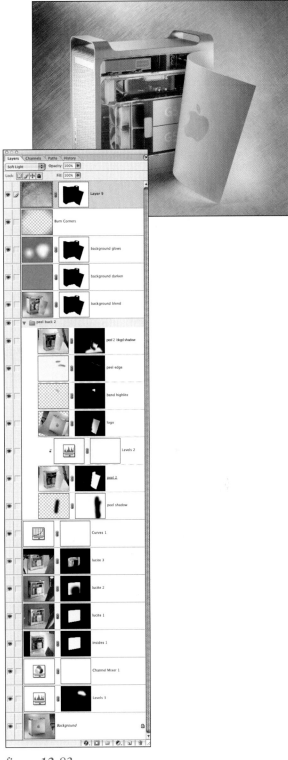

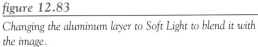

figure 12.83

Changing the aluminum layer to Soft Light to blend it with the image.

Creating Fantasy Light

Lighting effects can also be used to render realistic effects or add an "out of this world" feeling to an image (**figure 12.84**). Work with neutral layers and the Lighting Effects and Lens Flare filters to add rays, beams, bursts, and splotches of light.

Adding Lens Flare

To create lens flare lighting effects on your own images, read how Mark added the flare to the hourglass and then use the following technique on your own images:

1. To add a neutral layer that will serve as the lighting surface, (Option-click) [Alt-click] the New Layer button, change the mode to Soft Light, and select Fill with Soft Light Neutral Color, set to 50% gray.

2. Choose Filter > Render > Lens Flare and move the center point to the approximate area where the flare should start. Increase the brightness as desired (**figure 12.85**).

3. In this example, Mark strengthened the Flare effect by duplicating the flare layer, changing the blending mode to Hard Light, and using a layer mask to add a more dramatic effect in the center of the image (**figure 12.86**).

4. When adding light, it is often helpful to add darkness to the image to add visual tension in the contrast of light with dark. In this case, Mark used a Curves layer (**figure 12.87**) to darken the overall image, which made the flare even more dramatic.

figure 12.84

Twilight *by Mark Beckelman.*

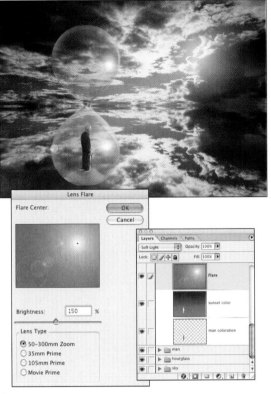

figure 12.85

Adding a dramatic flare on a Soft Light neutral layer.

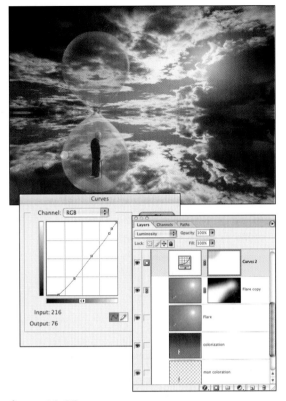

figure 12.87

Working with darkening to enhance visual impact is just as important as adding light.

Controlling Lens Flare Position

To add highlights onto a specific point of an image, such as the edge of the hourglass, follow these steps.

1. To add a higher-contrast specular highlight, (Option-click) [Alt-click] the New Layer button, change the mode to Hard Light, and select Fill with Hard Light Neutral Color (50% gray).

2. Open the Info palette and use the fly-out menu to change the Palette Options mouse coordinates to pixels.

3. Using the Move tool, click the point in the image where the flare should be placed. In this example, Mark clicked the upper-right edge of the hourglass and noted the pixel coordinates of 1275 × 437.

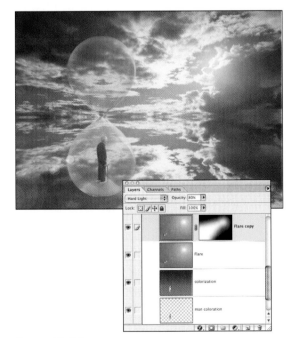

figure 12.86

Duplicating the flare and masking creates a Spotlight effect.

4. Mark chose Filter > Render > Lens Flare and (Cmd + Option-clicked) [Ctrl + Alt-clicked] the Lens Flare preview to bring up the Precise Flare Center dialog box and typed in the noted values. In this case, he entered *1275* and *437* (figure 12.88).

5. Since the flare is on its own layer, experiment with it by duplicating the layer, adjusting layer opacity, and moving it into a new position to fine-tune the Lighting effect (figure 12.89).

Working with neutral layers to create fantasy lighting can be an enlightening pastime that quickly changes an image from *ho-hum* to *Wow!*

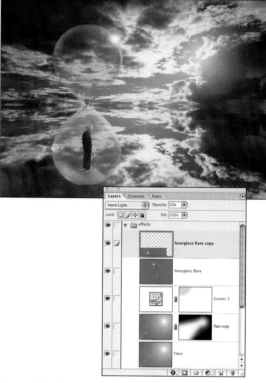

figure 12.89

Duplicating, moving, and transforming flare layers allows for creative enlightenment.

MATCHING COLOR AND IMAGE TEXTURE

Our eyes are attracted to color, and enhancing the color of an image or part of an image can insinuate the time of day, enhance emotional impact, create an intriguing mood, and add cohesiveness in an image. Juxtaposing cooler and warmer colors often adds a pleasing visual tension, which also attracts the eye.

Color is made up of three attributes—hue (the color), saturation (how much color), and brightness (how dark or light the color is), as illustrated in figure 12.90. Keep these three components in mind when making decisions to enhance and fine-tune your images. Often how much color or how bright the color is can be just as important as what color you are using.

figure 12.88

Adding flare in the exact pixel position.

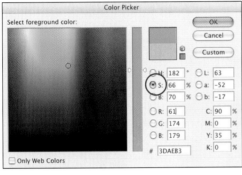

Hue

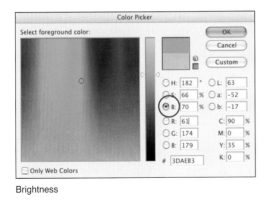

Saturation

Brightness

figure **12.90**

Color is a combination of three components.

Unifying with Color

Photoshop offers many methods to warm, cool, and enhance color, which include but are not limited to working with Curves, Hue/Saturation, Photo Filter, and Solid Color Fill Layers. The warmer reds, oranges, and yellows allude to early morning and evening, and the cooler colors such as blues and greens are better suited for midday and water-based scenes.

In the aerial joyride image seen in **figure 12.91**, Mark warmed the image with a subtle Fill Layer to create an evening mood as follows.

1. After completing the composite, Mark selected Layer > New Fill Layer > Solid Color and selected a sunny orange (**figure 12.92**), which covers the entire image with the orange color.

figure **12.91**

The contrast of scale and improbability add to the effectiveness of the image.

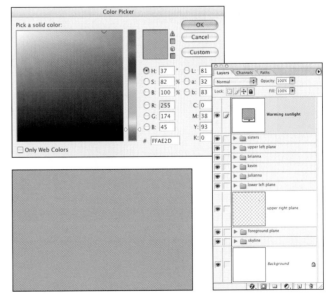

figure **12.92**

The sunny orange Color Fill layer will tint the entire scene.

2. To tint the image, Mark changed the blending mode to Color and reduced the layer opacity to 20% (**figure 12.93**).

3. After the color is established, Mark decided to reduce the amount of color ever so carefully by adding a Hue/Saturation layer and reducing the overall color saturation by –30% (**figure 12.94**).

When working on your own images, double-click the Solid Color and Hue/Saturation Layer icons to adjust the color and saturation as desired.

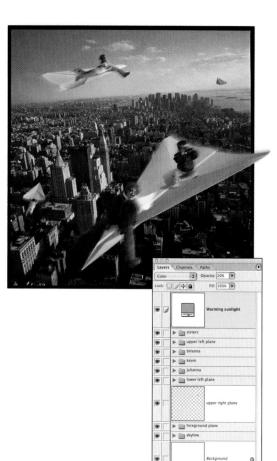

figure 12.93

The Color blending mode, set to 20% opacity, tints the image ever so slightly.

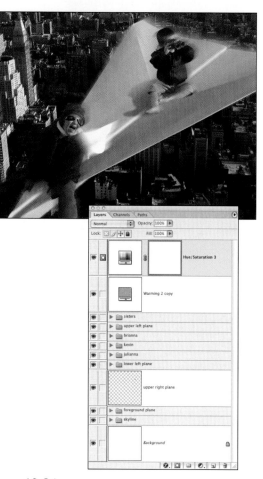

figure 12.94

Reducing the color saturation is a subtle and effective method for making the color a bit milder.

Enhancing a Scene Using Color

Combining color and black-and-white images can add new interpretations to images that are very exciting and completely change the mood in an image. A few years ago, Bruce McAllister, retired Black Star photographer and world traveler, was writing the book *Wings Above the Arctic: A Photographic History of Arctic Aviation*. He asked me to make the black-and-white image of the Hercules transport plane warmer so that the image could be featured on the back cover of the book (figure 12.95). I had never been to the Arctic and didn't understand what Bruce meant by warmer, so I emailed him and requested reference images. As soon as I received the reference images, I knew exactly how to create the scene to create the final image (figure 12.96).

1. I started by outlining the plane with the Pen tool, named the path *Herc*, and converted the grayscale file to RGB.

BEFORE

© Bruce McAllister

figure 12.95

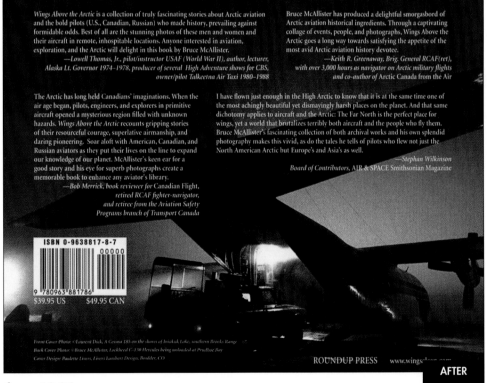

AFTER

figure 12.96

2. I dragged the sunrise image over to the plane file (figure 12.97). Of course, the sunrise layer obliterated the plane. To have the color interact with the plane image information, I changed the blending mode to Color and transformed the sunrise image to match the plane image (figure 12.98).

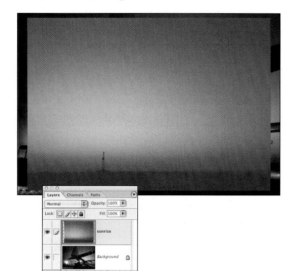

figure 12.97

Dragging the morning sky on top of the plane obliterates it completely.

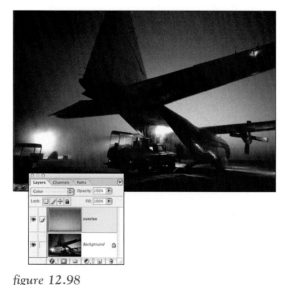

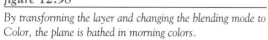

figure 12.98

By transforming the layer and changing the blending mode to Color, the plane is bathed in morning colors.

3. When reflective subjects are placed into colorful environments such as this, they will absorb some of the light and reflect some of the light—meaning the plane cannot have the same intensity of light as the environment. I added a layer mask and then activated the Herc path to be an active selection. Filling the active selection with 50% gray holds back half of the color (figure 12.99).

4. To reduce the intensity of the color on the ground, I painted on the layer mask with a 25% opacity black brush to reduce the strength of the reds (figure 12.100).

5. Bruce asked me to add taillights to the truck, which I did by selecting the blazing headlights in the second reference image with a 12-pixel feathered Lasso. After dragging the selected taillight over to the plane image, I scaled the light, set its blending mode to Hard Light, reduced its opacity to 67%, and blurred it (figure 12.101).

6. When the left taillight looked good, I duplicated and positioned it to add the light to the right side (figure 12.102).

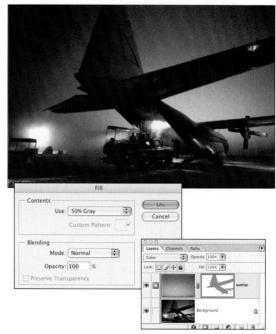

figure 12.99

The 50% gray fill blocks half the color from the plane.

7. After studying the tractor reference image, I noticed the colored reflections on the plane. To add these catchlights to the plane, I added a new layer. After sampling the headlight color, I painted along the plane's surface where the light from the truck's lights would hit it. By changing the layer blending mode to Color and reducing the layer opacity, the scene is starting to come together (figure 12.103).

figure 12.100

Painting on the layer mask with a soft, low opacity brush reduces the color intensity on the ground.

figure 12.102

The second taillight.

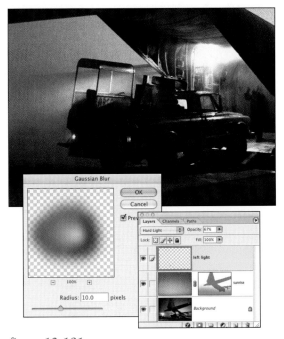

figure 12.101

Adding and blurring the first taillight.

figure 12.103

Painting in the color reflection from the truck headlights.

8. To frame the image with color, I added a new layer and used a Dark-Blue-to-Transparent gradient to darken down the upper-left and right-hand corners (**figure 12.104**).

The most important lesson I learned from working on this project was that when you don't understand what the client means, ask for a reference image. By studying the two files that Bruce sent me, I was able to solve the problem quickly and effectively.

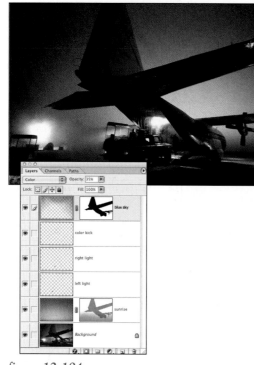

figure 12.104

Darkening the sky gives the plane greater visual presence.

Color Harmony

Whether it's a very large airplane or a small cell phone, subjects reflect the color of the environment and the light they are surrounded by. **Figure 12.105** shows the original files used to create the image in **figure 12.106**. To make the woman look as if she was in the window, I needed to tint her using the same color as the spotlight used in the showcase window and maintain the original window reflections.

figure 12.105

© Alex Beauchesne

figure 12.106

To harmonize subjects with color, use a Photo Filter layer, which allows you to simultaneously control the color, density, and luminosity of the color tint:

1. I used the Eyedropper tool to sample the color of the light from the center mannequin.

2. Since I only needed to tint the model, while not affecting the original scene, I pressed (Option) [Alt] while selecting the Photo Filter Adjustment Layer and then selected Use Previous Layer to Create Clipping Mask.

3. Rather than use one of the preset Photo Filter colors, I clicked the color square to open the Color picker and selected the color from the foreground Color picker. I adjusted the density to create a match and kept Luminosity selected (**figure 12.107**).

4. As you can see in the comparison of **figure 12.108**, without the Photo Filter the woman's natural skin color conflicts with the scene, while with the Photo Filter Adjustment Layer, the subtle tungsten tint effectively blends her into the window light.

I'll explain how I maintained the window reflections in the last section of this chapter.

Without correction

With correction

figure 12.108

Without the Photo Filter layer, the woman's skin is too natural. With the Photo Filter layer, she matches the light more closely.

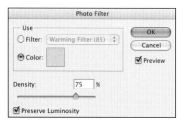

figure 12.107

Use custom colors to fine-tune color within a scene.

Working with Photo Filters

The Photo Filters in Photoshop CS mimic the filters that professional photographers use to correct for color temperature contamination and shifts. The two primary types of color compensation filters are warming and cooling. The Warming filters are orange to amber in color and subtract blues and cyan. The Cooling filters are blue in color and subtract red, green, and yellow.

- The 85 filter is a warming filter. Its color is amber; use it to accentuate the warm rendition of a sunset or sunrise and to enrich skin tones.

- The 81 filter is a milder warming filter. It's pale amber; use it to remove blue tones in photos taken on overcast days or to clear up bluish shadows in sunny scenes. It is also ideal for adding warmth to portraits.

- The 80 filter is a cooling filter. It's blue in color; use it to correct pictures with strong yellow-to-orange colorcasts created by taking the picture in tungsten or candlelight.
- The 82 filter is a milder cooling filter. Use it for waterfalls or snow scenes to turn them slightly blue, emphasizing the coolness of the subject.

The Preserve Luminosity option creates the Color effect while not adjusting density, similar to using a filter while photographing and adjusting exposure. Turning off Preserve Luminosity will darken the Color effect as if the camera exposure had not been adjusted.

Because the Photo Filters are Adjustment Layers, you have the additional advantages of being able to adjust their strength using layer opacity and layer blending modes and control where the corrections take place using layer masks.

Essential Sharpening Techniques

As soon as light passes through the atmosphere and your camera lens, it is being diffused, which softens images. Depending on the atmospheric conditions, subject matter, lens quality, and camera stability, this softness may be more or less noticeable. Sharpening digital files is an essential step in the image process and there are many third-party plug-ins and approaches to sharpening. The following section addresses the three popular methods of image sharpening in Photoshop.

Note

When and how to sharpen images has caused quite a few—to say it politely —"lively discussions." In this debate, I agree with the folks at Pixelgenius.com. They have developed a three-step approach for sharpening that takes into account the origin of the image (film format, type of digital camera, and subject matter), creative sharpening effects, and type of output (inkjet, monitor, offset press, and continuous tone). Applying image sharpening with the complete workflow in mind results in better images, and Pixelgenius PhotoKit Sharpener is an excellent product, which I use on all of my important images.

The Unsharp Mask Filter

The worst part of the Unsharp Mask filter is its name. If you haven't worked in a traditional darkroom or prepress shop, you might not realize that something called *Unsharp* is actually excellent for sharpening. In the dark pre-digital days of not-too-many years ago, separators made perfectly registered contact negatives of originals. To soften the mask, the repro artists would place a sheet of frosted mylar between the original and the masking film. This soft, *unsharp* mask increased edge contrast, making the image look sharper. Similarly, the Unsharp Mask filter looks for edges and differences to accentuate, making the image look sharper. There are three controls you use with the Unsharp Mask filter:

- **Amount**: This is similar to the volume dial on a radio—the higher you crank the knob, the stronger the sharpening becomes. For offset printing, start with a high amount, from 150% to 200%, and control the results with the radius and threshold controls. If you're outputting to CMYK offset, you should oversharpen the image by finding visually pleasing settings and then going a bit further. Continuous tone direct digital output devices, such as film or photographic paper writers, require a lower amount setting (in the range of 40% to 80%) and files should not be oversharpened. Sharpening for the Web or screen display is the easiest because you can judge the results on your monitor.

- **Radius**: This controls how far out Photoshop looks and determines the width of the edge contrast increase. An accepted rule of thumb for offset printing is to divide the printer's output resolution by 200 and use that as your starting point for the radius setting. This is the most critical setting—pushing it too high will cause ugly dark or light halos to appear along the edges of the image.

- **Threshold**: This scale goes from 0 to 255. Use it to tell Photoshop to ignore image tones that are very similar. For example, a threshold setting of 5 will ignore all tones that are within 5 level values of each other. A setting between 3 to 6 is a good rule of thumb to protect tonally similar areas from being sharpened. This is especially useful for avoiding sharpening image shadows and skin pores, wrinkles, and blemishes, as well as the grain in images that were shot on higher-speed film.

To use the Unsharp Mask filter with the great control and to avoid accentuating possible color artifacts:

1. Click on the top layer in the layer stack, add a new layer, and press (Option) [Alt] while choosing Layer > Merge Visible or use (Cmd + Option + Shift + N) [Ctrl + Alt + Shift + N), followed by (Cmd + Option + Shift + E) [Ctrl + Alt + Shift + E].

2. Change the blending mode to Luminosity to ensure that only the tonal information of the image is sharpened. Apply the Unsharp Mask filter as described previously.

To really understand what the Unsharp Mask filter does, download the canoe image from the Web site and apply various amounts of the USM filter to the entire image. Keep an eye on the differentiation between the rope lines holding the canoes, the edges of the canoes against the blue water, and the gray scale on the top of the image. The gray scale is a clear indicator of how the USM filter accentuates edge differences. Figure 12.109 shows the image with no sharpening, the right amount of Unsharp Mask sharpening, and sharpening that has gone too far.

Sharpening Tips

Sharpening an image effectively guides the viewer's eyes through the image as they move from softer areas to sharper areas.

- Images that are uniformly sharp often seem unnatural, so softening less important parts of an image will accentuate the sharper-image areas.

- Experiment with selective sharpening by masking out image areas that don't need to be sharp.

- Print your sharpening tests with the printer and paper that you'll use for the final document.

- Avoid resizing or retouching a sharpened file.

- When you send files to a service bureau, tell them whether you've already applied sharpening or you want them to do it. Too much sharpening can be just as bad as no sharpening.

When working with the Unsharp Mask filter:

- In the Unsharp filter dialog box, click and hold on the Preview box to see what the image looks like with and without sharpening.

- Use the Unsharp filter on the individual channels that contain the best image information—especially when sharpening CMYK files or when one channel is noisy, which should not be sharpened.

Neutral Sharpening

No matter how careful I am with the Unsharp Mask filter, I sometimes am still not happy with the results. When this happens, I turn to the High Pass filter to enhance image edges. That filter turns all non-edge areas to neutral gray but leaves image edges intact. The High Pass filter, combined with Soft Light or Overlay blending modes, yields a Sharpening effect that avoids ugly artifacts created when the standard sharpening filters are overused. Lee Varis has taken this technique, developed it further, and put it to fantastic use, especially on digital-camera files that do not benefit from the Unsharp Mask Threshold controls because they don't contain any grain.

To sharpen your digital camera files use the following technique:

1. Click on the top layer in the layer stack, add a new layer, and press (Option) [Alt] Layer > Merge Visible or use (Cmd + Option + Shift + N) [Ctrl + Alt + Shift + N), followed by (Cmd + Option + Shift + E) [Ctrl + Alt + Shift + E].

No sharpening

Correctly sharpened

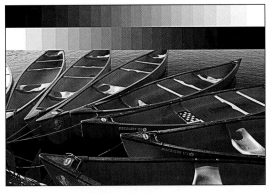

Oversharpened

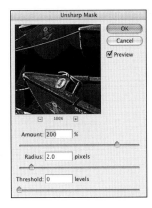

figure 12.109

Adjusting the radius and threshold settings controls how wide and apparent the sharpening effect is.

2. Select Filter > Other > High Pass and use the Radius slider to bring out the image edges. A very high Radius setting is less effective than a lower setting. Start with a setting between 2 and 5. Experiment with the Radius slider to increase or decrease the Edge Enhancement effect (figure 12.110).

3. Change the blending mode to Overlay, Soft Light or Hard Light to make the neutral gray disappear while maintaining the edge accentuation (figure 12.111). Using Hard Light adds a bit more contrast than Soft Light does.

4. If the image is too sharp, decrease the filtered layer's opacity to achieve just the right amount of sharpening.

Tip

When using the command keys to create a new layer and then merge all visible layers of (Cmd + Option + Shift + N) [Ctrl + Alt + Shift + N], followed by (Cmd + Option + Shift + E) [Ctrl + Alt + Shift + E], you can speed up the procedure by holding (Cmd + Option + Shift) [Ctrl + Alt + Shift) and then tapping *n* followed by *e*.

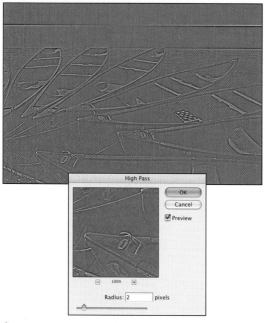

figure 12.110

High Pass sharpening is very effective for digital-camera files.

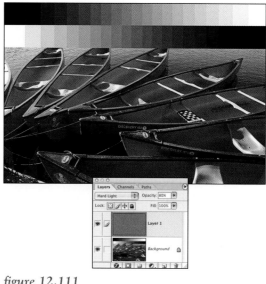

figure 12.111

Experiment with Overlay, Soft Light, and Hard Light to increase the Sharpening effect.

Neutral Softening

When sharpening files, the idea is to focus the viewer's eye on the essential image areas. Often, adding contrasting softening makes the sharp or in-focus areas seem even sharper. In addition to the focus control methods discussed previously in this chapter, try the following inverted sharpening method to soften images beautifully.

1. Click on the top layer in the layer stack, add a new layer, and press (Option) [Alt] while choosing Layer > Merge Visible or use (Cmd + Option + Shift + N) [Ctrl + Alt + Shift + N), followed by (Cmd + Option + Shift + E) [Ctrl + Alt + Shift + E].

2. Select Filter > Other > High Pass and use the Radius slider to bring out the image edges. Change the blending mode to Overlay or Soft Light to make the neutral gray disappear while maintaining the edge accentuation.

3. To soften the image, select Image > Adjustments > Invert or press (Cmd + I) [Ctrl + I] to invert the Sharpening effect and add a subtle glow (figure 12.112). Add a layer mask and use a soft black brush to conceal areas that do not require softening.

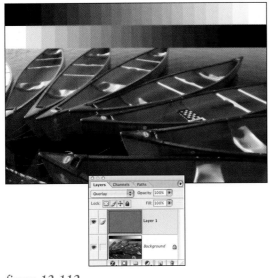

figure 12.112

Inverting the High Pass layer creates a delicate softness.

Smart Sharpening

Smart sharpening is a term Photoshop insiders use for a process that lets you sharpen image edges without sharpening noise, film grain, pores, or out-of-focus areas. In a nutshell, smart sharpening is a 10-step process that builds an edge mask based on image channel information and then sharpens only the image edges while ignoring the average midtones values, which is illustrated in grayscale in **figure 12.113**. Because this technique requires 10 steps, I've posted the action on the book's Web site. I also cover smart sharpening in detail in Chapter 8 of *Photoshop Retouching and Restoration, Second Edition.*

🌐▷⨍ **ch12_smart_sharpen.atn**

figure 12.113

Smart sharpening enhances the image edges.

The Value of Digital Noise

To make your images look more photographic, add digital noise as the last step in the imaging process. Even I—an avowed digital photographer—add noise to both composite and single images, not to mimic film grain but to give the image visual tooth. Digital noise also helps camouflage differences in image structure caused by different source materials and any softness that retouching or less-than-perfect masking may have introduced to an image.

1. After sharpening, (Option-click) [Alt-click] on the New Layer icon, change the blending mode to Overlay, and select Fill with Overlay Neutral Color (50% gray).

2. Choose Filter > Noise > Add Noise. Make sure to select Monochrome and add noise to the neutral surface. I add a lot of noise and use the layer opacity to fine-tune the effect.

3. To create clumpy noise, run the Median filter on the noise layer as shown earlier in this chapter with the baseball player.

Images without noise look too computery and artificial, while images with a hint of monochrome noise look more photographic. It is essential to add noise to gradient backdrops to help avoid possible banding, as I discussed in Chapter 8, "Selecting Hair and Fine Detail."

How much noise you add depends on your file size, type of printer, and personal taste. After you've added the noise layer, do not resize or scale the image, because this will soften the Noise effect.

SHAPING IMAGE ELEMENTS

We live in a three-dimensional world that, in its driest terms, can be described by height (y axis), width (x axis), and depth (z axis). Photographs inherently lack the capability to capture the z-axis. To add dimension to images using Photoshop, we can enhance light, shadow, and texture to insinuate shape, value, and volume. To add true dimensional realism versus faux effects, Photoshop images can also be combined with images or image elements in 3D applications (discussed more fully near the end of this chapter).

Adding Reflections

Reflective surfaces such as glass, water, marble, and windows have different reflective properties that depend upon the light, weather conditions, the angle at which they are photographed, and the curvature of the surface itself (figure 12.114).

In *Reflections of Youth*, Mark Beckelman portrays his father reflecting on his youth (figure 12.115). Here's how he did it:

figure 12.114

Observe and photograph natural reflections.

figure 12.115

Mark started with four separate photographs to create this final image.

1. The background, hands with water, and father's profile were all photographed separately so that Mark could better control the final placement. The face in the water came from an old picture of his father on a childhood football team (figure 12.116). After Mark restored it, he was ready to start the compositing process.

2. Mark used the Pen tool and luminance masking techniques to separate the hands with water from the background and to maintain the fine details (figure 12.117).

3. To better convey the sense of time, Mark aged his father's hands by duplicating the hands layer and using Filter > Stylize > Emboss (figure 12.118) to accentuate the wrinkles. By changing the blending mode to Soft Light, the gray disappears. After adjusting the layer opacity to 40%, the hands look older.

4. Mark brought in the boy's face, positioned and scaled it with Free Transform, and desaturated it with Image> Adjustments > Desaturate.

figure 12.117

Using the Pen tool on the fingers and luminance masking on the arms let Mark maintain important image detail.

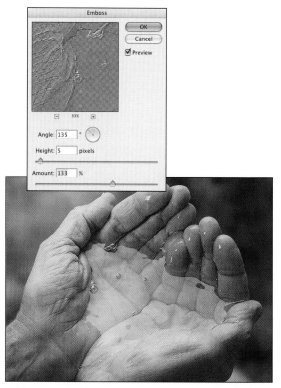

figure 12.118

Embossing a duplicate layer makes the hands look older.

figure 12.116

This football team photo served as the source of the face in the reflection.

5. He added a layer mask and refined the transition between the face and the hands with a soft, black brush.

6. To fine-tune the reflection, Mark removed cyan with a Color Balance Adjustment Layer, increased the contrast with a Levels Adjustment Layer, and reduced the face layer opacity to 66% (**figure 12.119**).

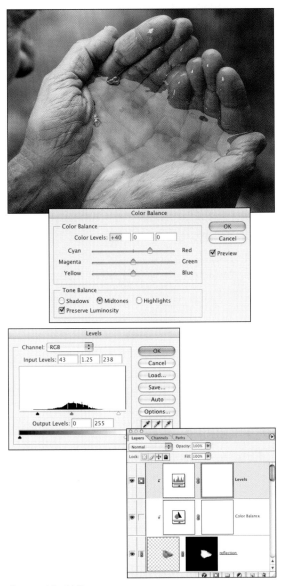

figure 12.119

Using clipped Adjustment Layers is essential in fine-tuning the reflection color and contrast.

Creating Water Reflections

As you can see in **figure 12.120**, reflections on water become more defined with smoother water. As the wind picks up, the water ripples and the reflections break up until they are just daubs of color and light. Before adding a reflection to water, decide on the weather conditions—is it a completely quiet day where the water looks like a mirror, a breezy one, or is there a storm on the horizon?

figure 12.120

Wind conditions influence the quality of the reflections.

Photoshop does have a Ripple filter, but I think its results are less than believable. The following technique relies on real water to create the Ripple effect, which in turn will create a much more believable reflection. I was inspired to experiment with the following water reflection technique after I read about it in Barry Huggins' book *Creative Photoshop Lighting Techniques*.

ch12_elfhouse.jpg

ch12_ripples.jpg

1. Double-click on the Background layer and name it *House*.

2. Select Image > Canvas Size, click on the middle top square, and increase the height by 200% (**figure 12.121**).

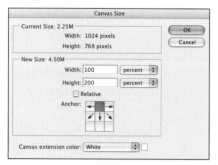

figure 12.121

Increasing the Canvas Size by 200%.

3. Use a 5 to 10 pixel feathered Marquee tool to select the top portion of the image and create the line where the water will meet the land. Copy and paste it or (Cmd + J) [Ctrl + J] and name the layer *Ripple*.

4. Choose Edit > Transform > Flip Vertical and position the Ripple layer in the lower portion of the image. Copy and paste or (Cmd + J) [Ctrl + J] the Ripple layer and rename the layer *Water*. Position the Water layer underneath the Ripple layer (**figure 12.122**).

5. To create a realistic ripple, we won't use the Photoshop filters, but reference real water ripples from a grayscale image. Open the ripples file and choose Edit > Define Pattern (**figure 12.123**) and close the Ripples file.

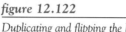

figure 12.122

Duplicating and flipping the layers to serve as water and ripples.

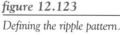

figure 12.123

Defining the ripple pattern.

6. Click on the Ripple layer and add a Pattern Overlay Layer effect, select the Ripples pattern, and set the blending mode to Hard Light (**figure 12.124**). If you see a distinct tile pattern, use the scale function to scale the ripple pattern up or down, while making sure that no telltale tiles appear. Click OK.

7. Where the water meets the land, the ripples should be smoother, which can be achieved by adding a layer mask to the ripple layer and using a Black-to-White gradient to blend the ripple and the smooth water layers together (**figure 12.125**).

8. Reflections shouldn't be as saturated as the world they are reflecting. Add a clipped Hue/Saturation Adjustment Layer and desaturate the reflection by approximately –25%.

9. Reducing the fill opacity of the Ripple layer to hide more of the Ripple layer pixels while maintaining the Ripple effect (**figure 12.126**) is an effective method for combining the original image with the rippled version.

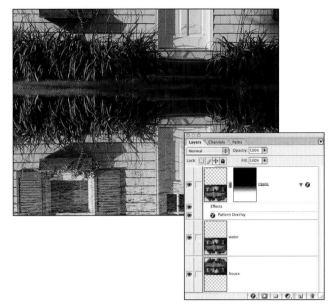

figure 12.125

The Gradient layer mask reduces the ripples near the faux shoreline.

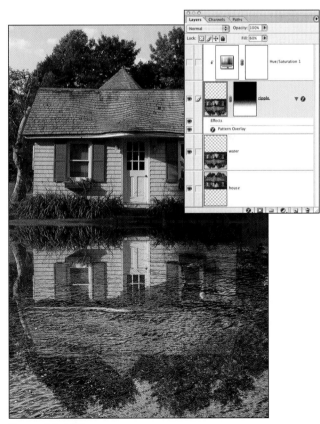

figure 12.124

Using a Pattern Overlay Layer effect to add the Ripple effect.

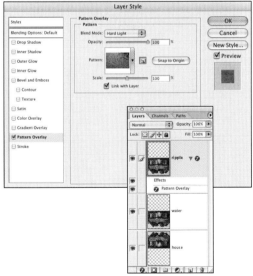

figure 12.126

Reduce the fill opacity to lessen the Ripple effect.

Maintaining Window Reflections

The primary features used to maintain existing reflections are layer blending modes, layer opacity, and the Blend If command. After compositing the fashion model into the window scene, I needed to add back in, i.e., maintain the window reflections by selectively using the original reflections as described here:

1. I duplicated the original window layer and placed it on the top of the layer stack. Changing the blending mode to Hard Light, set to 30% opacity, added the natural reflections back into the scene where the model had been added.

2. Just because something—in this case the reflections—are in the scene doesn't mean you have to keep them. Some of the reflections on the woman's face and arms (circled in **figure 12.127**) were not flattering, so I concealed them by painting with a black brush on a layer mask to flatter the model as shown in **figure 12.128**.

3. To better control how the model and the environment interacted, I placed them into a Layer Set and added a layer mask to the layer set, by clicking on the mask icon on the bottom of the Layers palette. To add a hint of window density to the image, I used a Light Gray-to-Transparent gradient to push the model back ever so slightly, as the comparison in **figure 12.129** shows.

figure 12.127

Some of the natural reflections are not flattering.

figure 12.128

Painting with a small black brush hid the bothersome reflections.

figure 12.129

The light gray gradient on the Model layer set makes the woman appear to recede into the window ever so slightly.

Bending and Distorting

Having image elements interact organically often requires that one subject take on the contours and surface characteristics of another subject. The Photoshop Distort filters offer classic bending, warping, and twisting options, including Displace, Shear, Pinch, and Spherize. Added more recently to Photoshop, the Liquify command lets you turn images into putty to make them look as if they're melting and flowing.

The Displace Filter

The Displace filter is the most powerful of the Distort filters, allowing you to shift and bend one image over the contours of another. Imagine how your shadow runs along the sidewalk and then up the side of a building—the sidewalk and the building is displacing your shadow. To use the Displace filter, you must first make a displacement map of the surface over which you are flowing or placing another image. The Displace filter is often used to make shadows interact with the surface they are falling onto or to have the hands and bottle seem as rippled as the water they are in (**figure 12.130**).

The Displace filter requires two images—the source image that you are distorting and a displacement map which is a file saved in the PSD file format, which can be in grayscale or color mode.

Grayscale displacement maps shifts the image horizontally based on lights and darks. Black (or 0) creates the maximum positive displacement shift, white (or 256) creates a negative displacement shift, and gray values of 128 produce no displacement. Color displacement maps are RGB files in which only the red and the green channel are recognized by the Displace filter; red controls the horizontal shift and green the vertical shift. The blue channel is completely ignored.

The behavior of grayscale displacement maps are often easier to predict as they distort in two directions, while RGB displacement maps are more complex to visualize as they distort images in four

figure 12.130

The Displace filter rippled the hands and bottle to match the water surface.

directions. Both grayscale and RGB displacement maps with transitional tones between dark and light displace smoothly as the illustrations in figure 12.131 show where the hard-edged dots displace abruptly, while the blurred dots gently push the grid pattern outward.

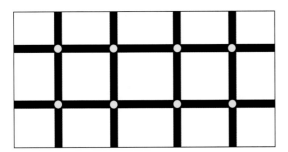

The original grid

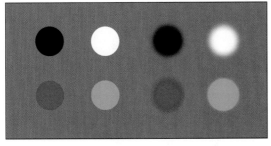

The displacement map

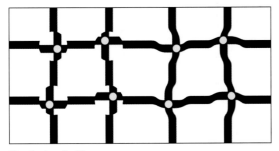

The displaced grid

figure 12.131

This example illustrates the impact of colors and hard and soft edges of a displacement map.

Building a Displacement Map

To build a grayscale displacement map for a color image that allows you to distort a thrown shadow over a textured surface, use the following technique:

ch12_kewpie.jpg

ch12_parkingsign.jpg

1. Starting with the surface image, in this case the rusty wall image, inspect the color channels to find the one with the most image contrast and detail. Use the fly-out menu on the Channels palette to duplicate the channel into a new document (figure 12.132). Select Image > Mode > Grayscale and save the file as a Photoshop document.

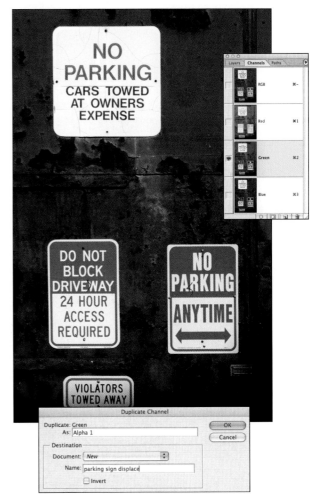

figure 12.132

Duplicate the channel with the most contrast and convert it to a grayscale file.

2. To create a smooth displacement that conforms gently to the image, use the Gaussian Blur filter with a setting of 1 to 2 and then use Curves to increase the image contrast (**figure 12.133**) to make the dark values darker and the light values lighter to make the displacement maps effect more dramatic. Save the file in the Photoshop PSD format.

figure 12.133

Blur slightly and increase the contrast.

Displacing a Shadow

Now that the displacement map is saved, the creative part can begin. In this image, I am showing how hard it is to find a parking space in Hoboken, NJ, and the Kewpie doll's shadow is going to fall on the wall and conform to the rusty texture.

1. Turn the path on the Kewpie Doll file into an active selection and drag her onto the rusty wall image.

2. Sample a dark brown from the rusty wall.

3. Duplicate the Kewpie Doll layer and position it to the right of the Kewpie doll.

4. Choose Edit > Fill > Use Foreground Color and make sure that Preserve Transparency is selected. Soften the shadow with a Gaussian Blur of 10 (**figure 12.134**).

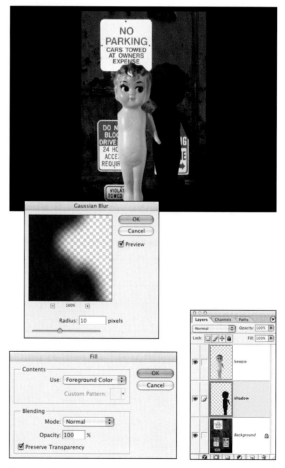

figure 12.134

Adding a soft drop shadow underneath the figure.

5. Activate the layer you would like to displace. In this case, I am displacing the doll's shadow over the rusty wall in the background.

6. Choose Filter > Distort > Displace and navigate to where you saved the displacement file. I usually start with the default settings to see how the displacement map is working (figure 12.135). Click OK and study the results. If you don't want more displacement, choose Edit > Undo and then press (Cmd + Option + F) [Ctrl + Alt + F], and change the parameters—increasing the horizontal and vertical settings applies a stronger effect.

7. To blend the shadow into the rusty wall, change the blending mode to Multiply and adjust the layer opacity. Increase the doll size to bring her into the foreground (figure 12.136).

Color Displacement Maps

Creating color displacement maps for more dramatic effects is similar to creating a grayscale displacement map.

1. Duplicate the file you wish to use as a displacement map, most often the defining surface of the composite image.

2. Activate the Move tool, open the Channels palette, and click on the word *Red*. Hold Shift and press the down arrow and then press the right arrow to shift the red channel down and over to the right by 10 pixels.

3. Click on the word *Green*. Hold Shift and press the down arrow and then press the right arrow key to shift the green channel up and over to the left by 10 pixels to create a bizarre image (figure 12.137).

figure 12.135

Start with the default settings of the Displace filter.

figure 12.136

Scaling the doll and adjusting the shadow layer opacity to fine-tune the image.

figure 12.137

The original image and the color displacement map in progress.

4. Click on the word *Blue*, select all and choose Edit > Fill with white.

5. Click on RGB or press (Cmd + ~) [Ctrl + ~] to return to RGB and use the Gaussian Blur and Curves, as described previously. Save the file as a PSD file and use it as the displacement map. **Figure 12.138** shows the shadow of the clarinet being displaced over the clouds.

The Displace filter creates unique and surprising image effects, and although I wish the Displace filter had a preview, I am willing to work blindly to achieve the creative effects.

figure 12.138

The displaced shadow follows the contours of the clouds.

Tip

The Displace Filter has not been improved in the many releases of Photoshop, and, worst of all, it does not have a built-in preview. If you are able to work with Adobe After Effects, I highly recommend you do your image displacing in that program because you can preview and control the effects. In Photoshop, the Displace filter forces you to work blindly, which often requires quite a bit of guesswork.

The Shear, Pinch, and Spherize Filters

The Shear filter lets you shift and bend an image as if it is in a wind tunnel. It is very useful to wrap labels onto cylindrical objects, to narrow a person's waistline, or to reduce the reflections of the studio lighting (**figure 12.139**) by adding cloud reflections onto the champagne glass (**figure 12.140**).

© Mark Beckelman

BEFORE

figure 12.139

AFTER

figure 12.140

After we photographed the champagne glass in the green screen studio and used Primatte 2.0 to extract the glass, I decided to replace the background with the dramatic sky as described here:

1. I started by outlining the studio reflection on the left side of the glass with the Pen tool.

2. I then generously selected a part of the sunset layer with the Marquee tool and pressed (Cmd + J) [Ctrl + J] to duplicate it onto a new layer and made sure that it was underneath the glass.

3. I chose Filter > Distort > Shear and implied the curvature of the glass with the filter control points (figure 12.141) and clicked OK. In this instance, I opted not to use the Wrap Around option, as it would envelop the clouds around the glass and ruin the effect.

4. I converted the path into an active selection and clicked the Layer Mask button to reveal just the clouds within the outlined reflection. By changing the layer blending mode to Lighten, the clouds interact more effectively with the glass (figure 12.142).

5. I refined the layer mask with a low Gaussian Blur of 2 to soften the edges of the reflection.

6. To create the reflection on the right side of the glass, I repeated the above steps with a newly selected area from the right side of the image.

Working with Pinch and Spherize is very similar: the Pinch filter pushes the image in or out from a center point, and the Spherize filter wraps the image around an invisible sphere to push the images in or out.

figure 12.142
The layer mask conceals unneeded reflection.

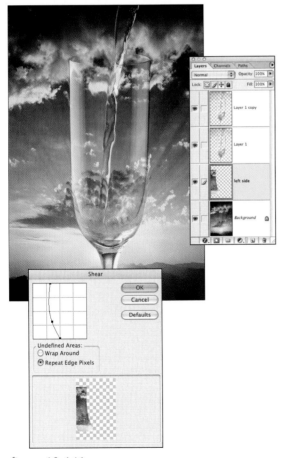

figure 12.141
Bend the shear handle points to create shape and movement.

Working with Liquify

As soon as I access Filter > Liquify, I feel as if I'm back in kindergarten, where I'm allowed to play with clay, paint, and goo to my heart's content. The Liquify interface is divided into three sections: Distort Tools, Preview, and the Options controls (figure 12.143).

When painting with the distortion tools, the distortion is concentrated at the center of the brush area, and the effect intensifies as you press the mouse button or repeatedly drag over an area. From top to bottom the distortion tools are:

- **Forward Warp** pushes pixels forward as you drag.

- **Twirl Clockwise** rotates pixels clockwise as you press the mouse button or drag. To twirl pixels counterclockwise, press (Option) [Alt] as you press the mouse button or drag.

- **Pucker** moves pixels toward the center of the brush area as you press the mouse button or drag.

- **Bloat** moves pixels away from the center of the brush area as you press the mouse button or drag.

- **Push Left** moves pixels to the left when you drag the tool straight up and moves pixels to the right when you drag down. You can also drag clockwise around an object to increase its size, or drag counterclockwise to decrease its size.

- **Mirror** copies pixels to the brush area. Drag to reflect the area to the left of the stroke. (Option) [Alt] drag to reflect the area in the direction opposite to that of the stroke. Use overlapping strokes to create an effect similar to a reflection in water.

- **Turbulence** smoothly scrambles pixels. Use it to create smoke, fire, clouds, and waves effects.

- **Freeze** and **Thaw** protect and unprotect areas from being changed. Use the Freeze tool to paint in a mask that blocks the Liquify tool and use the Thaw tool to remove the mask. You can also use an existing mask, selection, or transparency to freeze areas.

- The **Hand** and **Zoom** and their keyboard equivalents work exactly as they do within the main Photoshop interface.

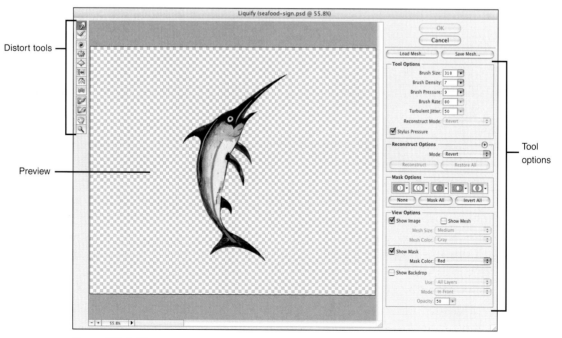

figure 12.143

The Liquify interface enables you to push, swirl, pinch, bloat, mirror, and reflect images.

From top to bottom, the Tool options include the following:

- **Brush Size** sets the width of the brush you'll use to distort the image.

- **Brush Density** controls how a brush feathers at the edge. An effect is strongest in the center of the brush and lighter at the edge.

- **Brush Pressure** sets the speed at which distortions are made when you drag a tool in the preview image. Using a low brush pressure makes changes occur more slowly, so it's easier to stop them at exactly the right moment.

- **Brush Rate** sets the speed at which distortions are applied when you keep a tool (such as the Twirl tool) stationary in the preview image. A high setting applies distortions quickly; a lower setting provides a slower change.

- **Turbulent Jitter** controls how tightly the Turbulence tool scrambles pixels.

- **Select Stylus Pressure** lets you use pressure readings from a stylus tablet. When selected, the brush pressure for the tools is the stylus pressure multiplied by the Brush Pressure value.

Reconstruct Mode is among the most interesting tools in the Liquify arsenal. Use it to reconstruct an area of the preview image based on the five types of reconstruction described here. Use the Reconstruct fly-out menu to increase or decrease the strength of the Applied Reconstruction effect.

- **Rigid** maintains right angles in the pixel grid (as shown by the mesh) at the edges between frozen and unfrozen areas and may produce disjointed edge effects.

- **Stiff** acts like a weak magnetic field. At the edges between frozen and unfrozen areas, the unfrozen areas continue the distortions into the frozen areas. As the distance from frozen areas increases, the distortions lessen.

- **Smooth** stretches the distortions from the frozen areas into unfrozen areas.

- **Loose** is similar to Smooth, with even greater continuity between distortions in frozen and unfrozen areas.

- **Revert** removes distortions as if using an undo eraser without any kind of smoothing effects.

On the bottom right, the View Options allow you to project a grid mesh over the image, which is helpful when creating depth effects. The Backdrop checkbox is an essential feature that lets you see through the layer being distorted to the underlying layers, allowing you to compare and monitor the distortion effects in relationship to the rest of the image.

The Beauty of True 3D

As discussed at the beginning of this section, Photoshop is a two-dimensional application and sometimes not having the true z-axis, the depth axis, to work with to change camera position, or wrap surfaces with color and texture, becomes painfully obvious.

Teaching at the School of VISUAL ARTS in New York has given me a great appreciation for the skills required to be an outstanding 3D artist. One of the best is Bob Bowen, who has worked with many successful photographers including Ryszard Horowitz, Eric Meola, and Howard Berman on campaigns for Johnnie Walker, Panasonic, American Express, Coca-Cola, Kodak, and Bacardi, to name a few. Bob is a painter, photographer, animator, and a true artist who appreciates art history and understands how the intricacies of light, atmosphere, and color interact.

When art directors or photographers cannot create an effect in the camera or with Photoshop alone, they turn to Bob to add the realism of 3D to maintain the illusion of believability. Bob has used many 3D software products including Softimage XSI, Alias Maya, Lightwave, 3D Studio Max, Cinema 4D, Form Z, and Side Effects Houdini. As soon as clients contact him with a potential job, he immediately starts figuring out strategies to accomplish the desired effect with both Photoshop and the best 3D application for the challenge at hand.

Rewrapping Candy Canes

The original composite seen in **figure 12.144**, a holiday season image for Millstone Coffee, was created with separate photographs of the candy canes, the bow, the spout, the coffee cup, the pour, and splashing coffee. After the composite was completed, the art director thought the candy canes looked too much like barbershop poles and not enough like delicious candy canes. It was time to call Robert Bowen. The challenge was to create and wrap the fine stripes in between the thick red stripes on the candy canes while maintaining the light and shadows in the original image. The final image was approved by the client (**figure 12.145**).

1. Robert started by finding reference materials of an ideal candy cane (**figure 12.146**).

2. He then painted image maps in Photoshop, which in this case are flat files with the color and pattern of the ideal candy cane (**figure 12.147**).

3. Robert built a 3D candy cane in Maya and rendered the Photoshop images around it to create candy cane variations and image masks (**figure 12.148**).

4. In Photoshop, he then meticulously rebuilt each candy cane, as the Layers palette in **figure 12.149** reveals.

5. By maintaining the candy cane pieces on separate layers, Robert was able to position each part perfectly and with clipped Adjustment Layers; Robert added subtle shading to create the final illusion.

figure 12.144   **BEFORE**

figure 12.145   **AFTER**

figure 12.146

Referencing a real candy cane is helpful.

figure 12.148

The new candy canes and mask as rendered in a 3D application.

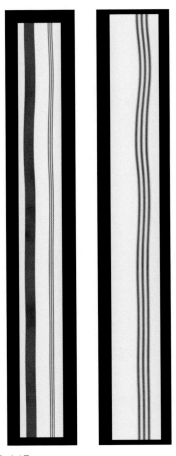

figure 12.147

Painted image maps created in Photoshop.

figure 12.149

Rebuilding the canes piece by piece.

Rainbow in a Jar

What would a rainbow in a jar look like? Would it be arched, swirled, or twisted? Who knows, but upon seeing the image in figure 12.150, I remembered catching fireflies on hot summer nights and watching them blink on and off inside the jar my mother had given us. The illusion of energy and light allow me to enjoy the image Robert created for Panasonic. Here's how he did it:

1. Working from the comp (figure 12.151), Howard Berman photographed the primary image—table, little girl, and the jar with rainbow color tape wrapped around it, which threw colored light reflections onto the table (figure 12.152).

    Having the actual jar in the image will serve as a useful reference for size and scale, and secondarily it serves as a focal point for the little girl. It is incredibly difficult for a model, especially a child to focus on nothing, and having the jar on the table gives the girl something to relate to.

2. In the meantime, Robert experimented with the shape of the rainbow (figure 12.153). Notice how beautifully the spirals and ribbons of light overlap with translucency.

3. Once the rainbow was rendered in Maya, Robert brought it back into Photoshop and dropped it into a new Mason jar (figure 12.154). He took advantage of the Screen, Soft Light, and Lighten blending modes to create the illusion of light. By painting with sampled rainbow colors on new layers, he added delicate details.

figure 12.150

Created for Panasonic, the image combines photography and 3D image elements wonderfully.

figure 12.151

The reference image comp.

figure 12.152

The initial photograph sets the scene.

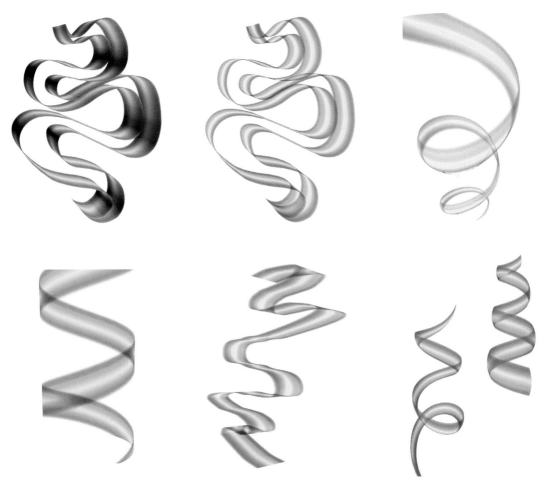

figure 12.153

Robert experimented with 3D swirls, ribbons, and swoosh-like rainbows.

figure 12.154

Dropping in the rainbow and painting rainbow colors onto the jar and table is only the beginning.

4. My favorite part of this composite is that Bob was thoughtful enough to punch holes into the lid of the jar just as we did as children to let the fireflies have air. The light coming out of the holes is completely impossible, yet 100% believable, and the hint of the background seen through the jar is intriguing (**figure 12.155**).

5. The final step was to fine-tune the image with careful cleanup and retouching.

figure 12.155

Reducing the jar opacity to let the background plate show though and punching holes into the lid ties the image together.

As Bob mentioned to me, "To maintain flexibility and just in case the client requests another change, I always archive all of my files with the layers." Well, if his clients do ask for a change, I know that Bob will finagle a way to bend, twist, light, and create it.

CLOSING THOUGHTS

To create believable photorealistic images, study nature and look at a lot of artwork. Notice how the play of light and shadow adds dimension and how your eyes tell you what looks right and what doesn't. In the next chapter, we'll depart from photorealism and enter the world of subjective fantasy images, but even there you should use the skills learned in this chapter to show the viewer your point of view of the world.

13

CREATIVE COMPOSITING

The creative process is simultaneously fulfilling, intimidating, and—in a way—addictive. It involves honing your craft, nurturing your muse, and creating images that express your values, perceptions, and sensibilities. In the process, you may doubt yourself and your abilities, but *don't*. Often we seek the recognition and approval of people we respect, and I know from experience that worrying about what others will think can have a paralyzing effect on working freely. In Chapter 1, "The Creative Process and Configuring Photoshop," I discussed finding your inspiration and turning off that nagging and critical voice. This chapter continues that discussion and addresses working freely and creatively with Photoshop to

- Discover inspiration with the simplest subjects
- Create images with your flatbed scanner
- Understand the essentials of image composition
- Add texture, shading, and personal meaning

The Photoshop techniques used in creative compositing are exactly the same as the ones that have been presented throughout this book—from making selections, to masking, to experimenting with blending modes, to adding shadow and texture. Therefore, this chapter includes fewer step-by-step examples to work along with because it concentrates on the artistic process. I hope you find the images and ideas inspiring.

IMAGES AND INSPIRATION

Every artist and designer I know is a flea-market walker, used-book-sale browser, junk-day gatherer, and inspiration scavenger. We are always on the lookout for an interesting background to be found in a discarded piece of metal or tossed-away canvas.

My husband and I found the baby Jesus figure shown in **figure 13.1** in a construction dumpster. Other objects we've found and brought home include a shattered golden halo; an ornately hideous wedding soup tureen replete with cooing doves and yellow roses; a flattened, dried-out squirrel carcass (**figure 13.2**); and numerous bugs and birds, which we scanned before burying them. All of these subjects are meaningful to us—often at the moment we don't know why—but we take pleasure in recognizing their stories, textures, and uniqueness.

Marcel Duchamp created the first *readymade*, or work of art created not by the hand and skill, but rather by the mind and decision of an artist. The Society of Independent Artists in New York held an open exhibition in 1917, and Duchamp entered a urinal mounted on its side, titling the piece *Fountain*. Although the piece was rejected, the idea of the readymade was born.

figure 13.1

Be open to inspiration—you may find it in a dumpster.

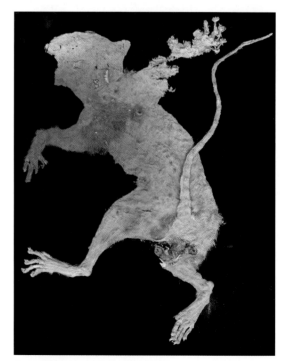

figure 13.2

Experiment with scanning three-dimensional subjects.

Galleries, Classes, and the Sunday Paper

Your inspiration may come in many forms—discover it and hang on to it like a bulldog. Visit galleries, go to lectures and presentations, take classes, read science fiction, go for a swim, and have a second cup of coffee with the Sunday paper. As I discussed in Chapter 1, keep a swipe book of pictures and articles that spark your interest. Mark Beckelman, whose images you've seen throughout this book, doesn't find inspiration in looking at photography; rather he takes the time to browse art and design books at local bookstores. He appreciates the abstraction that an illustrator brings to a topic as it helps him to think outside of the photographic framework.

For me, one of the most inspiring things I do is teach. Once my students realize they shouldn't be trying to please me, they take off creatively. I give weekly assignments, and I look forward to seeing their submissions. Their fresh take on a subject or topic always inspires me to develop assignments that will challenge both of us to make better art. In figure 13.3, Samuel Oh created a wonderfully textured image of New York. In figure 13.4, James Dick lends a refreshing take on Adam and Eve. James, a freshman at the time he created this image, started with the background, which he created by chopping up a lot of apples and photographing them. He photographed and printed his girlfriend and himself, and then tore out the figures and added them to the image, using lettuce as a background to signify the Garden of Eden.

© Samuel Oh

figure 13.3

Combining the textures and impressions of New York City.

© James Dick

figure 13.4

A quirky and insightful interpretation of Adam and Eve.

Travel and Inspiration

Lyn Bishop, a successful fine artist, finds inspiration in traveling and experiencing world cultures. Lyn appreciates the textures, lights, and colors found in the simplest settings of an early morning walk or along a weathered wall. Lyn makes use of both traditional printmaking and painting techniques and digital technology to express her inward and outward journeys, creating beautiful images such as the one shown in **figure 13.5**.

As Lyn explains, "The journey is the integral inspiration that propels my art. Traveling throughout the world, I look for the simple, unsophisticated, and organic details that define the beauty of that culture. I am always intrigued by the differing human elements and visual stimulation that I encounter. The internal artistic journey begins with a feeling or thought until the work takes on its own personality."

Lyn's images express her deep respect for the diversity of world culture. Her prints are rich and full of delicate details that you need to see firsthand to appreciate fully.

© Lyn Bishop

figure 13.5

Lyn Bishop likes to discover and combine a variety of sources to create quietly compelling images.

SCANNING FOR COMPOSITING

Being able to quickly translate your three-dimensional objects into pixels with a flatbed scanner can be a great way to input and experiment with image ideas. Even as a photographer, I often find it easier and quicker to plop a subject onto a scanner and make a quick scan, versus setting up lights and backgrounds, getting out the camera, taking the picture, and then having to clean up the set.

Figure 13.6 shows a sampling of objects I've scanned, from shriveled grapes to fantastic butterflies, to moths, stamps, and drips. To make an image for my mother's 80th birthday, I scanned the sunflowers in different positions (**figure 13.7**) and used layers, layer masks, blending modes, and the Blend If command to form the final bouquet (**figure 13.8**).

figure 13.6

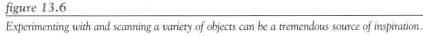

Experimenting with and scanning a variety of objects can be a tremendous source of inspiration.

figure 13.7

Repeated scanning allows for a variety of interpretations.

figure 13.8

The final image conveys the love of a child bringing home a handpicked flower bouquet.

To make successful scans of three-dimensional sub-jects with your flatbed scanner, try these tips and techniques:

- When in doubt, scan it. Often the very act of scanning a subject changes it from ordinary to beautiful, as the light of the scanner can add an iridescent quality to translucent and reflec-tive objects.

- Many flatbed scanners let you take the lid off completely—this can be very helpful when experimenting with self-portraits, large objects, and a variety of backgrounds.

- To avoid damaging delicate objects such as old photographs or old books, prop up the scanner lid at the corners using four empty film cans or four 2 x 2 building blocks.

- Experiment with a variety of backgrounds. **Figure 13.9** shows the difference between scanning the mackerel using a white versus a black background. To change your scanner background, you can either tape paper onto your scanner lid or simply drape cloth over the subject. **Figure 13.10** shows an experi-ment I did with a blue background. Because the doll's head was pink, using the opposite color as a background made making the selec-tion with Color Range very easy.

- Use an empty, plastic white food container, such as a half-gallon ice cream tub, to build an instant light box for your scans. Place the subject on the scanner and the tub over the subject. The light reflected back to the sub-ject will allow it to float in lightness. And you get to eat the ice cream first!

- Flatbed scanners have an inherent depth of field of approximately one-half inch to one inch. Often the transition from sharp to soft focus is both surprising and striking.

- Think of the scanner as an upside-down camera; position and place images on it as if you were building an upside-down still life from bottom to top.

- Don't be afraid to move the subject while scanning. Very often the streaks and trails can be very beautiful. If you don't like the results, simply close the file without saving it.

- To avoid scratching the scanner platen (the glass), use a clear sheet of acetate to protect the platen when scanning wet or gritty subjects.

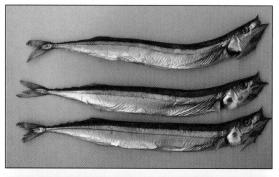

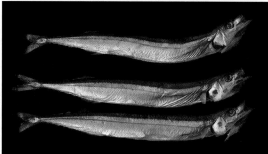

figure 13.9

Using a white or black background influences the look and feel of the image.

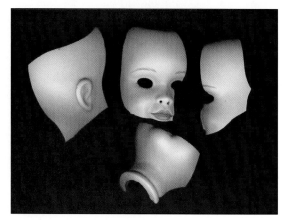

figure 13.10

Contrasting color backgrounds makes using Color Range for quick selections a snap.

- Keep your scanner clean. I avoid scanning fine particulates such as flour or ashes. After scanning a wet subject, such as a slice of kiwi, always clean the scanner right away. Spray glass cleaner on a lint free cloth (not on the scanner directly) and use the damp cloth to clean it. Please follow the directions in your scanner manual for cleaning the scanner platen.

- Use tape or Silly Putty to convince subjects that may fall, tilt, or move to stay in place.

N o t e

For additional information on scanning and determining scanning resolution please see "Input and Output Resolution," an appendix you can find on this book's Web site.

Creating Stories and Characters

Maggie Taylor finds inspiration by visiting flea markets and scavenging eBay for antique letters, photographs, dollhouse furniture, and small toys. She then scans the three-dimensional subjects with a flatbed scanner and creates beautiful and emotive images, such as those shown in **figures 13.11** and **13.12**.

Maggie is inspired by the stories that evolve as she creates her images. The backgrounds are her own paintings, and the subjects are dreamlike characters and stories she weaves together with humor and sensibility. Working at 360 pixels per inch, she then makes stunning inkjet prints, which are exhibited and collected worldwide. Her images are also commissioned for book and CD covers.

© Maggie Taylor

figure 13.11

After scanning the rabbit and the toy teacup, Maggie created a tableau for their mysterious interaction.

© Maggie Taylor

figure 13.12

Starting with an antique photo and scans of real fish, Maggie created an ambiguous and striking image.

ESSENTIALS OF IMAGE COMPOSITION

Entire art movements, countless books, endless lectures, and numerous courses of study have addressed the laws, rules, guidelines, and reasoning of good image composition. Digital compositing relies on and combines design principles from painting and drawing, design and typography, photography and filmmaking, and sculpture and 3D modeling. The best way to learn the fundamental design principles is to take classes in a variety of the listed concentrations and to look at a lot of different types of art.

Imagemaking is the art of making visual relationships, which the viewer can conceptualize and appreciate. Many of these concepts rely on how our visual perception system perceives and processes information:

- **Our eyes move from dark to light.** Lightening the important aspects of the image and darkening the less important will guide the viewer's eye through the image. Avoid light splotches near the edge of the image frame, because they will draw the viewer's eye out of the image.

- **Our eyes move from soft to sharp.** Use selective softening and sharpening with layers and layer masks to focus important image areas more than unimportant ones.

- **Our eyes move away from less detail to more detail.** To attract a viewer's eye, enhance or add detail and texture.

- **Our eyes are attracted to color.** By reducing color in less essential image areas, our eyes will not dwell on them for very long.

The next time you are in a gallery or looking at an art book, relax your eyes a bit and notice how they move through an image. Do they keep coming back to the subject? Or do they "fall" out of the frame because the edge of the image is too light? Noticing how your eyes look at an image is a useful exercise for appreciating image composition.

Note

If you're anything like most artists, just the idea of laws or rules of composition makes your skin crawl. The essentials of image composition are not a strict set of guidelines that you must follow; rather they are a visual reference for you to work with. The principles of good design and image-making are timeless, and learning them, to then forget them, will let you be a more accomplished and confident artist.

Creating Visual Relationships

Sometimes I stare at the screen and spend countless hours moving layers and objects around, and at other times, the images seem to flow together almost on their own. Working intuitively is the result of practice and confidence in your visual abilities.

Understanding the following elements of composition will help you create images, which viewers will appreciate more easily.

Position

The position of an image element in relationship to the overall image, other elements, and the frame plays a role in the perceived value of the element. Placing subjects off-center, for example, creates a pleasing visual tension that lets the viewer's eye move through the image and return to the subject.

You can create visual tension by placing subjects just within kissing distance of one another, which makes the space between the two vibrate with an intriguing relationship. You can also use the frame of the image as part of the composition. In the opera poster *Mourning Becomes Electra* (**figure 13.13**), Diane Fenster placed the arms within kissing distance and in a way that breaks the frame, leading the viewer's eye directly to the bottle of poison. Because of the resulting visual tension and the subject matter, there's no question this opera is not a lighthearted romp.

figure 13.13

The layering and framing draws your eye into the scene.

Size

The size of the image element connotes importance—larger subjects are more important than smaller ones. Size can also convey spatial relationships, since smaller objects recede. Overlapping, repeating, and varying the size of objects are all exciting image composition schemes with which to experiment.

One approach to sizing elements that can produce interesting results is exaggerating their size relationships. Think of the visual tension that images from *Alice in Wonderland* or *Gulliver's Travels* have. Alice can barely fit into the house, and Gulliver is tied down by hundreds of Lilliputians. These examples play with our perception of reality and are intriguing as they bring into question what we know and feel to be real.

In figure 13.14, the viewer surely realizes that the people aren't really that small and that the flag can't be that big. But in this image created after September 11, 2001, Mark Beckelman wanted to show that the American flag could be that big.

© Mark Beckelman

figure 13.14

The small figures make the flag look even larger.

Shape and Form

Two-dimensional attributes, from mechanical geo-metric to natural abstract, define the shape of an object. The more unusual the shape, the more our eyes are attracted to it. Whenever you separate a subject from its environment, you draw attention to it. Use layer and vector masks to refine the shape and flatter the image composition.

Form is the dimensional quality of an image. Although Photoshop is a 2D application, you can insinuate depth using shadow, lighting, and per-spective to add the dimension to the subjects in the image.

Figure 13.15 is an image by Lyn Bishop, which is based on shape, texture, and color. *Gyotaku* is the ancient Japanese folk art of creating fish rubbings. *Gyo* means fish, *taku* means rubbing. In Japan, gyotaku is practiced by anglers to make a record of their catch. Lyn's piece, *Talking Fish*, plays off of this ancient artform. Initially, Lyn began the piece traditionally, by inking the fish with sumi ink and then tried to make a print impression onto thin washi paper. Lyn told me that she was unhappy with the results after repeated tries so she washed the ink off the fish and scanned it instead. "The simple act of scanning the fish created surprising color and intriguing textures in the fish," Lyn said.

Texture and Details

The surface quality of an image or subject can add tremendous visual interest to an image, and we enjoy looking at the details, as shown in an opera poster for *Percival* (**figure 13.16**.) by Diane Fenster.

Subjects that are too smooth and perfect seem arti-ficial, cold, and computery. Adding texture mimics natural media, such as painting, drawing, and even photography, where the film grain can be an inte-gral aspect of the image. To draw a viewer's atten-tion to an area, accentuate the texture and details, as addressed later in this chapter.

© Lyn Bishop

figure 13.15

Repeating and contrasting shapes add to the pleasure of viewing this image.

figure 13.16

The variety of color, texture, and line is intriguing.

Focus

Making less important image areas softer and more important ones sharper focuses the viewer's attention on the sharper of the two, as shown in **figure 13.17**. By blurring the background, Maggie Taylor pushes it further back, which in turn brings your eye to the woman in the foreground. Our visual system is a comparative one, so by softening less important image areas, the sharper ones will look even sharper as the contrast between soft and sharp is accentuated.

© Maggie Taylor

figure 13.17

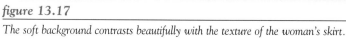

The soft background contrasts beautifully with the texture of the woman's skirt.

Negative Space

The space of the image is defined by the object's shape, size, and placement. But just as important is the space that is not full—also referred to as the *negative space*—because it sets the stage for the subject. Negative space supports the image and allows the eye to leave the subject, rest for a moment, and find its way back to the subject. For this reason, the negative space, or background, should not compete with the subject.

In graphic design, negative space is often a blank white surface, while in compositing it is more likely to be a blurred photograph or a subtle color or texture. **Figure 13.18**, another beautiful image by Maggie Taylor, makes wonderful use of negative space. The seemingly empty space of the sky on the right carries the small butterfly that the figure on the ladder is watching. Notice how your eye moves back and forth between the two? That is good use of negative space and visual tension.

© Maggie Taylor

figure 13.18

Empty space can be just as important as the subject.

Tone and Color

The tone of the image is the value from black to white. Our eyes are attracted to contrast, but too much contrast results in loss of shadow and highlight detail and can become tedious to view. To quickly see how the tonal values of your composite are working, add a Channel Mixer layer, set to 30, 60, 10, and click Monochrome (**figure 13.19**). Leave this layer at the top of your layer stack and turn it on and off to see how the tonal values of your image are working.

Color is one of the most essential imaging attributes with which we work. Full of cultural, psychological, and emotional references, color can attract or repel a viewer's eye. Too much color, or chaotic use of color, is deemed incomprehensible, and too little color is deemed unstimulating by our visual system.

Color is a three-dimensional entity and is broken down into the following:

- **Hue**: the color it is—red, green, chartreuse, and so on
- **Saturation**: how much color there is
- **Brightness**: how light or dark the color is

Colors can contrast or harmonize, and the best way to learn about color is to take a painting class. It was in my early attempts to paint that I first saw and appreciated how color bounces from the environment into the subject and varies from shadow to highlight. French Impressionist Claude Monet studied the ways that colors interact, which is reflected in a series of haystacks he painted in 1890 and in a series of the Rouen cathedral he painted in 1894, which shows the façade changing color and character, depending on the change of seasons, weather, and times of day.

I often have trouble choosing colors from the Photoshop Color picker, because the choices are too wide and seem artificial. Rather than using the Color picker, you might try collecting photographs or subjects of color schemes that you find intriguing or attractive. Choose Filter > Pixelate > Mosaic and use a high enough setting to create squares of color you can use as reference material (**figure 13.20**).

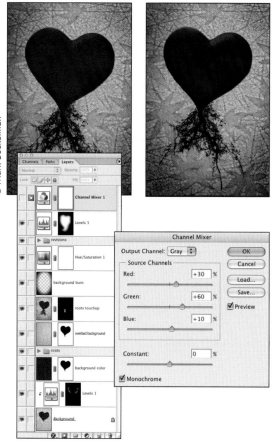

© Mark Beckelman

figure 13.19

Check the tonality of your image using a Channel Mixer Image Adjustment Layer.

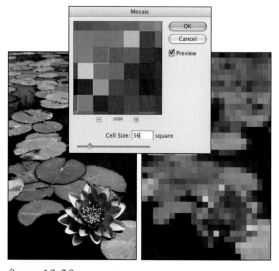

figure 13.20

Use the Mosaic filter to simplify an image into its component colors.

Lines and Grids

A line connects two points and is often employed as a graphical or typographic element that leads the eye through an image. Lines can vary in length, width, texture, direction, and curve. They can be one of five varieties: vertical, horizontal, diagonal, curved, and zigzag.

Dividing an image into a grid creates an "image in an image" effect as seen in figure 13.21, in which Julieanne Kost explores the artifacts of memory. I especially like the shadowed dimension that Julieanne added to the image, as it insinuates that the image was folded and carried in someone's pocket for a long time.

figure 13.21

The balanced grid structures the image harmoniously.

© Julieanne Kost

Creating a Body of Work

Creating one good image in Photoshop is easy, creating two or three more takes a bit of effort, and creating an entire body of work is the sign of a true artist.

A body of work is a series of images that form a coherent collection signified by a unity of theme and subject matter. It is a thorough artistic investi-gation of an idea, concept, perception, or style. Visual signifiers, such as the format, size, color palette, style, output media, and technique, are all used to tie a series together. Artists may create a body of work over a short period of time or over the course of a lifetime as they veer in and out of artistic inspiration.

figure 13.22

Working on a variety of projects keeps you inspired.

Figure 13.22 shows two of an ongoing series of postcards by Robert Bowen, a highly regarded digital artist with a worldwide client list (his commercial work is also shown in Chapter 12, "Photorealistic Compositing"). The postcard series is a personal project that Bob works on to offset the demands of his professional work.

COMBINING IMAGES SUBJECTIVELY

An essential aspect of being creative is being aware of and appreciating how the act of creating images will evolve as you work. The act of putting two image elements into one image frame creates a relationship and new meaning. Listening to what is happening on screen is very important. Be open to discover the surprises that working with Photoshop can reveal.

Inspiration and Input

I was asked to be a visiting artist at the Marlborough School, which is a private girls' school in Los Angeles. Before I create a show, I like to visit the gallery, because the environment of the space always resonates within me and is reflected in the images I create for the space.

The gallery was large and sunny and wrapped around an enclosed courtyard. The day I arrived, the trees in the courtyard had just been trimmed down to bare nubs of branches and trunks, and my heart went out to them. As the gallery director explained how the walls would be repainted, I blurted out, "I'm not going to use the walls—I'm going to use the windows!" As you can see in **figure 13.23**, the large windows were framed with strong squares that looked like picture frames to me, and I wanted to make full use of them.

Before I left, I knew that this exhibit would address my relationship with nature—the way in which I look within myself to understand the universe and, inversely, how by looking at the universe, I learn more about myself. I also wanted to explore and express the evolution of time and nature in the images I created for this show.

Source Material

I am a very practical person, meaning I am aware of the time, materials, and constraints within which I need to work. For this exhibit, I had three weeks to prepare ten final images—from photography to compositing to output and installation. That is not a lot of time, but that is all I had, so I needed to work with images and source materials that were close at hand.

figure 13.23

The trees were the inspiration, and the windows acted as the frames.

I had a ready source of nature backgrounds and textures that I had photographed over the years with medium format film (**figure 13.24**), which I had digitized onto a Kodak Photo CD Pro. So I was able to open each image up to approximately 48 MB.

I've always been intrigued by how our understanding of our bodies has changed with the changes in medical research. So I decided to portray the "looking within" aspect of the exhibit with antique medical illustrations, which I found online at `www.visuallanguage.com`. (The quality of Visual Language stock images surpasses any antique collections I have ever seen.)

Another aspect of the images that I wanted to incorporate was black-and-white self-portraits that I photographed with a Leica digital scanning camera. The "rules" say not to photograph anything that moves or breathes with a scanning camera. But guess what—the motion artifacts caused by the scanning camera, which takes pictures by moving a linear CCD over a period of minutes, became an integral aspect of the images.

figure 13.24

Photographs taken over the years served as image backgrounds.

My shooting area was 4 feet by 6 feet. Because my light source was the sun, I had an approximately 60-minute to 90-minute window of shooting time. It was in that week that I realized how quickly time passes, as I followed the fleeting beams of light every afternoon. As **figure 13.25** shows, I photographed my hands in the proper position to facilitate quick compositing with the medical illustrations.

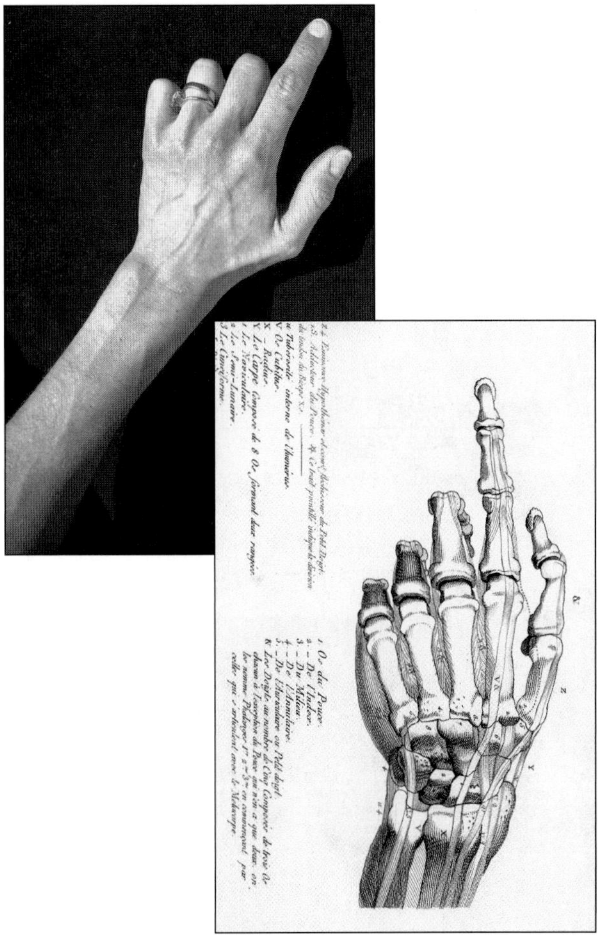

figure 13.25

Photographing my hand in the position of the illustrations made compositing easier.

Resolution Issues

Each image was to be 48 inches square. I was planning on outputting the images onto Kodak Duraclear material, a completely transparent material used for backlit displays, using a Kodak Durst Lambda printer, which at the time wrote at 200 ppi. A 48-inch square file without any layers would have been 263.7 MB. At that time, my computer couldn't handle such a large file, so I consulted with Ihor Makara, owner of Infinite Photo and Imaging (www.infinitephoto.com), to make the prints for me. Ihor told me to work at half size and that the RIP (raster image processor) they use to drive the Lambda would scale the images up better than Photoshop could.

© Visual Language

Am I recommending you work at half size for all your composites? Of course not. But professional equipment with savvy operators and good communication can make all the difference in the world. (Infinite Photo and Imaging in Virginia is just outside of Washington, D.C., and I highly recommend them for all types of large format printing and digital services.) Before starting out on an important project, take the time to work through the entire process to uncover any pitfalls, such as file size limitations or output constraints.

Note

Outputting to watercolor papers and creative surfaces can help conceal possible artifacts caused by scaling files up or working with lower-than-ideal-resolution source materials. Always test the

print resolution before committing to a project by making a series of test prints at various resolutions and onto different papers. In my experience, working at 240 ppi while printing onto matte or watercolor paper creates (for my eye) pleasing results. When going out to glossy paper, work at 360 ppi because the glossy paper absorbs less ink and therefore maintains greater detail.

Creation and Refinement

Having the hand break the frame and point into the image leads the viewer's eye to the impossibility of touching a shadow (figure 13.26). The hand position insinuates that the hand is the viewer's hand—thereby including the viewer in the image cycle.

figure 13.26

The position of the hand transforms the viewer from observer to participant.

I started by preparing the background images with this incredibly easy, yet effective technique:

1. To first load the image luminosity, I opened the Channels palette and clicked on the Load Channel as Selection button (**figure 13.27**). You can also use (Cmd + Option + ~) [Ctrl+ Alt + ~] to load the image luminosity.

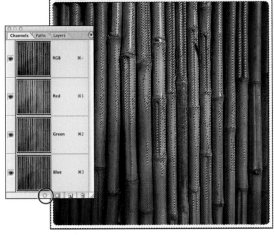

figure 13.27

To improve the contrast of flat files, begin by loading the image luminosity.

2. I chose Layer > New > Layer via Copy or (Cmd + J) [Ctrl + J].

3. To quickly add a kick of contrast and bring the texture to life, I changed the blending mode of the luminosity layer to Hard Light. To further intensify the image, I duplicated the Hard Light layer and set it to Multiply (**figure 13.28**).

4. To add my shadow to the bamboo, I dragged the shadow over to the bamboo file. By changing the blending mode to Multiply, the shadow starts to meld with the bamboo (figure 13.29).

5. The Multiply blending mode made the bamboo too muddy. So I turned off the shadow layer and selected Edit > Copy Merged to copy all of the bamboo layers. I turned on the shadow layer, added a layer mask, and (Option-clicked) [Alt-clicked] on it to make only the layer mask visible.

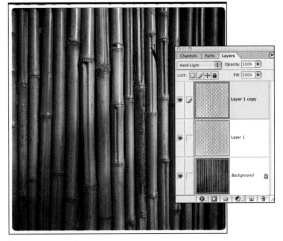

figure 13.28

Changing the blending mode to Hard Light kicks up the contrast; duplicating the Hard Light layer increases the effect.

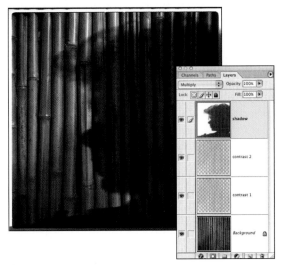

figure 13.29

The Multiply blending mode lets the shadow interact with the bamboo.

6. I selected Edit > Paste to paste the bamboo information into the layer mask to create the image shown in **figure 13.30**. By duplicating the shadow layer and adjusting the opacity, the shadow melded with the bamboo just the way I wanted it to (**figure 13.31**).

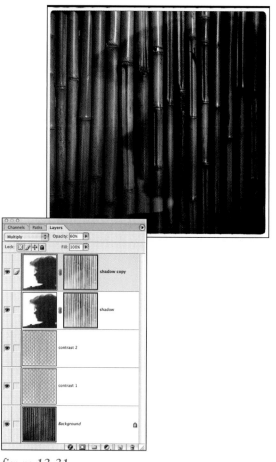

figure 13.31

Duplicating layers and adjusting opacity gives you tremendous creative control.

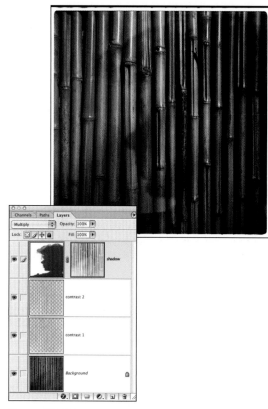

figure 13.30

Using the texture of the bamboo to mask the shadow lets the bamboo shimmer through.

7. Adding the hand and the skeleton required a combination of Free Transform and the Darken and Luminosity blending modes so that the layers would interact. To add a hint of unreality, I inverted the hand layer to turn it into a negative image.

8. To separate the hand layer from the background, I added a subtle glow with the Outer Glow Layer Style.

Color and Shadow

In the archetype image for the show, I harmonized the image elements using a layer filled with the brown that was sampled from the image with the Color blend mode (**figure 13.32**) to change my hands from black and white to a warm brown tone. The shadow on the right is the actual shadow created while photographing. I had initially removed it, but after living with the image for a few days, I decided that its graphical character would balance the image.

Work in progress

Toned hands

With shadow

figure 13.32

Working with layers let me add color and shadow to tie the image together.

Proofs and Discussion

Even when working under such a tight deadline, I find it very important to make proof prints. Looking at, living with, passing by, and catching glimpses of proof prints is a good way to learn from your work. The prints talk to you, telling you what is missing, wrong, or needs refinement. They also help you decide about the sequencing of the images, which is a very important aspect of both page layout and exhibit installation.

After discussing the images with my husband, I was able to refine and proof print each image two to three times. By the time I was finished, I had created a coherent body of work that was ready for output.

Output and Display

When I was finished, I flattened all the files, burned them to a CD, and overnighted them to Infinite Photo and Imaging to make the prints. While I was on the plane flying from New York to Los Angeles—it hit me. I had never seen these images output to size, so I wasn't sure if the color and density was going to be right, if the CDs had even arrived, or if the files could be opened. Me, panic? Well, it was too late and I had to have faith in my vision and Infinite Photo and Imaging's extensive experience.

If you ever plan on hanging an exhibit, I can only give one important piece of advice—give yourself extra time. Hanging a show is a time-consuming endeavor that is best done without rushing. I arrived one day ahead of schedule in LA, and the yellow Kodak boxes were waiting at the gallery. It was with great trepidation that I opened the first box. You cannot imagine the rush of relief and pride I had as I pulled the first image from the box and saw how the light streamed through it.

To mount the images on the window frames, I had double-sided matte cut from pure black-foam core board which would hold the prints and could be taped to the metal frames without showing.

As viewers looked at an image, they could look through the image to see another image on the other side of the courtyard and the trees swaying in the background. One thing I had not imagined was how, over the course of the day, the images were projected across the gallery floor, similar to how stained-glass windows sprinkle church floors with color (figure 13.33).

figure 13.33

The transparent material let the sun shine through and painted the room with the images over the course of the day.

OVERCOMING A CREATIVE BLOCK

Sometimes coming up with an idea or creative spark under pressure just doesn't click. When I feel that emptiness, I do the following:

- Don't think about it. I clean the office, take care of the plants, or go for a run—anything to get me into a relaxed mindset where I am processing but not thinking.

- Browse through my swipe book or image collection.

- Keep a notepad next to my bed. Many people find the time between sleep and dream to be where they latch onto fleeting ideas. But if you're like me, you won't remember the idea in the morning.

Often trying out new tools or techniques is a fantastic way to break out of a creative rut. For example, Julieanne Kost, whose work was featured earlier in this chapter, has been working for Adobe Systems since 1993. I can only imagine how much time she spends working on a computer. To balance her work with her art, Julieanne takes classes in encaustic painting, which allows her to work with actual physical materials such as wax, inks, and handmade paper to create beautifully textured images (figure 13.34).

Alternative Digital Photography

Experimenting with new lenses or digital cameras always gets me out of a creative rut. My latest endeavors are in digital pinhole photography and working with a Lensbaby (www.lensbabies.com) to create softly abstracted images that really show how I feel about the world. These images are much less about strictly recording the world; they are about experiencing and interpreting it. I have not yet used any of these images in my composites—but they will make exquisite backgrounds.

Digital Pinhole

Pinhole photography is photography without a lens. It has been an insider artform for decades. Pinhole photography requires long exposures from a half-second to many seconds, creating images that are soft and low in contrast and often have rainbow flare whenever sunlight falls directly onto the pinhole (figure 13.35). On a more positive note, you're never quite sure what you're going to get, which is always intriguing.

To do digital pinhole photography, you need a camera with removable lenses, such as a digital SLR by Nikon, Canon, Kodak, or Olympus, and a pinhole (figure 13.36). The one I used to create the images shown was purchased online at www.pinholeresource.com.

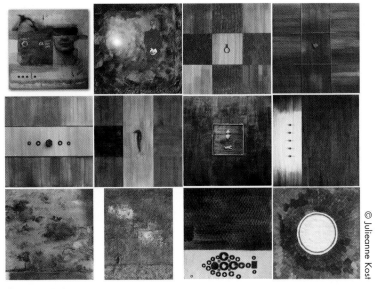

© Julieanne Kost

figure 13.34

Julieanne Kost's explorations of encaustic painting offers her a respite from
constant computer work.

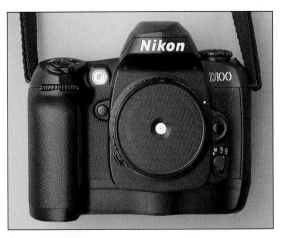

figure 13.35

Experimenting with alternative types of image input and
photography is a great way to avoid boredom and burnout.

figure 13.36

A pinhole body cap on a Nikon D100 digital SLR.

Lensbaby

When I showed some of these Lensbaby images to my Advanced Photoshop class, one student proclaimed, "I can do that with a feathered selection, Gaussian Blur, and Free Transform." And I imagine he could. But for me, it is much more important to get away from the computer, to feel the sun on my back, to take a different street home just to see what surprises it holds, and to look through a viewfinder, which is always surprising—while working on a computer often isn't.

Lensbaby is a rubber-mounted lens available for SLR (single lens reflex) cameras. You focus by squishing the rubberneck in and out, and squishing more on one side than the other creates off-center focus images that are romantic yet soberingly photographic, as shown in the tree portraits in **figure 13.37**.

Photomerge

When you're looking through the camera viewfinder, take a moment and look to the left, to the right, and up and down. Often trying to frame an expansive or interesting scene with a single exposure may not do the subject justice. With a digital camera, you can expand your horizons and create spacious images simply by shooting a number of overlapping images and then using the Photoshop CS Photomerge function to merge them together.

1. After shooting and downloading your source images, access the Photomerge command by either choosing File > Automate > Photomerge or highlighting the targeted images in the File Browser and selecting Automate > Photomerge from the File Browser menu. (The latter is my preferred method.)

figure 13.37

These images inspire me to continue to look at things with fresh and open eyes.

Photoshop will open previews of all the selected images into the Photomerge interface and do its best to overlap and merge the images into a panoramic scene, as shown in figure 13.38.

figure 13.38

Position the sequential frames automatically or by hand.

2. If Photoshop has a problem or cannot find enough overlap, a warning message will pop up that says Photoshop couldn't complete the task. But you can drag files into the Photomerge window from the image hopper at the top of the Photomerge interface and visually align files by rotating them with the rotate (R) and arrow (A) tools.

3. Because I didn't use a tripod to take the initial pictures, the resulting Photomerge has ragged edges (figure 13.39). With a bit of cloning and creative cropping, the final image portrays the grandeur of the California coastline (figure 13.40).

figure 13.39

Because a tripod wasn't used, the image edges won't align perfectly.

figure 13.40

With a bit of cloning and cropping, my vacation panorama is finished.

In the Photomerge interface, I recommend keeping Advanced Blending enabled because it uses a sophisticated color matching process to blend the images, which cannot be duplicated with layer masks. Although it may sound counter-intuitive, make sure the Keep as Layers option remains deselected because maintaining the layers will defeat the advanced color matching blending that is built into Photomerge.

Panoramic images do not have to be rectangular (**figure 13.41**) or even panoramic in subject (**figure 13.42**). Photomerge is a great way to blend and create both realistic panoramas and abstract image backgrounds.

figure 13.41

An image does not have to be rectangular.

figure 13.42

Use Photomerge to create backgrounds for image composites.

PERSONAL SIGNIFIERS

Adding textures, symbiotic references, historical artifacts, or a signature lends a personal touch to an image. Textures can represent experience, time passing, or challenges overcome. Including a handwritten note or historical document connects a contemporary image with your family history. Texture can also be used to tie a series of images together. How you sign a print and what you print an image on adds to the personal expression of the image. Applying this finishing touch is not a time for plug-ins or tricks—it is a moment for introspection and reflection to express your uniqueness.

Texture and Details

Some images are all about texture. In **figure 13.43**, for example, Jeff Heller has added visual interest to his image by adding texture. Texture can be reminiscent of natural media and the world away from computers. You can add it with a variety of techniques, which I hope you will experiment with.

figure 13.43

The viewer's eye is drawn to the texture and the detail.

Blend Modes

People used to have nicer handwriting. Even a cookbook my grandmother made notes in looks better than anything I could ever scribble down. To add handwriting or text from documents such as sheet music or immigration papers, follow these simple steps:

1. Drag the document with the text onto the composite.

2. Change the blending mode to Multiply (**figure 13.44**). To strengthen the effect, duplicate the layer.

3. To drop out the type and create a reverse effect, use the Lighten blending mode.

Figure 13.45 shows a DVD project I designed in which the images on the cover and the disk used blending modes to add depth and tactility.

figure 13.44

The Multiply blending mode lets the writing from the postcard layer show through.

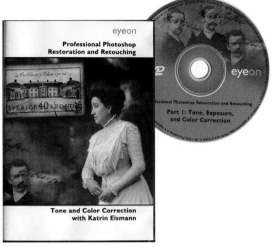

figure 13.45

The texture and detail added by the handwriting gives the product a reminiscent quality.

 T i p

When scanning documents, use grayscale mode, not line art. After scanning, use a Levels Adjustment Layer to make the dark areas darker and the light areas lighter (**figure 13.46**). Flatten the file before dragging it onto the composite image.

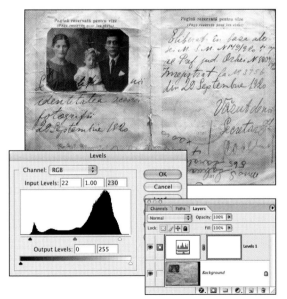

figure 13.46

Increasing image contrast exaggerates the difference between the handwriting and the paper, making it easier to composite the two into an image.

Layer Masks

Adding texture via Adjustment Layers and layer masks is a flexible method for experimenting. To create the initial texture, scan in or photograph textures that appeal to you—from tree bark, to dog fur, to gravel, or rusty metal.

To create the initial texture (which you can download from the book's Web site), I taped over a film scanner slide mount holder with multiple layers of standard office tape. I then scanned the tape texture (**figure 13.47**). I enjoy using this as a homage to the Starn Twins, the New York-based artists who, in the late 80s to early 90s, created a body of work with beautiful texture created by applying tape to their negatives and prints.

ch13_tape.jpg

1. Select > All and Edit > Copy the tape-texture source file.

2. In the target file, (Option-click) [Alt-click] on the layer mask so that only it is visible (**figure 13.48**).

figure 13.47

I layered tape on a film holder and scanned it to capture the quirky texture.

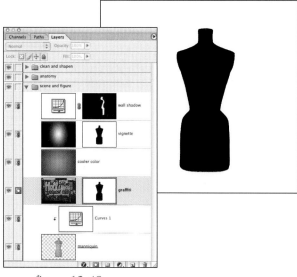

figure 13.48

The texture has been copied using (Option) [Alt] on the layer mask.

3. Choose Edit > Paste and immediately select Edit > Fade > Multiply (**figure 13.49**) to let the dark areas of the existing mask resurface. In case you are pasting the texture into a layer mask that does not have existing information (such as an Adjustment Layer mask), you do not need to use the Edit > Fade step.

4. Use the Move tool or Free Transform to position and scale the texture (**figure 13.50**).

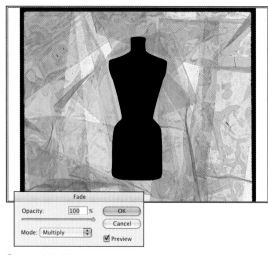

figure 13.49

Immediately after pasting, choose Fade > Multiply to let the dark values of the original mask show through.

5. Click on the Layer icon of the texturized layer to view the effect (**figure 13.51**).

Figure 13.52 shows a comparison of a corner of the image with and without texture.

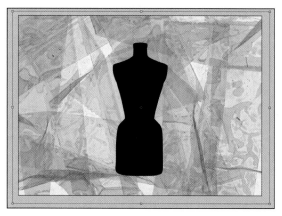

figure 13.50

Scale the texture as needed.

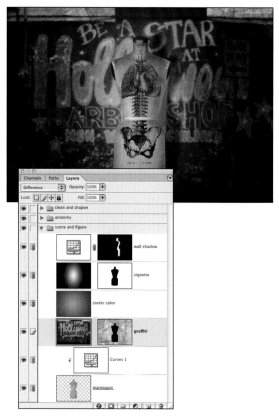

figure 13.51

Click on the Layer icon to see the effect of the added texture.

figure 13.52

I find the texturized version (on the bottom) much more appealing and fitting for the image composition.

Active Selections

Use the luminosity information from any layer or channel as an active selection to add texture to an image:

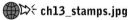 **ch13_stamps.jpg**

🌐▷ **ch13_poppy.jpg**

1. To load the image luminosity of the desired texture, open the Channels palette and click on the Load Channel as Selection button (**figure 13.53**). Or use the shortcut (Cmd + Option + ~) [Ctrl + Alt + ~].

2. To move an active selection, make sure you use a selection tool and not the Move tool—in most cases I use the Marquee tool. Use a selection tool to move the active selection over to the poppy picture (**figure 13.54**).

🖐 **C a u t i o n**

It can be tricky to move a selection without dropping it. Keep an eye on the Tool icon—if the mouse looks like a selection tool, such as the Lasso, as soon as you click, the selection will be dropped. When the Tool icon looks like a small arrow with a dotted rectangle, then it is safe to drag the active selection to the next image.

figure 13.53

Loading the image luminosity always results in very abstract selections.

figure 13.54

After dragging the selection to the second image, the structure of the stamps becomes more apparent.

3. Add an Adjustment Layer and change the blending mode to Multiply (**figure 13.55**).

4. Transform the textured layer mask (**figure 13.56**) and try increasing contrast and color (**figure 13.57**), which I limited to the upper-right corner by painting on the layer mask with a large, soft black brush.

T i p

To create a selection based on image luminosity, (Cmd + Option + ~) [Ctrl + Alt + ~].

To create a selection based on an individual channel, (Cmd-click) [Ctrl-click] on the channel icon in the Channels palette.

To activate an existing layer mask, (Cmd-click) [Ctrl-click] on the layer mask.

figure 13.55

Adding a Curves Adjustment Layer, set to Multiply, adds a hint of the texture.

figure 13.56

Scale the textured layer mask as desired.

figure 13.57

Painting on the layer mask refines the image and creates a letter in the sky effect.

Filters

Photoshop comes with well over 100 filters, many of which can be used to add texture. I highly recommend you use the filters either on neutral layers or on merged layers to avoid destroying valuable image information. Use the Photoshop CS Filter Gallery to add and combine textures as explained in the following list.

ch13_grapes.jpg

N o t e

All filters work in 8-bit images, but only a small handful of the production filters work in 16-bit.

1. Click on the topmost layer in the layer stack.

2. To add a new layer with merged image information to the layer stack, use (Cmd + Option + Shift + N) [Ctrl + Alt + Shift + N], followed by (Cmd + Option + Shift + E) [Ctrl + Alt + Shift + E].

3. To apply filters cumulatively or individual filters more than once, choose Filter > Filter Gallery and work with Artistic, Brush Strokes, and Sketch filters. You can also rearrange filters and change the settings of each filter you've applied to achieve the effect you want.

4. Filter effects are applied in the order you select them. You can rearrange filters once you apply them by dragging a filter name to another position in the list of applied filters (figure 13.58).

   Rearranging filter effects can dramatically change the way your image looks. Click the Eye icon next to a filter to hide the effect in the preview image. You can also delete applied filters by selecting the filter and clicking the Delete Effect Layer button.

5. When trying various filters, you can speed up filter previews, which will encourage more experimentation, by selecting a small, representative part of your image. After clicking OK, use Edit > Undo (Cmd + Z) [Ctrl + Z], Select > Deselect (Cmd + D) [Ctrl + D], and (Cmd + F) [Ctrl + F] to rerun the last used Filter Gallery settings.

After using the Filter Gallery to apply Artistic > Smudge Stick and Sketch > Reticulation and changing the layer blending mode to Hard Light, my shriveled grapes are looking much more artistic (figure 13.59).

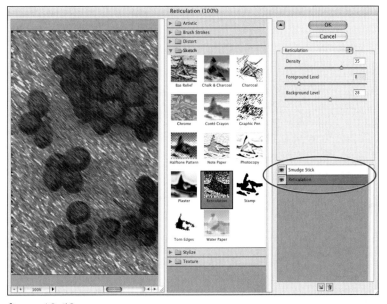

figure 13.58

The Filter Gallery interface lets you combine and control a large variety of filters.

figure 13.59

The original shriveled grapes have changed into a moody sketch.

Brushes

Use the textured brushes in Photoshop to add a hand-painted or etched quality to your images and picture edges:

🌐 ⟫ **ch13_pear.jpg**

1. Choose Image > Duplicate. If you are working on a multilayered file, select Duplicate Merged Layers Only. Save the file to your project folder.

2. Select an appropriate background color. White or black are both effective choices.

3. Press *f* to enter full screen mode, and frame the entire image with the Crop tool. Pull the Crop handles out to create a larger working surface (**figure 13.60**) and click OK.

4. Choose Select > All and press the Delete key. In this example, I used black as my background color, so the image is filled with black.

5. Activate the History brush and select a large textured brush by scrolling down to the bottom of the brush palette or by loading the Dry Media brushes (**figure 13.61**). Choose a rough brush. I am using a large charcoal brush (**figure 13.62**). Press the right bracket to increase the brush size.

figure 13.60

Use the Crop tool to visually increase the image canvas size.

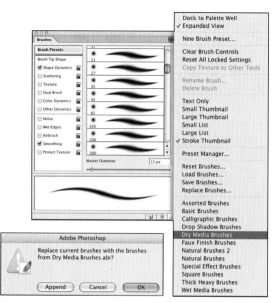

figure 13.61

Photoshop comes with a large variety of brushes; loading and appending them is very easy.

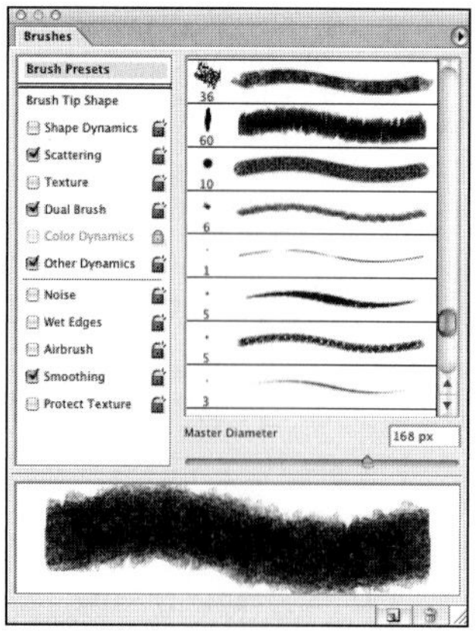

figure 13.62

Use a large charcoal brush.

6. Open the History palette and click the source point to the left of the Select Canvas and brush over the image with the large brush to create the effect shown in **figure 13.63**. Continue painting to roughly reveal the essential part of the image (**figure 13.64**).

7. Use the standard paintbrush with the same rough brush to paint over the edges to make them more natural (**figure 13.65**).

This technique is an effective way to catch someone's eye on a Web site, postcard, or gallery invitation.

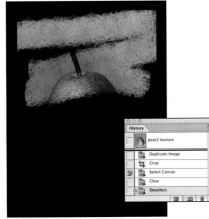

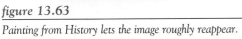

figure 13.63

Painting from History lets the image roughly reappear.

figure 13.64

The roughness of this rendition adds grittiness to the pear.

figure 13.65

Painting with the same rough brush and using black finishes the image edges.

Creative Edges

The edge of an image is an area that traditionally showed the artist's hand. Sketches, paintings, etchings, and fine art prints often have very interesting images that surround the image with the signifier of the craft and artistic touch used to create the image. Scan in interesting edges from cloth, torn paper, film frames, and so on, and use them to build up roughened image edges with the Multiply blending mode (**figure 13.66**).

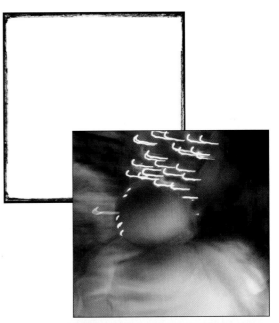

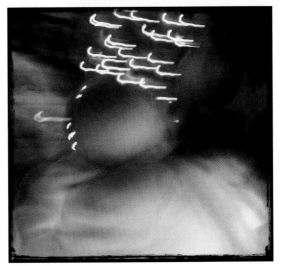

figure 13.66

The Multiply blending mode lets the dark frame show through.

Signatures and Chops

Signing a print or including a symbol as a signature or artistic mark is a long-standing tradition. In Chinese painting and calligraphy, the use of the name seal or *chop* is an ever-present element. Lyn Bishop likes to make use of a chop in her work: "I use a Chinese character, pronounced *rin*, as my name seal (**figure 13.67**), which means *small grove of trees*. It represents my love for nature."

In addition to the name seal, traditional Chinese paintings often include another seal with a poetic meaning, which Lyn also makes use of. "These two chops (**figure 13.68**) represent breathing, and in this context the flow of the air, or wind, around the heavens." Lyn always signs her images with her personal chops (**figure 13.69**). If you wanted to use a chop on your own images, you could scan in a family seal, a signature, or develop your own.

To sign inkjet prints, use either a sharp #2 pencil or a Micron Pigma acid-free pigment ink pen, which you can find in most good art supply stores for approximately $3.00. Traditionally, prints are signed, dated, and numbered by edition near the lower-right corner.

© Lyn Bishop

figure 13.67

Lyn Bishop's name seal.

figure 13.68

Additional chops add personal significance to Lyn Bishop's work.

figure 13.69

Lyn signs her images using her personal chops.

Unique Media and Format

The surfaces and media you can print on are almost limitless. From dozens of paper types to canvas, cloth, metal, and lenticular printing, experimenting with unique media can add visceral dimension to your images.

Unique Editions, an artistic collaboration formed by Bonnie Lhotke, Dorothy Krause, and Karin Schminke, has explored, pushed, and prodded more types of media through the print process than any group or individual I know. They have written a wonderful book, *Digital Art Studio: Techniques for Combining Inkjet Printing with Traditional Art Materials* (Watson-Guptill Publications), which explains and demonstrates how to prepare alternative surfaces for printing and reworking the prints using gold, dyes, and paint.

CLOSING THOUGHTS

Being an artist is invigorating, intimidating, essential, and one of the most valuable contributions we can make to this world. Find what speaks to you—scan it, photograph, sleep with it. It will tell you what it needs. Explore the possibilities and enjoy learning about yourself and the world around you.

APPENDIX

CONTRIBUTORS

This book would never have come to fruition without the generous sharing of Photoshop knowledge and techniques by these very talented professionals. I thank them all for their time and help.

NEO AFAN

afanofneo@yahoo.com

Specialties: Motion graphics, design, compositing

Inspirations: My wife and family, all unique artwork, movies, and popular culture

ALEX BEAUCHESNE

www.johnturnerphotorep.com

Specialties: Beauty and fashion photography, high-end digital photography

Inspirations: Seeing other countries and their traditions, classic photography of early Hollywood, any landscape at sunrise

MARK BECKELMAN

mark@beckelman.com • www.beckelman.com

Specialties: Digital imaging, compositing, and conceptual illustration

Inspiration: My local Barnes & Noble (strong tea combined with art and graphic design books and magazines), beautiful light, Jerry Uelsmann

LYN BISHOP

lyn@lynbishop.com • www.lynbishop.com

Specialties: Digital mixed media and alternative digital printmaking

Inspirations: Diverse cultures, journeys, and organic textures

ROBERT BOWEN

bowenbob@aol.com • www.Bowenstudio.com

Specialties: Visual effects, personal projects, and teaching

Inspiration: Architectural theory as analysis of form; the calming but also speculative interrelation of yoga asana and 3D computer graphics—like a horse and carriage; Flan O'Brian's *The Third Policeman*; baseball; and Clarice Lispector for weird and yet profound insights into motion design

SHAN CANFIELD (A.K.A.) PHOTOSHOP MAMA

www.shanzcan.com • www.moidesignstudio.com

Specialties: Tutorials, digital art, digital photography, and retouching

Inspirations: Appreciation for life and my innate curiosity.

JAMES DICK

jd@sagacious.net • www.sagacious.net

Specialties: The digital grotesque

Inspiration: Everything from the Elizabethans, to the surrealists, to contemporary album art

SEÁN DUGGAN

www.seanduggan.com

Specialties: Slow shutter speed; pinhole cameras; detail views of things that are easy to pass by; finding the unusual or extraordinary in every day, ordinary scenes

Inspiration: The many incarnations of light; the unexpected; visiting galleries, museums, bookstores and Web sites keeps my creative spark burning brightly

DIANE FENSTER

diane@dianefenster.com

www.dianefenster.com

Specialties: Photography, photomontage and photo illustration, and antique rose growing

Inspiration: My dreams and the shower oracle, gardening, Miles Stryker (not necessarily in that order)

JEFF HELLER

jeffheller@jhgfd.com • www.jhgfd.com

Specialties: Graphic/Web design, motion graphics and video editing, vector illustrations

Inspirations: Nature, the art deco posters of Cassandre, and the music videos of Michel Gondry

JULIEANNE KOST

www.adobeevangelists.com

Specialties: Photography, digital imaging, and mixed media

Inspiration: Found objects, the effects of time, psychology of the mind, and the sacred feminine

MIKE MCCORKLE

mike.mccorkle@vedros.com • www.vedros.com

Specialties: Compositing and retouching

Inspiration: Music, and lots of it; the Arts and Crafts Movement

JOHN MCINTOSH

jmacsva@earthlink.net

Specialties: Digital fine art education and Photomerge

Inspiration: Morning fog on the first green, Walker Evans, Neil Young, and Iggy Stooge

SAMUEL H. OH

samueloh@optonline.net • www.ohansol.com

Specialties: Digital photography, dynamic and static computer graphics, and 3D animation

Inspiration: Life, death, and everything in between

WAYNE R. PALMER

pmi@palmermultimedia.com

www.palmermultimedia.com

www.waynepalmer.com

Specialties: Photo restoration, digital imaging and Photoshop education, multimedia projects and conversions, photography and videography

Inspiration: Finding artistic abstracts in everyday things, seeing new sights, and the desire to make better, not just make do

MAGGIE TAYLOR

info@maggietaylor.com

www.maggietaylor.com

Specialties: Creative digital images

Inspiration: Gardening, flea markets, museums, travel…

JERRY UELSMANN

www.uelsmann.com

Specialties: Black-and-white multiple printing (in the darkroom)

Inspiration: Museums, folk art, travel, hiking in Yosemite, and the blues

LEE VARIS

varis@varis.com • www.varis.com

Specialties: Digital photography and photo-digital illustration

Inspiration: Nature, music, family

NICK VEDROS

www.vedros.com

Specialties: Advertising photography, humor, people, animals, sets, and digital photography

Inspiration: Great films, my music collection, and my motorcycle

JOHN WARNER

john@warnerphotography.com

www.warnerphotography.com

Specialties: Architectural, advertising, industrial, panoramic, and annual report photography using 80-percent digital capture.

Inspiration: Light and pixels. Music too.

INDEX

C